MW01049019

Race and Ethnicity in
the American West

Black Gun
Silver Star

The Life and Legend
of Frontier Marshal
Bass Reeves

Art T. Burton

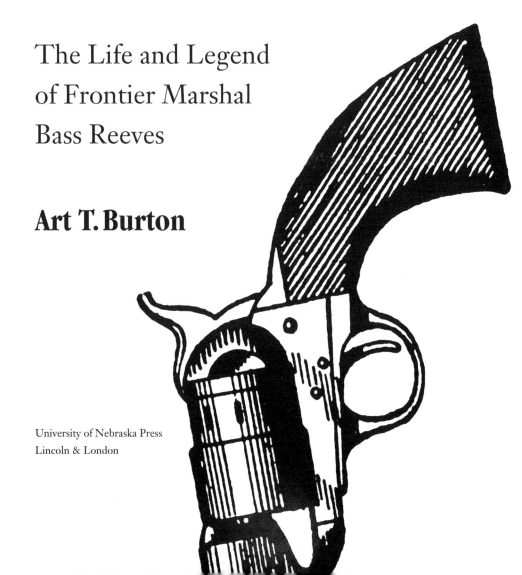

University of Nebraska Press
Lincoln & London

© 2006 by the Board of Regents
of the University of Nebraska
All rights reserved
Manufactured in the
United States of America

∞

Library of Congress Cataloging-
in-Publication Data
Burton, Arthur T.
Black gun, silver star: the life and legend
of frontier marshal Bass Reeves /
Art T. Burton.
p.   cm.—(Race and ethnicity in the
American West)
Includes bibliographical references and
index.
ISBN-13: 978-0-8032-1338-8 (cloth: alk.
paper)
ISBN-10: 0-8032-1338-7 (cloth: alk.
paper)
ISBN-13: 978-0-8032-1747-8 (paper: alk.
paper)
1. Reeves, Bass.   2. United States
marshals—Indian Territory—Biography.
3. United States marshals—Oklahoma—
Biography.   4. African Americans—
Oklahoma—Biography.   5. African
American police—Oklahoma—Biography.
6. Frontier and pioneer life—Indian
Territory.   7. Frontier and pioneer
life—Oklahoma.   8. Indian Territory—
Biography.   9. Oklahoma—Biography.
10. Outlaws—Indian Territory—Hisotry.
11. Outlaws—Oklahoma—History.   I.
Title.   II. Series.
F697.R44B87   2006
363.28'2089960730766—dc22
2005032827

This book is dedicated to law enforcement officers of the past, present, and future, with a special salute to the late great historian Arthur Schomberg. It is also dedicated to two men, Richard Fronterhouse and Nudie Williams, who illuminated the path.

Bass Is Coming
by Wallace C. Moore

Murder has been done in the Creek Nation, and them that is
    Guilty will soon have to pay.
Down in Fort Smith, the law has got the word, and everybody knows
    That soon Ole Baz is coming this way.
His name is Bass Reeves, but we just call him Ole Baz. They say he
    Was the baddest Deputy U.S. Marshal in the land.
Killed himself fourteen men in combat, rode thirty-five years for the
    Law, but to this day hardly anybody knows that he was a black man.
Sometimes he comes in wearing a disguise, clowning, a laughin' and a joking.
Other times he comes in on a running horse, his Winchester be
    Barking, and them Colts be a-smoking.
All you outlaws, killers, whisky peddlers, and thieves had better
    Watch your back trail, because soon down in Fort Smith you will have
    your day.
Judge Parker's court is where all you hard cases is a heading, cause
    We just got the word that Ole Baz is on the way.

Contents

Illustrations

Foreword

My introduction to Bass Reeves came in an Oklahoma history course at Oklahoma State University in the late 1950s. The teacher was Angie Debo, a temporary replacement, as I recall, for Berlin B. Chapman, who was on leave. Even in my late teens I was struck by the quality of her teaching, and although nearly fifty years have passed, I remember that classroom experience remarkably well. Angie differed in many ways from most historians of her generation. As she said in an *American Experience* film, made when she was ninety-five, she committed the cardinal sin for the historian: she told the truth. She ultimately chose to expose the means by which white Oklahomans preyed on the Indians and Freedmen and their resources rather than to glorify the land rushes and the "triumph" of white settlers and entrepreneurs. For that choice she was blacklisted by the wealthy and politically powerful of Oklahoma and could obtain only substitute or temporary teaching positions in institutions of higher learning in the state, like the one she held that summer in the late 1950s when I enrolled in her class.

In some ways, however, Angie was like the other old-style historians. Her vision of history was beset with blind spots. Whether it was her wry sense of humor or her spirited teaching method that made the lasting impressions, I remember that her comments on Bass Reeves were offhand and had a tone about them that treated Reeves as an oddity. But he was not an oddity at all. He was one of many African Americans and African Indians, such as Grant Johnson, Crowder Nix, and Robert Fortune, who served as peace officers in the region that later became Oklahoma. Angie probably did not know that in the African American communities of northeastern Oklahoma in the late 1950s, particularly in the Muskogee area, there lived many people who had known Bass Reeves and had vast repertories of stories about him and his exploits. In retrospect, had she been asked she would probably have admitted her blind spot, as she did to me some years later regarding the Freedmen of the Five Civilized Tribes. "I knew those people were there," she said. "I just didn't know their history. You write about them."

By the time she made this statement to me in the early 1970s, I had already begun to pursue some of the ideas for writing that I had gleaned from her class. One of them was the story of Bass Reeves. Although by then the study of African American history had become fashionable in academic history departments and historical research institutions, it was abundantly clear that decades of racial bias in historical research and in development of research collections had resulted in a dearth of resources for African American history of the Trans-Mississippi West. In addition, there was a general lack of access to what existed. It simply had not been deemed important enough for serious historians or professional archivists. Thus, during the next decade, William L. Katz, Lonnie Underhill, and I, and later Nudie Williams and others, worked from limited resources and lack of access to potential resources. By then, most people who had known Reeves were gone, so the stories we produced about him often failed to separate fact from fancy or reality from rumor. We had to wait for the emergence of another generation of researchers who, though facing the racial politics of research that we had faced, had better access to more resources to tell the story of Bass Reeves.

One of those researchers is Art Burton, who, intrigued from childhood by the story of the bigger-than-life African American marshal, has been indefatigable in his pursuit of the trail of Bass Reeves. He has poured over archival collections, interviewed people in far-flung geographic regions, cranked roll after roll of microfilmed newspapers, and tirelessly traced each lead that came to him. The result of many years of such efforts is the largest assemblage of information about Bass Reeves known to exist. The story Burton's research tells is more than just a tale of the exploits of a feared and fearless law enforcement officer of the Indian Territory that later became a part of Oklahoma.

Bass Reeves's story is one of racism in the Old Southwest. A former slave, Reeves found a niche for himself in law enforcement by virtue of his intelligence, his abilities as a tracker, the confidence placed in him by the citizens of the tribal nations of Indian Territory, his facility with a Winchester, and his effectiveness in "getting his man." The Indian Territory became his beat, in part, because of racism. The Indians, Indian Freedmen, and African American criminals in Indian Territory preferred being taken in by someone who was not white to being taken by someone who was. White criminals of Indian Territory were opposed to, and at times adamant against, being taken by an African American. Even the lowest of white criminal offenders exercised what he considered his "right" to deny the authority of a person of African descent. For decades Reeves successfully negotiated the boundaries between the racial groups who occupied the region that was his beat.

Bass Reeves's story unfolded against the backdrop of struggle between the United States and the tribal nations for jurisdiction over Indian Territory. For Americans, the struggle was to achieve the fulfillment of manifest destiny; for the tribal nations, it was to defend national sovereignty. During the decades following the Civil War, thousands of U.S. citizens took up residence in Indian Territory, either as renters of Indian land or as intruders, whom the United States refused to remove. With their influx came increased crime. The tribal courts had no jurisdiction over these interlopers, and in the waning decades of the nineteenth century jurisdiction over them rested with the U.S. courts at Fort Smith, Arkansas, and Paris, Texas. These courts provided the opening for a marshal like Bass Reeves. In the whole of Indian Territory, the only active U.S. court officials were the marshals. During Reeves's career, over a hundred of them were killed in the line of duty. Obviously, their job was extremely dangerous and became less so only after establishment of the U.S. courts in Indian Territory in the late 1890s.

Ironically, the work of Bass Reeves and other marshals helped bring an end to the societal atmosphere that made Reeves's career possible. It created sensational news, which often circulated throughout the states, and although it was exaggerated greatly at times after the popular fashion of yellow journalism, it was often taken as fact. Additional public attention focused on the courts the marshals served. The courts were big business. They were lucrative for hordes of attorneys and for marshals who worked under a per diem fee system. The long distances the marshals like Reeves had to travel generated large fees, but they also made enforcement inefficient. Thus the public claimed that the U.S. courts were too expensive and ineffective in containing crime in Indian Territory, and people in the surrounding states stereotyped the territory as a place where crime was rampant and lawlessness prevailed. Politicians took up the cry and argued that the tribal courts were inefficient, even though those courts had no jurisdiction over the majority of criminals. They argued that the tribal courts should be eliminated and jurisdiction turned over to the U.S. courts. Momentum for the argument grew, and by an act of Congress, the United States finally usurped tribal court jurisdiction in the late 1890s.

Against this backdrop of shifting jurisdictions and its attendant dangers, Bass Reeves plied his trade with a success that was due in part to his effectiveness as a lawman and in part to his rapport with a large portion of the population of the territory. His career survived the federal dissolution of the tribes and spanned the transition from Indian Territory into Oklahoma statehood. In the process, his image transformed from the hard riding, tough-as-nails lawman of the "Wild West" to the suit-dressed cop on the beat in Muskogee, a modern Oklahoma town of the early twentieth century.

In the latter role, instead of negotiating racial boundaries among four societies—Indians, Indian Freedmen, African Americans, and whites— Bass Reeves walked his beat between two—"colored" and white. Oklahoma statehood had been founded on racial separation. State constitutional convention delegates who stood for white superiority won overwhelmingly. Jim Crow was the longest-debated issue at the convention, and Jim Crow legislation was among the first bills introduced in both houses of the first Oklahoma legislature. Because the Oklahoma legislature declared Indians white, the Jim Crow legislation, without regard for historical, social, and cultural differences, arbitrarily and legally divided Oklahoma society in two—the Indians and whites on one side and the Indian Freedmen and African Americans on the other. That Bass Reeves remained effective as a policeman in the virulent racial atmosphere of the early twentieth century is a testament to the man. Thus from Art Burton's research emerges the story of a man both intelligent and persistent. To compensate for his illiteracy, the former slave devised a system that helped him determine which writ to deliver to which suspect. To succeed as a marshal, he kept on the trail for long periods of time, and unfortunately, away from his large family. Some of his children ultimately went astray. His unwavering attachment to duty led him to arrest his own son, who had run afoul of the law, as well as the preacher who had baptized him. As Burton's research separates the man from the myth, the man emerges as the more interesting of the two. The story of Bass Reeves the man adds another thread to the rich fabric of Oklahoma history and of the Trans-Mississippi West.

Daniel F. Littlefield Jr.
Sequoyah Research Center

Acknowledgments

Many people have given me significant information and vital assistance in my research on Deputy U.S. Marshal Bass Reeves over the last fifteen years. I belong to an organization titled Oklahombres, an educational association for the preservation of lawman and outlaw history in Indian Territory and early-day Oklahoma. I am a past president of the association. Many of the members have assisted me in finding archival and oral resources about Bass Reeves's career. Diron Ahlquist, an expert on frontier law enforcement from western Oklahoma, located court documents on Reeves that came from the Fort Sill and Anadarko areas. Both Edward Herring and Roger Bell sent me newspaper articles from Muskogee, Indian Territory, that proved essential. Retired Oklahoma City police officer Herman Kirkwood assisted with information from the Seminole Nation and Pottawatomie County that concerned Reeves. Ken Butler of Shawnee, Oklahoma, was able to locate photo images that enhance the narrative of the text.

Judge Paul L. Brady of Atlanta, Georgia, a great nephew of Bass Reeves, was an asset in understanding the family history and oral stories of Reeves that were passed down in the family.

Personnel at the Oklahoma Historical Society (OHS) have been very supportive and considerate. Executive director Bob L. Blackburn appointed me as the director of the Scholarly Review Committee for Black Programs at OHS in 2002. Bill Welgie, director of the Archives and Manuscripts Division, assisted with my search for archival materials and images. Bruce T. Fisher, director of cultural diversity at OHS, has found newspaper articles on Reeves that proved to be indispensable. Bruce is a noted advocate for the preservation of Oklahoma's African American history; his wife, Sharon, produced a play on black pioneers titled *Oklahoma Bound*.

I had many conversations with the staff of the Fort Smith National Historic Site, National Park Service, in Fort Smith, Arkansas. In 2002 they sponsored a mock murder trial of *United States vs. Bass Reeves*, which was very successful. Park Superintendent Bill Black supplied me with information on his distant relative, Deputy U.S. Marshal J. Mershon, who worked for the Fort Smith federal court. Park Ranger Tom Wing found information on Reeves's fees and receipts that assisted in my research. Al Drap, an architect and resident of Fort Smith, located information on where Reeves resided in Van Buren and Fort Smith that no one else had been able to find. Drap is a meticulous researcher and a devout fan of Bass Reeves. I couldn't have finished the book without his assistance. Richard and Judy Young, storytellers from the Ozark region, have done insightful research in trying to document Bass Reeves's life. Information they shared with me helped to substantiate facts and delineate from fiction. Angela Walton-Raji, who grew up in Fort Smith and is an expert on Indian Freedman genealogy and black Fort Smith history, also provided information and archival material that has aided immensely with my research. In locating information concerning Van Buren, Arkansas, my manuscript was enhanced by the findings of local Van Buren historian and genealogist Tonia Holleman.

The late Dr. Nudie Williams, University of Arkansas at Fayetteville, shared much of his research and ideas with me over the past fifteen years. He was one of the first historians to research and document the history of black deputy U.S. marshals who served in Indian Territory for the Fort Smith federal court.

I am especially indebted to two people. Dr. Daniel F. Littlefield Jr. of the University of Arkansas at Little Rock allowed me to review his research on the Indian Freedmen. The major focus of this material was the African American community in the town of Muskogee and the Creek Indian Nation. Dr. Littlefield is the foremost scholar on the history of Indian Freedmen of the Five Civilized Tribes. His reflections and insights on the territorial era and lifestyle have been truly indispensable in my research for this book. I value his knowledge and scholarship in this area of history more than of anyone I have met. Thank you, Dr.

Littlefield. Also, Mrs. Shirley Hill of Okmulgee, Oklahoma, sent me the unpublished research papers of her late husband, Richard Fronterhouse, who had conducted the first empirical research on Bass Reeves as an undergraduate at the University of Oklahoma in the late 1950s. This allowed me to view information I had never seen before and put my previous research into proper perspective.

Linda Moore, director of the new Three Rivers Museum in Muskogee, Oklahoma, was essential in assisting me with images and information on early Muskogee. The Three Rivers Museum has a permanent display on Bass Reeves and is doing a terrific job in documenting the early history of the Muskogee area.

On my many research trips to Muskogee, Oklahoma, the police department did a magnificent job in helping with my logistics and coordination for research purposes. I owe a big thank you to Chief Rex Eskridge, Lt. Reggie Cotton, and, last but not least, my late dear friend Maj. Steve Caywood.

While conducting research at the Southwest Branch of the National Archives in Fort Worth, Texas, everyone I came into contact with was very helpful and supportive. Three of the staff members, Cindy Smolovik, LaVern Owens, and Meg Hacker, were of great assistance in my research.

At the National Archives in College Park, Maryland, archivist Fred Romanski assisted me in my research and was very knowledgeable of records pertaining to the U.S. marshals and their deputies. My cousin Jabari Parks and his wife, Renata, were gracious with lodging and transportation while I was in the District of Columbia area doing research at the National Archives. Robert Ernst, one of the foremost historical researchers on the U.S. Marshals Service, also supplied me with pertinent information on Bass Reeves. Ernst is very active in the western history organizations, National Outlaw and Lawmen Association, and Western Outlaw and Lawmen Association.

Last but not least, I would like to thank my lovely wife, Patrice, and loving daughter Aisha, for assistance on research trips and editing of the manuscript. I couldn't have completed the task without their encouragement and love. If I omitted someone's name it was inadvertent, and I truly thank you for your consideration and assistance in this project.

Introduction

Uncovering the History of Black Deputy U.S. Marshals

The research on Bass Reeves has not been easy to obtain. One of the first responses I received from a local town historical society in Oklahoma after inquiring about Reeves was, "I am sorry, we didn't keep black people's history." Due to the discriminatory practices in the twentieth century, much African American history was not retained in local towns of the South or Southwest. Information that could be located on Reeves was like a rare jewel. This book is part and parcel of a journey I have been on for the past twenty years, back to the era of the American Wild West. My first book, *Black, Red, and Deadly: Black and Indian Gunfighters of the Indian Territory, 1870–1907*, published in 1991, was the first book to highlight exclusively the exploits of black and Indian outlaws and lawmen of the western frontier. My inspiration for the book was the story of Deputy U.S. Marshal Bass Reeves. The longest chapter in *Black, Red, and Deadly* is on Reeves, and initially I felt there wasn't too much more I would be able to research on his career. Numerous people who read my book told me they felt Reeves needed a book of his own. After some trepidation, I decided to see how much more material on Reeves might be available. After realizing that many of his federal criminal court cases were available in the National Archives, I decided that I would be able to use this material as the foundation for a book on Reeves. Further research uncovered more newspaper articles from the Indian Territory and oral stories from individuals in Oklahoma and around the country. In this book you will find direct testimony from witnesses, defendants, and Reeves himself in various criminal cases. How Reeves made an arrest is often not apparent in the criminal case document. We only know this information, if it was not available in the case report, from newspaper stories or oral accounts. I am sure the most exciting aspect of his relationship with a desperado was the arrest. When this information is available, I have included it in the text. Many of Reeves's exploits in subduing criminals and who they were, we will never know.

My first book generated national interest in Bass Reeves, for the first time in history. Hollywood became interested in the Bass Reeves story, and producers and actors who considered development projects included Suzanne DePass, Louis Gossett, Don Johnson, Maury Povich, and Morgan Freeman. As of this date, these projects have not come to fruition. In the spring of 2002 Marlon Edwards produced a small-budget, independent movie about Bass Reeves in Oklahoma titled *The Black Marshal*. Reeves was also featured in a docudrama entitled *It Took Brave Men: Deputy U.S. Marshals of Fort Smith*, produced by the Fort Smith National Historic Site, National Park Service. He was also briefly discussed in a documentary produced by the History Channel for cable television on the history of the U.S. Marshals Service. Reeves has been featured in several yearly calendars that are distributed nationally. The most prominent publication was the *365 Days of Black History Calendar* for 2001, in which Reeves was the highlighted personality for the month of February. Bass Reeves was also included in the Lawmen of the Old West Card Game produced by U.S. Games System, where his image is shown with Wild Bill Hickock on the cover of the box. His image was also included in the historical wall map titled *The American West*, along with dozens of other frontier heroes and heroines, that was produced by White Mountain Puzzles in 1996.

Recently, Bass Reeves was included in several fictional books in a supporting role or was mentioned in works such as *Zeke and Ned* by Larry McMurtry and Diana Ossana (Pocket Books, 1997). Reeves appears in nonfiction books as well. He is given a passing glance in *The Taming of the West: Age of the Gunfighter* by Joseph G. Rosa (Salamander Books, 1993). The Time-Life Books' *African Americans: Voices of Triumph: Perseverance*

(1993) includes a brief biography on Reeves. There were chapters on Bass Reeves in *Best of the West* by Bill O'Neal (Publications International, 1997) and *Black Profiles in Courage* by Kareem Abdul-Jabbar and Alan Steinberg (William Morrow, 1996). In his book *Lawmen of the Old West* (Republic of Texas Press, 2000), Texas author Del Cain writes that of the fourteen diverse lawmen of the Old West chronicled in the book, "Bass Reeves was perhaps, the greatest 'good guy' of them all."

Reeves is also featured as one of the noted lawmen of the Old West in *The Wild West: Lawmen, Outlaws, Ghost Towns and More* by Bill O'Neal, James A. Crutchfield, and Dale Walker (Publications International, 2001). A recent book, *Isaac C. Parker: Frontier Justice on the Frontier* by Michael J. Brodhead (2003), states, "Some of the Fort Smith court's most valued deputy marshals were black; the most notable example was Bass Reeves."

W. David Baird and Danney Goble's 511-page school textbook entitled *The Story of Oklahoma* (University of Oklahoma Press, 1994) contains a chapter titled "Eight Notable Oklahomans." One of the eight Oklahomans they profile is Deputy U.S. Marshal Bass Reeves, about whom they wrote:

> Bass Reeves won a reputation as the "most feared U.S. marshal in the Indian country."
> . . . Bass Reeves was one of those rugged lawman who brought law and order to the American West, and more particularly to nineteenth-century Oklahoma. He is especially important, but not because of his thirty-two years as a marshal or his feats of bravery. He is important because he represents the way Oklahoma really was—the early multicultural Oklahoma, when the men who "wore the star" were not necessarily white but sometimes were black.

Leon Claire Metz included Reeves in his book *The Encyclopedia of Lawmen, Outlaws, and Gunfighters* (Checkmark Books, 2003). Metz commented, "In places such as the Indian Territory (Oklahoma), U.S. deputy marshals provided practically the only law enforcement. Bass Reeves, a black man, did an exceptionally fine job."

The Bass Reeves story is without a doubt one of the greatest stories in American history. Reeves's record as a peace officer on the western frontier is exemplary and outstanding, although he did have a couple of bumps along the way. But what lawman during that era didn't? Reeves had to overcome more obstacles than most in his line of endeavor. Given the real danger confronting peace officers in the Indian Territory, Reeves walked through "the valley of death" for thirty-two years and never blinked. He may have been the greatest lawman of the Wild West era. His law enforcement record will stand the test of time. Even if you doubt that he was the best, this book should at least convince you that he was as good as any rural or urban peace officer on the American western frontier.

One of the things that made Bass Reeves special was the fact that he was an African American who lived his early life as a slave in Arkansas and Texas. As a former slave, Reeves was illiterate and remained so throughout his life. Illiteracy was common on the western frontier, but it was uncommon in deputy U.S. marshals, who had to fill out reports, vouchers, and the like. It was reported that some of the clerks in the federal offices complained about Reeves's handicap, but his ability as a man hunter was far more important.

Reeves was not the only African American deputy who worked the Indian and Oklahoma territories, but he became the most famous of them all during his lifetime. Other black deputy U.S. marshals who worked the territories included Grant Johnson, Rufus Cannon, Crowder Nix, Ike Rogers, Clint Scales, Robert Love, Neely Factor, Robert Fortune, Lee Thompson, Zeke Miller, Bynum Colbert, Charlie Pettit, John Garrett, James Garrett, Jim Ruth, Dick Roebuck, Dick Shaver, Jack Walters, Wallace McNac, Dennis Cyrus, and Barney Cleaver, who later became the first black policeman in the town of Tulsa. Ike Rogers captured the infamous black Indian outlaw Cherokee Bill, and Wallace McNac, also a Creek Indian policeman, killed the notorious Indian outlaw Wesley Barnett. The majority of these men were Indian Freedmen (former black slaves in the Indian nations) or a descendant of one. In the Indian Territory before the Civil War, members of the Five Civilized Tribes (Cherokee, Choctaw, Chickasaw, Creek, and Seminole) owned African slaves. African Choctaw Bill Colbert never became a commissioned deputy but worked for more than twenty years as a posseman for various federal deputies in the Indian Territory. Colbert was essentially a professional gunman for the federal police. Another, Cherokee Freedman Daniel Walker, was a federal posseman who worked full-time as a top cowboy on a big ranch near Claremore. He taught the ranch owner's offspring, Oklahoma's favorite son, Will Rogers, how to ride and rope.

The truly unique aspect of these black lawmen of the Southwest was that they were active primarily after the end of Reconstruction. During Reconstruction, it was quite common to find African American men who were hired as police officers in various cities and towns, especially in the South. But with the demise of Reconstruction in 1877, black men generally were not hired. After 1877, if black men were hired at all, they were only hired to police areas where black people lived. Given the unusual circumstance of black lawmen in the Indian Territory, I note in the text the race of the arrested party, regardless of ethnicity, whenever possible to help give clarity to Reeves's arrest record.

In the book *The Western Peace Officer: A Legacy of Law and Order* (University of Oklahoma Press, 1972), author Frank Richard Prassel wrote of the black deputy U.S. marshals who served in the Indian and Oklahoma territories:

> A surprising number of the deputies were Negro. Apart from a few policemen in urban areas, however, the black peace officer was a rarity in the frontier West. In Oklahoma the presence of many former slaves, existence of Indian subcultures, and the continued dominance of federal authority led to commissioning many Negroes. These included Grant Johnson, Ike Rogers, Ed Robinson, Wiley Escoe, Robert Love, Edward Jefferson, and Bass Reeves. The Negro deputies performed all the usual duties, often with outstanding valor and distinction. While many were themselves former slaves with virtually no educational background, they successfully carried on the functions of office and had relatively little attention paid to color.

Blacks reportedly made up a third to a half of the Texas State Police. Many white Texans called them the "Negro Police" or worse. Prior to the end of Reconstruction, they were disbanded and replaced by the all-white Texas Rangers. The Texas Rangers didn't have a black member until the late twentieth century, when Lee Young of the Texas Highway Patrol was appointed. At least one Ranger of the nineteenth century may have been black but passed for white, but I have not yet been able to verify this report.

There was one Texas lawman who, though he appeared to have African ancestry, claimed to be a full-blood Cherokee Indian. Tom Threepersons became a famous lawman in El Paso, Texas, during the 1920s. He was born in Vinita, Oklahoma, and grew up in Canada. In El Paso, Threepersons was a federal customs officer and later worked for the El Paso County Sheriff's department. He was involved in numerous shootouts on the Mexican border and designed a fast-draw holster, which was named for him. In fact, the holster that actor John Wayne wore in his later films was based on Threepersons' design.

It was truly unusual in American history for such a large group of black men, after Reconstruction, to have federal police powers as they did in the Indian and Oklahoma territories. It should also be noted that the Indian Territory was the most dangerous location for U.S. marshals to be. In its long history, the U.S. Marshals Service has lost more than 200 deputies in the line of duty. Of those, more than 120 deputy U.S. marshals were killed in the Indian and Oklahoma territories prior to Oklahoma statehood in 1907. No other place in the Wild West comes even remotely close to the danger presented to federal peace officers as the "Twin Territories."

Only one Hollywood movie depicts a black man on the western frontier as a deputy U.S. marshal. *Tracker* starred Sammy Davis Jr. and was made as a television movie in the 1970s. In the film, Davis assists a reluctant rancher whose daughter was kidnapped by the Comanche Indians in the Texas panhandle. The script is historically inaccurate in basing Davis in Amarillo, Texas. I have never come across any African American who was commissioned as a deputy U.S. marshal in Texas, during or after Reconstruction, who wasn't assigned to work in the Indian Territory.

African Americans were hired as deputy U.S. marshals in the Indian Territory because they had been an important part of the Five Civilized Tribes community since the late eighteenth century and were familiar with the languages and customs. A significant number of white deputies didn't speak the languages or understand the customs of the Indians, and this put them at a disadvantage. Many Indians didn't trust white lawmen because some of them had proven to be unscrupulous and had falsified evidence, such as planting bottles of illegal whiskey on Indians.

Many African American deputies were part Indian. All Indian Freedmen were declared tribal members by the 1866 treaty between the Five Civilized Tribes and the United States. Black men also served as possemen and scouts for federal peace officers in the Indian Territory. The archival records show that the majority of these black lawmen carried out their duties just as well as any others in Indian Territory. Black deputies, such as Reeves, however, excelled in their work.

There was one brief television series in the late 1960s entitled *The Outcast*, which starred Otis Young, a black man, as a bounty hunter. The independent bounty hunter is pretty much a fabrication of Hollywood. Most real-life bounty hunters in the Old West were deputy U.S. marshals, railroad detectives, sheriffs, special investigators for a state or territorial governor, or military scouts. More on this can be found in my second book, *Black, Buckskin, and Blue: African American Scouts and Soldiers on the Western Frontier*, published in 1999.

Charles Pettit and a few other black deputy U.S. marshals served in Oklahoma Territory, formerly Indian Territory, when it opened for settlement in 1889, . Yet the vast majority of black deputy U.S. marshals, many of them Indian Freedmen, served in the Indian Territory. Some of the white deputies of the Fort Smith and Muskogee courts, such as J. H. Mershon, Paden Tolbert, G. S. White, A. J. Trail, and Heck Bruner, deserve their own books. The same goes for Indian deputy U.S. marshals such as Charlie LeFlore, Jackson Ellis, and Sam Sixkiller. The deputy U.S. marshals who worked the Indian Territory got very little national press notice. Sometimes the white Arkansas and Indian Territory press were hostile toward black deputies such as Bass Reeves, or simply did not report the exploits or the presence of black deputies, as I will discuss in the book. One thing was certain in the Indian Territory, whether you were a black, white, or an Indian deputy U.S. marshal, you could lose your life "at the drop of a hat." The majority of killings of deputies in the Indian Territory happened within a fifty-mile radius of Muskogee, the wildest town in the Wild West, and most of these killings happened in the Cherokee Nation. I believe the best peace officers, white, black, or Indian, during the Wild West era were found in the Oklahoma and Indian territories, a tradition that continued in later years. Possibly the most accomplished policeman in the United States during Prohibition in the 1930s was Oklahoma City detective Jelly Bryce, part Kiowa Indian, who later worked for the FBI as an agent and firearms instructor.

It is interesting to note that in the 1898 book *Hell on the Border*, which is considered the "bible" by some on the Fort Smith federal court, author S. W. Harmon does not mention Bass Reeves once in the text, nor does he mention any other black deputy unless he was killed in the line of duty. Harmon mentions that a black deputy U.S. marshal was killed by the Rufus Buck gang in Okmulgee but doesn't give his name, John Garrett. Names of black Indian policemen are given but are not generally recognized as being African Americans. Harmon, however, does mention the black outlaws by name. There are several criminal cases in *Hell on the Border* that Reeves was actively involved in, which I will discuss later.

While visiting my grandparents in Arcadia, Oklahoma, as a youngster, I watched an old Hollywood movie on Wyatt Earp. After the movie ended I asked my grandfather, Frank B. Traylor, if there had been any black deputy U.S. marshals. He told me he had seen black deputy U.S. marshals ride through Arcadia when he was a young man but he didn't know their names. During the frontier era, Arcadia was part of Oklahoma Territory, not far from the territorial capital of Guthrie. I asked him if any of them became famous like Wyatt Earp, and he replied, "No." Then he asked my grandmother, Ida Traylor, "What was the name of that famous black marshal from Muskogee?" Grandmother answered that she remembered the marshal but couldn't remember the name. Then, after a long pause, he remembered: "Bass Reeves." I asked him if he knew much about Reeves. He said no but went on to tell me that Reeves had attained quite a reputation during Oklahoma's territorial era. Then I asked him if he was like Wyatt Earp. Again he said no. Grandpa was referring unwittingly more to Earp's national popular recognition. This stopped any further questions from a young inquisitive grandson. But he was correct; Bass Reeves was nothing like the more famous Wyatt Earp. In reality, Reeves was a much better lawman than Earp, real or imaginary. While doing research for my book, one old black man in his nineties from Coweta, Oklahoma, told me, "Wyatt Earp couldn't have been a patch on Bass Reeves's pants leg."

The next time I encountered Bass Reeves, many years later, it was in the book *The Black West* by William Loren Katz (1971). I was proud to learn there had been black lawmen on the western frontier. By the time I read the book, I had forgotten about the conversation with my grandfather concerning Reeves. Katz later discussed Reeves briefly in his book *Black Indians: A Hidden Heritage* (Atheneum, 1986).

In the mid-1980s my wife and I attended an African American rodeo in Chicago that featured a skit in which a stagecoach loaded with passengers is robbed by a gang of outlaws. Before the outlaws can get away, a black man with a badge rides up and saves the day. I remarked to my wife that it was a good skit, but there was no literature to substantiate this occurrence or any other in history. Shortly thereafter, I attended a family reunion in Arcadia, Oklahoma, near Oklahoma City. While hanging out with my cousin, Jabari Sangoma Parks, we visited with his former college roommate, who said he was from Reeves Addition in Muskogee and that Reeves Addition was named for Bass Reeves. This information highly intrigued me—a town having a section named for a peace officer. I subsequently learned that Reeves Addition, which is predominantly black, was named for a white banker named Ira Reeves, but the information I found on Bass Reeves started me on my research, which has culminated in this book.[1]

In 1992 Bass Reeves was inducted into the Hall of Great Westerners at the National Cowboy and Western Heritage Museum in Oklahoma City. I was honored to initiate this campaign and witness Reeves receive this recognition posthumously. Bass Reeves became the first African American inducted into the Hall of Great Westerners. It is my hope that with the release of this book, his life and legacy will receive more national attention. He received so little recognition during his lifetime that it is time that we honor him today.

Oklahoma has one of the most fascinating frontier histories of any state in the union. Its Western cowboy frontier culture and history can rival any on record. It includes Indians, fur traders, European settlers, buffalo soldiers, outlaws, lawmen, more than thirty black frontier towns, cowboys, cowgirls, cattle trails, railroad towns, mining towns, oil towns, huge cattle ranches, Wild West shows, Sam Houston, Col. George Custer, Indian chiefs Quanah Parker and Geronimo, Cherokee Bill, silent movie cowboy star Tom Mix, cowboy entertainer Will Rogers, cowboy movie stars William "Hopalong Cassidy" Boyd and Ben Johnson, black cowboy Bill Pickett, who invented bulldogging, and Bass Reeves.

Many of the federal cases in which Bass Reeves was involved during his career are not found in the archives. I have selected available federal cases that I believe give a descriptive overview of his distinguished law enforcement career as a deputy U.S. marshal in the Indian Territory. Many of the stories and exploits concerning Reeves's law enforcement career will never be known. Because Reeves didn't read or write, his correspondence with the U.S. marshals at Fort Smith was written by individuals he found in the territory who were literate or semiliterate and who always signed Reeves's name for him.

If there are any errors in the book, I take all responsibility for them. I hope you enjoy this trip back to the Old West and the dangerous trails of the Indian and Oklahoma territories. Deputy U.S. Marshal Bass Reeves, the former slave from Arkansas and Texas, is a frontier hero for all Americans and a role model for those who work in law enforcement today. If Reeves were fictional, he would be a combination of Sherlock Holmes, Superman, and the Lone Ranger. William Loren Katz in *Black Indians: A Hidden Heritage* said that Bass Reeves's story was an Oklahoma legend. This, then, is that story.

1.

The Lone Ranger and Other Stories

Much of what we know today about Bass Reeves persisted in oral stories told by individuals and families whose origins are in frontier Oklahoma. I was able to collect a few of these stories from persons who currently reside in Oklahoma or have lived there in the past. This chapter will focus on these folktales. After I finished writing *Black, Red, and Deadly*, I thought about the uncanny similarities between Bass Reeves and the TV and radio character, the "Lone Ranger." Federal law mandated that deputy U.S. marshals have at least one posseman with them whenever they went out in the field. Oftentimes the men who assisted Reeves were Native Americans, like the character Tonto who assisted the Lone Ranger. It was common practice for Reeves to work in disguise while trying to capture fugitives from justice, à la the Lone Ranger, who wore a black mask. Many times the white settlers in the territory didn't know Reeves's name and called him the "Black Marshal"; likewise, many didn't know the name of the Lone Ranger. For most African Americans during this time in American history, their dark faces became a black mask to white America—they became "invisible."

David Craig, a fellow member of Oklahombres, the Association for the Preservation of Lawman and Outlaw History of the Indian Territory, and an employee of the juvenile criminal court in Tulsa, told me a story about his family during one of my research trips to Oklahoma. Craig's

MAP 1. Indian Territory, 1889

MISSOURI ARKANSAS

KANSAS

TEXAS

No Man's Land

Cherokee Outlet

Osage

Kaw

Pawnee

Cherokee

Verdigris

KANSAS & ARKANSAS VALLEY RR

Arkansas

Langston

Guthrie

Unassigned Iowa and
Lands

Sac and Fox

Kickapoo

Pottawatomie and Shawnee

Creek

Deep Fork

Canadian

Seminole

Wewoka

Sacred Heart Mission

Chickasaw

Cherokee Town

Choctaw

Tishomingo

Tahlequah

Fort Gibson

Muskogee

Okmulgee

McAlester

Atoka

Durant

Paris

Van Buren

Fort Smith

ST. LOUIS & SAN FRANCISCO RR

MISSOURI, KANSAS, & TEXAS RR

TOPEKA, & SANTA FE RR

Vinita

Pawhuska

Wichita

Tulsa

ROCK ISLAND, & PACIFIC RR

ATCHISON, TOPEKA, & SANTA FE RR

CHICAGO,

Cimarron

North Canadian

Cheyenne and Arapaho

Darlington
Fort Reno

Wichita and Caddo

Wichita Agency

Anadarko

Fort Sill

Comanche, Kiowa, and Apache

Greer County

Red

Fort Supply

1. Peoria
2. Quapaw
3. Modoc
4. Ottawa
5. Shawnee
6. Wyandotte
7. Seneca
8. Tonkawa
9. Ponca
10. Oto and Missouri

N

0   miles   50

grandfather, D. H. Brown, was from a Quaker family originally from Indiana. During the territorial era the Browns settled in a sod house east of Kingfisher, in western Oklahoma, near the home of the mother of the Dalton brothers. The Dalton gang—Grattan, Bob, and Emmett— were lawmen who became train robbers in the Indian Territory. A story about Reeves remains in the family lore. According to D. H. Brown, Reeves showed up one day at their prairie dugout home with a posse of two white men and a Pawnee Indian on the hunt for the Dalton gang. Reeves hired D.H., who was about fourteen at the time, to show Reeves and his posse where abandoned dugouts and caves were located near the Cimarron River. Before they went out on the hunt the posse ate breakfast and Reeves paid for the meal with a silver dollar. The family told Reeves a silver dollar was way too much money for the meal. Reeves told them it was quite all right, he would get reimbursed later. After being out all night with D.H. and finding recently used campsites but no outlaws, Reeves paid D.H. with another silver dollar. We all know that the Lone Ranger's calling card was the silver bullet. Quite possibly Reeves's was the silver dollar. This particular hunt by Reeves and his posse would have occurred after the Dalton gang robbed the Santa Fe train at Red Rock, Oklahoma Territory, on June 1, 1892. A large number of federal posses in the Indian and Oklahoma territories were put into the field to hunt for the Daltons after this robbery.[1]

In another interesting similarity to the Lone Ranger, Reeves may have ridden a white horse during one period of his career. During the trial of Bass Reeves for murdering his cook, which will be discussed at length in chapter 8, witnesses testified that the cook threatened to shoot Reeves's gray horse. A gray horse can look anywhere from near black to near white, so it was possible that Reeves rode a horse that appeared to be white.

Another possible connection, though tenuous, is that the original story of the Lone Ranger began on the radio, in Detroit, in 1933. Many of the fugitives arrested by Bass Reeves and later convicted at Fort Smith, Arkansas, were sent to the Detroit House of Corrections in Michigan.[2]

In his book *Black Pioneers: Images of the Black Experience on the North American Frontier* (1997), author John W. Ravage asked the question,

"Could Bass Reeves be the prototype for the Lone Ranger character?" I doubt we would be able to prove conclusively that Reeves is the inspiration for the Lone Ranger. We can, however, say unequivocally that Bass Reeves is the closest real person to resemble the fictional Lone Ranger on the American western frontier of the nineteenth century.

Many of the oral stories about Reeves are lost to time, but a few are still extant. Sandy Sturdivant, who grew up in the Osage Nation of Oklahoma, as a small girl heard the following three stories about Bass Reeves on the Oklahoma frontier.

Dog Story

Bass Reeves was known to be an animal lover. He cherished not only his own animals but also other people's. Once, up near Vinita in the Cherokee Nation, he came upon a man beating his hound dog. The dog had just had puppies and was apparently in somewhat poor condition. It grated on Reeves's nerves that someone would beat an animal, let alone one that had just given birth. Reeves grabbed the stick from the man, who was a Cherokee Indian, and threatened him with bodily harm if he didn't stop thrashing the dog. Reeves told the man he would be back, and then left. He returned with a box to collect all the puppies and the mother dog. He then tossed some coins at the dog-beater and rode out, leading the mother dog along on a rope. Reeves took the animals to a friend somewhere up in that area whom he knew would take care of them. Several months later, after Reeves had conducted his business in the area, he passed by this same friend, took one of the now lively puppies, and headed home.

Skunk Story

On one occasion down in the Choctaw Nation near Robber's Cave, Bass Reeves and his posse had stopped for the night and made camp. They had been out rounding up felons and were on their way back to Fort Smith with a contingent of prisoners. After dinner, when everyone was asleep, a skunk crawled up around Reeves. Now, some skunks don't carry odor around themselves unless they are riled up. Well, when Bass awoke, the skunk was curled up, blissfully sleeping next to him. One of the prisoners woke up at the same time and proceeded to yell and carry on, trying to rouse the skunk into doing something obnoxious. Bass reached over, gently stroked the animal and talked soothingly to it, whereupon it moseyed off without spraying anyone. The Reeves charm had won out again.

Lynch Party at Oolagah

Ms. Sturdivant's grandmother told her this story, which occurred near Oolagah, Cherokee Nation, the home of Will Rogers. Her grandmother said Bass Reeves was afraid of no man. It was like he had a destiny, and until that destiny was fulfilled he was invincible. This is a belief of many Native Americans. Since Reeves operated in the Indian Territory, it is quite possible he adopted this line of thought. While out making his rounds, Reeves came across a lynch mob near one of the large cattle ranches. Evidently a rustler had been caught and was about to be strung to a tree on the prairie by a group of cowboys. Without any thought to the danger he might be in, Reeves rode straight up to the lynch mob, cut the man down with his knife, and rode off with the man—without saying one word to anyone. It so astonished everyone that he was not pursued. Sturdivant's grandmother said Bass was probably seething under his breath.[3]

The following stories come from interviews Richard Fronterhouse conducted in Oklahoma during the late 1950s.

Expert with Firearms

Bass Reeves's ability with firearms was legendary. He was ambidextrous with pistol or rifle. Reeves never carried silver- or nickel-plated pistols with ivory or pearl handles, or fancy rifles of any type. He preferred his firearms to be plain, ordinary, and inconspicuous. Reeves was possibly the greatest gunfighter of all the lawmen of the Old West. He could shoot so well and so consistently that he was barred regularly from competition in turkey shoots that were common to the local fairs and picnics of the Indian Territory. I was told that a turkey shoot in the Seminole Nation consisted of tying a turkey upside down on a clothesline, after which a rider with a rifle would attempt to shoot the head off the turkey while galloping at full speed down the line. Reeves's speed with a pistol has been likened to that of a "Methodist preacher reaching for a platter of fried chicken during Sunday dinner at the deacon's house." It was fast and sure, with no wasted or unnecessary motion. Reeves could draw and shoot from the hip with great speed and accuracy if necessary, but he favored the slower, even more accurate method of taking his time, planting himself solidly, and drawing "a bead as fine as a spider's web on a frosty morning." When he shot this way, "he could shoot the left hind leg off of a contented fly sitting on a mule's ear at a hundred yards and never ruffle a hair." But Reeves claimed to be "only fair" with a rifle. This characteristic modesty belies the truth, for Reeves was truly an expert with a rifle. For example, he once rode over the crest of a rise, way out on the fringes of the Kiowa-Comanche country, and interrupted six wolves as they were in the process of pulling down a steer. Shooting at the wolves from the back of his horse with his Winchester rifle, causing them to scatter in all directions, he killed six with eight shots. True, he broke one wolf's leg and "gut-shot" another, thus missing a clean, one-shot kill. But he did stop them both, using a second shot only to end their suffering. Eight shots for any six kills that are moving targets is fine shooting in any man's language.

Superhuman Strength

Reeves's physical strength was also legendary in the territory. Once, while riding in the southern portion of the Chickasaw Nation, Reeves came upon some cowboys attempting to extract a full-grown steer from one of the bogs along Mud Creek, which emptied into the Red River. The cowboys had roped the steer and were attempting to bodily drag it back to solid ground using their horses. Several ropes had broken under the strain. The steer was big and was buried so deep in the bog that only its head and upper back were visible. Its eyes rolled back into its head, its neck had been pulled and stretched until its tongue lolled out of its mouth into the mud and slime of the bog, and its windpipe was so restricted by the ropes that its breath was only an occasional labored, rasping wheeze. In fact, the cowboys were almost ready to give him up as lost. They were seriously considering riding off and leaving the steer where they found him, with a bullet in his brain to soothe their consciences and mark their defeat.

Bass rode up, watched for a few minutes, and grunted his dissatisfaction. Then, stepping down from his horse, he began to strip off his clothes. Without saying a word, he stepped into the bog and began to work his way out to the trapped steer.

First, he removed all the ropes so that the steer could breathe again. Then, grabbing the steer by the horns, he began to lift and pull, all the while talking in a low, steady voice to the steer. He pulled and heaved and lifted and grunted under the strain until he sank into the mud almost to his waist before the cowboys could detect the first progress in moving the steer. Stopping to catch his breath, he wiped his sweating, muddy hands dry on the back of the steer, and stooped to lift and pull again.

Ever so slowly, the steer was lifted until the lethal suction of the bog holding the forequarters of the steer was broken. Reeves then moved to the steer's flank and began the tortuous process again. By this time, the steer had regained its breath and began its first attempts to help itself. These attempts were feeble at first but grew stronger with each great, sucking breath.

Reeves repeated this process of lifting and pulling, first at the steer's head and then at its flank, until the steer, with great, convulsive twists and turns, was able to lunge toward solid ground under its own power. Upon reaching solid ground, the steer, without so much as a glance at its savior, wobbled off into the brush and disappeared, bawling its triumph for all the Chickasaw Nation to hear.

Reeves waded out of the mud, scraped himself as clean as he could with the flat of his hands, stuffed his clothes into his saddlebags, mounted his horse, and rode off stark naked while mumbling something about "damned dumb cowboys." He rode off without saying a word to any of the dumbstruck cowboys, even though he had been there for almost a full hour.[4]

One of the most fascinating stories I collected concerning Bass Reeves came from a retired Muskogee, Oklahoma, schoolteacher. Alice Hendrickson told me a story in the summer of 2001 after I gave a talk at the Three Rivers Museum. During Ms. Hendrickson's senior year at the University of Arkansas at Fayetteville in 1959, she took a folklore class with Prof. Mary Celestia Parler. The professor had the students in the class research and find native folk songs. Worried that she might fail the assignment and not be able to maintain her straight-A average for graduation, Ms. Hendrickson contacted her parents, who lived in Muskogee, and told them about Professor Parler's assignment. They advised her to contact an elderly white man named Stewart who sang local folksongs.

When Ms. Hendrickson visited Mr. Stewart at his home near downtown Muskogee, he was glad to sing a number of folksongs for her. One of the songs she remembered, due to its content, concerned Deputy U.S. Marshal Bass Reeves. Mr. Stewart told her he had worked with Bass Reeves, and that Reeves was a legendary black lawman. Ms. Hendrickson said that, though she had grown up in eastern Oklahoma, she had never heard of such a man.

Professor Parler was so happy with the songs Ms. Hendrickson had gathered that not only did she give Ms. Hendrickson an A for the class, but she had Mr. Stewart record a number of his folksongs.[5] Many of the folksongs that Mary Parler recorded have been archived in the University of Arkansas Library at Fayetteville, but the Bass Reeves song has not yet been located. The main impediment is that the title of the song is not known.

The late Hortense Love, a noted African American vocalist and choir director in Chicago, told me she was originally from Muskogee, Oklahoma, and that her grandmother was a Creek Indian and very good friends with Bass Reeves. Ms. Love said she was told that whenever Reeves was preparing to go into a gunfight, he would sing softly to himself. When others nearby heard Reeves softly break into song, they knew it was time to take cover, for Reeves meant business.[6]

This book documents the law enforcement career of the man known in his day as the "Invincible Marshal." It begins with what I have been able to discover about his early life before the Civil War and takes us through the tumultuous frontier years when Bass Reeves became a legend. We end after the turn of the twentieth century, as Oklahoma becomes a state, while Bass Reeves continues to work until nearly the end of his life. Along the way I include other oral stories that fit into the chronological sequence of the amazing life of Bass Reeves.

2.

Arkansas Son

Once upon a time on the Arkansas frontier, there was a young slave who was given the name of Bass. As an adult he would take the surname Reeves, that of the family who owned him as a chattel slave. From all the records available, I believe that Bass Reeves was born in July 1838 in Crawford County, Arkansas. It appears that Bass was named after his grandfather, Basse Washington, whose name appeared on Bass's mother's death certificate. Bass Reeves's obituary notice in the *Muskogee Phoenix* newspaper stated that he was sixty-nine when he retired from the U.S. Marshals Service in November of 1907. The same article stated that Reeves's mother was living in Van Buren, Arkansas, and was eighty-seven years old. This would place her date of birth in 1823. Reeves was interviewed by a territorial newspaper in March 1907, where he gave his age as sixty-eight. The 1870 census report gave Reeves's age as twenty-three and his birthplace as Arkansas. The 1880 census report gave Reeves's age as forty, his birth month as July, and his birthplace as Arkansas. The 1900 census report gave Reeves's birth month and year as July 1840 and birthplace as Texas.[1]

According to Paul L. Brady, Bass Reeves's mother's name was Pearlalee and he had a sister named Jane Reeves. Brady is a grandson of Jane, who married a man named John Brady. According to a list of persons buried in Van Buren cemeteries, a Paralee Stewart is buried in Fairview Cemetery. Her date of birth is given as October 16, 1821, and date of death is January 28, 1915. However, her death certificate lists her date of birth as March 16, 1818. The 1880 census report for Crawford County, Arkansas, lists Paralee Stewart as either a widowed or divorced housekeeper. Her birthplace is given as Tennessee. At the time, she had a fifteen-year-old daughter living with her named Belle Stewart, whose birthplace was Texas. The 1880 census also shows that living two houses away from Paralee Stewart is John and Jane Brady. Jane's age in the 1880 census is given as thirty-five. On some official documents Paralee's last name is spelled as Steward or Stuart. Buried near Paralee in Fairview Cemetery is J. M. Stewart, a Civil War veteran, presumably her husband.[2]

Bass Reeves and his family were slaves of William Steele Reeves of Crawford County, Arkansas. William S. Reeves was born in Pendleton District, South Carolina, on March 9, 1794, to parents who had immigrated to the United States from Ireland. He was reared in Nashville, Tennessee, by an uncle. He served in the War of 1812 and in the Creek Indian War. William Reeves represented Hickman County in the Tennessee legislature, and later he represented Crawford County in the Arkansas legislature. As a slave, Bass worked alongside his parents as a water boy and later a field hand. While carrying out his duties as a water boy, Bass caused concern for his mother because he spent quite a bit of time singing original songs about guns, rifles, butcher knives, robberies, and killings. She felt he might turn out to be an outlaw, since he spent so much time in the field singing about them. When Bass was eight years old, the William S. Reeves family, including eight of twelve children, some in-laws, and six slaves, packed up thirty covered wagons and moved to northern Texas, just across the border from the Choctaw and Chickasaw nations in the Indian Territory. They settled in the Preston District of Grayson County, northwest of the city of Sherman, as a member of Peter's Colony. According to Brady, in addition to serving as water boy, as Bass got older he tended the mules and horses. His way with animals led to his becoming the blacksmith's helper. Accordingly, because he was swift with his work at the forge and eager to take on additional duties, the blacksmith never grumbled when Bass spent more time with the master's prize horses, and indeed, the horses thrived under his attention. William S. Reeves died June 7, 1872.[3]

In the book *A Certain Blindness*, Paul L. Brady wrote:

> Bass was selected as his master's "companion," a position of
> prestige among his fellow slaves. His mother, Pearlalee, was
> pleased because now each member of her family was an upper
> servant, able to eat at the "house table." Bass's sister, Jane, had
> worked inside the house for years, where her needlework was
> esteemed. Pearlalee herself had long been her mistress's per-
> sonal attendant and the household favorite, and she sang on
> most occasions when her master entertained.
>
> Bass accompanied his master nearly everywhere, serving as
> valet, bodyguard, coachman, and butler. Compared to field-
> work, smithing, and stable tending, his new duties seemed light.
> But Bass took advantage of his opportunities to be close to white
> people, listening to them and trying to understand them. He
> even asked his master if he could learn to read, because Bass
> wanted to be able to read the Bible. Like other slaveholders,
> Bass' master refused this permission, but he did permit Bass,
> who had quick hands and a good eye, to learn to use a gun.
> Being himself a poor shot, Bass' master indulged his loyal and
> trusted slave and appreciated the vicarious prestige when Bass
> invariably won the turkey shoots and other trials in which Bass
> was entered, regardless of whether the opponents were black or
> white.[4]

In November 1901 Bass gave an interview to a Muskogee newspaper
in which he stated he had been the slave of Col. George Reeves of
Grayson County, Texas. He stated he was a body servant and accompanied his master into battle during the Civil War. Colonel Reeves was
a member of the Eleventh Texas Cavalry. Reeves said they were together
in the battles of Chickamauga and Missionary Ridge. Interestingly, the
article states that later they were in the Battle of Pea Ridge in Arkansas,
where Reeves says he saw Texas hero Gen. Ben McCulloch killed, but in
fact Pea Ridge was fought before Chickamauga and Missionary Ridge.
The story given by Reeves cannot be verified because records were not
kept concerning body servants of Confederate officers, and Col. George
R. Reeves does not mention Bass in his known war memoirs.[5] Before we

examine further this slip in chronology, let us take a closer look at the life of Colonel Reeves.

Col. George R. Reeves was the son of William S. Reeves, fifth of twelve children, born January 3, 1826, in Hickman, Tennessee. He was married in Arkansas, on October 31, 1844, to Miss Jane Moore. In 1846 George moved to Grayson County, Texas, west of the present city of Sherman. In 1848 he was elected tax collector and served two years. In 1850 he was elected sheriff and served until the close of 1854. In 1855 George was elected to the Texas House of Representatives from Grayson County. He remained a legislator until the outbreak of the Civil War, at which time he became a member of the Eleventh Texas Cavalry Regiment under the command of Col. William G. Young. George fought at the Battle of Chustenahlah in Indian Territory, the Battle of Pea Ridge (Elkhorn Tavern) in Arkansas, and later in engagements east of the Mississippi. After the war, in 1866, George Reeves was elected again by Grayson County voters to the Texas state legislature. He remained in that body until the time of his death, September 5, 1882, at Pottsboro, Texas, from hydrophobia after being bitten by his dog. At the time of his death, George was the Speaker of the House of Representatives for the State of Texas. Reeves County in West Texas was named for George Reeves.

Before the war, George was reported to have owned seven slaves that lived with him in his house in Grayson County. These slaves, one of whom was Bass, could have been the same slaves owned by his father, William Reeves. The original command roster for the Eleventh Texas Cavalry Regiment lists George Reeves, who was second in command, as having a wealth of fifty-six hundred dollars and owning no slaves, whereas the commander of the regiment, William Young, had a wealth of $129,988 and owned forty-seven slaves. So it is quite possible the ownership of the slaves stayed under George's father's name.[6]

Returning to the newspaper interview, Bass stated he was with his master at the battles of Chickamauga, Missionary Ridge, and later at Pea Ridge, but the order in which he placed these battles is incorrect. Pea Ridge took place in March 1862, Chickamauga in September 1863, and

Missionary Ridge in November 1863. It is probable, at least in my mind, that Bass Reeves was not at the latter two battles with his master.

The Eleventh Texas Cavalry Regiment was involved in the Battle of Chustenahlah on December 26, 1861, in what is today the Osage Nation. Though a relatively early battle in the war, it was the last battle in which the Indians loyal to the Union under the leadership of the Creek Chief Opotheyahola, also known as Gouge, put up a fight. They were crushed by the Confederate troops, mostly Texans and Confederate Indians, in pursuit. The loyalist Indians had put up an excellent fight in two earlier engagements. These Indians were primarily Creeks, Seminoles, and African Americans. After this battle, Chief Opotheyahola and his Indians and blacks were forced to flee in disarray from the Indian Territory into Kansas, freezing and starving.

Paul Brady, Bass's great-nephew, states that Bass had found a home as a fugitive slave with the full-blood Creek and Seminole Indians of the Indian Territory. As such, he was with Chief Opotheyahola at the Battle of Chustenahlah, where the chief advised Bass to stay in the northern Cherokee Nation and fight. In the Cherokee Nation, there was a sect called Keetoowah, who were abolitionist. They were also called Pins because of the crossed pins they wore on their lapels. They carried on a guerilla war against the Confederates in the territory throughout the duration of the Civil War and inflicted heavy damage. Bass Reeves may have joined up with this group after the Battle of Chustenahlah in 1861. Or Bass could have left his master after the Battle of Pea Ridge in March 1862; a number of Cherokees left the Confederacy not long after this battle and joined the Union cause in July 1862.

An interesting side note is that William "Wild Bill" Hickock, the famous gunfighter, was also at Pea Ridge serving as a Union scout. Is it possible Reeves and Hickock met during or after this particular engagement? Since Reeves said he saw General McCulloch, of Texas Ranger fame, receive a fatal gunshot at Pea Ridge, could he have been the one who pulled the trigger?[7]

According to Bass Reeves's daughter Alice Spahn, Bass parted company with his master over an altercation during a card game. Though body servants became on many occasions their master's best friend and confidant, in this case young Reeves got into a heated argument and gave his master a beating. He "laid him out cold with his fist and then made a run for the Indian Territory north across the Red River, with the hue and cry of 'runaway nigger' hounding him up until the Emancipation." It is said that everyone who knew anything or might have been involved refused to talk about the incident or events leading to it. This fight, if it happened, could have occurred before the Battle of Pea Ridge or it could have happened earlier and placed Bass with the Creeks and Seminoles under the leadership of Opotheyahola.

I believe that the fight between Bass and his master probably occurred earlier rather than later in the war. The main evidence for it is that Bass learned the lay of the land in the Indian Territory like "a cook knows his or her kitchen," and he learned to speak Muscogee, the language of the Creeks and Seminoles, and conversed reasonably well in the languages of the other Five Civilized Tribes that inhabited the Indian Territory. If Bass went east of the Mississippi River during the war, it is unlikely that he would have had time to learn the languages and the landscape of the Indian Territory.

One old-timer claimed that Bass Reeves had been a sergeant in the Union army during the Civil War. There were numerous African Americans enlisted who served with the Union's First Indian Home Guard Regiment, which was composed mostly of Seminole and Creek Indians and Freedmen. Many blacks in the regiment served as noncommissioned officers, namely sergeants. All the officers in the regiment were white, and the blacks served as interpreters. Countless black sergeants went only by Indian names on the rosters, so it is possible that one of these men was Bass Reeves. The Civil War years are the haziest in the life of Bass Reeves, but we know one thing for sure. During this period, Reeves perfected his ambidextrous mastery of firearms, both pistol and rifle.[8]

3.

Van Buren and Fort Smith

Bass Reeves and his family moved to Arkansas sometime around 1870; the exact date is not known. In the 1870 census for Crawford County, Arkansas, which was compiled in the month of June, Bass's wife, Jennie, is given the name Jane and her age is given as twenty. At that time they had four children: Sarah, age six; Robert, four; Harriet, two; and George A., six months, who was actually a girl named Georgia. The three oldest children are listed as being born in Texas and the youngest in Arkansas. Bass's wife, Jennie, was evidently living somewhere in Texas during the last years of the Civil War, or that is what was told to the census recorder. It is not known if Bass was making periodic visits or if they lived together in Texas or elsewhere as a couple during the war. Bass Reeves is listed on the census as a farm laborer with a personal estate valued at one hundred dollars. At this time in his life, Reeves was definitely not in the middle class.[1]

Brady states that Reeves sought to assist law enforcement officers who were headquartered at the U.S. marshal's office in Van Buren, Arkansas. Using his knowledge of the Indian Territory and his tracking skills, Reeves was able to make substantial sums as a scout and tracker throughout the territory. According to Brady, Reeves abandoned an earlier plan to settle in Kansas and instead bought a small farm near Van Buren, a town adjacent to the Indian Territory. Reeves relocated his mother, Paralee, and his sister, Jane, to Van Buren as well, and married Jennie. An excellent horse breeder, Reeves established himself in the community and minimized his contacts with the locals, many of whom were former Confederate soldiers and sympathizers.[2]

According to the 1870 census, Bass Reeves and his family lived in the First Ward in Van Buren. From the 1880 Crawford County tax records, we know today that Bass Reeves lived on the corner of Second and Vine streets, block 54, lot 1. His house was across the street from the tracks of the Little Rock and Fort Smith Railroad that ran alongside the Arkansas River. Bass's neighbor across the street on the east side was a white man named Augustus J. Ward. Ward was originally from Connecticut and had lived previously in the Indian Territory. Ward was the treasurer of Crawford County, Arkansas, for twenty-four years, from 1846 to 1860. He owned the whole block in which he lived, opposite the Reeves home.[3]

The town newspaper of Van Buren reported in the early 1880s that Reeves built a nice cottage on the site of his original dwelling. His daughter Alice stated that Bass built this particular home himself, the first by blacks in Van Buren proper. She called the house, with its eight rooms, a "showplace." Alice said it was her brothers' job to keep the place up and looking good. She said they had a big barn, with spotless stalls and well-tended horses. Alice's brother Newland was assigned to taking care of the horses. By the time of the 1880 census, the Reeves family included, besides Bass and his wife, eight children: Sally, 16; Robert, 14; Harriet, 12; Georgia, 10; Alice, 8; Newland, 7; Edgar, 4; and Lula, 2. Alice also stated that on a regular basis attorneys William H. H. Clayton and William M. Cravens took the train from Fort Smith to Van Buren to visit Reeves to talk about cases. She said they always stayed to eat dinner with the family. Clayton was the prosecuting attorney and Cravens was appointed to defend many of the felons arrested and brought to Fort Smith.[4]

Bass Reeves sold his Van Buren home in 1887 during the time he was on trial for murder, to free up monies for his defense. He moved to North Twelfth Street, Park Place, on the outskirts of Fort Smith, Arkansas, in 1889. At that time, this house would have been on the outskirts of Fort Smith.[5]

In 1871 the federal court for the Western District of Arkansas, which also included the Indian Territory, was moved from Van Buren to the nearby town of Fort Smith, which had been an important frontier military post. In 1872 an incompetent lawyer named William Story was appointed to the federal judgeship at Fort Smith. After slightly more than one hundred murders were committed in Indian Territory, Story had to resign to avoid impeachment for bribery. A two-term representative to the U.S. Congress and a member of the House Committee on Indian Affairs from St. Joseph, Missouri, Isaac Charles Parker was named the new judge for the Fort Smith court in March 1875. One of Judge Parker's early moves after being appointed in 1875 was to order his marshal to hire two hundred deputies, mainly to police the Indian Territory. However, Juliet Galonska, park historian of the Fort Smith National Historic Site, estimated that there were no more than forty or fifty deputy U.S. marshals at any time. The area covered by the Western District of Arkansas included all of the Indian Territory (present-day Oklahoma) and western Arkansas, a total area of seventy-four thousand square miles. This was the largest federal court, in terms of area, in U.S. history. The task for a deputy U.S. marshal of the Fort Smith court was a large one, where the outlaws knew every trail and hideout. A year's imprisonment was the only penalty for resisting a federal officer.[6]

Parker's marshal, Daniel P. Upham, hired some deputies who later turned to crime. He also hired some suspicious and shady characters who remained honest and died in combat for the law. Altogether, somewhere between seventy-five to a hundred deputies would die in shootouts with felons during Parker's two decades at Fort Smith.

Sometime after March 1875, Bass Reeves was approached by officials and asked to serve as a deputy U.S. marshal. He accepted the offer and became one of the first men who "rode for Parker." Around this same time, Reeves was arrested by the local Arkansas authorities and brought up on state charges of assault with the intent to kill. According to the *Van Buren Press*, a jury found him not guilty in September 1875. No other information has been found on this incident. The case was known as "The State of Arkansas vs. Baz Reeves."

It has been assumed that Reeves was the first African American commissioned west of the Mississippi River as a deputy U.S. marshal, but this may not be true. According to one story in the Indian Pioneer Papers at the Oklahoma State History Museum, a federal posse was sent out from Van Buren under the leadership of a man known as "Negro" Smith. The posse investigated a stagecoach robbery near Atoka in the Choctaw Nation in 1867, during which the stagecoach driver, Fred Nickolds, was murdered. We know, however, that the majority of black deputy U.S. marshals that worked for the Fort Smith court were appointed during or after 1890. Reeves's outstanding record in the preceding decade no doubt was an impetus for these hirings.[7]

In 1907 an Oklahoma City newspaper article discussed Reeves's early career as a deputy U.S. marshal:

> When Reeves commenced riding as a deputy marshal all of Oklahoma and Indian Territory were under the jurisdiction of the Fort Smith court and deputies from Fort Smith rode to Fort Reno, Fort Sill and Anadarko for prisoners, a distance of 400 miles. In those days the Missouri, Kansas & Texas railroad, running south across the territory, marked the fringe of civilization. Eighty miles west of Fort Smith it was known as "the dead line," and whenever a deputy marshal from Fort Smith or Paris, Texas, crossed the Missouri, Kansas & Texas track he took his own life in his hands and he knew it. On nearly every trail would be found posted by outlaws a small card warning certain deputies that if they ever crossed the dead line they would be killed. Reeves has a dozen of these cards which were posted for his special benefit. And in those days such a notice was no idle boast, and many an outlaw has bitten the dust trying to ambush a deputy on these trails.
>
> In the early 80's there were two principal trails that led up from Denison, Texas into the Indian country that were frequented by horse thieves, bootleggers and others. They were known as the Seminole trail and the Pottawatomie trail. The former led up via old Sasakwa and on toward Sacred Heart Mission. The Seminoles hated the Pottawatomies and the two trails, though they practically paralleled each other, were never used by the same Indians. It was along these two trails, which also led to Fort Sill, Anadarko and Fort Reno, that most of the scenes of encounters with outlaws were laid.

There were three principal classes of outlaws—murderers, horse thieves and bootleggers. Added to the Indians and mixed Negro and Indian were the white outlaws that had fled from Texas, Kansas and other states.

Whenever a deputy marshal left Fort Smith to capture outlaws in the territory he took with his wagon, a cook and usually a posseman, depending on what particular outlaws he was after. The government allowed seventy-five cents a day to feed the prisoners captured and mileage for the distance they traveled at ten cents a mile. A deputy going west was not allowed to arrest a man east of the M.K.&T. railroad, however, he was entitled to pay both for feeding and mileage, both ways, if he carried him 300 miles west to Fort Sill and back again to Fort Smith. A deputy was allowed thirty days time to make a trip as far west as Fort Sill and return. If he had to stop for high water he was paid for the delay. Every deputy was then on fees and took chances making a living. It was a hazardous business and the deputies made big money. Reeves says that he never made a 30 day trip and back with less than $400.00 worth of fees and expense money. He went to Mud Creek and brought in sixteen prisoners at one time and the fees amounted to $700.00, while the total overall expense to him was less than $300.00. The biggest killing he ever made was one time when he captured seventeen prisoners in Comanche county and took them into Fort Smith. The fees for that trip amounted to $900.00. A deputy was allowed to take a posseman, guard and a cook. The posseman drew $3 per day, the guard $3 and the cook $20 per month. The deputy paid his own expenses and got all the fees. The deputy of course rode horseback and ranged wide from the wagon, which was simply his base of supplies and his prison.

Each wagon was equipped with a long heavy chain. When a prisoner was captured he was shackled with old-fashioned brads. At night all the prisoners were shackled in pairs and the shackles passed through a ring in the long chain. One end of the chain was locked around the rear axis of the wagon. In this manner one man could handle thirty prisoners if he wished to. His only precaution was to prevent the prisoners from ever getting within reach of the six-shooters. This danger was ever present. No guard or cook was ever allowed to gamble with the prisoners for fear they would lose their six-shooters. The first thing a prisoner wants after he is captured and shackled to chain is to gamble.[8]

Deputy U.S. marshals for the Western District of Arkansas were ordered to make arrests for murder, attempts to murder, manslaughter, assault with intent to kill or to maim, arson, robbery, rape, burglary, larceny, incest, adultery, and willfully and maliciously placing obstructions on a railroad track. For these offenses a warrant was desired but not mandatory. For other offenses, such as violations of the revenue laws or introducing liquor into the Indian country, a warrant was necessary unless the felon was caught in the act. Deputies were also made aware of the types of crimes for which Indians could be arrested. These crimes were specified by the jurisdictional treaty restrictions of the sovereign Indian nations, who policed their own citizens. The deputies usually traveled on horseback accompanied by a "grub" wagon. The officer and his guards, posse, and cook were called an "outfit." The grub wagon was commonly provisioned with bread, beans, coffee, bacon, beef, molasses, sugar, flour, potatoes, venison, and ham. Sometimes the residents in the territory called the deputy's wagon the "tumbleweed wagon."[9] The deputies typically left Fort Smith, traveled to Fort Sill, then headed north to Anadarko, Fort Reno, and on occasion Fort Supply before returning to Fort Smith.

The court at Fort Smith ran nonstop in the fight against the lawless. Between May 10, 1875, and September 1, 1896, Judge Parker tried 13,490 criminal cases and won better than 8,500 convictions. Approximately one in every hundred of those found guilty was sentenced to death; for the others, it was imprisonment from one to forty-five years in one of the state penitentiaries that accepted federal prisoners by arrangement with the U.S. government. Parker's court was in session for six days a week, from 7:30 a.m. to 12:00 p.m. and from 1:00 p.m. to 6:00 p.m. Eighty-five percent of the offenses were committed in the Indian Territory. It was Parker's theory, often expressed, that certainty of punishment rather than punishment itself was the only way to combat crime. When the territory's hardest criminals heard his name, they cringed, for it was synonymous with the gallows. From 1875 until 1889 there was no appeal from his decision; his word was final except on those very rare occasions when the president intervened. Parker sentenced eighty-eight men to be hanged, but only seventy-nine came to their death on the gallows. One was killed trying to escape, one died before the execution date, and seven won reversals, after it became possible in 1891, and received lesser sentences on being retried. Of the seventy-nine who were hung, thirty were white, twenty-six were Indians, and twenty-three were black.[10]

Each tribe in the Indian Territory had their own highly regarded police force called Lighthorse police, but treaties prohibited them from arresting criminals who were not citizens of their Indian nations. This reality enticed some of the worst criminals in the West to take up residence in the Indian Territory. It then fell to the undermanned federal court at Fort Smith to arrest white or black men who perpetrated crimes against Indians or Indians who committed crimes against noncitizen white or black men. The U.S. attorney general in 1888 estimated that of the twenty thousand white persons residing in Indian Territory, only five thousand were law abiding. Out of every eleven men convicted in Parker's court, seven were white, three were black, and one was Indian.[11]

The country would never see another federal court like Fort Smith, nor would it see lawmen like those who worked for the court, especially the one named Bass Reeves.

4.

On the Trail

Among the numerous deputy marshals that have ridden for the Paris (Texas), Fort Smith (Arkansas) and Indian Territory courts none have met with more hairbreadth escapes or have effected more hazardous arrests than Bass Reeves, of Muskogee. Bass is a stalwart Negro, fifty years age, weighs one hundred and eighty pounds, stands six feet and two inches in his stockings, and fears nothing that moves and breathes. His long muscular arms have attached to them a pair of hands that would do credit to a giant and they handle a revolver with the ease and grace acquired only after years of practice. Several "bad" men have gone to their long home for refusing to halt when commanded to by Bass.[1]

D. C. Gideon, 1901

On numerous occasions in Reeves's early career as a deputy U.S. marshal, he rode out of Fort Smith as a posseman for another deputy. This was not an uncommon practice in the Indian Territory. Less experienced deputies frequently went on patrol with more experienced deputies so they could gain knowledge from seasoned lawmen. Sometimes a deputy would request another deputy to go out with him because he respected his skills and dependability. Oftentimes a deputy U.S. marshal's posse did not consist of another commissioned deputy unless specially requested. But the deputies traveling in Indian Territory were mandated by law to have at least one posseman with them. A person hired as a posseman was considered an acting deputy U.S. marshal. Sometimes the posses would range from one to six people or more depending on the circumstances. Larger posses were always evident after a train robbery or similar crime.

Bass Reeves worked as a posseman for various deputies of the Fort Smith court. He was acting as a posseman for Deputy U.S. Marshal Robert J. Topping on June 25, 1877, in the Choctaw Nation near Atoka when they arrested Austin Ward. Ward had stolen one yoke of oxen, valued at sixty dollars, from a Frenchman named William Deshon on December 10, 1876.[2] In November of 1878 Reeves served in a different capacity for the federal court when he and his wife were subpoenaed to serve as character witnesses for a detained suspect. John Adams claimed he was mistaken for his half-brother William Ausley, an escaped convict. Adams stated that Reeves and his wife, Jennie, of Van Buren had known him and his brother for fifteen years and could vouch for his veracity in this case.[3]

The next month, on December 20, 1878, Reeves served as a guard at the executions of James Diggs and John Postoak at Fort Smith. Diggs, a black man, had murdered a cattle drover, J. C. Gould, in the northern portion of the Indian Territory near the Kansas border on August 4, 1873. Postoak, an Indian, was convicted on August 16, 1878, for the murder of a white man, John Ingley, and his wife in the Creek Nation. When an Indian or Indian Freedman committed a crime against a non-Indian-nation citizen, or vice versa, it fell under the federal court to pursue and adjudicate the case. In the summer of 1879, Reeves arrested a black man by the name of Taylor for the murder of a woman in the Indian nations. On his return to Van Buren, Arkansas, with the suspect for the purpose of identification by witnesses, he found out he had arrested the wrong man.[4]

On May 20, 1880, Bass Reeves was along as a posseman for Deputy U.S. Marshal James H. Mershon when they arrested Simon James and General Cooper for introducing illegal whiskey in the Indian Territory. Reeves and Zack Moody, also a member of the posse, served as witnesses in the court case. The defendants went to trial on June 14 during which

On the Trail   33

Mershon testified that he saw them with a load of whiskey in kegs and quart and pint bottles, estimating that they had ten to twelve gallons between them. He said there were bottles in their saddlebags and in their shirts and pockets. Between ten and twelve o'clock at night the posse picked up James and Cooper about four miles from the Texas border heading into the Indian Territory. Mershon said he tasted the goods to make sure it was whiskey, and Reeves and Moody said they also did a taste test. Simon James was convicted and given eighteen months at the Detroit House of Corrections and fined twenty dollars. It is not known what happened to Cooper, as the case file has no record of a judgment on his conviction. Most likely he was sent to Detroit also. Reeves would work quite a bit in the 1880s with Mershon in the Chickasaw Nation.

Mershon was one of the most noted and outstanding deputies who worked for the Fort Smith court. Originally from London, Kentucky, and of French descent, Mershon served in the Civil War, originally with the Confederates in Texas, and later joined the Second Kansas Cavalry with the Union Army in Arkansas, attaining the rank of sergeant during the war. Mershon worked as a deputy U.S. marshal for about fifteen years, from 1875 to 1890. His most famous capture was of the notorious black outlaw Bully Joseph in the Chickasaw Nation. On his tombstone in Oak Cemetery in Fort Smith, Arkansas, the title of captain precedes his name. Many people were called captain after the war due to their position in life. It was a badge of respect. Mershon was born in 1838, the same year as Bass, and died in an asylum in Terrill, Texas on April 16, 1899, after going insane at his home in Denison, Texas, in 1898. He is one of eighty-two deputy U.S. marshals of the Parker court buried in Oak Cemetery.[5]

In late May of 1881, Reeves served as a guard for the transportation of prisoners from the Fort Smith federal jail to the House of Corrections in Detroit. U.S. Marshal Dell personally accompanied the twenty-one prisoners on this trip by rail. Other deputy U.S. marshals who served as guards on this assignment were Jacob T. Ayers, Thomas E. Lacy, J. M. Caldwell, Addison Beck, and George Maledon, who was also the official executioner at the Fort Smith jail. One of the prisoners being transported was a female named Arena Howe who had been given a ten-year sentence. She was accompanied by her two children, one age six years and the other an infant who was born in the U.S. jail at Fort Smith.[6]

On July 19, 1881, Reeves was riding as a posseman for Deputy U.S. Marshal Jacob T. Ayers when they arrested Bill Wilson for assault with intent to kill in the Chickasaw Nation near Atoka. Atoka itself was in the Choctaw Nation but not far from the Chickasaw Nation line west of town. Frank Tucker was the guard for Ayers on this trip. There is nothing in the case file indicating whether Wilson was convicted of the charges.[7]

Ayers and Reeves on the same trip went into Texas after a white man named William Watson. Watson was wanted for larceny in the Indian Territory, and after being apprehended he tried to bribe Ayers into releasing him. He was then brought up on charges of trying to bribe a peace officer. Ayers stated in the hearing before the U.S. Commissioner of Indian Affairs:

> I arrested Defendant about the 16th of August near Burlington, Texas, either in Montague or Cook County. I put him on my horse with me and we proceeded to Rasstin Turner's house, I failed to get Turner and came back by King William's house. Watson said he wanted to stop there and make some arrangements for some money. Williams came out and asked Watson how much money he wanted, Watson said he did not know how much money he would need and Williams told him he had better take $100. Watson then asked me to ride to one side that he wanted to speak to me privately. I rode five or six steps away from where Bass Reeves was sitting on his horse. Watson then asked me how much money I would take to release him. I replied that there was no use of talking any more about that and turned and rode back to where Bass was, we then crossed the river and stayed the remainder of the night at William R. Watkins. Before going to bed that night I took the money that Watson had, $110, and gave him my due bill for the same. . . . We went the next day to Courtney Flat, that night I moved

camp to Simon Creek. I was admiring a mare that belonged to John Watson, defendants brother, The defendant told me he would make me a present of the mare. He said you had better let me make you a present of that mare. The next day I move camp to Spring Creek, we were camped there four days, while there he asked me how much my fees would be in his case. I told him near a hundred dollars, he said he would give me more than any fees would amount to if I would release him. I told him I could not release him under any circumstances.

Bass Reeves gave the following testimony in the hearing:

I was out with Deputy Marshal Jacob Ayers on his last trip. I was his posse, we arrested defendant in Texas then went to Rass Turners then to King Williams, while standing there he asked Ayers to step to one side he wanted to speak to him. They stepped one side a little and I heard defendant ask Ayers what he would take to release him, or drop it or something to that effect and Ayers told him he could not do it. We went on to camp. We then moved to Spring Creek. While there Defendant asked me what I thought Ayers would take to release him. I told him I did not know, that he must talk to Ayers about it. I told him that Ayers could not release him, that one deputy had already gone to the penitentiary for such as that. At Cherokeetown he told a man to write some more in a letter that he had asking them to send $300 in the letter to McAllister. He told me that King told him to slip $150 in his boot so he could give it to one or to Tucker to release him. At Spring Creek I heard defendant tell Ayers to set his price. I heard Ayers tell him to send his letter.

Reeves testified on cross examination:

I heard defendant and Ayers talking something about a sorrel mare that his brother was riding. Defendant then asked Ayers if he wanted her and said he could get her if he did want her. I was in camp when Joe Smith was released. Joe was charged with larceny, I suppose Ayers had a writ for him he had him under arrest.

Frank Tucker testified:

> I was out with Jake Ayers on his last trip where he brought in
> Watson. I was guarding and cooking. I heard defendant and
> Bass and Ayers talking about releasing Watson for money. I
> heard them two or three times. But I did not pay much attention
> to it. On Spring Creek defendant asked me how much I would
> take to turn him loose and I told him I could not do it.

Evidently Watson was released by the U.S. commissioner on charges of
attempting to bribe an officer, but he was charged later with committing
a murder, that of John Phelps, on October 1, 1882. Then, on September 15, 1884, Watson was charged with another larceny. A warrant for
the murder charge was written up on February 17, 1887, and on June
16, 1887, in the Chickasaw Nation near Courtney Flats, Deputy U.S.
Marshal Heck Thomas arrested Watson for the murder.[8]

Ayers and Reeves arrested a black man named Randall Stick for horse
theft on August 27, 1881, in the Chickasaw Nation. Stick claimed the
horse was given to him because he helped an old woman through an
illness. It is not clear in the case file whether Stick was convicted on
this arrest, but it would not be his last run-in with law. He was arrested
numerous times later for various thefts in the Chickasaw Nation.[9]

One early Indian Territory pioneer said, "Bass Reeves was a very big
man, told jokes, was boastful and lusty, full of life and wore a large black
hat." He had a deep and resonant voice that could be very authoritative
when it had to be but assuring just the same. Reeves's laugh was thunderous and booming. Due to his size, he always rode a large horse. Bass said,
"When you get as big as me, a small horse is as worthless as a preacher
in a whiskey joint fight. Just when you need him bad to help you out,
he's got to stop and think about it a little bit." Reeves rode mostly bay,
sorrel, and gray horses when he made trips into the Indian nations.[10]

Deputy U.S. Marshal Jacob Ayers, with a posse that included Bass
Reeves, arrested two peace officers, one white, one Indian, for murder
on December 30, 1881, near the Wichita Indian Agency. James Jones,
chief of the Indian Police at the Wichita Agency at Anadarko, and Indian
Police officer John Mullins, alias Comanche Jack, were indicted for the
murder of two white men, Charley Hard and James Davis. Hard was a

fugitive from Texas and Davis worked at a wood camp east of Fort Sill. In October of 1881 Jones, with a contingent of Indian Police, had arrested Hard. Davis was taken into custody as an accomplice, since Hard was living with Davis's family. The lawmen informed Davis that he was not under arrest but would be required to accompany the detachment of Indian Police back to Fort Sill. Davis brought along his wife, Mattie, and their two small children.

The Wichita Agency Police had an encampment about a half mile northeast of Fort Sill. Chief Jones went to Fort Sill and telegraphed to the Wichita Agency at Anadarko that he had arrested Charley Hard and taken James Davis in custody. The telegram was given to Deputy Jacob Ayers who had arrived at the agency with his posse shortly before the arrival of the telegram. Ayers sent a telegram back to Jones that he wanted James Davis to be placed under arrest and brought to him for transfer to Fort Smith on an unstated criminal charge. Ayers made no mention of Hard, who was wanted by Texas authorities.

Jones went back to his camp and made preparation for the trip to Anadarko. Jones told Davis that before they departed he would allow him a short visit with his family at their camp southeast of Fort Sill. This was five days after the Indian Police had made the arrests. On Friday, November 4, 1881, according to witness Isaac Lorantz, Jones took Davis and Hard southeast to the camp of Mattie Davis. Strangely, the men never arrived at the Davis camp. According to Jones, before they arrived at the camp, three men identifying themselves as deputy sheriffs from Texas requested that Davis and Hard be turned over to them to answer criminal charges in Texas. Jones testified that he turned the men over to the Texas lawmen after being satisfied that they were legitimate peace officers. However, no one can recall seeing Jones after he departed the Indian Police until the next day when he told the story about turning Davis and Hard over to the Texas lawmen.

A few days later Chief Jones and his Indian Police returned to the Wichita Agency in Anadarko where he reportedly told Deputy U.S. Marshal Jacob Ayers that he had released Davis and Hard to the Texas authorities. Jones went on to tell Ayers that he felt sorry for Davis as he had a family to support and he feared that Davis and Hard would be lynched before returning to Texas. Becoming immediately suspicious,

Ayers ordered Jones to surrender his pistol, which Reeves took possession of. Bass noticed the pistol had four out of a possible six cartridges in the cylinder, so he took these bullets and returned the gun to Jones. Many times a person would leave the pistol hammer down on an empty chamber so no firings would occur accidentally. This would then leave five cartridges in a pistol loaded.

Isaac Lorantz, a civilian employee for the military, stated he was at the beef issue pens east of the Davis camp when he saw three unknown men riding north toward the area where Jones claimed to have turned Davis and Hard over to the Texans. In addition, a woman named Mary Daily was camped with her husband, James, about a half a mile south of the Davis camp on what was called the Texas Crossing of East Cache Creek. She stated that she saw five men riding south and that she recognized one of the men as James Davis, whom she had seen as a prisoner in the Indian Police camp earlier that day. Mary Dailey was well acquainted with James Jones and stated positively that Jones was not a member of this group of riders.

Davis and Hard were not seen or heard of again until about a month later when their remains were discovered about three miles southeast of Fort Sill in a bend on the east bank of East Cache Creek opposite the present site of the Fort Sill Indian School. After Davis and Hard's arrest, John Mullins had left the contingent of Indian Police before they reached their camp near Fort Sill. One day in early December, Mullins, also known as Comanche Jack, showed up at Fort Sill and told the post adjutant, Lieutenant Jacob R. Pierce, that he had found two bodies. Upon inspection of the bodies, Pierce estimated that the men had been dead about twenty days. The body of James Davis was in a good state of preservation in a deep gulch that ran into East Cache Creek. Lieutenant Pierce ascertained that Davis had been both hanged and shot. Davis had suffered two bullet wounds, one in the breast and one in the head. A bruise on his neck indicated he had been either hanged or dragged by the neck with a rope. The lieutenant was able to recognize that Davis was a man he had seen frequenting the Fort Sill trader's store saloon. Charley Hard was found about one hundred yards away, but his body was harder to examine because prairie wolves had eaten most of it. They could ascertain that Hard had suffered a bullet wound to the head. About twenty feet from Hard's body, the soldiers located a dried pool of blood and a spent copper-cased .45 Long Colt cartridge casing.

Ayers and his posse were back in the Fort Sill vicinity in late December and took Jones and Mullins to Fort Smith to face charges of murder. At the preliminary hearing before the U.S. commissioner, Bass Reeves testified:

> I am a posse under Deputy Marshal Jake Ayers. I was at the Wichita Agency at the time Davis and Hard were said to be under arrest. I saw Jones he told me that he had two prisoners. Jones came to the Agency and left his hack mule at the store and went down to the camp and told Ayers he had two prisoners that he intended to bring down but he said the Sheriff of Henrietta came up with writ for them and he turned them over to him. Ayers asked him what the Sheriff's name was but he said he had forgotten. He said he felt sorry for Davis for he feared they would lynch them before they went far. I don't remember his calling the other prisoners name, he said he said he felt sorry for Davis because he had a family. Ayers asked him if he knew these men and he said he did not but that they were from Henrietta. Ayers asked Jones if he did not know his name and told him he ought to know it that he ought to have taken down the name. I saw Jones around there the next day after he reported this to us. Jones never talked with me at another time about Davis and Hard. I saw him about two weeks afterwards at Tishomingo, he did not tell me anything about the men having been killed. I saw him again on Christmas Eve at Wichita Agency he did not then say anything about their being killed. When we arrested Mullins he told me he was with Jones when he arrested the first man, but was not with him when he arrested Davis but had gone home. (The witness here presents a pistol cartridge which he says he took out of Jones pistol.) I took the pistol from Jones at Wichita, they are .45 caliber copper cartridges, they are different from the .45 caliber cartridges I use. Mine are brass cartridges, the cartridges I took out of Jones pistol are

the same kind as those used by soldiers and the Indian Police up there.

On cross examination Bass testified:

I think it was in the evening of the third day after I first went to see the agent that Jones came from Fort Sill.

Another posseman, William Hunter, testified:

I helped arrest Jones. Bass Reeves took the pistol off of him. When he took the pistol from him, Bass said there ain't but four barrels of this pistol loaded. He took the cartridges out of the pistol and gave these to me and I have had them in my possession ever since. They are government cartridges, the kind issued to the soldiers. I tried to buy some of these at Fort Sill but could not do it.[11]

The U.S. Indian agent for the Wichita Agency, P. B. Hunt, wrote a very interesting letter to the Commissioner of Indian Affairs in regard to this case:

United States of America
Indian Territory
Kiowa, Comanche, and Wichita Agency

Personally appeared before me this 11th day of February 1882, John Mullins, whose Indian name is Comanche Jack, known to me as the person who after being duly sworn makes the following statement to wit:

I am a member of the Indian Police force of the Kiowa, Comanche, and Wichita Agency and live about 12 miles south of Fort Sill.

On the 1st day of January, 1882, two men, whom I afterwards learned were in the employ of Deputy U.S. Marshal Ayers came to my place and told me that James N. Jones, Chief of Indian Police, and Lieut. Pierce, U.S. Army Post Adjutant wanted to see me at Fort Sill. I at once got ready and proceeded with them to Fort Sill to see Jones who I found was under arrest and in the custody of the Deputy Marshal. A few minutes after my arrival at his camp the

Marshal came to me and told me had had a paper for me and that I would have to go to Fort Smith without showing me any paper he arrested me and then asked me for my pistol, but I did not have it with me, he then sent me into his tent, where Jones and a Seminole Indian were held and soon afterward put shackles on me and the Seminole.

That night the marshal told me I was charged with hanging or aiding in the hanging of two white men near Fort Sill.

On the night of the 2nd of January while still in camp at Fort Sill the Marshal and one of his posse took me out of the tent a short distance away near their wagon and in sight of where a crowd of Soldiers had gathered as there had been the night previous and then told me that I had helped to hang those two white men and that now these men pointing to the crowd of soldiers had come and would hang me unless I would tell all about the hanging of those men and that If I would tell all about the hanging of those men and that if I would tell that, Lieut. Pierce would release me and let me go, that if I had anything to say it must be said then.

All this was said and done in a manner to intimidate me, but as I had nothing to do with the hanging of these men and knew nothing at all about it I told the Marshal to this effect and if they hang me that is all I can say. I was then taken back to the tent and the next day the Marshal and the posse employed by him started with the two other prisoners and myself to Ft. Smith traveling 19 days in a two horse wagon reaching Fort Smith on the 21st of January when I was placed in jail and kept there four days, was then taken before a U.S. Commissioner and after an investigation of the charge against me and others lasting two days, I was released from arrest by the Commissioner and told that I could go home.

When I was arrested at Fort Sill I had no money with me and had no opportunity to provide myself for the trip or for my defense and when I was turned loose at Ft. Smith, Ark., no means were offered or furnished me for my return home a distance of about 350 miles and I was compelled to work my way back as best I could. I was also put to the necessity of employing a lawyer at Ft. Smith to conduct my defense before the U.S. Commissioner whom I had to agree to pay $200 for which I was compelled to give mortgage being the least he would do it for and said if the case went to Court he would charge an additional fee.

I was unable to pay this amount at present and I do not know when or how I am to earn or can raise the money to pay him without depriving myself of the means of living and I further say not.

[signed] John Mullens

Subscribed and sworn to before me at the Kiowa, Comanche, and Wichita Agency on the day date first above written. The alterations and interlinsation [interlineations] made before signing

[signed] P. B. Hunt
U.S. Indian Agent[12]

Evidence was lacking to indict Mullins and he was discharged from custody following the examination of evidence before U.S. Commissioner Stephen Wheeler.

The U.S. Indian agent of the Wichita Agency sent a follow-up letter to Washington DC:

I have the honor to acknowledge receipt of your letter of 21st ultimo asking for more specific information concerning offending Deputy U.S. Marshals and in reply thereto I first beg leave to state that in presenting this subject to the Department by letter of Feb'y 1st   82 my object was to make a general complaint regarding the manner of arresting accused persons of my reservation and not for the purpose of having past offences punished but to prevent in the future a recurrence of irregularities and wrong doing on the part of the Deputy Marshals. As to more definite information concerning the same, I have to state that the only U.S. Marshals, or Deputies, who have served processes to my knowledge within the limits of my jurisdiction belong to the Western District of Arkansas and in regard to recent arrests referred to in my said letter, these were made by Deputy J. T. Ayers, who is the same person referred to by the Commandant at Fort Sill in his communication to me of Jany 10 from which I quoted in my letter of the 1st ultimo to the effect that Ayers was drunk while camped at Fort Sill, and it was he who about this time arrested John Mullins, a Comanche Indian referred to in the Commandant's letter as Comanche Jack, the circumstances of which are set forth in the affidavit of said Mullins, a copy of which is herewith submitted. I have been informed by Mr. E. C. Suggs, Beef Contractor at Fort Sill, lately returned from Fort Smith, Arkansas, that Ayres and his party spoke of their trip to the Indian Territory in December last as a very successful one and that the costs accessed [assessed] against the Government in making the arrest of Mullins, J. N. Jones, Washington, and one other, here and at Fort Sill, amounted to $1,200 or about $300 for each arrest. I particularly invite your attention to the case of Mullins, who ought not to have been arrested, as the proceedings had in his case before the U.S. Commissioner at Fort Smith demonstrated, but who was arrested as it appears, without the formality of serving a warrant, and subjected to treatment, unauthorized by law such as is usually resorted to by mobs and when intimidation failed of its purpose, to carry him 300 miles or more by wagon to Fort Smith to be subjected there to a fleecing by exorbitant attorney fees that taken altogether is not flattering to the administration of justice.

[signed] P. B. Hunt
U.S. Indian Agent

Chief of Indian Police James Jones was indicted by a Fort Smith grand jury on February 6, 1882. Jones was released from jail due to his bond being paid by Indian agent Philemon B. Hunt and cattleman Eli Suggs. Jones was tried in the Fort Smith federal court in March 1883 and was found not guilty of the double lynching of James Davis and Charley Hard. If Jones was inebriated, as Hunt claims in his letter, the source of his spirits most likely was the trading post at military forts, where whiskey was sold legally. Peace officers would not take the chance of drinking illegal whiskey in camp. James Jones, who had started his tenure with the government as an army scout, continued his service with the Indian Police and as a deputy U.S. marshal for the Fort Sill area for many years afterward.[13]

For Reeves, speed in a horse was important, but of primary importance was strength and endurance, for Bass felt that being certain of getting where he was going was far more important than how fast he got there. However, Bass did own at least one horse that was famous for its speed. He took great pride in demonstrating this speed, backing up this demonstration with hard money whenever possible.

Once, along the upper reaches of Hellroaring Creek, deep in the Chickasaw Nation, Bass rode up on a man named Allen Thompson. Reeves was on his way to the Creek Nation with a pocketful of warrants and Thompson was working the brush along the creek for stray cattle. As was the custom of the travelers of that day, Bass stopped to "palaver" for a little bit before riding on.

Bass was riding a big sorrel gelding that stood almost a full nineteen hands tall, and Thompson was riding a little gray mare hardly bigger than a Spanish mule. Both men admired the other's horse, discussing the finer points of both, and after a few minutes the question of speed was mentioned. Bass, with a great display of calculated indifference, said that his horse was pretty slow, but he might be able to get a race out of him as long as it was a short one and over good ground, because the sorrel was old and had traveled many a hard mile already that day. Thompson rose to the bait and "allowed his gray might could run just a little bit" if he encouraged her along with the liberal application of his quirt because, after all, she was only a poor, hard-working cow horse that had been popping cattle out of the brush all day, and chasing cows was mighty poor training for racing speed in a horse.

With each man belittling his horse's ability as a racer, a matched race between the sorrel and the gray was reluctantly arranged. Just to make it interesting, a twenty-dollar gold piece was to be put up by each man to help the winner of the race reconcile the strain and effort his "poor old wore-out hoss" would have to exert in running the race. The loser was to receive the best wishes and deep sympathy of the winner, with maybe just a smattering of heel dust from the winner thrown in to help even things up.

In short order, a two-mile course was picked out. Reeves was to toss a rock over his shoulder into the creek and the splash it made was to be the signal to start. Bass selected the rock, tossed it back, and there, down the fertile bottomland of Hellroaring Creek, with perhaps not another soul closer than forty miles, the race was on.

Thompson and his little gray were off like "a guinea hen in a hailstorm" to take an extremely easy lead, leaving Bass and his sorrel "sitting and wondering" what kind of cows that gray was used to chasing. Reeves cut loose with a bellow "louder than any cow-chasing range bull" advertising his availability and gave the sorrel his head. He leaned low in the saddle and shifted his weight as far forward as possible, and the sorrel settled down to the job of catching the upstart gray.

The gray was running easy. Its ears were flat and laid back along its stretched neck, and Thompson was laid so far out over the saddle, chuckling and encouraging the gray, that it was hard to tell where the gray's ears ended and Thompson's began. He and the gray did not intend to lose the race, for this gray mare was one of the top horses in the Chickasaw Nation, and Thompson had a reputation to maintain of beating all comers in a matched race. Bass's sorrel began to unlimber and answer the challenge of the gray with the long, powerful, ground-eating strides that had served Reeves so well in his official capacity as a lawman, and which had won countless matched races before.

When the gray reached the half-mile mark, Reeves and his sorrel were back in the race and closing fast on the gray. By the three-quarter-mile mark, the gray didn't stand a chance; though fast and truly a horse among horses, her short-coupled, small size was no match for the long-bodied, rangy sorrel. The sorrel passed the gray so fast that Thompson grunted in disbelief. He spoke to the gray and even used his quirt in an effort to increase her speed, but the daylight between the two horses increased until Thompson felt that there was a "Tuesday 'til next Sunday night" difference between them. He sat back and pulled up the gray, letting her finish the race in an easy lope. The size and power of the sorrel were too much for the gray over a two-mile course, and Thompson didn't want to break her heart by letting her finish a race in which she was so greatly overmatched. He simply pulled her up to wait for another day and another race, and above all, a race with another horse.[14]

Being a big man who rode on his horse erect, Reeves could be identified at great distances on the prairie. For outlaws looking to ambush him or elude capture, Reeves would have to alter his appearance in the saddle. Richard Fronterhouse told me that Bass learned to disguise himself on horseback by learning riding tricks from the Indians. They taught him how to look smaller in the saddle at great distances. Also Reeves wouldn't always ride his best horses when he was in disguise, for that would be a dead giveaway that he was a peace officer. Deputies always had very good saddle horses that wore horseshoes; they were noted for riding the best horses in the Indian Territory. So Reeves always kept a couple of regular saddle ponies for undercover work. Outlaws many times would ride inferior horses that were unshod.[15]

On March 22, 1882, Reeves arrested Jim Grayson, a Creek Freedman, twenty-five miles west of Stonewall, Chickasaw Nation, for an assault on a white man named Sy Cochran. Reeves had a letter written to Fort Smith for the warrant. It said:

> Stonewall, C.N.
> April 4th 1882
>
> Hon. Thos. Boles, U.S. Marshal
> Dear Sir:
>
> Please send me a writ for Jim Grayson who committed an assault on one Sy Cochran about the last of March, 1882. He done it by striking him across the head with a spike knocking him senseless for one hour and he has not been able to do anything since. The following are the names of the witnesses: Ben Underwood, Indian Police; Sy Cochran and two others. Your Obedient Servant
>
> > [signed] Bas. Reeves
> > Dep. U.S. Marshal

Reeves brought Grayson into Fort Smith on April 24, 1882, and turned him over to the jailer.[16]

That same day, Reeves sent a letter requesting a warrant for another outlaw operating in the Chickasaw Nation:

Stonewall, C.N.
April 4th 1882

Hon. Thos. Boles U.S. Marshal

Dear Sir:

Please send me a writ for Frank Wilburn for introducing five gallons of spirituous liquors into the Indian country last May. The witnesses names are as follows: Owen Hennessy and Joe Smith and one Henderson. The Chief of Police of the Indian Nation has got him under charges and wants to turn him over to me, he sent for me yesterday and I went and saw him but would not receive him until I got a writ from you.

> Your Obedient Servant
> [signed] Bass Reeves
> Dep. Marshal

P.S. Please send the writ to Stonewall, C.N. for[th]with as he promised me that he would hold him until I could get an answer. He is a very bad man and the citizens of this country wish to have him taken out. He is a white man.

Reeves did receive the warrant for Wilburn's arrest. Subpoenas for witnesses were issued on April 15, 1882, for the crime noted as having taken place on May 15, 1881.[17]

In June of 1882, Bass Reeves was working with Deputy U.S. Marshal Zack Williams when they arrested Banks Grayson and Boston Williams for introducing and selling whiskey in the Chickasaw Nation. The crime supposedly took place on Christmas Day of 1881. The warrant was written on May 18, 1882, on the oath of Bass Reeves, and the parties were arrested on June 1, 1882. There was a hearing before U.S. Circuit Court Commissioner James Brizzolara in Fort Smith on June 20. At the hearing Richard Herrod testified:

> I reside at near Sacred Heart Mission and know the defendant in this cause. I have known him ever since I was a boy. Defendant lives about five miles from me. I have never seen him with any whiskey, never saw defendant sell any whiskey; never

seen anyone get any whiskey from him. I was down at Bank Stephenson's church on Christmas eve night. Defendant was there; there was whiskey flying around there; but I did not get even a chance to taste it. Defendant lives close to this place. Boston Williams was there that night.

Dan Grayson, being duly sworn, testified:

I live in Seminole Nation; know defendant; am no kin to defendant; have known him ever since I was a little boy. The river is between defendant and I. I have never seen defendant with any whiskey. I never bought any whiskey from him; never saw anyone buy any whiskey from defendant. On Christmas eve night I was at the meeting house in defendants settlement; if there was any whiskey around there I do not know it. Defendant was there when I first got there . . . he came late in the night. Boston Williams was there too.

U.S. Commissioner Brizzolara discharged Banks Grayson in this case because he was exonerated by the witnesses' testimony. There was not enough evidence to bring it before a jury.[18]

On July 31, 1882, Reeves arrested Charleston Holmes near Stonewall, Chickasaw Nation, for stealing the horse of a black man named George Nelson. The horse was valued at twenty-five dollars. Witnesses for the prosecution included George Nelson, Henry Kemp, and Israel Colbert, all from Stringtown. The case was thrown out because all parties were citizens of the Chickasaw Nation.[19]

On July 25, 1882, Reeves arrested a black man, Bass Kemp, in the Chickasaw Nation for attempted murder with a pistol of another black man named Elijah Jackson. This case was also thrown out. Evidently as in the previous case, these individuals both turned out to be citizens of the Chickasaw Nation.[20]

The following month in the Choctaw Nation, Reeves arrested a white man for an assault upon a white woman. Charles McNally was picked up on August 5, 1882, for striking with the butt of his rifle a lady named Sarah Kenzie near Skullyville. The case went before a jury trial on August 8th in Fort Smith. It came out during the trial that Sarah did not have a good reputation in the community in which she lived. Kenzie had unlawfully took possession of a horse McNally had loaned to W. H. Winn, and when McNally found it in a field tied to a tree he retrieved it. Kenzie physically attacked McNally and grabbed him in the collar and in defending himself he slapped her in the face. She proceeded to pick up a big rock and attacked him; in defense he pushed her away with the butt of his rifle. The jury found McNally not guilty on August 14, 1882.[21]

Frank Guion, a white man, brought charges against another white man named William Horton for attempted murder. The warrant for Horton's arrest dates the incident May 28, 1882, but the testimony during the hearing dates the incident July 4, 1882. Reeves arrested Horton in August and it went to trial on August 11. The case was thrown out because according to testimony there was a family feud with bad blood between the parties. Also, little physical evidence existed of an attempted murder except the complainants' testimony.[22]

A notorious Seminole Indian outlaw named Greenleaf and a confederate of his named Pana Maha were selling whiskey in the Creek Nation. Bass Reeves swore out a warrant for the arrest of Greenleaf and Maha on July 1, 1881. He arrested Maha in Fort Smith on August 8, 1882, but the hunt continued for Greenleaf. On September 11, Reeves had another writ of arrest made up for the elusive Greenleaf. The hunt for this Indian outlaw would last almost a decade.[23]

Traveling through the Indian Territory on a regular basis allowed Reeves to become familiar with a significant number of the residents. This was especially true of individuals who had some relationship, as witness or defendant, with the Fort Smith court. Reeves's hometown newspaper, the *Van Buren Press*, ran a story on August 26, 1882, that involved Reeves identifying a person who died mysteriously:

A Woman Found Dead

The woman found dead on the sand-bar, just above the mouth of Lee's Creek, last Saturday, was identified by United States Deputy Marshal Bass Reaves, as a woman by the name of Lydia Combs, who lived in the Choctaw Nation, and was a witness in a case pending in the United States court at Fort Smith. A post mortem showed that the woman was dead before she was put in the river. The Fort Smith Herald says that the "description is said to suit a Mrs. Suttle, who came in on Friday, via the Muscogee stage, to this city, bringing with her a daughter by her first husband, a Mr. Davis. Suttle, her present husband, is in jail, under a charge of assault, and lives at Atoka, I.T. Mrs. Suttle was not of sound mind, and escaped from her daughter last Friday, the 17th, since which time her whereabouts have been unknown. The whole case is enshrouded in mystery, and the evidence of a foul and damnable crime are not wanting. We trust our authorities will be vigilant, and get to the bottom of this tragic affair. We conversed with Miss Davis yesterday, and she manifested a singular, if not stoical indifference to the sad fate that had overtaken her mother, and did not seem to care whether it was investigated or not. Whether Mrs. Suttle was an important witness or not we do not know, or how far she was mentally unsound is unknown to us."[24]

While searching out felons in the Indian Territory, Reeves arrested John Lynch for murder on October 9, 1882, on Deep Fork Creek of the Creek Nation. Lynch was indicted for murder along with Robert Gentry and Willie Fisher. In connection with this arrest, Reeves served subpoenas on Sugar George, James Stick, and Dick Glass on October 12 at Cane Creek. George and Glass are two of the most famous personalities in the history of the Creek Freedmen in the Indian Territory. Sugar George was prominent in the political and economic development of the Creek Freedmen and Creek Nation and was one of its wealthiest citizens. Dick Glass was the most famous Creek Freedman outlaw in the history of Indian Territory. In 1885 Glass was killed in a shootout with the noted Cherokee Indian policeman Sam Sixkiller. Evidently, Reeves did not have a warrant for Glass's arrest at this time. Most of Glass's crimes fell under the jurisdiction of the Creek Nation Lighthorse police and the U.S. Indian Police. There is no information in the case file in regard to the outcome of the trial for Lynch, who evidently was also a Creek Freedman.[25]

An early resident of the Indian Territory, Lem F. Blevins, stated that

"Bass Reeves was a Negro U.S. marshal. I have heard Bass say he took his U.S. marshal's commission just to get to kill Dick Glass and George Mack, both Negroes. These two Negroes were bad outlaws and they caused the U.S. marshals lots of trouble." Reeves may have made the remark but knew he couldn't shoot an outlaw in cold blood. Judge Isaac C. Parker would bring a deputy up on murder charges as fast as he would an outlaw.[26]

Prior to the Lynch arrest, on October 2, 1882, Reeves arrested Isaac Frazier for stealing a fifty-dollar horse. Evidence points to Frazier being released. Reeves arrested Frazier again on April 3, 1883, on the Canadian River at Mumford Johnson's ranch in the Chickasaw Nation for stealing a gray horse valued at $160 that belonged to a man known as Doctor John of Shawneetown. Doctor John died before the case went to trial, and the court file indicates that Frazier was again released from custody.[27]

In 1938 Adam Grayson, a resident of the former Indian Territory, was interviewed about the frontier days of Oklahoma before statehood. He recalled Reeves at length:

> Bass Reeves, a colored man, was a noted and well-known United States marshal. He was a fearless man when it came to fulfilling his duty as an officer of the law. He was a broad shouldered man, standing fully six feet and had very broad hands. He owned and always rode a sorrel horse which he loved next to his duty. He was known in Oklahoma and in the Indian Territory for his deeds as U.S. marshal for at least thirty-five years. He is said to have missed only one time in capturing his man and that was a man named Hellubee Sammy who lived at that time in what is now the Boley vicinity. Hellubee Sammy owned a large black horse that was a swift runner, and that was the only reason why he was not captured—Sammy's horse outran the U.S. marshal's horse.
>
> At another time, Reeves made a trip to Seminole to return with a prisoner who was being held there and who he wanted. While they were on their way back, the prisoner bargained with Reeves. The prisoner bet that his steed could outrun Reeves'

steed, and if it did, Reeves would tear up the warrant. Reeves was so confident in his horse that he said it would not be necessary to tear it up as he (the prisoner) couldn't outrun the horse of Reeves. In the outcome, the U.S. marshal Reeves was very surprised to see how the prisoner's horse outran his sorrel steed so that in the end, he actually tore up the warrant and prisoner kept on riding fast and was never captured.

One mile south of what is now Pharoah or Springhill, Oklahoma, in eastern Okfuskee County, Bass Reeves had made a camp in some thickets. It was his custom to hold several prisoners until he had several in camp when they would be loaded into wagons and hauled off to Ft. Smith. He had a man named Campbell, who stayed all the time in camp with the prisoners, as guard and as the camp cook. All the prisoners were seated on a large log cut especially for this purpose. The prisoner's feet would be shackled together and the shackles pinned to the ground near the end of the log and rest of the loose shackles pinned to the log itself.

In his free and spare moments, Reeves would walk up and down before the prisoners and preach to them for he was a deacon of the church. Reeves hated to think that he took men to prison but it was his duty to carry out the law enforcement so that he would take the time to tell his prisoner and preach to them of right and wrong.

There was a time when notices were issued offering $5,000.00 reward for the capture of two bad men. Reeves decided that he wanted the reward. He studied the many ways in which he might make a capture and he finally heard that the two men were somewhere along the south near the Texas border so that he journeyed in that direction with a following of a few select men.

Reeves knew just about where the two men were staying and where they could be found. It is said that Reeves pitched his camp about twenty-eight miles from where he thought the notorious outlaws might be found. He established the camp at this distance so that he could take his time in making a plan of procedure for a capture without creating any suspicions and look over the lay of the surrounding land.

He had made out one plan to see if he could successfully carry it out and if this failed he was going to try other plans. The first plan was successful. It is told that he disguised himself as a tramp. From all outward appearances he was a tramp but inwardly he was the fearless U.S. marshal with his duty to fulfill. With him he had every aid that a U.S. marshal could need, handcuffs, six shooter . . . while over all this he wore very ragged clothes. He removed the heels off an old pair of shoes, carried a cane and wore a very floppy old hat in which he shot three bullet holes. He started out walking in the direction of the probable hideout of the two wanted criminals. He walked the twenty-eight miles before he reached his destination which was the home of the mother of the two boys.

When he reached the home, the mother of the two boys came out to see what he wanted. Reeves played the part of a real tramp and asked for a bite to eat, remarking that he was very hungry and that his feet were blistered as he had come a long way and this was his first stop; that the men of the law were hard on his trail and had even shot at him making the three bullet holes in his hat. The women replied, "I will be glad to give you something to eat." She invited Reeves into her house. While he was eating, the woman gave an account that interested Reeves. Her two boys were always wanted by the law and that they were always pursued by the law.

After night had fallen, Reeves thought he heard a sharp whistle from the creek. The old woman went outside and gave an answer. Then two riders rode up where the mother talked to them for a long while but they all finally came into the house. They all finally agreed to join forces and work together.

When they were preparing to go to bed, a bed for Reeves was made in a separate room but he suggested that they all sleep in one room by saying, "Something might happen and if we are separated we couldn't be much protection to one another." So they all prepared to sleep in one room. The two brothers slept on the floor.

While in bed, Reeves kept a watchful eye on the boys. Just as soon as the boys were asleep, Reeves left his bed and managed to handcuff the pair without awakening them. He waited until early morning before he awoke them but he was ready to leave out when it was time. He kicked the boys from their sleep and said, "Come on, boys, let's get going from here." When the two boys were fully awake they realized that they were in the hands of the law. When Reeves started out with the boys to his camp twenty-eight miles away, the mother following him for three miles cursing him and calling him all sorts of names. The two prisoners were forced to walk every bit of the twenty-eight miles.

Upon reaching his camp, Reeves found all his followers there waiting for him and he remarked, "Maybe you think my money won't turn green now, boys." He meant that he expected to obtain the $5,000.00 reward.[28]

This undercover police work in Reeves's career helped to cement his legacy as a detective. Working in disguise became a regular component of his crime-fighting skills.

5.

"No Sunday West of St. Louis, No God West of Fort Smith"

In the Indian Territory, whiskey profits were high and attracted tough and dangerous men. Whiskey bought on the Arkansas or Texas border for two dollars could be resold to the Indians for as much as twenty dollars. Many people were willing to take the chance of arrest for the high profits of a crime analogous to the illegal drug trafficking of today. Four-fifths of the criminal cases in the Fort Smith court were liquor related. The principal offenders in "introducing and selling" liquor in Indian Territory were white men and women. In January 1883 Bass Reeves arrested an Indian for selling whiskey in the Seminole Nation and sent this note to U.S. Marshal Thomas Boles:

> Sasakwa Seminole Nation Ind. Ter.
> Jan. 30, 1883
>
> Hon. Thomas Boles
> U.S. Marshal West Dist. Ark.
>
> Dear Sir
>
> I have captured a Seminole for selling whiskey Saturday night January 27th. He had 2½ gallons. His name is Sammy Low. Please issue a writ and forward to me at McAllister. The witnesses are Parmaskah & Jim Kinder. I have also captured Cantille the Man that escaped from Mershon. Please hold the writ—I am getting

along very well and Will be in about the 13th Feb. I remain Very Respectfully

> [signed] Bass Reeves
> Deputy U.S. Marshal

Low went to trial on March 17, 1883, on charges of "introducing spirituous liquor in the Indian Country," a misdemeanor. Judge Parker gave Low a sentence of thirty days in jail and a fine of twenty dollars.[1]

On March 19, 1883, Reeves arrested an Indian named Cutsee Homachte, ten miles west of the mouth of Little River in the Creek Nation for the same crime. Homachte went before Judge Parker on April 25 and was given sixty days in jail and fined twenty dollars.[2]

A day later, March 20, Wilson Willow was arrested by Reeves for horse theft and selling whiskey. The arrest was made on the Canadian River, five miles west of the mouth of Little River. Reeves sent a note to U.S. Marshal Boles:

> Mill Creek, I.T.
> March 27, 1883
>
> Hon. Thos. Boles
> U.S. Marshal
> Fort Smith Ark
>
> Send me a writ for Wilson Willow for introducing and Selling one gallon of whiskey also for stealing two horses one from John Taylor and the other from Willie Garrett, one horse was valued at $75.00 and the other $50.00. Witnesses in the larceny case are Willie Garrett and John Taylor and a man named "Aaron" Witness in the whiskey case are "Simon" and one "Lowey." The horses were stolen about the 12th or 13th of March 1883. The whiskey was introduced on 1st of January 1883
>
> > Respectfully
> > [signed] Bass Reeves. Deputy.

Reeves sent an addendum to the above note:

Hon Thos Boles

The Creek Lighthorse arrested Wilson Willow and turned him over to me. Please send the writ to McAllister, C.N. I am getting along very well Will go from here up on Caddo Creek west of the Washita River.

Respectfully
[signed] Bass Reeves Deputy

The town of McAllister that Reeves is referring to is now spelled McAlester. Willow was taken to Fort Smith by Reeves, placed in the jail, and given a five-hundred-dollar bail. The bail wasn't paid. There is no information on the outcome of the case.[3]

Reeves sent another note to Boles in June requesting a writ for murder:

McAlister I.T. June 18/83

Thos. Boles Esq.
Fort Smith

Please issue a writ Sparney Harjo for murder was done 5 years ago. Killed a Seminole named Isaac. Sometime Nov. Witness Jennie "Wollie Lusta" Sampson Please issue writ and hold it as I have the man. This is the party that [illegible] had and he got away from him.

[signed] Bass Reeves
US Dpt

Harjo was placed in the Fort Smith jail on June 20. On the arrest warrant he is said to be a "white man." A case involving a Sparing Harjo is mentioned in the book *Hell on the Border*, but there he is said to be a Seminole Indian. Harjo was indicted for murder in October 1883. On October 4 the jury, ready to declare the prisoner guilty as charged in the indictment, found that his victim also was an Indian. This fact released Harjo from the federal court's jurisdiction, and he was turned over to the Seminole authorities for punishment. The book makes no mention of Reeves arresting Harjo.

The names and dates correspond too well for this not to be the same case. The only interesting thing is that in the warrant for Harjo the victim is clearly noted as being a Seminole Indian.[4]

On July 18, 1883, aboard a ferryboat on the Arkansas River at Fort Smith, Reeves arrested a man named William Haines for introducing whiskey in Indian country. Reeves gave the following testimony at the hearing:

> I went down to the river being informed that defendant went across. I found defendant down on the ferry boat; when he saw me coming he laid the saddle riders [bags] down on the boat and came off and met me and tried to get me to come back up town; I told him I did not have time to come on up town and I walked up on boat; he followed me on back and told me there was no engineer on the boat and there would be none come for two hours; at that time we got to where his saddle riders were and I was standing looking down on them; I told him that I was not going across the river that I came down after him and I asked him if they were not his saddle riders and he said yes. I asked him what was in them he said he did not know I told him to open them and he took out two bottles; then I brought defendant and saddle riders to U.S. jail at Jailor's office we examined the saddle riders; we found five bottles of alcohol and one quart of whiskey; this was on yesterday. The ferryboat was in the bottom. I found the saddle riders and defendant in the Nation.

> **Cross examination**

> I seen it taken out; there were two flat pints of alcohol and two round bottles of alcohol; they were white, there was one quart bottle white; and one bottle of whiskey it was a quart bottle; there was some medicines besides; when I arrested he took a paper out of his pocket and I took it from him and gave it to Mr. Burns to not know what it was; I am certain it was in the Nation.

Mr. W. L. Jones from Fayetteville, Arkansas, testified at the hearing:

> All I know is that Defendant was in a saloon in the city here and

I heard him asking about the price of whiskey and that he had to hurry back across to a dance that there was going to be a dance last night; I saw him leave the saloon and go down towards river; I came on down behind him until he got to Meyer & Leo then I stopped and he went on; he had saddle bags on his shoulder; I could see the top of one quart bottle in saddle bags; in almost fifteen or twenty minutes saw Defendant again he came into the Jailors office in custody of Mr. Reeves; they took whiskey and alcohol out of them; I first seen defendant just after dinner; Did not see him get the whiskey; it was down at the old C[——] Saloon that I first saw him; this was yesterday in this city.

Bill Haines was convicted in Judge Parker's court and given thirty days in jail and a twenty-dollar fine.[5]

Reeves arrested three white men named George Scruggs, Nezzie Scruggs, and Albert McCarty on July 20, 1883, in the Choctaw Nation, seven miles west of Fort Smith. The men were charged with stealing seventeen head of cattle from Milo Hoyt on the July 17. John Hoyt gave testimony at the U.S. commissioners' hearing at Fort Smith on July 21, 1883:

On the night of Tuesday last, I was informed that defendants had penned at Parson McCarty's seventeen head of stock; and I got right on my horse and followed them. I heard of the cattle on the way clear on until I got . . . to Poteau. Then I came to town and swore out a writ against defendants. I saw these cattle at old man Scruggs. I suppose I asked him to let me see the cattle; he told me that he did not know anything about any cattle that they were all scattered to the devil. Bass Reeves was with me and (I) had him arrested. Reeves told him he must see the cattle and he said he would let us see the cattle provided he would not let me drive them away. We went down to where the cattle were in the field and I saw them and recognized them. There were ten head, they were Milo Hoyt's cattle. They were in Milo Hoyt's mark and brand. . . . I saw them today one week ago, for I sale them. They were on Milo Hoyt's place. It is about 68 miles from Milo Hoyt's to Scruggs place where I saw the cattle. . . . These cattle were worth $15.00 per head. This was in the Choctaw Nation.

On September 5, 1883, Reeves had a warrant written up for the arrest of two white men, John McAllister and James Wasson. They had assaulted John Smothers with pistols in the Chickasaw Nation on July 3, 1883. McAllister was arrested more than a year later, on October 17, 1884, in Sherman, Texas, by Deputy U.S. Marshal William Grant of the Northern District of Texas Federal Court. It appears the court had problems locating most of the witnesses, and McAllister was released after a trial in 1885.[6]

The *Fort Smith Weekly Elevator* reported on September 21, 1883, that Deputy U.S. Marshal Bass Reeves had brought in Thomas McKinney for larceny, and McKinney had been subsequently released on bond.

The next month found Reeves involved in a manhunt for a killer of a deputy U.S. marshal. During the twenty-one years Judge Isaac C. Parker held office at Fort Smith, sixty-five of his deputies were killed in the line of duty. On this sad occasion it was the death of the popular Deputy U.S. Marshal Addison Beck, who lived in the Indian Territory. The *Fort Smith Weekly Elevator* printed:

Johnson Jacks, the Murderer of Deputy Beck, Brought In

On Sunday evening last, about 5 o'clock, Special Deputy C. C. Ayers, with a posse of ten men, was sent over into the Cherokee nation to arrest Johnson Jacks, who so wantonly murdered Deputy U.S. Marshal Addison Beck and young Morrell, a few days ago. The marshal and party made a forced march in the night, arriving in the neighborhood of where the tragedy occurred about daylight. From Dick Anderson, who lives near there, they learned that Jacks who was badly wounded in the fight with the officers, had been taken to the house of Tom Bearpaw, about a mile from where Beck was killed and about forty miles from here. The marshals surrounded the cabin, but no resistance was offered, and they quietly loaded Jacks into a wagon and arrived here with him Monday evening late. Jacks' wound is in the left breast, and is very severe, though not necessarily dangerous, and he will probably recover. He is half negro and half Indian. Bark, the man Beck had the writ for, is still at large and on the scout. Jacks made a statement to Marshal Boles on Tuesday in which he says Beck shot him first, and then he fainted, and don't know whether he shot Beck or not. The circumstances of the case go to show that his story is all a fabrication and does not bear the semblance of truth on its face . . .

The following are the parties that went with Ayers to arrest Jacks: G. H. Fanin, John Williams, Wiley Cox, Bass Reeves, Geo. Delaughter, Hiram Moody, Bynum Colbert, John Phillips, Sam Mingo and one Pittock.

The editor of the *Fort Smith Weekly Elevator* wrote: "Addison Beck was one of the oldest, most efficient deputies on the force. He was a gentle, quiet and sober man. His wife and three small children reside at Muscogee and are left almost destitute."

On October 17, 1883, the *Arkansas Gazette* in Little Rock reported on the case:

Fort Smith: Arrest of Murderer Jacks . . .

Fort Smith, October 16.—Last night John Jacks, one of the murderers of Deputy Marshal Adison Beck and posse, was brought to the jail here by Deputies Ayers and Cox. Jacks was dangerously wounded in the fight with Beck and posse, and was expected to die. He says he killed both men while they were attempting to arrest Bark, who escaped and has not yet been found. Jacks, it is supposed, makes the statement, expecting to die himself, in order to shield Bark in case of his capture.

The correct name of the posseman who was killed with Beck was Lewis Merritt, who was twenty-two years of age. Beck was thirty-eight years of age at the time of his death. It is not known if the deputies ever arrested Bark for this crime.[7]

In early November 1883 Reeves arrested three white men for taking a horse from a black woman in the Creek Nation. M. B. Donaghey was arrested November 2 in the Choctaw Nation near the mouth of the Little River. John Hoboy was arrested near Stonewall in the Chickasaw Nation on November 3. John McColslin was arrested at the same location of Donaghey on November 4. This incident no doubt helped to spread a rumor that Bass Reeves was in with the outlaws in the Indian Territory. The black woman was said by the defendants to be associated with notorious outlaw Dick Glass, her son being one of the members of Glass's gang. Reeves had a warrant written up on September 15 due to the testimony of Rose Brown, Sandy Bruner, and Rector Rogers. John McColslin bonded out and wrote a letter to Judge Isaac C. Parker concerning the arrest and asking for assistance:

11/12–1883
Stonewall
I.T.

Hon. Judge Parker
Ft. Smith Ark
Dear Sir, Marshal Reeves

Arrested . . . young Donagee charged with stealing a horse from . . . Rosie. I write you this to state the matter to you just as they are and that (Donagee) is a good moral & industrious young man and the whole thing is given up through prejudice. Last spring a year ago one Joe Loving a son of this (Rose) stole a Horse from (Donagee) and (Donagee) traced the horse up to this Rose house, and learned that Joe Loving had disposed of the horse and thinking thus there would be no chance for him to secure his horse that was stolen he (Donagee) proposed to this woman (Rose) mother of (Joe) that if she would give him (Donagee) another Pony he would drop the matter and say nothing more about it so (Rose) & her husband (Fred) agrees to this and gives this Pony to (Donagee) willingly and then she has Donagee arrested for stealing the horse. Thinking she will get the Pony Back These other two men charged with stealing the same pony had nothing to do with it at all was simply with Donagee assisting him to trace his (Donagee) horse that was stolen by (Joe Loving). Young Donagee is working on my farm and is hard that he should be kept away from his work by a set of Ignorant Negroes. She (Rose) has been told by some one that if she would have these Boys arrested she could get his Pony back she says I have to [do] all she wants (Rose) own husband say that they give the Pony up willingly a short time after Joe Loving stole (Donagees) horse he shot and killed himself accidentally. So now she (Rose) don't find the law on (Joes) Part There is a written agreement . . . (Rose) & (Donagee) signed by both parties showing that these was no thefts on part of (Donagee) which (Rose) has in her possession. Rose harbors such men as (Dick Glass) and her son (Joe) was one of that gang. You will please investigate this and release (Donagee) as his mother is a widow woman and they need him at home.

Yours Respectfully
[signed] J. McColslin

At the commissioners' hearing in Fort Smith on December 7, 1883, Rose Brown made the following statements concerning the theft:

Rose Brown being duly sworn, deposes and says:

I reside at Little River, Creek Nation . . . they came to my house one day, and my old man called me out. The defendant Hobaugh said to me I am after a horse your son has taken. I told him I knew nothing about it, he said well it has been proven that he took a horse and we are after it. I told him I could not give up a horse when I knew nothing about it. He had his Winchester in his hand and said the horse I must have Donagee said yes I must have it for Joe McCaslin shot my mare the other day then Hobaugh said he has the damnest luck of any man I ever saw, he bought a mule from old man Tutler and gave $100 for it and he was just riding along and the mule stubbed his foot and fell and broke his neck. Donegee said yes I am out a horse and a horse I must have. I said have you proved that he has taken a horse from you all, Joe McCaslin said yes I am a witness that he took the horse. I then said if I could help myself you would not take my horse but I am nothing but a poor woman. I told them that my son was of age and I could not help what he had done. Donagee had a pistol and I was frightened. Then they went to work and made me a piece of paper and handed it to me, Donagee wrote the paper They then took my horse and rode off. The horse was standing out by the lot near the house. It was a balled face glass eyed horse, the two fore feet white, branded R I think. I raised the horse from a colt, I always owned the horse. My son never owned the horse. The horse was worth $100 to me, but it would not probably sell for that much. This occurred in the Creek Nation in September last I think. The defendants live across the Canadian River. Defendants are considered white men, they are renters in that country. My sons name was Joe Richards, he was never arrested for horse stealing. If he ever stole a horse it was not the one that defendants took away from me. After defendants were arrested Colbert and Grayson came to me and told me that I must write to the Commissioner at Fort Smith and tell him to throw the case out, if I did not they would break me up. The next day he came back with two white men and the white men wanted me to give up the paper the defendants had given me but I would not do it, they then wanted me to let them take the paper and copy it but I would not do it. I have never seen the horse since it was taken from me.

Cross examination

Defendants did not tell me where they were going after they took my horse. My son was sometimes called Lovett. MsCaslin's wife passes for a Creek Citizen. I am a Creek Citizen. I never saw the horse that defendants claim my son stole. My son killed himself accidentally. My husband was there when the defendants came and took the horse. There were two Indians there Birdhead and another whose name I did not know. My son Caesar came about the time defendants left with the horse. My husband did not have his pistol on, I don't remember whether Caesar had his on or not. When defendants came up they were on their horses but got down and were sitting on the fences. The defendants told me that they came to see if I would not give them a pony in place of one my son had taken. I did not send my boy to get the horse for defendants that I know of. I was scared. Paro Bruner was at my house after defendants were arrested, he did not speak to me. I did not tell defendants that the horse belonged to my son. I did not tell them that it was the last piece of property he had on the place and that no one else need come there for any of his property. I don't know exactly why the defendants came to my house and took the horse.

Direct resumed

The witness here presents the paper given to her by defendants which is in words and figures as follows.

September 1, 1883

Mrs. Rosio brown gives me thirly sadisfaction of my horse She gives me a nother horse in the Place of mine that her son dispose of this thing is settle

[signed] M. B. Donaghey
[signed] John Houghboy
[signed] J. P. McColslins

The witness says that neither she nor her husband can read and that the paper was not explained to her.

I did not tell defendants that they could take the horse. I told them that I did want to give up the horse.

Fred Brown being duly sworn says:

I am Rosa Brown's husband. Defendants came to our house and said they wanted a horse and it was their determination to have a horse. John Hobaugh said this. They were armed and took a horse neither myself nor wife gave our consent to their taking it the horse belonged to my wife. I saw the horse afterwards, one of the defendants had it hitched to the wagon and was working it. We told the men that they had no right to take the horse but they took it. Joe Richards never owned the horse in his life.

Cross examination

My gun and pistol were both in the house. Defendants told me that they tracked the horse Donaghee had lost right up to my house. I told them that I saw some men tracking something to the house but that I did not know what it meant. I was at work in the field that day and Donaghee and another man came to the field and inquired if they had seen any thing of the horse they were hunting. I told them I had not seen it and knew nothing about it. . . . I did not see Dick Glass about there along about that time. . . . When my wife came out I explained to her what the men had come for and asked her what she thought about it. She said she did not think that she had any right to give a horse for anything her son had done. . . . I did not hear my wife tell the defendants that she gave the horse to her son when it was two years old.

Sanderson Bruner being duly sworn says:

I know the horse in question and know that It belonged to Rose. It was a bald faced glass eyed white legged horse branded R. This is Rose's brand.

Cross examination

I know that Joe rode the horse to my place once and I saw him riding it one other time when I was up there, he had to borrow it from his mother. I never heard him claim that his mother had given it to him.

Fred Brown recalled by defendants says:

Only two of these men had arms there that day that I know of. Hobaugh had a gun and one of the other men had a pistol. . . . I did not have Hobaugh's gun in my hand while he was there. I remember of seeing gun setting by the fence close to Hobaugh at the time. I don't recollect whether he left the gun in the fence corner when he went into the house to write the paper or not.

Mark Wallace a witness for defendants being duly sworn says:

I was a guard with Deputy Marshal Reeves on his last trip, he sent one to Brown's house to tell Fred and Rose to [come] down to camp. I was afterwards at their house. I asked Rose if they used their arms in taking the horse and they said they did not. It is my best recollection that she told me that she told defendants that they could take the horse. I never heard the old man Brown say whether they took the horse by force or not. Sandy Bruner saw Paro Bruner there that day.

Cross examination

I did not pay much attention to what Rose said about defendants taking the horse, and will not be certain as to what she did say.

The defendant Joseph McCaslin being duly sworn says:

About the fifth of May 1882, Donaghe had a horse stolen. Cal Donaghe, Zack Donaghe, Bud Donaghe and Ed Wilkins and perhaps some other person came tracking the horse by my field where I was at work, they hailed me and I went out to where they were and they asked me If I had seen Buds horse. I told them I had not, they went out and showed me the tracks in the road. . . . I went up to Bud Donaghes brother about 16 miles in the Creek Nation. I saw Jerry Bruner a lighthorse Captain who informed me that he had seen Dick Glass with a horse answering to the description of the one we were looking for. He deputized us all to go and hunt Dick Glass. About a week and a half after that Joe Lovett killed himself. One morning I started up to my brother-in-laws John Hobaughs. On the way I met John and Donaghe on their way to Fred Browns. They said they were going down to Roses to see if she would let Donaghe have a horse for the one Joe had taken. Fred spoke to us as we rode up and asked if we were just riding around or hunting stock. I told him that as far as I was concerned I was just riding around, but that the other boys had some business with him. One of them told him that they had come up to see if he would not give them a horse in place of the one Joe had taken from Donaghe. Fred said well as to that I could not say, you will have to talk to Rose about that and he called Rose. Fred said that he had found out that Joe did undoubtedly get the horse. . . . So they consulted among themselves and agreed to let Bud have a pony. Bud said will thee get me a paper and pen and ink and I will give you a paper showing perfect satisfaction. So Caesar went in the house and hunted up paper pen and ink and into the room and we all went in. Bud sat down and wrote the paper. . . . While Bud was writing the paper he told her son Cammy to go get old Baldy and he went and got it and brought him up and hitched him to the fence . . . We went out to our horses and got on an I think Fred handed the rope to Bud. I was not armed. There was no force or threats used there at all. Hobaugh came up with his guns laying beside him and he stood it up in the corner of the fence where it remained until we got ready to start. John picked it up and handed it to Fred and showed him how it worked. . . . Hobaugh did not take his gun in the house with him. Casear had a pistol on when he came there, it was a blue barreled .44 or .45. Fred also had a pistol on, it was a white handled pistol, he always carry's his pistol. There was no threatening language used there at all, there might have been some cursing but none to amount to anything. If the Browns were frightened it was on account of the manner in which we rode up. . . . If anybody has been to see Rose about the case since we were arrested I knew nothing about it.

Cross examination

I did not have any interest in the transaction whatever, I signed the paper just because the others asked me to. They asked Rose to sign the paper but she would not do it. Rose had some ponies beside the one Bud took.

The hearing was carried over to Saturday, December 8, 1883.

John Hobaugh being duly sworn says:

On Sunday after the Thursday that Donaghes horse was stolen I helped search for the horse and became satisfied that it was not in that neighborhood. The next morning 6 of us went in pursuit of the horse. We went by Jerry Bruners a lighthorse Captain, we found him at home and told him what our business was and described the horse to him. Bruner took us to a trail where Pink Donaghe recognized the tracks of the stolen horse.

We were out six days hunting the horse but failed to get it or find it. On the day before went to Browns we had stated the case to Tuttle where we lived. So the next day we wanted to go over on the river hunting. So Donaghe wanted me to go over to Browns with him to see if they would not let him have a horse in place of the one he charged Lovett with taking, we met McCaslin and he went with us. . . . When Joe Lovett died he had in his possession a large bay horse, Rose Brown told me that she did not think it was good property and did not want to have anything to do with it and turned it over to Joe Barnett a lighhorseman and told him to keep it an if the owner came for it to let him have it. Barnett kept the horse until he was killed and then it was turned back to Rose and still she did not want to have anything to do with it and turned it over to Sandy Bruner and that a man by the name of Clark came along afterwards and claimed the horse and got it.

Cross examination

The reason we thought Rose ought to give us a pony was because we supposed Joe had a pony there. They said Joe had a wife and I don't know why we didn't go to her instead of his mother. It seems to me that if Joe had had any horses or ponies his wife would be the one that would have had possession of them.

Direct resumed

I had seen Joe Lovett riding the pony time and time again. I never saw him riding anything else. I have heard the pony called the Joe Lovett pony. . . . Rose said he had a pony there that she had raised and given to him and that was the pony that she turned over to us.

M. B. Donaghe cross examined by Commissioner says:

I lost a horse in May 1882 and tracked it to about 100 yards of the house where Joe Lovett lived. I became satisfied that Joe Lovett stole the horse. I was thinking about have Joe arrested when I heard he had killed himself. I did not know he had a wife. So I went to his mothers to see if she would give us a poney.

Direct resumed

The Brown place is a harbor for horse thieves, they are connected with the Bruners.

After the hearing at Fort Smith the charges against the three white men were dismissed by U.S. Commissioner Stephen Wheeler. Reeves in the immediately following years, in spite of his accomplishments, would be accused on occasion of collusion with shady characters. In this particular case, he made the arrest only after a warrant was requested for the implicated parties.[8]

On November 3, 1883, Reeves arrested a young black man named Miles Jordan at Birneyville for murder. . Birneyville, which no longer exists, was a community in the Chickasaw Nation near the Texas border.

Jordan had shot a fifteen-year-old black youth named Charles Percy in August of 1882. Percy's mother and brother both testified that Charles on his deathbed said he was shot deliberately by Jordan. They claimed Jordan had whipped young Percy and threatened him not to tell anyone, and when he did tell this was the consequence. The gun belonged to his older brother, Loney Percy. Evidently the youths found the gun in the house and were playing with the gun outside near a creek bottom. At the time of the incident Jordan was living with the family. Jordan had other witnesses who could confirm his story that the shooting was an accident, and on February 8, 1884, he was found not guilty in Fort Smith.[9]

Reeves sent a letter to Marshal Boles on November 23, 1883:

Sasakwa, Seminole Nation Ind. T.
Nov. 23, 1883

Mr. Thomas Boles
U.S. Marshal
Ft. Smith Ark

Dear Sir

I have two prisoners turned over by Thos Cloud, Indian Police, both Seminoles. Tommy Caesar who stole a saddle from C. B. Trotter, a white man living in the Seminole Nation [and] Pe fat-hoh-che who stole a revolver from J M States a white man living in the Seminole Nation Thomas Cloud, Caesar Monday and other witnesses In the Tommy Caesar case Car pih che Emartha, Billy & Lilly witnesses against Pe fat hoh che—Please issue a writ for them and hold it in the office until I arrive I will subpoena the witnesses. These are good cases We have a load and are On our road home I am well and so are all the rest

> Very Respectfully
> Bass Reeves
> Deputy US Marshal

Perfathohche and Caesar were picked up near Brown's Store at We-woka in the Seminole Nation. Perfathohche plead guilty before the U.S. commissioner on December 5, 1883. The outcome of Tommy Caesar's case for stealing the saddle is not known. Capt. Thomas Cloud, Seminole Indian Lighthorse Police, would later be killed by a black Indian outlaw named Rector Rogers, on March 29, 1885. Cloud, with a seventeen-man posse, was looking for outlaws in a black settlement south of the Canadian River near Sacred Heart Mission. They came across Rogers, who had murdered his brother the year before. They had a gunfight in which another policeman, the Freedman Sam Cudgo, was also killed. Cloud was wounded and died at the Seminole Chief John Jumper's home in Sasakwa. The Seminole police killed Rogers during the shootout.[10]

Reeves sent a letter from the Patterson and Foley General Merchandise Store in Eufaula, Creek Nation, to Marshal Boles:

> Eufaula, I.T.
> Nov 29 1883
>
> Hon Thos Boles
> Ft Smith
>
> Dear Sir
>
> Pleas issue a writ for the following num. Gent. Emarthle chee. Salt and attempt to kill Sandy Bruner with a Pistol on the 28th day

of November 1883. Witnesses Mark Wallace "Bass Reeves" Sandy Bruner We have him in charge Will bring him with us.

Very Truly
[signed] Bass Reeves

Sandy Bruner and Paro Bruner were acting as Bass Reeves's posse when Sandy almost lost his life in November 1883. They were looking for a Creek Indian known as Little John who was selling whiskey in the Creek Nation. At the U.S. commissioners' hearing on December 10, 1883, Bruner gave the following testimony:

Sanderson Bruner being duly sworn, deposes and says:

I reside on Canadian I.T. and know the defendant in this cause when I see him. I was helping Deputy Marshal Bass Reeves and I went to arrest Little John, I drew my pistol and told Little John we had a writ for him and that he was my prisoner. The defendant and Little John were both in the yard and as I did this the defendant; I looked around at defendant and saw that he had a pistol and Paro was taking it from. I warned the defendant who had attempted to shoot me and that Paro had grabbed the pistol away from him. This was while we were on the way down here not more than about two weeks ago. I am a Creek Negro and have the rights of a Creek citizen. The defendant is a Creek Indian.

Cross examination

Little John cannot speak the English language that I know of. The pistol, defendants pistol was loaded all around. I do not know whether it was cocked or not. Bass Reeves shot all the loads out of the pistol and left it at the house.

Paro Bruner being duly sworn says:

Early in the morning we went to defendants house to arrest Little John. Sandy and I were a little ahead of Reeves. Sandy spoke in Indian to Little John to give up, he had his pistol in his hand but did not have it presented on Little John. The defendant was standing at a wagon about 20 steps from the door, and as he saw that Sandy had the best of Little John he started towards Sandy with his pistol out and I caught him. I hailed Sandy and told him he was about to be shot. I was there tussling with defendant for the pistol and I being the strongest got it away from him. After I wrung the pistol out of his hand he said no one could arrest Little John. I told him that officers were there and they were bound to arrest him and that he ought not to act as he did. He said that if they had seen us before we got to the house they would not have let us come up. Bass told him that he was an officer. Defendant replied he did not care that he would just as any soon kill an officer as any other man. When I got the pistol away from him it was loaded and capped all around and full cocked. I gave the pistol to Reeves and he fired it off and left it at the house. Bass arrested Little John and the defendant too and brought them along. They way I came along to interpret as Sandy could speak very little of the Creek language.

Cross examination

Defendant had his pistol presented on Sandy when I caught him. Little John is defendants nephew.

Emarthla Chee the defendant being duly sworn says:

The reason I did the way I did was because I did not know what the men were about to do when they came up. I did not know they were officers. I did not know what they were after and for that reason I thought I would help my nephew out.

Cross examination

I am sort of deaf and I did not hear Sandy tell Little John to give up. I was going out to make medicine that morning and if I had seen the men coming up to the house I would have let them come up. Paro Bruner told me that Reeves was an officer. Little John has no family and sometimes stops with me and sometimes somewhere else. I don't know whether he goes to the brush or not when the officers come around.

The U.S. commissioner felt the evidence warranted the case going before a jury. It did so in February 1884. Emarthla Chee was held on a five-hundred-dollar bond, which he didn't have bail for to be released prior to trial. There is no information on the outcome of the jury trial.[11]

Bass Reeves spent more time in the Seminole Nation than did any deputy who worked for the Fort Smith court. From its inception, Africans were always major players in the history and politics of the Seminole Nation. Reeves was respected by Seminole blacks and Indians alike.

6.

Gunman's Territory

The year 1884 had a major impact on Bass Reeves's career as a peace officer in the Indian Territory. He was involved in several deadly shootouts with outlaws, and he had a tragic incident happen in his camp on one of his trips—he shot and killed his cook.

Bass Reeves's family had grown larger by 1884. The 1880 census for Crawford County, Arkansas, listed his children as Sally, 16; Robert, 14; Harriet, 12; Georgia, 10; Alice, 8; Newland, 6; Edgar, 4; and Lula, 2 years. There would be three more boys born during the decade.

Reeves sent a note to the U.S. marshal on January 28, 1884 from the Patterson and Foley General Merchandise store at Eufaula:

> Hon Frank Boles
>
> Dear Sir
>
> Please hold the following Writs issued for the following parties George Barr Intr 4 Gall Liquor one Jessie Introducing 2 Gall W and sold it Witnesses Colbert Lasley Chir wi La Mar du All the above parties are Creeks I have them in charg Issue the writ and hold until I come
>
> > Yours Truly
> > [signed] Bass Reeves

On February 7, 1884, Bass Reeves swore out a warrant for the arrest of Mitchell Bruner, a Creek Freedman also known as Michael Grayson, who had murdered his brother Josh Bruner on September 1, 1883. Before Reeves could arrest Bruner, the principal chief of the Muskogee Nation, J. M. Perryman, interceded by writing a letter to the John Tufts, U.S. Indian agent for the Five Civilized Tribes at Muskogee on October 18, 1884:

> Hon J Q Tufts
> U.S. Indian Agent
> Muskogee I.T.
> Dear Sir.
>
> The friends of one Michael Grayson Colored Citizen of the Muskogee, desire me to say to you that said Michael Grayson committed Murder of his own brother sometime ago and was tried before the Criminal Court of Eufaula Dist. and was released and now for the same crime a warrant had been issued by authorities of the United States at Ft Smith for his arrest and trial before the U.S. States Court. I would refer you to the fact of his citizenship in the Muskogee "statue book" Chapter 7 and Article 2nd there his name is recorded and his bro Josh Grayson he killed. I would be glad if you will explain this fact to the proper officer at Ft Smith, that said Grayson may not be arrested by the U S deputy Marshals any longer.
>
> Very Respectfully
[signed] J. M. Perryman
Princ Chief M N

This problem of jurisdiction in criminal cases would continue to arise until the Indian Territory became the state of Oklahoma, and would became prevalent again a century later, in the 1980s, when Indian tribes were granted police powers in Oklahoma. Agent Tufts responded by writing a letter to Marshal Boles concerning the matter:

Union Agency
Muskogee Oct. 20, 1884

Hon W Boles
U.S. Marshal
Ft. Smith Ark
Dear Sir.

I enclose herewith letter of Chief Perryman which explains truly. Both Mitchell Grayson and Josh Grayson were adopted by act of council with others and can be found on page 58 of the Laws of the Muskogee Nation. If this is the charge for which Mitchell Grayson is wanted, the warrant must have been issued on the statement of some parties who know nothing of the action of the council. (action of Council was prior to 1880)

> Yours Truly
> [signed] Mr. J Tufts
> U.S. Ind. Agt

The Creek Indian Nation was also known as the Muskogee Nation. Muskogee is also the name given to the language spoken by these Indians from the southeast United States. Evidently the U.S. federal court in Fort Smith did not destroy the warrant because on September 28, 1886, Bruner was again arrested for murdering his brother. This time, he was arrested fourteen miles west of Okmulgee in the Creek Nation, and the arresting deputy didn't sign the arrest card. Reeves might have made the arrest. Bruner was also wanted at that time for the theft of a horse that belonged to a white man named Ebenezer E. Weldon near Eufaula, Creek Nation, in October 1885. The murder charges were dismissed on December 3, 1886. The outcome of the horse theft trial is not clear.[1]

Cotcher Fixico was a Seminole Indian who was doing big business selling whiskey in the Indian Territory. Deputy U.S. Marshal W. J. Grey had sworn out a warrant for Fixico's arrest on January 15, 1880, and Deputy U.S. Marshal Addison Beck had sworn out a warrant on December 25, 1881. The wily Fixico was able to elude the lawmen until Bass Reeves arrested him ten miles west of Wallace Wannack's store on the North Fork of the Canadian River on March 15, 1884.[2]

Reeves told the following story about the capture of an Indian medicine man to D. C. Gideon, a writer chronicling the development of the Indian Territory:

Bass Reeves, the invincible deputy United States marshal related to the writer an instance of the supernatural power at one time exerted over himself by Yah-kee, who made his abode on North Fork. "I was up there," said Bass, "to arrest a lot of men for horse theft, and had two wagon-loads of prisoners encamped in the woods in care of my posse. Among them were two Indians who had each made Yah-kee a present of a pony for medicine and the old man had furnished them, guaranteed to render them 'invisible' should the officers attempt to serve a warrant upon them for horse theft. As I also had a warrant for Yah-kee I went back and got him, too, and when we camped for the night I was feeling very stiff and sore, although having felt well all the day. We started for Fort Smith the next morning and although I rode a saddle horse I was unable to keep within sight of the wagons. When I reached their camp at noon they were done eating and prisoners shackled together, were lying under the trees asleep. With the greatest difficulty I dismounted, and fell forward against a tree, aching in every limb, and my eyes were so swollen that I could scarcely see. I could eat nothing and seemed possessed of a consuming thirst. Believing that old Yah-kee had bewitched me, I felt that all hope was gone. My knees refused to bear the weight of my body, and feeling that my last hour had come I thought to take a last look upon the man whom I felt was responsible for my present condition. He was lying on his back asleep, and his coat had turned partly over so that a concealed inner pocket was in view. I saw a string dangling from it and made up my mind that it was attached to his 'conjurbag.' Gently I dragged myself to his side and with a jerk drew from his pocket a mole-skin bag, filled with bits of roots, pebbles and tiny rolls of short hair, tied with blue and red strings. I tossed it as far as I could, and saw it float away on the bosom of a creek that flowed alongside the camp. With a start

Yah-kee awoke. 'Bass,' said he, 'you stole my conjur-bag.' 'Yes, I did,' said Bass, 'and it is now sailing down the creek.' The old man promised all kinds of pay if I would return it, but I feared it less as it sailed down the creek than when it was in the hands of Yah-kee. 'I don't conjur any more,' said the old man; 'my power is gone. Take off this chain and I will follow you like a dog.' I declined to do this, however, and the prisoners started on. From the moment the bag touched the water I began to feel relieved. I later mounted my horse and when I caught up with the party in the evening I felt as well as ever." Yah-kee told him afterward that if he had not lost his "conjur-bag" Bass would have been dead before they reached Fort Smith; and he believes it, too.[3]

On March 22, 1884, twenty-five miles west of Stonewall in the Chickasaw Nation, Reeves arrested a Creek Freedman named Jim Grayson for attempted murder. Grayson had been in numerous previous scrapes with the law. In one, Grayson attacked a white man named Silas Richardson in March 1882. In the hearing before the U.S. commissioner on April 23, Richardson made the following statements:

> I was at Eastman Fraziers working in March and Jim came over there and asked me if I was going to the [illegible]. I told him no, he said if I wouldn't go he would came and tie me and carry me. I told him you all are not going to do it, he said he was a man, I said I was a man too, he went home and came back on Saturday on his way to the "[illegible] city." And Saturday night after dark I went to the fence and he had his rifle and knocked me down with it and I never knew anything until after breakfast the next morning. My teeth are loose yet, a piece of bone came out of my jaw. This happened two years ago last March towards the latter end of the month.

> **Cross examination**

> This was after dark, there was no moon but it was starlight. I did not have any knife in my hand. I had my right hand up with a pipe in it when he hit me. I do not know whither the gun was loaded or not. I was not cursing him when he hit me.

The other witnesses here were in the house at the time. This happened two years ago last March. Jim has been staying at home since that. I live in the Chickasaw Nation and my wife is a Chickasaw Nation. I have always lived in that country. I have been living with her as my wife for three years. Defendant passes for a Creek darkey up there.

Grayson was found guilty by a jury trial at Fort Smith on May 8, 1884. There was an appeal made with more witnesses for the defense, and another trial took place in November. Grayson was found guilty again on November 12, 1884. Judge Parker sentenced him to eighteen months of confinement in the Detroit House of Corrections on January 10, 1885.[4]

On April 9, 1884, Reeves and his posse made camp near Cherokee Town in the Chickasaw Nation east of Pauls Valley in current Garvin County. The posse had five prisoners in custody on their way east to Fort Smith. An argument ensued between Reeves and his cook, William Leach. Late that night while sitting around the campfire, Leach was shot in the neck by Reeves and seriously wounded. He later died from the wound. According to Reeves, a cartridge got lodged in his rifle, and while trying to extract it the gun went off and a bullet hit Leach. The next day Reeves sent for a doctor but Leach expired from the wound. This incident would cause Reeves much mental and financial misery.[5]

The popular story before and after the trial, which took place in 1887, was told by a group of deputy U.S. marshals, Christie Madsen, Heck Thomas, Allen Goff, John P. Jones, A. Jacobsen, and D. A. Hadden, who were meeting in Guthrie, Oklahoma, in January 1911, and was recorded by an Oklahoma City newspaper:

> Makes me think of that old story of Bass Reeves, said the taciturn Goff, referring to Bass Reeves, a negro deputy United States marshal who was a celebrity in Indian Territory until he died at Muskogee two years ago. "You recollect, Chris, when Bass killed his Negro cook—hired all the good lawyers in Fort Smith to keep them from being on the other side, you know, when they tried him for it two years later. Well, Bass was coming back into Fort Smith with a string of prisoners and a Negro

cook that he allowed to carry a gun. Now Bass had a little dog that he was mighty fond of—carried him with him all the time and he had taught the dog to beg for something to eat by standing up on his hind legs. That negro cook got a grudge against Bass while they were still several days away from Fort Smith, and took it out on the dog. Bass—this was the way he told it, of course—told the cook to quit several times and this must have made him sullen. One night, when the prisoners were lying by the campfire chained together and Bass was back on his elbows with his Winchester by his side, that little dog got up on his hind feet and danced up to the cook begging with his front paws, and cook didn't do anything but empty a skillet of boiling grease down the dog's throat and grabbed for his pistol. Bass slipped his Winchester forward quicker and it went off right in that cook's face, and he pitched forward into the fire. Bass didn't pay any attention to him for a minute, since he knew he had winged him, but tried to help the little dog, which was dying a few feet away. Bass saw the dog die and then turned round to finish the nigger cook, but found his bullet had hit him right in the neck and shot his head so nearly off that when Bass kicked the body it rolled into the fire.[6]

The testimony at the trial was completely different from this story, but this was the tale most told. We will take an in-depth look at this shooting and the trial in chapter 8.

On April 25, 1884, the *Arkansas Gazette* in Little Rock published the following:

> Deputy Marshal Bass Reeves brought in twelve prisoners from
> the Indian Territory yesterday, charged with various offenses.

Sometime in 1883, a cowboy named Jim Webb from Texas drifted into the Chickasaw Nation. He found employment with the celebrated rancher Billy Washington, who at that time was a partner with Dick McLish, a prominent Chickasaw Indian, in an extensive ranch in the southern portion of the Chickasaw Nation. Webb was hired as the foreman of this ranch, with forty-five cowboys under his supervision, many of them being African Americans.

The ranch was isolated, the cowboys were tough, and the cattle were wild and scattered. Jim Webb was an ideal choice as foreman because he ran the ranch with an iron hand. The cowboys he couldn't whip with his fists, he fired, and his gun was always ready to argue any point if anyone was foolish enough to stand up to him. This tendency to argue with a gun led to his clash with Bass Reeves.

Rev. William Steward, a black circuit preacher, had a small ranch adjoining the Washington-McLish Ranch which he worked between his preaching jaunts. In the early spring of 1883, Reverend Steward started a small grass fire on his ranch, which got out of control fast and spread over into the vast Washington-McLish range. Jim Webb blew his top and rode over to chastise the preacher, and a bitter but short argument started. It soon ended with Jim Webb killing the preacher.

Reeves took the warrant to arrest Jim Webb for murder. At this time he had a white man named Floyd Wilson riding as his posseman. Reeves and Wilson reached the Washington-McLish Ranch about eight o'clock one morning several days later.

As Reeves and Wilson rode up to the ranch house they noticed only three men there: Jim Webb, a cowboy named Frank Smith who was a trusted friend of Webb, and the ranch cook. Reeves had never seen Webb but thought he recognized him from the description he had been given before leaving Fort Smith. To make sure that this man was Webb, however, Reeves and Wilson rode up like any traveling cowboys and asked for breakfast. Webb, however, had not lived as long as he had by being foolish; he was immediately suspicious. When Reeves and Wilson walked up to the porch, both Webb and Smith had their pistols in their hands, holding them nonchalantly at their sides, yet conveying the idea that they were ready for immediate use, if necessary. Reeves than began to wonder how he was could arrest Webb without someone getting killed or seriously wounded.

The ranch house was a typical one for those days in the territory. It consisted of two large rooms, built of logs, which were completely separated by a long "dog run" or breezeway. One side served as a kitchen and dining room, and the other served as a bunkhouse. Reeves and Wilson were escorted into the kitchen–dining room side and told to wait until the cook could fix their breakfast.

Reeves didn't like the situation a bit. He felt he must do something to ease Webb's suspicions if he was to have any chance at all of arresting him. After talking for a few minutes, he asked if he could feed his horses while they were waiting for breakfast. Webb grunted his permission, but he followed Reeves out to the barn, watching Reeves every second with his gun still in his hand. Reeves, talking easily and steadily, with no hint of his uneasiness, fed his and Wilson's horses, loosened their saddle girths, and casually pulled his Winchester rifle from its saddle boot and leaned it against a corn crib, hoping this would convince Webb he was honestly a traveling cowboy just passing through the country.

Reeves thought for a few minutes that he was successful in convincing Webb he meant him no harm, because when the cook called out that breakfast was ready, Webb did not follow him back into the dining room. But when Webb called Smith out of the room into the dog run and they began to whisper and gesture toward Reeves and Wilson, Reeves knew he had failed. Watching Webb and Smith by their reflections in a mirror on the opposite wall, Reeves took a chance and whispered to Wilson that at his signal he was to jump Smith while Reeves concentrated on Webb.

After eating, Reeves and Wilson walked out into the dog run. Webb followed Reeves and stood directly over him when Reeves sat down on a bench; Smith and Wilson were similarly arranged at the far end of the bench. Both Webb and Smith still had their pistols in their hands, and they were watching Reeves and Wilson so intently that Reeves didn't have a chance to signal Wilson. Reeves simply kept talking and hoping for the best.

After this watchful waiting had continued for a few minutes, with Reeves talking his head off about absolutely nothing, one of those incidents you usually see only in movies occurred that saved the day. Something drew Webb's attention from Reeves for a split second.

When Webb looked away, Reeves made his move. He leaped to his feet, knocked Webb's gun away, wrapped his large left hand around Webb's throat, and drawing his own pistol with his right hand, he shoved it into Webb's face. Webb, with a giant of a man choking the life out of him and looking into the ignorant end of a Colt .45 as well, gurgled out a meek surrender.

In the meantime, Wilson was so overwhelmed by the suddenness of the attack that he was unable to move, and made no attempt to seize Smith. Even as Webb surrendered, Smith whirled and fired two shots at Reeves, but missed with both shots. With Webb completely controlled by his left hand, Reeves turned his attention to Smith and fired one shot. Smith fell to the ground, the fight completely taken out of him by a .45 slug in his belly.

Reeves, never loosening his grip on Webb's throat, ordered Wilson to put the handcuffs on Webb. This was done immediately, and Reeves made his plans for returning his prisoner to Fort Smith. Quickly, two horses were hitched to a wagon. Webb and the wounded Smith were loaded into it, and the long trip back was started.

On the return trip Frank Smith died from his wounds by the time they reached Tishomingo, the Chickasaw capital. Smith was buried there without ceremony, and Reeves, Webb, and Wilson traveled on to Fort Smith.

Upon reaching Fort Smith, Reeves placed Webb in the federal jail and proceeded to forget all about him. But Webb and Reeves were destined to meet once more before their story was finished.

Webb was given a hearing before the U.S. commissioner and bound over for trial. However, he had friends who were hard at work in an effort to assist him. After spending almost a year in jail, two such friends, Jim Bywater, a store owner, and Chris Smith, managed to have him released on $17,000 bond. But when the time for Webb's trial for murder finally came around, Webb had completely disappeared and the $17,000 bond was forfeited.

Reeves rankled under the knowledge that Webb had escaped. Finally, Reeves received word that Webb had drifted back into the Chickasaw Nation and could be located at Jim Bywater's general store on the south side of the Arbuckle Mountains. This store was located near where the Whiskey Trail entered the mountains and where a spring supplied large quantities of water. It is now known as Woodford, Oklahoma.

This time Reeves took a posseman named John Cantrell with him. When Reeves and Cantrell came within sight of Bywater's store, Reeves sent Cantrell ahead to see if Webb was actually there. Cantrell rode ahead, slipped up to the store, and sure enough, there sat Jim Webb near one of the windows on the opposite side of the store. Cantrell eagerly motioned for Reeves to ride on up.[7]

D. C. Gideon described what happened next:

> As he went dashing up, Webb espied him, and jumping through the open window armed with both revolver and Winchester, ran for his horse that stood about one hundred yards away. Reeves cut him off from his horse and Webb turned toward a clump of bushes, ran about six hundred yards, turned and fired. The first shot grazed the horn of Reeves' saddle; the second cut a button from his coat, and the third cut off both bridle reins below his hand, allowing them to fall to the ground. As Reeves jumped from his horse another bullet . . . cut the brim from his hat. Reeves then fired his first shot, and before Webb could fall had sent two Winchester balls through his body.
>
> By this time Reeves' posse and Messrs. Bywaters and Smith came running up. Webb lay on the ground with his revolver in his hand, calling Reeves to come to him. Reeves advanced, but while keeping his gun trained on him told Webb to throw the revolver away. He flung it into the grass out of his reach and the whole party walked up to the dying man.
>
> "Give my your hand, Bass," said Webb, as he extended his own with an effort to grasp it. "You are a brave man. I want you to accept my revolver and scabbard as a present and you must accept them. Take it, for with it I have killed eleven men, four of them in Indian Territory, and I expected you to make the twelfth." Bass accepted the present, and has it now carefully stored away. The dying declaration of Webb was taken in writing by Mr. Bywaters, and thus ended the career of another "bad" man.[8]

While being interviewed by a newspaper in 1907, Reeves made the following remarks about the Webb shootout:

> "The bravest man I ever saw," said Reeves, "was Jim Webb, a Mexican that I killed in 1884 near Sacred Heart Mission. He was a murderer, I got in between him and his horse. He stepped out into the open 500 yards away and commenced shooting

with his Winchester. Before I could drop off my horse his first bullet cut a button off my coat and second cut my bridle rein in two. I shifted my six-shooter and grabbed my Winchester and shot twice. He dropped and when I picked him up I found that my two bullets had struck within a half-inch of each other. He shot four times, and every time he shot he kept running closer to me. He was 500 yards away from me when I killed him."[9]

Reeves had teamed up with Deputy U.S. Marshal J. S. Mershon on this particular trip into the Chickasaw Nation. Reeves took a batch of warrants for the area and Mershon did the same, then they split up and met later after making their arrest and traveled to Fort Smith as a group. The *Fort Smith New Era* of June 26, 1884, made the following remarks about the trip:

> Deputy Marshal Mershon and posse attempted to arrest Jim Webb near Bywater's store, in the Arbuckle mountains, a few days since, which resulted in a running fight, in which Webb was wounded and died that night. Webb was boss of Washington's ranch. He was charged with killing a negro for burning the ranch last winter.—Cor. Champion.

The *Fort Smith Weekly Elevator* on June 27, 1884, printed:

> Jim Webb the boss of Washington's cattle ranch in the Chickasaw Nation, who was charged with killing a negro last winter for burning off the range, was shot and killed near Bywater's store in the Arbuckle mountains on the 15th inst. by Deputy U.S. Marshal Mershon and posse, while resisting arrest.

After the deputy U.S. marshals arrived in Fort Smith with their prisoners from the Indian Territory, more articles were written about the trip. The *Arkansas Gazette* on July 4, 1884, wrote:

> ***Fort Smith: Rough Encounter with Criminals in the Territory***
> Fort Smith, July 3.—Deputy United States Marshals J. S. Mershon and Bass Reeves came in late this evening from the Chickasaw country, with twelve prisoners, five charged with assault with intent to kill, five with larceny and two whiskey peddlers. Ed McCurry of the number is badly wounded in the groin,

having been shot while resisting arrest, near Tishomingo, about three weeks ago. The officers had some rough experience on the trip. A man named Webb, charged with murder engaged them in A RUNNING FIGHT and was fatally wounded, dying the next day. One Hamilton, a full-blooded Chickasaw, also resisted arrest, and in the fight Mershon's horse fell, and his posse's ran over him, bruising the officer up badly. Hamilton was wounded, but escaped to the woods where it is reported he has since died. He was also charged with murder. This fight occurred near Fishertown, in the Creek nation.

The *Fort Smith Weekly Elevator* on July 11, 1884, reported:

U.S. Prisoners: A Trip Not Entirely Devoid of Interest

We mentioned last week the arrival of deputy U.S. marshals J. H. Mershon and Bass Reeves with a load of prisoners from the Choctaw and Chickasaw nations. We find them registered at Jailor Burns' office as follows: Cash Benton (white), Robert Colbert (Indian), Eli Riddle (negro), assault with intent to kill; Sterling Williams, A. P. McKinney (negroes), Joquin Thawes, Ike Rose, George Seeley (Indians), Ed McCurry (white), larceny; Thomas Logan, Wash Taylor (negroes), Colbert Moore (Indian), J. D. Williams (white), introducing and selling whiskey in the nation. Colbert Moore immediately gave bond. Ed McCurry is badly wounded in the groin, having made such a vigorous resistance when arrested that the officers were compelled to shoot him. His arrest was made by the Indian police. In the fight, Ed's partner was killed and one of the police wounded in the knee. He is charged with peddling whiskey in the Territory and also with larceny. He was brought all the way from near Tishomingo laying on a mattress in the bottom of a wagon bed, and stood the trip remarkably well considering the severity of his wound. On the trip the Marshals killed a man named Webb who was charged with murder and would not submit to having the writ served on him. An account of this killing has already been published. Near Fishertown, Mershon attempted to arrest one Hamilton, a full-blood Creek Indian, on a charge of murder, when he resisted by firing on the officer and his posse and running. In the melee Mershon's horse fell with him, and the posse coming up at full speed behind run over the prostrate man and horse, bruising them both up considerably, while Hamilton escaped to the woods, where the officers learned he soon afterwards died.

Being a U.S. Marshal may appear to some a regular picnic, but we don't want any of it in ours.

The (Vinita, Oklahoma) *Indian Chieftain* on Thursday, July 17, 1884, made the following comments:

Territory and Border Notes

Fort Smith, New Era, 10th.—Dep. U.S. Marshals J. H. Mershon and Bass Reeves came in last Thursday with twelve prisoners, all hard cases. One of them is badly wounded having been shot while resisting arrest. Two others charged with murder resisted and were killed.

It is interesting that Reeves was not singled out in the press as the deputy who shot Webb, possibly because of Reeves being an African American in an area that at best tolerated black deputy U.S. marshals who had power to arrest white people. Most of his shootings were not reported in the territorial newspapers. Later, in 1906, as mentioned earlier, Reeves stated that Webb was a Mexican. He may have or may not have been a Mexican. Reeves could have said this to deflect any criticism that he had killed white men, even if they were criminals. At the end of his career the territorial newspapers stated repeatedly that Reeves had killed fourteen men in the line of duty. This could be the correct number or could be a conservative number. We have no fixed record of his shootings or his participation in shootings with a posse. In looking at the years that Reeves served as a peace officer we can safely say he was undoubtedly in more than a few shootings in the dangerous Indian Territory. The outlaws he shot no doubt reflected the ethnic diversity of the territory. If we embrace the number fourteen, as the newspapers did, Reeves would have killed more outlaws in the line of duty than any lawman of that era. This would make him the preeminent gunfighter of any Old West lawman on record.[10]

Later in the month of July 1884, Reeves arrested an Indian who went by the name of Hanna. He also had the alias of George Washington. It was reported by citizens in the Creek Nation that Hanna had killed a white man. Reeves made the arrest on July 21 on the Canadian River twenty miles west of Eufaula.[11]

Deputy U.S. Marshal James H. Mershon sent U.S. Marshal Boles a note a few days later where he remarked about Reeves:

> McAlister I.T.
> July 29/884
>
> Col Thomas Boles
> U.S. Marshal
> Ft. Smith Ark
> Dear Sir Please
>
> Get writ for One Arnie Stone a white man for stealing ($5) five Dollars in United States Currency from James Allen a white man about July 20th 84—Witnesses James Allen J Golsby and two others now we followed this man Stone to Colbert and arrested him the Case is a good one he confessed it and will plea guilty. Please get the writ it is not any great amount of course that he stole. Yet he is known to be a thief and we have the positive proof besides his own confession. Send the Writ to Atoka. I have now 11 Prisoners. I will leave them hear tomorrow and visit the Chickasaw country. Bass did not stop here. I heard of him up on Canadian yesterday he had two Prisoners. Send all my papers to Atoka unless other . . . orders. Please don't forget to look after that writ for Vinsen and this man Arnie Stone. Very Respectfully Yours.
>
> > [signed] James H. Mershon
> > Deputy U.S.M.[12]

The next month, on August 28, 1884, the *Muskogee Indian Journal* made the following comments about Reeves's work in the territory:

> Bass Reeves, one of the best Marshals on the force, reported at Atoka, Monday from the Chickasaw, Pottawotamie and Western Creek country with the following prisoners: One Hanna,

Creek, murder; Chub Moore, murder; Jedick Jackson, Jno. Bruner, colored, Jim Mack, Chickasaw for larceny; Jno. Hoyt, Dr. A. Smith, J. M. McConnell, whites, Alex. Baker and Daniel Dorsey, Creeks, all for introducing.

Another article in the same edition reported on a shooting that Reeves was involved in:

A Thrilling Tragedy

Bass Reeves on his last trip had an experience that came near cutting short his usefulness and did send one man where he won't fool with other peoples horses. He had warrants for two men, Frank Buck and John Bruner. While up the Canadian looking for prisoners he came on these men but did not know them. He enquired for other parties whom he was after and Buck and Bruner volunteered to guide him. At noon all parties camped, and while they were getting dinner he noticed Bruner stealthily pulling his pistol. Suspecting something he stepped behind his horse and around to the front of Bruner and grabbed his pistol before he had time to use it, and at the same time pulled his own. Glancing over his shoulder Buck was seen getting out his weapon, when as quick as a flash Reeves still holding Bruner's pistol in one hand, threw over his other and shot Buck dead. Bruner was then secured and is now on his way to Fort Smith where he will have to answer to a double charge.

A third article from the same newspaper reported on activities by Frank Pierce, who was acting as posseman for Reeves on this trip into the Chickasaw Nation:

Frank Pierce, a deputy marshal had a writ for Chub Moore, charged with killing a negro who raped a white woman. Chub being at the head of a party of about 75 who went to capture him over seven years ago on the Canadian. Pierce says that in the morning that Chub and himself went down to the spring alone and that Chub asked him if he had any papers for him and Pierce told him he had none. When they came up from the spring and got opposite the house Pierce told Chub to halt, that he had a writ for him. Chub swung his leg over to get off his horse when Pierce shot him on the inside of his thigh, the ball ranging up into his body. It is thought that he will lie but a few days as they cannot find the ball. There is a party over from the Pottawatomie country looking into the matter and there may be considerable more to add next week. Pierce is still there. Champion.

The Little Rock *Arkansas Gazette* reported on Reeves arrival into Fort Smith on September 2, 1884:

A Good Haul: Fifteen Prisoners Brought to Fort Smith from the Nation

Fort Smith, Sept. 1—Deputy Marshal Bass Reeves came in this afternoon with fifteen prisoners, two of whom, Chubb Moore and one Hanna, are charged with murder. Chub was severely wounded in the leg at the time of his arrest, on the 7th of August, but nevertheless was hauled down here, a distance of 265 miles, lying flat on his back on a mattress, and stood the trip very well. He was at the head of a gang of men who hung a negro about two years ago, who was charged with having attempted to commit a rape. On the trip Reeves killed one Frank Buck in self-defense. Buck was charged with larceny.

On September 5 the *Fort Smith Weekly Elevator* gave a more descriptive report on Reeves's arrival:

U.S. Prisoners

Deputy U.S. Marshal Bass Reeves came in on Monday last with fifteen prisoners as follows: Chub Moore and one Hanna, alias George Washington, murder; James McJohnson, Zedick Jackson, John Bruner, (negro) Ellick Bruner, (Indian) Isaac Deer, larceny; W. R. Burnett, assault with intent to kill; John Hoyt, John McConnell, Dan Dorsey, John Lodcar, J. A. Smith, Alex Baker, introducing whiskey in Territory; Jack Riddle, violating revenue law.

Club Moore is charged with being the leader of a party of men who seven years ago hung a negro for an assault upon a white woman in the Chickasaw Nation. In making the arrest on the 7th of August, Frank Pierce, acting as posse for Reeves, shot Chub in right thigh, the ball ranging up, inflicting a severe wound. He was placed in a covered hack on a mattress and made the trip here, a distance of some 265 miles, and is now doing remarkably well. He is a full blood Chickasaw. Hanna, the other party charged with murder, is a full blood Creek, and killed a white man on the 24th of February last.

Frank Pierce, who shot Chub Moore, turned out to be a notorious horse-thief, and has fled the country to avoid arrest.

The Marshal was out six weeks, and on the trip killed a Negro named Frank Buck.

The *Fort Smith Weekly Elevator* seven days later reported on the death of Chub Moore:

Took a Change of Venue: Chub Moore Dies in the U.S. Jail
He Made a Statement

On the 7th of August Chub Moore, a Chickasaw Indian charged with murder was shot near Johnsonville, Chickasaw Nation, by the posse of Bass Reeves, while making his arrest. The wound was in the right thigh, the bone being badly shattered. After receiving the wound Chub was placed in a covered hack on a mattress and conveyed to this place, a distance of about 265 miles, arriving here on the 1st of September. He immediately received the attention of Dr. J. E. Bennett, jail physician, who did all he could to relieve the sufferings of the wounded man, but came to the conclusion on Friday last that the only chance to save the man's life was to amputate the wounded limb. Before deciding on the matter, however, he called in several other physicians, and after a thorough examination of the case all agreed with Dr. Bennett that the only remedy was a amputation and the odds were largely against the patient even then. Saturday the operation was performed, the leg being amputated near the hip joint by Dr. Bennett, assisted by Drs. Bailey, Dunlap, Eberly, King, Kelleam, Smith and Leo Bennett, but Chub never recovered from the shock of the operation, dying on the table.

About an hour before the operation was performed the wounded man made a statement to Mr. John Patterson of the Marshal's office in which he "gave away" several parties who have been engaged in stealing horses in the Territory. In regard to the case for which he was brought here—that of being one of a party who hung a negro near Erin Springs about seven years ago, while under arrest charged with assaulting a white girl—he declared his innocence, saying that after the negro had been arrested, himself and a man named White started with the prisoner to Fort Sill to turn him over to the U.S. authorities. While en route, between Erin Springs and Fort Sill, they were overtaken by a party of men who seized the negro and took him off, and that was the last he ever saw of him; did not know whether the negro was hung or shot, though he heard afterwards that the negro was killed. While making the statement he had hopes of recovery.[13]

The case of Chub Moore is very interesting because here we have an African American peace officer bringing to justice parties accused of lynching a black man in the nineteenth century. This action by Reeves was a rarity in itself at this time in American history. Lynching was mob violence carried out against the African American population at regular intervals during the late nineteenth and early twentieth centuries by the white community. Most of these crimes, which were seen as a means of intimidation and control of the black community by violence, occurred in southern states. But lynchings also happened in northern states. The Indian Territory was the scene of very few racial lynchings before statehood. Most crimes of mob violence were committed against cattle and horse thieves. After statehood in 1907, the majority of lynchings in Oklahoma were perpetrated against African Americans. This would not be the last time Reeves would investigate crimes of racial violence in the Indian Territory.[14]

A very descriptive rendering of the Frank Buck shooting was given in the newspapers, as shown previously. The shooting took on another scenario when testimony was given before U.S. Commissioner James Brizzolara on September 22, 1884, in the federal court at Fort Smith on the arrest of John Bruner for obstructing justice by resisting arrest. Bass Reeves gave a statement:

Bass Reeves being duly sworn, deposes and says:

I reside at Van Buren, Arkansas and I had a warrant for defendant for Larceny; and am and was at the time Deputy U.S. Marshal. I went down to his fathers got there almost twelve o'clock in daytime tethered my horse to the wagon and got over the fence. I had my gun in my hand. I started on up to house and I saw two men; one jumped out at one door and one out of the other. Defendant had a Winchester, the other fellow had his hand on a six-shooter. One was John Bruner and the other was John Bucks; had writs for both of them. I went on over to the horses and the both jumped to the cornfield. I did not know who they were until the old man I met at house told me who they were. I told him to go out and [tell] him that I had no writ for him. Defendant never came back they both left their horses there; I stayed there until dark. I told his brother that I wanted defendant to help me catch Perry Bruner. I left and went home and defendants brother told me he would meet me the next morning. I started over there and met them before I got over to Ransom, [I] met them on the edge of a little prairie like they were all down off their horses. Defendant had his Winchester in his hands. I got down and walked up to them and spoke to them. Defendant said he heard I had a writ for him. I asked him who told him; he did not say; he asked me if I had it. I told him I did not know that I did but would tell him all about it before I left him. Ransom, defendants brother left us and defendant told me to go with him and he would show me Perry Bruner; we went on about four miles. Then he told me to stop, for me to stay there and he would go and locate him and so defendant and Frank rode off. When they rode off I seen things were not exactly right so I moved off from my horse. I got out where I could watch them, they went off, both were gone a little bit and they came back. I waited till they both came back and then I went to where my horse was hitched and when they came to where my horse was they got down. Defendant got down on the far side of his horse and put his hand on his six-shooter. We all squatted down then and commenced talking while we were there talking defendant commenced drawing his pistol. I seen that he was drawing his pistol and I told him, "John [all] I want is get you to serve a subpoena for me," he said, "a dollar and a half." I then said very well I will have to give it. I handed him the subpoena and he opened it. I asked him what day of the month it was I had book in my hand and I got between defendant and his horse and Winchester and I told him to look at name next to his thumb. When he done this I seen he had his pistol almost out of his scabbard with his hand on handle and then snatched my pistol before I got to him he had gotten his pistol out and I just grabbed his pistol and as I grabbed his pistol I threw mine down in his face. I took pistol from him and handcuffed. I told defendant I had a writ for him as soon as I jumped and threw my pistol in his face. John Hoyt was with me. Defendant knew all the time I had a writ for him. He had been told by a dozen. I had writ for him. This was about four weeks ago in the Chickasaw Nation. Frank Buck was killed at that place. When I jumped towards defendant. Frank jumped up with his pistol drawing it and I called to Hoyt to shoot him and he done so. This was after I told them I had a writ, as I jumped I told him to throw up his hands, that I had a writ for him.

Cross examination

It was on Wednesday or Thursday; had arrest John Hoyt about a week before this for introducing and had him as a prisoner. I told the old man to tell defendant that I had no writ for him. John Hoyt was with me and Ransom and Frank were with defendant when I met them. Had made arrangement with Ransom for them to meet me the next day. Ransom told me that if he knew what the charge was and there was only one charge he would go to Ft. Smith. Ransom and these boys were to meet me and carry me on to Perry Bruner's. Ransom did not go with us, when I first met defendant he said I heard you had writ for me and I saw who told you think he said Perry Bruner told him I had no writ for him. I never remember defendant ever saying that if he knew I had a writ he would come with me to Ft. Smith. I recollect Hoyt going over three or four writs for me. This was when we first met and defendant was present.

Case was continued to Sept 24/84

Bass Reeves recalled for cross ex. says: I went on the field that evening and staid there until night to try to catch them. Ransom came to me in field but not before sundown. Hoyt was with me. Ransom saw that defendant told him that if he knew that I had a writ for him and there was only one charge against him he would come to Fort Smith. I never told defendant for certain that I had a writ for him until I went to pull my pistol on him. Defendant aimed to grab me with his left hand. He never said he would surrender until I jerked his pistol, he went to grab me and I told him that if he moved I would kill him. I threw my pistol down on him and told him if he moved I would kill him.

John M. Hoyt duly sworn says:

Bass and I started one evening and went see about George Mack and we went to Tecumseh Bruner's place when we rode up to house, I saw Frank step out of the east door and John out of the south door and we walked right on into the house. When we got into the house Bass remarked to Tecumseh Bruner, "What are these boys running for?" Tecumseh said that they understand that he, Bass had paper for John. Bass say no not that I know of I have no papers for him; that he came to see about George Mack. We sat there and talked and Bass made the remark to Tecumseh to go and call the boys back that he wanted to see them. He started and went out to cornfield and called for the boys. He came back in and said he couldn't find them that he guessed they had gone on home. We ate dinner there, after we ate dinner we went to Ransom about two miles off, a brother of defendant and after getting there he was not at home we waited there a short time and Ransom came in. When he came Bass told him how defendant and Frank did when we rode up there and he told him he wanted him to go over and see them and that he wanted them to help him to catch George Mack and Perro Bruner; and that he wanted him, Ransom to bring them over that he wanted to see them. He made the remark that he would do so. The three of us got on our horses and rode over to Tecumseh's. When we got there Ransom went across to defendant and we went around back in the cornfield where we had agreed to meet. Ransom when he came back from defendant we went in field and waited until nearly sundown when Ransom came back. When Ransom came back into field I went to where we were to meet him and saw his horse hitched there. When I got up to where Ransom's horse was I saw Ransom coming up through the field. I went back and told Bass that Ransom had come. Bass and I went up to where Ransom was under the tree. We all got together and Bass asked him what he had done, if he had seen them. He said he had then we got on our horses and went out of cornfield on over way to camp. . . . Bass asked him if he could get John, Frank and Ransom to catch Perro Bruner and George Mack. He made the remark that he thought the three could go and help him. Bass told him to go back and see the boys, and see if he could get them to go back that night or come in the morning and meet him in the morning at forks of the road. He made the remarks that he and the boys would be there as early in the morning as possible at sun up. We separated at forks of road, he went on home and we went on to camp. The next morning we all met at forks of the road where we had agreed to. When we rode up Ransom, defendant and Frank were there we bid time of morning and shook hands. Ransom making the remark, Mr. Bass the boys and I are now all here. Bass made the remark to defendant and Frank, "boys why did you for yesterday?" John said, "I understand you have papers for me but since I found out that you have got no papers for me I came over to see, and if you have papers for me I want to give up to you, if not will try and help you all I can if you will satisfy me for my trouble." Bass remarked, "I shall satisfy you for your trouble," and Ransom said to Bass, "now these boys will do you as much good without me than with me," making the remark he had to go to Stonewall to get a steer and Bass said, "very well." Defendant then said, "now I am going to do all that I can and if George and Perro are there I am going to do my best to take them. We shook hands and Ransom left for Stonewall. We on our way to Perro Bruner. After reaching bottom before we got to Perro Bruner field the four of us separated. Defendant and Frank went to Perro Bruner's and we stopped where we had separated at; and in course of half an hour . . . they came back. When they came back we had a slicker spread down on ground where they had left us at. Bass invited him to get down and asked them what they had done. They got off their horses and sat down on and by the slicker; John being to my right and Frank to my left. Bass was to John's left but Bass to my right. Bass pulled a subpoena out of his pocket after asked these boys what they had done. They told him that Perro and Rector had left that morning with some horses. Bass handed the subpoena to John asking him if he knew where this man was. John and Frank's horses were in front of us. Bass picking up a book that was lying in the slicker asked what day of the month it was stepped up to Frank's horse making the remark, "I will put that down," as Bass stepped to horse he looked at me nodded his head and winked as he did this. I rose to my feet making the remark that I would take a chew of tobacco when Bass got to the horse, he nodded his head at me and I made the remark to Frank, "I have a writ for you." As I said this Bass pulled his pistol and threw it to the right side of John's head. Then I caught Frank by his right wrist with my pistol in my right hand demanding Frank to give up. As I demanded of Frank to give up he commenced getting up on his feet saying, "I will give up," as Frank rose to his feet I turned and looked at Bass, as I looked at Bass, Bass had thrown John's pistol away from him three or four steps and when Bass saw me he made the remark to me, "shoot him, God damn him, shoot him," and Frank had his hand in a manner on his pistol. His left hand was on a pistol hanging on his right. I demanded of Frank to give up, shoving him away with my left hand and Bass made the remark to me again, "shoot him!" As he made that demand of me I fired on him. Frank threw his left hand up when I fired reaching with his right hand to the pistol hanging on his left. I made the remark, "give up Frank," and as I made the remark I fired again. When I fired the second time he threw his right hand up, catch his pistol on the right with his left hand and drawing it out past the cylinder in the scabbard. And I fired a third time on him and he turned with his back directly to me running in a southerly direction from me and as he did this my pistol failed to fire a fourth shot. As that I heard a racked and some one saying I will give up, when I turned I seen John was lying on his left side just almost the place he was sitting. . . . When I saw them Bass had John caught by the right arm with his left hand and his pistol pointed to the side of defendants head to the right side of his face. I stepped up to where our Winchesters were sitting up by the root of a tree. Bass said give up again. John said I give up but Mr. Bass you did not do me right. Then I stepped to John's mare to get his Winchester and when I got to the mare, Bass made the remark, "You have played hell haven't you." And I made the answer, "Why Bass?" And he said, "You have let your man get away from you." I made the remark that I done the best I could that there is where he got into the brush and I was not going in after him. Then I took John's Winchester and scabbard from off his saddle. Then put the handcuffs on John. John getting on his mare, the three of us struck out for camp taking Frank's horse with us. I forgot to state that in going up to Ransom's we got to him and he asked him if he had a writ for defendant. He handed me the writ book and he told him he had no writ for defendant. When he handed me the book he told me that I could read the writs over to Ransom to show him that he had no writ for Frank or John. I read them over and Ransom said that was all right that he should go and see them. When Frank and defendant ran out of house, one of them had a Winchester, think it was Frank. When we met them at the forks of the road the following morning. Ransom had a Winchester and six-shooter, John had a Winchester and six-shooter and Frank had two six-shooters. We got down off of our horses in bottom by Perro Bruner's field just before they left. We sat down there and took out the writs. They left as soon as we got off our horses. When we took writs out they were not present. We were to stay where we were until they returned. We looked over the writs and some court subpoenas. We spoke there and arranged about arresting defendant and Frank when they came back I was to arrest Frank and Bass John. We had the writs out when they came back. . . . They got down off their horses, tied them to bushes with their heads toward us. Our horses were tied to our back with their heads away from us about five steps away. Defendant and Frank's horses were about four steps from us we were standing up when they came. . . . All four of us sat down. After we all sat down they told us that Perro and Rector had gone off that morning and they were not at home. When he first sat down defendant had his pistol in front of him like and after he sat down he moved it to his side from in front of him, after he done this, the pistol was out of the scabbard to the cylinder. As soon as he done this, Bass handed him the subpoena and defendant took it and looked at it. Then Bass got with his book. Frank's pistols as he was lying on the ground in the scabbard and the one on his right with the butt towards the other, the butts were in a drawing position. Frank's were in the scabbard. Defendant had one in coat. Frank had his pistols buckled on him over his coat. When I caught Frank I heard Bass say throw up I have a writ for you. When Bass made the remark, defendant was sitting on the ground with his feet under him and the subpoena in his hands. I seen nothing more after this until I seen Bass have defendant on the ground. Frank when I arrested him I held him by the right hand and he got up with his left. I had hold of him all the time until he got on his feet. When he got on to his feet I turned and looked at Bass still holding him by his right hand. When Bass called me to shoot, Frank was trying to get away from me, going sideways and trying to pull his pistol out with his left hand, his right hand pistol and kept saying, "I will give up." He had his hand on his pistol and drawing it when I shot. Do not know if I turned him loose or whether he jerked loose from me. It seems to me that I pushed him from me before I fired. He was in the act of drawing his pistol with his left hand when I fired first. When I fired the second shot he had thrown up his left hand from his right hand pistol and caught his pistol on his left with his right hand. He was in the act of drawing it then when I fired a second time. When I fired the third he turned his left hand pistol loose out of his right hand catching his right hand pistol again with his left hand. When I fired the third shot his pistol was drawn out of the scabbard to the hilt extractor. There were two or three inches of muzzle sticking yet on his scabbard. He said a time or two I will give up but still he this but kept getting away from me. He never threw both his hands up. This was in August last. We had writs for these parties. At this time I was a prisoner of Bass Reeves, but he employed me to make these arrest from the time he first arrested me until we came into Fort Smith. This was the contract between him and I and that he would allow me guard wages. This was in Indian country.

Cross examination

I was arrested on Monday, August 1, 1884 for Introducing. This was almost two weeks after I was arrested. When he told them he had no writs for them he pulled his book out to hand me but defendant saw that will do. Ransom said, 'Yes, I knew Bass to be a gentleman.' The writs against Frank and John were not in the book. I had read the writs. Bass thought that we could not arrest the defendant and Frank unless we got the drop on them and they were hard characters. When they were together with Ransom. That if we met them in a crowd we could show the book and show that we did not have them. This was why the writs were taken out of the book.[15]

This testimony from the hearing differs completely from the stories about the shooting that the newspapers published before and after Bass

Reeves came in with the prisoners. John Bruner was released on the charges of resisting arrest. Also, the hearing points to the posseman, John M. Hoyt, as the shooter of Buck. This is very interesting, since Hoyt was arrested by Reeves on this same trip and then promised guard wages if he assisted in capturing some felons. In the testimony it isn't clear if Frank Buck was wounded or killed. But in the newspaper articles it is clear that Buck was killed. On January 1, 1886, John Bruner was arrested by Deputy U.S. Marshal Heck Thomas for murdering the notorious black outlaw George Mack. Deputy Thomas subpoenaed Bass Reeves on February 10, 1887, at the Fort Smith federal jail for the murder trial. At this time in 1887, Reeves was in jail for the murder of his cook. The outcome of the Bruner murder trial is not indicated in the case file.[16]

Did Reeves actually shoot Mack and then paid Hoyt to take the heat? Why were the newspapers stories so off base with only portions of the story correct? Why would Reeves deputize a felon he had arrested only a few days earlier? Reeves might have done this due to Hoyt being literate and could help read the warrants. These are just a few questions we can ponder while analyzing this particular case. This shooting sounded similar to another shooting that occurred during 1884, which Reeves talked about in the 1906 newspaper interview:

> Reeves says that the tightest place he ever got into was in 1884, when he was riding the Seminole whiskey trail, looking for two white men and two negroes. He was ambushed by three Brunter brothers who knew he was looking for them. They had their guns on him and made him dismount. He got down and showed them the warrants for their arrests and asked them to tell him the day of the month as he could make a record to turn in to the government.
>
> "You are just ready to turn in now," remarked one of the outlaws, but they relaxed their guard for the merest instant and instant was enough.
>
> Reeves whipped out his six-shooter and killed one of the men as quick as lightning and grabbed the gun of the other in time to save himself. He also killed the other Brunter while he was

still holding the gun of the third one, who shot three times with Reeves gripping the barrel of the gun. Reeves finally struck him over the head with his six-shooter and killed him.[17]

Were the "Brunter" brothers referred to in this article actually the Bruner brothers? In a newspaper article from 1901, Reeves states he killed two of the Bruner brothers who belonged to a notorious black outlaw family in the Indian Territory.

A story with some similarities was told by Nancy Pruitt, a white resident of the Creek Nation prior to statehood:

> This Bass Reeves had the name of being a good officer and when he went after a man he got him. One time he went after two mean Negroes and knew when he left that if he didn't kill them they would kill him, for it would be impossible to bring them back alive. When he found them they were lying under a tree asleep but before he could get to them one awakened and got up. Bass started talking to him and gave him a letter to read. By that time the other one was up. When the first had read the letter Bass told him to let the other one read it. When he turned to give the letter to the other one, Bass shot him and then the second before he could draw. That looks like a cold blooded murder to us now but it was really quick thinking and bravery.[18]

In Fort Smith on September 20, 1884, Bass Reeves arrested a man named James Grier for selling whiskey to Indians. At the hearing before U.S. Commissioner Brizzolara, witnesses against Grier testified:

Gilbert Collins being duly sworn, deposes and says:

> I reside at Choctaw Nation, the defendant, (here pointing at Grier,) sold me the whiskey. I got eight bottles [from] him. They called it two gallons. I paid him four dollars for it. I bought it right there at P. R. Davis store. It was the Wednesday I got arrested. Shendan Huggins was with me. I am an Indian, a Choctaw Indian. I asked him if there was any danger, he said no if I would not get drunk. This was about one or two o'clock in the evening.

Cross examination

My mother was a white woman. My father was an Indian, he said he was an Indian. I am 21 years old. Have seen defendant before this time. Knew him from his general appearance. I just came in and got it.

Shendan Huggins duly sworn says:

I was with Collins when he got whiskey at P. R. Davis' he got it off defendant. (here witness points to defendant) He got two gallons in eight quart bottles. This young man sold it to him. I was in the store when he gave him the whiskey. This was almost past two or three o'clock in the evening.

Cross examination

I am a white man. I live in Choctaw Nation. I live close to Collins. I came with him when Collins got whiskey. We went in to Mr. Davis'. We sampled the whiskey before he bought it. We got it in saddle riders. I did not pay for the whiskey or get the whiskey. I was there and seen it bought. I talked about the whiskey and sampled it. I was there all the time Collins was there. I has no interest in the whiskey. I had no money.

Re-direct

Collins bought the whiskey. The whiskey was given to Collins. Think defendant carried saddle riders to door. Collins done the trading and pricing of the whiskey and paid for it.[19]

The *Muskogee Indian Journal* on October 16, 1884, printed the following story about Bass Reeves's posseman, Frank Pierce (spelled Pearce in the article):

Frank Pearce

Frank Pearce is getting quite a reputation in the Chickasaw Nation, first by shooting Chub Moore and later being shot at himself. It was claimed it was done by officers trying to arrest him, but we learn he has been passing himself off as an U.S. Marshal and as such visited Dick Glass. To prove it he shows a certificate from Mr. D. N. Robb, of Atoka, dated sometime in July last. As a marshal he took possession of four horses which he claimed had been stolen by Dick Glass or by the Ward brothers. The Ward brothers followed a[n]d waylaid him, shooting his horse and leaving him lying supposedly dead. At the time there seemed to be considerable mystery attached to the shooting but our information comes direct from the scene of the affair and probably is correct.

Reeves was mentioned in another article in the same edition of the *Muskogee Indian Journal*:

Bass Reeves, John Williams and Bud Kell, U.S. deputy mar-shals have been around the past week disturbing the peace and quietude of some of our violators of the law in this vicinity (Fishertown).

Bud Kell would later become a member of the United States Indian Police stationed at Muskogee.

It appears Deputy U.S. Marshal Bass Reeves was having problems of his own at the time. Apparently Reeves was temporarily relieved from the U.S. marshals' office at Fort Smith until some charges made against him could be investigated. The *Fort Smith Weekly Elevator* on October 17, 1884, reported:

Bass Reeves, one of the most successful of the marshals "doing business" in the Territory, has been discharged from the force by Marshal Boles. It seems he had a habit of letting a prisoner escape when more could be made than by holding him and that is where the trouble came in.

The *Muskogee Indian Journal* printed another article a few months later, on Christmas Day, 1884, that attacked Reeves's character and linked him to outlaws in the Chickasaw Nation:

News around Sacred Heart Mission

Horse stealing has commenced rather lively again, David Bruner and Rector Rogers seem to be at the head. Our citizens may well watch their stock for the man that goes by the name of Frank Pearce and who ran such a narrow chance for his life is in this part of the country again. He is stopping at the residence of

George Young. My informant says that he is cheerful although expresses great sympathy for his old partner Bass Reeves, the ex-U.S. Marshal. It was these two men that caused the death of Chub Moore, of Johnsonville. It is to be regretted that a man in the standing of George Young would harbor such an outlaw as Pearce has proven himself to be. If any one wishes to find out about Pearce, Hill Phillips, merchant at Johnsonville, can satisfy the most skeptical.

The Wade boys have left this part of the country. King Berry and his gang have retired from doing business, and there has been less horse stealing done here since Bass Reeves was taken off the force than has been for many months.

Apparently U.S. Marshal Boles couldn't find enough evidence to substantiate the charges against Reeves and reinstated him on the force. The *Fort Smith Weekly Elevator* the day after Christmas printed:

E. D. Jones was arrested in Franklin county by Deputy Marshal Reeves. He was lodged in the U.S. jail on the following night, and of Friday Chief Deputy C. M. Barnes left with him for Louisville, KY., where there is an indictment against him for altering a mail contract. He was formally a Kentucky mail contractor. He has a family in the Blue Grass State. He sent his wife $100 the morning he left.

Franklin County is just east of Crawford County, where Reeves lived in the county seat of Van Buren. If, as this article indicates, Bass Reeves arrested E. D. Jones, Reeves must have been reinstated as a deputy by December 1884. Incidentally, it was one of the few arrests on record that he made in Arkansas outside Sebastian County, the home of Fort Smith.

7.

Hell on the Border

T he year 1885 found Deputy U.S. Marshal Bass Reeves riding hard on the trail of outlaws deep in the interior of Indian Territory. In February, Reeves sent a note to Marshal Boles asking for writs on lawbreakers he had arrested in the Seminole Nation:

> Eufaula, Creek Nation
> Feb 2nd 1885
>
> Thomas Boles
> United States Marshal Western Dist
> Ft Smith Ark
>
> Dear Sir
>
> Please send me a writ for Jimmy Shepard for selling whiskey which he sold yesterday The witnesses in the case are Ruben Miller Davis & Taylor Hardwich Also a writ for H A Rumsford for selling whiskey he was the assistant Telegraph Operator at this place The witnesses in the case are Lori Crow & Lee & others Also a writ for Adam Fields for selling whiskey he had six quarts that was taken away from him by the Lighthorse named Ham-mi-tibbie and two

others who are witnesses against him Please send the papers to me
At Sawsaqua [Sasakwa]

Respectfully

[signed] Baz Reeves

P S Fields had been to the Penitentiary once for 18 months
the other two are White men

The Seminole policeman's name mentioned in the above note was
Hammetubbee.[1]

Being a former slave, Reeves was never exposed to even the slightest
hint of a formal education, and as a result, he never learned to read or
write. Whenever he signed a formal document he would always write an
"x." If he had to write a note, he would always dictate it to someone who
could write. This fact complicated matters when he was given a group
of subpoenas to serve on the numerous witnesses the Fort Smith court
required during a regular court session, because in most instances, the
people who were to be served with a subpoena could not read or write
either.

Reeves had several approaches to solving this problem. He would
study each separate subpoena until he could associate the symbols of
a written name with the sounds of the name as it was spoken. Then he
would have someone read the entire subpoena to him until he memorized which name belonged to which subpoena. Thus armed, he would
take to the field to locate his person.

When he located a man or woman that answered to one of the names
he had memorized, Reeves would search through his file of subpoenas
until he located the one with the proper symbols, thrust it into the
person's hands, and gruffly command, "Read it." If the person could
read, he had nothing to worry about, but if he couldn't, Reeves was
forced to locate somebody who could read to ensure the right person
had been served.

Finding someone who could read was not always an easy task. There
were two factors involved that must be considered. Reeves had to keep
the person he had located in tow because many of them had a tendency
to disappear as they had no desire whatsoever to participate in any trial.

Appearing as a witness in a trial generally entailed making a long trip over rough country, losing several days and possibly weeks of work, and there was always the danger of reprisal if the person they were testifying against was acquitted or had family or friends who wanted to get revenge. As a result, Reeves often had to resort to out and out threats to keep the person with him until he found somebody who could read.

For another reason, the persons Reeves found to read for him were usually in the most isolated and thinly populated areas in the entire Indian Territory. This meant sometimes riding as far as a hundred miles before locating someone who could read. This long ride was not necessarily because people were scarce, but because in reality even a rudimentary education was rather rare during these frontier times in many areas.

As a possible third minor factor, only incidentally contributing to Reeves's difficulty, the weather almost invariably turned bad when Reeves was out in the open on subpoena services. He even went as far as to warn the other deputies, "Get ready for bad weather, boys. I got a stack of subpoenas to serve, so Mother Nature is bound to go crazy. Hope I don't drown or freeze before I get back."

In spite of these difficulties, Reeves always served the subpoenas he was issued, and he was proud of the fact that he never made the mistake of serving one on the wrong person. Many of the courts he rode for specifically asked for Reeves to serve the subpoenas because of his dependability.[2]

On February 25, 1885, Reeves arrested a murderer named Luce Hammon who was a young citizen of the Creek Nation. Hammon was brought before the U.S. commissioner on March 13. The book *Hell on the Border* had this to say about Hammon:

> Luce Hammond, Hewah-na-cke, and one Wiley, three half-civilized Creek boys were tried for the murder of a white man named Owens, March 8, 1883, in the Creek Nation near the Seminole line.
>
> Owens traveled alone, and while camped at night he was visited by the boys and asked by each for a chew of tobacco. He

gave each of them a chew and they left, but returning soon after he had fallen asleep, they shot him for the purpose of robbery; they secured a few dimes.

Owens lived three or four days in a house nearby; he made a dying statement but did not identify the murderers, and they remained at large. Indian like they boasted of their crime, and told of killing a white man; they were arrested soon after and convicted. They were from seventeen to twenty years old.

After their conviction by the jury they were recommended for commutation by Judge Parker and District Attorney Sandels, on account of their youth and ignorance, and they were finally sent to the penitentiary for life.

There is no mention in *Hell on the Border*, which was written in 1898, of Reeves making the arrest. The boys were convicted on December 4, 1885. They were sentenced on January 30, 1886, to be hung on April 23, but their sentence was commuted and they were sent to the Detroit House of Corrections.[3]

Reeves served a subpoena on a white man named Weaver on March 11, 1885, twelve miles west of Eufaula in the Creek Nation. It concerned a larceny case involving a man named Al Baker.[4]

The *Fort Smith Weekly Elevator* on March 27, 1885, published a story on Reeves traveling to Texas for apparently the wrong reason:

The Wrong Man

Deputy U.S. Marshal Bass Reeves found a Negro man in jail in Gainesville, Texas, last week that he was sure was John Williams, the murderer of Constable Houck, of Van Buren. The Texas authorities turned him over to Bass, who brought him to Van Buren by rail, but he proved to be the wrong man. A Gainesville correspondent of the Fort Worth Gazette says Bass paid $100 reward to the Texas officers to get possession of the man. If that's the case Bass is the loser.

Jonas Post and Jonas Stick committed a murder on July 15, 1879, in the Creek Nation. Bass Reeves arrested Jonas Stick on April 20, 1885, at Grave Creek, fifteen miles west of Oklmulgee. On June 5, Reeves subpoenaed Billy Naconney and Wiley Blackbird as witnesses in the case, and another witness was in the jail at Fort Smith. Reeves sent Marshal Boles a note in regard to the subpoenas:

Eufaula, Ind. Ter
June 24, 1885

Thomas Boles
Ft Smith Ark

D Sir

Enclosed please find Subpoena I served it on Wm Naconney and Wiley Blackbird 10 miles west of Eufaula on Monday. Shelton Bruner is in Jail at Smith.

> Yours
> [signed] Bass Reeves[5]

When Reeves's former posseman Frank Pierce was killed by Texas peace officers in April 1885, the newspapers still tried to connect Reeves to the outlaw even though there was no evidence. The *Fort Smith Weekly Elevator* gave a report on the story on April 24:

A Gainesville, Texas dispatch reports a fight between Texas officers and cattle thieves from the nation, a few days ago in which Frank Pierce, alias Roberts, one of the thieves, was killed. Pierce is the man who was acting as posse for Deputy Marshal Bass Reeves some time since, and shot Chubb Moore, who was brought to this place and died of his wound in the U.S. jail. It has been frequently charged by correspondents to the Indian papers that Pierce was a thief and that Bass Reeves was in with him, though Marshal Boles has been unable to get evidence here to substantiate the charges against Reeves. The above indicates that the reports about Pierce must have been correct. Later advices say that the four thieves who were with Pierce, were "rounded up" in the Territory by a lot of cowboys who killed all four of them. The names of the thieves are not given.

On Reeves's next trip into the Seminole Nation he arrested Charles Coley and an Indian named Fegley for theft and arson on May 13, 1885. They stole a suit of clothes valued at twenty-five dollars from a Dr.

Smith, a white man, and then burned his house down. At the hearing at Fort Smith before U.S. Commissioner James Brizzolara, Reeves's posseman David Pompey made the following statements:

David Pompey being duly sworn, deposes and says:

I reside at Seminole Nation and know the defendants in this case. Defendant Coley was under arrest by the Lighthorse and delivered to me. Dr. Smith came to my house and asked to see defendants. I told him he could go ahead. He went over there. I seen defendant Coley with vest belonging to Dr. Smith, he was wearing it. I knew the vest, seen him wearing the vest when we had him prisoner. The house was burned, it was Dr. Smith's house. This was about 21st of March 1885.

The defendants were discharged on the theft charge and there is no information on the outcome of the arson charge.[6]

In Fort Smith, the *Weekly Elevator* reported on May 29, 1885, that Reeves brought prisoners into the U.S. jail from his latest trip into the Indian Territory:

Deputy Bass Reeves came in Sunday from an extended trip through the Territory bringing seventeen prisoners who were registered at the jailer's office as follows: Jonas Stake, Two-a-nuck-ey, one Wiley, (Indians) charged with murder; Chas. Cosey, one Feglin, arson; Ben Bowlegs alias Ben Billy alias Williams, (Indian) John Pickett, larceny; Robert Ken-a-wah, Joseph Dorsey, one Hawkins, Robert Kelly, Wolf alias Ya-gha, Barney alias Hillis Harjo, one Winnie, one Siller, one Jennie, (Indians) Adam Brady (negro), Introducing and selling whiskey in Territory. John Pickett gave bond.

It is quite possible that the Indian named Ya-gha reported in the newspaper article is the Indian medicine man Yah-kee, mentioned earlier in the book who tried to put a spell on Reeves. Fort Smith newspapers were notorious for misspelling individual's names, especially Indians, who were brought in to the federal jail.

A white man named George Perryman murdered a doctor named Stephenson in the Creek Nation on July 2, 1883. The court had trouble procuring witnesses for the case. Bass Reeves was called in to deliver the subpoenas. He served two of them five miles west of Eufaula on the Canadian River and near Brooken in July 1885. Reeves sent a note to the marshal:

> I served Subpoenas on Brassfield On Canadian 5 miles east of Eufaula & Mrs. Piercy near Brooken
>
> [signed] Yours Bass Reeves[7]

A little earlier, Reeves sent a request to Marshal Boles for the arrest of a black railroad employee who was trafficking in whiskey:

> Eufaula, Ind. Ter.
> June 24, 1885
>
> Mr. Thomas Boles
> Ft. Smith Ark
> Sir
>
> Send writ for one Hall for Introducing and selling whiskey He is Porter on train has been selling whiskey for the last 2½ years Most every trip he delivers to his customers from 1 to 4 gal a trip. Witnesses W. F. Gabler & Wm. Sorb Adam Brady. R. J. Miller Send to Wewoka store.
>
> Yours Truly
[signed] Bass Reeves[8]

On June 25, 1884, Bass Reeves arrested two white men for selling whiskey. Bass had arrested one of the men, Henshaw, in September 1882 for selling whiskey. On this trip, Reeves had his oldest son, Robert, along as a guard. Reeves sent a note to Marshal Boles asking for a writ and describing the arrest of these two men:

Eufaula, Ind. Ter.
June 27, 1885

Thos Boles
Ft Smith Ark

Sir

Send me Writ for Henshaw for Introducing and selling whiskey also one for Harper who was with him it is supposed that Henshaw brought in the whiskey and Harper sold it they brought in 5 gal. Witnesses Nate Colbert & Wash Collins & George Wailey. I have them in Custody—send writs forth with to Wewoka Sem. Nation. Bass Reeves Over Henshaw and I had a fight he crippled me up considerable, he snapped his Revolver at me 3 times then he went to fighting with it. I will be [in] as soon as I can owing to high waters. I have made slow progress when I caught Henshaw & Harper there was another one got away. I think it was Henry Shepard.

> Your Truly
> [signed] Bass Reeves
> I Captured these two men
> on the night of the 25th

A warrant for their arrest on charges of introducing whiskey was written and signed by the U.S. marshal on July 2. Reeves arrested the men September 22 at Eufaula and brought them to the Fort Smith jail. It was November before a hearing was held before the U.S. commissioner. A writ for resisting arrest was drawn up on November 3, 1885. Bond was posted for the two defendants on the same day. Three men signed the $500 bond, one of whom was William Cravens, the popular defense attorney in Fort Smith, and another was Crowder Nix, a black man from the Creek Indian Nation who worked as a posseman and later became a commissioned deputy U.S. marshal.

One of the defendants was named Debkerker Harper and the other was only called Henshaw. The hearing for introducing liquor was heard on November 3 by U.S. Commissioner James Brizzolara. The men serving in Reeves's posse when he arrested Harper and Henshaw testified.

Nathan Colbert being duly sworn and deposes and says:

I reside at Choctaw Nation and know the defendant in this cause. I never seen defendant with whiskey.

George Whaley duly sworn says:

Knew defendant, Mr. Henshaw had a pint and seen him drinking it. Do not know of his introducing any whiskey. Defendant is discharged

The hearing for resisting arrest was heard the next day, November 4, before Commissioner Brizzolara. Colbert and Robert Reeves gave testimony:

Nathan Colbert being duly sworn deposes and says:

I reside at Choctaw Nation and know the defendant in this cause. Got acquainted with him after he was arrested. We had Henshaw and defendant under arrest I was a guard I was driving up a hill and they were in same wagon with me. Henshaw jerked my pistol away from me then he said stop this wagon then I stopped pretty quick. Then defendant and Henshaw jumped out of the wagon. They were shackled together and Henshaw had the pistol up just so. I looked around and jumped out of the wagon and then they jumped out. When they jumped out of wagon they wheeled and went back towards hind end of the wagon towards wagon that was behind me; by this time Henshaw had fired off pistol. I went on around the wagon and called for Bob Reeves to bring me his pistol. I was running when Henshaw fired pistol, they wheeled and came back to wagon. Then defendant got the axe out of the wagon I was driving and the other got the hatchet. They both got out to the left of the wagon; do not know if he ran after me with the ax or not. Defendant made no attempt towards me with ax. When they got loose they left.

Robert Reeves duly sworn says:

When I heard report of pistol I looked and Henshaw was coming towards me. I turned and ran back to back of wagon. They

stopped and defendant got ax out of wagon and they went towards front of wagon and after this I seen no more of them.

Defendant Harper is discharged.

It is evident that Reeves and these two white defendants didn't get
along, given the fistfight Reeves said he had with them. The evidence
was not strong enough on the whiskey-selling charges. Even his own
possemen were weak witnesses to the charges of introducing liquor. This
must have impacted Brizzolara's decision in dismissing the obstruction-
of-justice charges leveled on them for escaping from the deputy's posse.
On the latter charges one wonders if ethnicity came into play during the
hearings, with the posse being predominantly African American. On the
flip side, one of the men who signed for the defendants' bond was an
African American.[9]

On June 24, the same day as previous mailings, Reeves sent a note to
Marshal Boles for yet another writ:

Eufaula, Ind. Ter.
June 24, 1885

Mr. Thomas Boles
Ft. Smith Ark

D Sir

Please send me writ for the Arrest of one Addie Grayson for breaking in valise and taking there from $17.00 stolen from Henry John-
son. Witnesses Mrs. Johnson & Alfred Rose. The offense is for
Larceny. Please send forthwith to Wewoka They had her in custody
here for stealing and they turned her over to me.

> Yours Truly
> [signed] Bass Reeves
> They caught her with the money
> & took it away from her

Reeves placed Adeline Grayson under arrest on July 3, 1885, ten
miles west of Eufaula in the Creek Nation. While in the Fort Smith jail

an additional charge of selling whiskey in the Indian country was also lodged against Ms. Grayson.[10]

A few days later, on the sixth, eight miles west of the town named Seminole in the Seminole Nation, Reeves arrested a white man named W. A. Gibson for assault with intent to kill. Four days later he served the writ of subpoena on John Pickett and Prairie Bill in the Seminole country for this case against Gibson. On July 25, Gibson was found not guilty before a jury trial and released.[11]

The last letter we have that was sent by Reeves from Eufaula on June 24 has to do with a charge of attempted murder with a deadly weapon. Reeves's note stated:

> Mr. Thomas Boles
> Ft. Smith
> Dr Sir
>
> Send writ for One Thomas Post for committing assault on Jo Young by shooting at him. One shot when he was caught and prevented from shooting any more. Thomas Post is a Creek darky and Jo Young is a State darky. The witnesses one by the name of Will and another John & Jo Young. I have him [in] custody Send writ to Wewoka. The shooting was done Sunday.
>
> > Yours Truly
> > [signed] Bass Reeves

White people would refer to blacks as darkies quite frequently in the nineteenth century. In the Indian Territory, the indigenous group of African Americans were known as Indian Freedmen. They called themselves "Natives." African Americans who came into the territory were known as "State Negroes" or "State Raised" because they originated from a state outside the territory. At the hearing before the U.S. commissioner on July 30, Joseph Young gave the following statement:

> I reside at Eufaula, I.T. and know the defendant in this cause, he is my stepson. On one Sunday in June, defendant had a pistol in his hand and I told him to give it to his mother; and he would not obey me and we had a little scuffle over it and the pistol

went off accidentally in his hand; and that is all there was to it, he made no attempt to shoot me.[12]

After the testimony by the stepfather was heard, the case was dismissed by the U.S. commissioner. On July 31, 1885, the *Fort Smith Weekly Elevator* printed the following under "Court Notes:"

> Deputy Bass Reeves came in same evening with eleven prisoners, as follows: Thomas Post, one Walaska, and Wm. Gibson, assault with intent to kill; Arthur Copiah, Abe Lincoln, Miss Adeline Grayson and Sally Copiah, alias Long Sally, introducing whiskey in Indian country; J. F. Adams, Jake Island, Andy Alton and one Smith, larceny. Island, Alton, Lincoln and Smith gave bond. The others went to jail . . .
>
> The jail contained one hundred and twenty prisoners last Sunday, with the thermometer registering 93 in the shade.

According to information from the National Historic Site at Fort Smith, Arkansas, the jail in 1885 was known as "Hell on the Border." The jail was located under the courtroom. It consisted of two rooms divided by solid masonry walls in the basement of the federal building. The rooms were approximately twenty-nine feet by fifty-five feet each. There were no individual cells in these rooms, leaving prisoners free to mingle with one another in the large space. The ceilings rose only seven feet above the flagstone floors. Each room had eight grated windows, four on the front and back walls, but they were under veranda porches, allowing little light or ventilation into the basement. Some people called the jail a "dungeon" or a "black hole." It was estimated that the space could hold a total of 150 prisoners. Female prisoners were kept in another location. The jail had a heterogeneous mix of men of every age, ethnicity, and criminal background, but nearly all from Indian Territory. Guards set urinal tubs in unused fireplaces in the hope that the flues would carry the odor out of the building. This rarely proved successful and often the stench was present in the courtroom on the first floor. A single sink for cleansing was in each cell, but the jail staff did not ordinarily allow baths. When the prisoners slept on the rough flagstone floor, the dampness caused their blankets and straw-filled mattresses to become soaked and moldy. The guards tried to keep the smell and dirt down by using whitewash, lime, and copperas. A new jail addition was built at Fort Smith in 1888, which helped to ease the crowding and congestion.[13]

On September 11, 1885, Deputy U.S. Marshal Bass Reeves swore a warrant and received it for the arrest of Fayette Barnett and the infamous female outlaw Belle Starr. They were accused of stealing a horse from Albert McCarty, whom Reeves had arrested a few years earlier for cattle theft. McCarty's horse was valued at one hundred dollars. It has been said that Reeves and Starr were friends and it is quite possible he told her he had a warrant for her arrest. Oftentimes during his career, Reeves would tell acquaintances and friends that he had a warrant for their arrest and to turn themselves in at the federal court so he would not have to haul them around the country. On January 21, 1886, Belle Starr appeared in Fort Smith at the federal jail and surrendered to the U.S. marshal. She stated that she "did not propose to be dragged around by some federal deputy." This would be the one and only time Belle Starr surrendered to the federal authorities. On February 8, 1886, Starr entered a not-guilty plea before Judge Parker and filed an application for witnesses:

> The defendant says . . . she cannot safely proceed to trial without the testimony of the following . . . William Hicks and James Johnson who live at Eufaula, Creek Nation, I.T. by whom she can prove the day after said mare is alleged to have been stolen they fell in with her on the road and nooned with her; and the next day she came into Fort Smith and hired up her train at the wagon yard publicly and stayed all night at a hotel where she registered in her own name—that she was traveling in her horse wagon with her daughter, and that she did not have said mare in her possession at this time.
>
> Edwin Reed who lives in Canadian district Cherokee Nation . . . by whom she can prove that Fayette Barnett [was] in the country near where said Albert McCarty lived—that he at the request of Fayette Barnett took the horse to John Middleton out in the woods . . . That this defendant had no connection with the taking of said mare nor anything to do with her after she was stolen.

Judge Parker set a court date in September 1886. Starr proved her innocence in the horse theft case, largely because Fayette Barnett testified that he was present when John Middleton paid "a stranger" fifty dollars for the McCarty mare. On September 30, the jury returned a verdict of "not guilty as charged in the within indictment." Belle Starr was a free woman from this charge and returned to her home on Younger's Bend in the Cherokee Nation.[14]

Dr. Jesse Mooney was Belle Starr's personal physician in 1888. Mooney's son, Col. Charles W. Mooney, recounted a story told him by his mother:

> While Dr. Jesse and Ella were visiting with Belle Starr one Sunday afternoon, the loud barking of Belle's Great Dane warned them someone was approaching. Soon a lone rider came into view. He was a big, broad shouldered man, riding high in the saddle, was clean shaven except for a bushy mustache. As he rode into the clearing in front of Belle's house, they saw he was a Negro wearing a deputy U.S. marshals badge pinned on his shirt.
>
> "It's Bass Reeves," Belle said, as she walked out of her cabin door and called off the dog.
>
> "Howdy, Miss Belle," the Deputy said politely, dismounting.
>
> "What brings you this way, Bass?" Belle asked.
>
> "Jest ridin' through and thought I'd stop, but didn't know you had company."
>
> "That's alright, Bass, yore welcome any time yore near here. This is Doc Mooney and his wife, Ella," Belle said.
>
> "Please to meetcha," the Deputy responded, tipping his hat politely. "Your Uncle Isaac told me about you, Doctor. I've know'd him a long time."
>
> "Bass Reeves here is one of the few deputy marshals I trust," Belle remarked to Jesse and Ella. "He's been a friend of mine for several years. He was raised around Van Buren."
>
> "Jest thought I'd warn you," the deputy said, "I'm on the trail of Bob and Grat Dalton. They may be headed this way.
>
> "Much-a-bliged, Bass. But them rascals won't be comin'

round here for no help. Bob Dalton knows what I think of him," Belle remarked.

When Deputy Bass Reeves rode away, Belle told Jesse and Ella all about him. She explained that it was unusual for her, who had fought for the Confederacy, to be a friend of a Negro. But Bass Reeves was a dedicated, fearless deputy U.S. marshal. He would "shoot it out" if necessary, and made a reputation throughout the Indian Nations as a lawman second to none.[15]

The *Muskogee Indian Journal* ran a story on the Fort Smith federal court on October 22, 1885:

History of the United States Court at Fort Smith

This court is without doubt the largest criminal court in the United States. It is a district court with circuit court powers. Its jurisdiction extends over sixteen counties in Western Arkansas and the five civilized tribes of Indians . . .

The House of Corrections in Detroit, Mich., has been designated by the Attorney-General as a place of confinement for the convicts of this district and to that place all convicted are sent unless they be so fortunate as to receive a jail sentence . . .

The Deputy U.S. Marshals for Creek and Cherokee Nations are Andrew Smith, Elias Andrews, W. F. Jones, Bud T. Kell and Sam Sixkiller; for Choctaw Nation, Tyner Hughes, John Farr, Sam Wingo and J. W. Searle; for Chickasaw Nation, J. H. Mershon and John Williams; Seminole, Creek and Chickasaw Nations, Bass Reeves. There are many local deputies scattered throughout the district. This court has the following commissioners with full power:

Stephen Wheeler and James Brizzolara at Ft. Smith; E. B. Harrisson, Esq., at Fayetteville; Geo. O. Linbarger, Eureka Springs; John Q. Tufts, at Muskogee, I.T., besides many others who are only appointed for special purposes.

Some idea of the magnitude of this court can be had from the following:

Since the 6th of July there have been thirteen persons tried for murder, and of these, six were convicted and are now awaiting sentence, four were acquitted and three resulted in hung juries. There are now about thirty prisoners confined in jail charged with murder, awaiting trial. Since the 6th of July forty-six prisoners have been sent to the House of Correction at Detroit and about twenty others who have been convicted recently, are awaiting to be transported.

Back in the field, Reeves sent a note to Marshal Boles:

Thomas Boles
U.S. Marshal
Fort Smith

Dear Sir

Send me writs for the following named persons. Send to Sasakwa Seminole Nation I.T. I caught them in the act of selling myself. Amos Gray. Introducing & selling 3. gal. Whiskey Sunday. Oct. 4, 1885 Witnesses James Canard Nix, Crowder Bass Reeves William Anderson Introducing and Selling 2½ gal. Whiskey Oct. 4 1885 Witnesses Samuel Haynes. Mont Moore I am doing well. I have all under arrest. I will start for Sasakwa tomorrow. Hoping I will receive the O.K. I am

Yours Respectfully
[signed] Bass Reeves

Reeves arrested Amos Gray twenty miles west of Okmulgee in the Creek Nation for selling whiskey. He had been arrested in 1884 for larceny and sentenced to one year at the Detroit House of Corrections. At the hearing before U.S. Commissioner Stephen Wheeler, the following testimony was given by Reeves and his posse:

Crowder Nix being duly sworn, deposes and says:

I reside at Eufaula, I.T. and know the defendant in this cause when I seen him, I was at a camp meeting and saw defendant three different times take money from persons there at the meeting and go off and get them a bottle of whiskey and bring it there. I saw one man give him $2. at two different times. I saw defendant bring the whiskey back and deliver it to the persons he got the money from, but I do not know the names of the men as I was not acquainted there. He brought the whiskey in quart bottles.

Bass Reeves being duly sworn says:

I saw defendant at the camp meeting, and saw him take two quarts of whiskey out of his bosom at one time and give it to a man by the name of Sanker [Sanger]. He sold whiskey all night there that night. I watched him but did not arrest him until the meeting was over as I did not want to disturb the meeting.

Here the defendant says by his attorney that he will plead guilty.

Crowder Nix, a Creek Freedmen, would later become a commissioned deputy U.S. marshal by 1890. Amos Gray was given six months of confinement at the Detroit House of Corrections and fined fifty dollars on December 2, 1885. He was delivered to Detroit authorities on December 6.

William Anderson was arrested in the same locality as Gray. At the U.S. commissioners' hearing on October 29, Samuel Haynes said:

I reside at Okmulgee, I.T. and know the defendant in this cause. I know nothing about the case except that Willie and I threw in and bought a gallon of whiskey off a whiskey peddler sometime during the present month up at Okmulgee.

Anderson was released on the charges of peddling whiskey.[16]

John Carroll signed the documents for Gray's incarceration as U.S. Marshal for the Western District of Arkansas. A Democrat, Carroll was appointed U.S. marshal in October of 1885. During the Civil War, Carroll received a commission as a colonel in the Confederate army. Prior to the Civil War, Carroll had married a woman named Susan Ward in the Cherokee Nation. Ward was a quadroon, one-quarter African. She died in 1856. They had two sons. Thomas Boles, who preceded Carroll, was a Republican and served as a captain during the Civil War with the Third Arkansas Federal Cavalry. Carroll's appointment as U.S. marshal was made official by the U.S. president on May 21, 1886. Carroll would become the first former Confederate soldier and Democrat who served as U.S. marshal at Fort Smith that Reeves served under as a deputy.[17]

Bass Reeves delivered subpoenas for the Luce Hammon murder trial to John Coy and Major Coy on October 17, and Leab and Jimmy Anderson on October 20. All of the recipients resided in the Creek Nation.[18]

Reeves sent a message to the U.S. marshal in late October:

Eufaula, Ind. Ter.
Oct 21, 1885

Mar. Boles
Ft. Smith Ark

Dr. Sir

Pleas issue a Writ for Tobe Hill for selling 5 gal whiskey along the last of July Names of witnesses are George Chupco and one Wiley & David Frank. & one other. Issue the writ and hold in office for me I have him. He is an old hand at the business. I will be in Sunday or Monday a.m. if nothing happens. I had some one shoot in my camp at Wetumka at 12 o'clock at night but I turned the duel on him and he left.

> Yours
> [signed] Bass Reeves

Tobe Hill was released in Fort Smith for this particular case on October 26 because no witnesses appeared. According to earlier testimony for previous arrest, Hill had once served as a captain with the Seminole Lighthorse Police. In the note, Reeves alluded to one of the many assassination attempts on his life during his law enforcement career.[19]

On October 30, 1885, the *Fort Smith Weekly Elevator* reported on Reeves's arrival into Fort Smith with a load of prisoners:

U.S. Court: Close of the August Term: Big Docket for the November Term—Notes, etc.

The November term begins of Monday next with some . . . already indicted and a large number on the grand jury docket. The jailers register shows the following cases, the parties to which are now in jail awaiting trial:

Murder 31
Assault with intent to kill 6
Larceny 17
Arson 2
Rape 1
Introducing and selling whiskey
    in Indian country 10
Total 67

. . . U.S. Marshal, Bass Reeves, came in on Monday evening last with 17 prisoners, among them were Hens Posey and one Deidrick, charged with murder. The others are John Robinson, assault with intent to kill; Robert Johnson, Wiley Kelly, Colbert Lasley and old man Cintop, larceny. The balance are all whiskey cases.

Thus ends the record on Bass Reeves's exploits during 1885.

8.

Trial of the Century

The most important murder case Deputy U.S. Marshal Bass Reeves was involved in was his own. Some details of the incident in which Reeves killed his cook, William Leach, in April 1884, were presented in chapter 6. Public notice of Reeves's arrest and trial for the shooting began when several articles appeared in Arkansas newspapers. The first is from the *Arkansas Gazette*, published in the state capital of Little Rock, on January 22, 1886:

Caught Up With: An Ex-Deputy Marshal's Misdeeds Brought to Light

Fort Smith, Ark., Jan. 21—Ex-Deputy United States Marshal Bass Reeves was arrested and lodged in jail today, charged with the murder of Wm. Leach, in the Chickasaw nation, in April, 1884. Leach was cooking at Reeves camp when the murderous official shot him dead for some trivial offense. Reeves has been constantly on the marshal's force here for several years, and notwithstanding rumors reached here frequently that he was in league with some of the worst cutthroats and outlaws in the Indian country, he managed to cover up his tracks so effectually as to retain his commission until the recent marshal took charge, when he was removed. During his long service as an official he has stained his hands with the blood of several of his fellow-beings, and now languishes in jail with many others whom he has been instrumental in placing there. One of the eye-witnesses to the killing of Leach is now in prison at Detroit, where he was sent for some minor offense, but his pardon will be asked for in order that his testimony in the case may be taken.

The next newspaper story appeared the following day in Reeves's hometown newspaper, the *Van Buren Press*. The article showed him no sympathy. Rather, it slandered Reeves at best, and at worst convicts him before the trial.

Bass Reeves, A Noted Character, in Limbo, Charged with the Murder of William Leach

Fort Smith Times: the mills of the Gods grind slow but exceedingly fine. Ex-Deputy United States Marshal Bass Reeves (colored) is in the clutches of the law, charged with murder. The fact of the killing had been known for a long time but the circumstances attending it and the evidence tending to establish foul murder, committed in pure wantonness, have just been brought to light. Reeves at the time reported the killing to have been in self defense.

Deputy U.S. Marshal, S. J. B. Fair went to Van Buren yesterday and arrested Reeves on a warrant, charging him with the murder of William Leach in the Chickasaw Nation in April 1884. Leach was a colored man and was a cook for Deputy Reeves and posse, and the murder was committed while they were in camp. Leach was cooking supper when a dog belonging to him came up and stuck its nose in one of the cooking vessels. Reeves kicked the dog and threatened to kill it, when the cook interfered, saying it was his dog. Reeves replied, "G-d d—n you, I'll kill you then, and drew his revolver and shot the negro in the head blowing his brains out. Bass Reeves has a reputation throughout Western Arkansas and the Indian Territory that no man need envy. It is said that when he was riding as deputy he was in the habit of holding "kangaroo court" in camp and extorting small sums of money from prisoners by fining them for small imaginary offenses and would use the money to buy tobacco, etc. It is charged that at one time he made an insulting proposal to a white woman in the territory and his conduct was investigated by the grand jury and his dismissal was the force recommended by that body, but for some reason he was not dismissed but let go on making history, all of which will come to light in due time. Bass is in the toils at last and will find that the Territory is full of people who will interest themselves in his case. We have heard it stated that there are about one hundred men in the B. I. T. to whom he is indebted in sums ranging from $3 to $25 for provisions and feed furnished him while he was riding over the country looking (?) for criminals. One of the eye witnesses to the killing of Leach is now in prison in Detroit where he was sent for some minor offense, but his pardon will be asked for in order that his testimony in the case may be taken.[1]

The warrant for Bass Reeves arrest read:

United States of America
Western District of Arkansas.

I DO SOLEMNLY SWEAR AND BELIEVE FROM RELIABLE INFORMATION
IN MY POSSESSION THAT
Bass Reeves
Did in the Indian Country, within the Western District of Arkansas, on or about the 10th day of April 1884
Feloniously, willfully, premeditatedly and of his malice aforethought kill and murder William Leach a Negro and not an Indian
Against the peace and dignity of the United States, and I pray a writ:
S. J. B. Fair
Subscribed and sworn to before me this 18 day of January 1886
   [signed] Stephen Wheeler, United States Commissioner
   Charlie Jones
   Sill Stanton
   Isaac Chisholm

John Brady
Richard Cochran
Mary Grayson
James Grayson
Hardy Blue
Joe Bell
Big Wiley
Isaac Colbert

Reeves was relieved of his duties as a deputy marshal at the time of his arrest and placed in the federal jail. We have no information that sheds light on why it took the court two years to arrest Reeves for this shooting or on whether U.S. Marshal Carroll being a former Confederate and a Democrat had anything to do with it. Park ranger Tom Wing of the Fort Smith National Historic Site has commented that it is interesting that Reeves was charged with murder, not manslaughter or negligent homicide, speculating that a white deputy would have received a lesser charge in such a case. It is not known if Reeves was housed with the general population of the Fort Smith federal jail or given trustee status. In the preliminary hearing before Stephen Wheeler, U.S. commissioner in Fort Smith, Arkansas, Bass Reeves's nephew John Brady gave testimony on January 27, 1886. He testified that he was Bass' cousin and had been a member of Reeves's posse on that fateful trip when Leach was shot. Leach's name is also spelled Leech in the following transcription:

John Brady being duly sworn, deposes and says:

I reside at Van, Buren, Arkansas and know the defendant in this cause. I was along at the time William Leach was killed. I was driving team for Bass Reeves. We stopped at night to camp and had a dog along and he was eating some meat out of a skillet. Bass told Leach to not let the dog eat the meat out of the skillet, he drove him away. . . . Leach replied that if he killed the dog he (Leach) would kill him (Bass) or his gray horse. Bass got his gun and was putting a cartridge in it and it went off and shot Leach. Defendant said then, "I have shot Leach but didn't aim to do it. I aimed to kill the dog." Bass sent for a doctor but could not get any that night and next morning he took him to a doctor and told him to cure him if he could and that he would pay the bill, and if he got well to get a hack and send him home and that he would pay all the bills. I have never seen Leach since. I have heard that he died. This occurred in the Indian Territory. Defendant and I are cousins.

Cross examination

Bass gun was a .44 caliber Winchester rifle. He had been working with his gun trying to get a cartridge out that was too big. I think he was on one knee working with his gun when it went off. I asked Leech if he was badly hurt and he said he was and that he did not believe that Bass shot him on purpose. They had always been perfectly friendly. Leech was shot in the neck. I heard Leech tell the doctor that he did not think Bass shot him on purpose. I had been with Bass and Leach on the trip about two months and I never heard a cross word between them. I thought Bass and Leech were just joking when they were talking about shooting. I did not see Bass strike Leech with the gun. Bass had had the gun working with it about a half hour before it went off. There was a tent up and the prisoners were in the tent. Bass and Leech and I were out at the fire where the shooting occurred. If anybody else was there I don't remember it. There was no one else present but the prisoners and us three and a woman, I think it was one of the prisoners wives. The dog was one that came to us in camp and we all claimed him.[2]

On May 16 Reeves made an application for witnesses:

United States v. Bass Reeves
Application for Witnesses

The defendant says he is indicted in said court for the alleged crime of murder and that he cannot safely proceed to trial without the testimony of the following witnesses:

> David Pompey
> Nat Hawkins
> Philip Cyrus
> James Young

Robert Johnson Jr.

Mrs. Cassey Foster

Jesse Kemp

Cy Abraham

Tom Brown

Edward Cohee

He can prove by the said Pompey, Hawkins and Cyrus. That they were with the defendant the day after and for several days after the alleged murder. That the prosecuting witnesses—Tobe Hill, Chas. Jones, Mary Grayson, and others who were the prisoners of the said defendant at the time of the said alleged murder. Defendant at that time a deputy U.S. marshal, stated on several occasions that the killing was an accident and not intentional. He can prove the same thing by the said Johnson and also by Chee that as he can prove said Chee that Mary Grayson and Blue said that the killing was an accident. He can prove by the said Foster, Kemp, Abraham and Brown that this defendant with his prisoners and deceased had staid several days at said Fosters, immediately, preceding the day of the killing and that the said defendant and deceased often together and that they were cordial, friendly and jovial with each other. That defendant and prisoners left the said Foster's place the day before the killing, then the killing occurred about twenty miles from said Foster's where defendant had been camping.

He can also prove by said Foster and Kemp that deceased had been for several days very much afflicted with diarrhea, he expects to show by Dr. Nathan Cochran who attended deceased to the time of his death the deceased did not die of the wound inflicted by the said accidental shot, but that he died from the effects of diarrhea.

By said Young he can prove that he was present at the time of the killing saw all that occurred and that said Hill, Jones and others of the defendants prisoners were at all the time of the killing in the defendants tent nearby and did not see the said killing. He will also prove that the said killing was purely accidental, that defendant and that there was no difficult or hard fillings manifested between defendant and deceased.

Said Young lives at Fort Reno, said Pompey, Cyrus, Johnson and Hawkins reside near Wewoka, I.T.

Said facts are then when provided, that this application is not made for delay but that Justice may be done. That he has not the means and is actually unable to pay the fee of said witnesses.

Therefore he prays that said Witnesses by summoned at the expense of the United States.

> [signed] Bass (his mark) Reeves
> Sworn to subscriber before me this 22nd May 1886
> Stephen Wheeler
> Clayton, . . . and Marcum
> Defendants Attorneys[3]

On June 19 the *Van Buren Press* reported that Bass Reeves, who had been confined in the United States jail, had been released on June 15 on a $3,000 bond. He had spent almost exactly six months in jail, being incarcerated on January 21. Besides Reeves signing for the bond himself, other co-signers were James Mershon, Cassius Barnes, Thomas Marcum, and William H. H. Clayton. Mershon was a deputy U.S. marshal and Bass' good friend, and Barnes, Marcum, and Clayton were attorneys.[4]

While the trial for murder was being processed, Reeves had another court appearance on a contempt charge against a white juror who had confronted him on the streets of Fort Smith. This is a highly interesting item considering the visibility and notoriety of Reeves in Fort Smith. The name of the juryman was A. J. Boyd. At the hearing before the U.S. commissioner on September 22, 1886, the following testimony was given:

> In the matter of contempt of this Honorable court, alleged against this respondent, upon the information of one Bass Reeves, respondent, A. J. Boyd comes into court and answers, as follows: He states that he a juror on the regular panel for the August turn, 1886, of this court. But he denies positively that he was willfully guilty of conduct violative of the instructions

given by the court to him and the balance of the panel for the August turn 1886, at the opening thereof, as charged. In further response, he said A. J. Boyd States, that it is possible that he approached the said Bass Reeves and, as a juror, used improper words, but he denies all consciousness of having done so—and, if he did have such improper communication with the said Bass Reeves, he states positively he did not do so knowingly and willfully. But he believes that if any communication or conversation was had between him and the said Bass Reeves about the case pending in this court of the said Bass Reeves, that the said Bass Reeves approached him and was repulsed.

He states, in further reply and explanation, that unfortunately some years ago he acquired an appetite for intoxicant, which at times is very strong and violent. And that after taking several drinks his mind becomes a blank. That prior to the alleged misconduct, in seeking to have improper conversation with the said Bass Reeves he had abstained from drinking intoxicating liquors for the period of about fifteen months. That he did not drink anything while a juror as aforesaid, until about the date laid for the conversation with said Bass Reeves. But he states that about the time of the alleged meeting with said Bass Reeves he was drinking heavily, and commenced to so do against his will, but will-power was not strong enough to resist the appetite for whiskey that at periods assails him.

He knows nothing whatever about the conversation detailed or occurring between himself and said Reeves, and as to the same his mind is a blank—and he states if anything was said that he ought not as a juror to have said, it was not willful, nor was he conscious of what he was doing or saying. With his answer, he submits himself to the order of the court.

[signed] A. J. Boyd

John Williams next gave testimony:

One day the latter part of last week I saw A. J. Boyd and Bass Reeves talking together on the sidewalk over on the Avenue and afterwards Bass Reeves came to me and told me that Boyd told him that if he was on the jury that tried him he would hang him in spite of hell. I advised Reeves to go and report the matter to Judge Parker.

Bass Reeves testified:

I was standing between City hotel and Bolingers Store, on the sidewalk a few days ago, I think it was last Monday, when A. J. Boyd came up to me and tapped me on the shoulder with his walking cane, and asked me how it was about that killing and said he wanted me to tell him about that killing and all about my case. I said to hear you and a juryman and I have no statement to make until I go on the stand, and more than that I have no business talking to you about my case. He said, "Yes I am a juryman and if you want to save your neck you had better make a statement to me." I told him again I had no statement to make, he then said, "you damned black son of a bitch, I am just as certain to break your neck as I have this cane in my hand. Me and three others have got it in for you." I turned to walk away and he caught me by the coat and led me off by the sidewalk and said now you had just as well tell me about your case and I again told I did not want to talk to him. I turned to walk away again when he raised his cane and shook it at me and said, "God damn you I am just as certain to break your neck as I have got this stick in my hand." I said, "well that is all right," and walked away. Dave Pompey, Phil Cyrus and John Williams overheard all or a part of this conversation. Other persons were also near by and perhaps overheard also.

Dave Pompey gave his version of the incident:

On Saturday last, I think it was Saturday. John Williams, Bass Reeves, A. J. Boyd and myself came out of the City Hotel Saloon, as we came out Boyd pulled Bass Reeves one side and was talking to him but I did not hear what Boyd said to Bass but I heard Bass say, "No Sir, I haven't any statement to make now." John Williams called Bass over and they stepped off ten or fifteen steps and Boyd stepped up to me and said what do you know about Bass' case tell me all about it. I said no, I don't think it is the time to tell it here, he then said you had better tell me all about it if you want to save his neck. I said there is plenty of time for me to state what I know about it and you may not sit on the jury anyhow. He then said all right you will see how it will be. He then left me and went over to where Bass was. I followed on and as he came up to where Bass and Williams were, Williams started off and said come on Bass, come away from here. Boyd then caught Bass by the coat and said stop, stop now and tell me about your case. Bass told him again that he had nothing to tell him. Boyd then said, "well your neck is just as sure to break as I hold this cane in my hand. I and three others have got influence." Bass and I then walked away.

Judge Isaac C. Parker, made the following statements in regards to the case on September 27, 1886:

In having been brought to the knowledge of the Court that one A. J. Boyd while on the regular panel of the Petit Jury for this the August Term of Court. Was guilty of Conduct violative of the instructions given him as well as the balance of the panel of Jurors at the opening of Court for the said term in this to wit. That on or about the 20th inst. he went up to one Bass Reeves tapped him on the shoulder with his walking cane and asked him how it was about that killing and said he wanted the said Reeves to tell him all about the case. (He the said Reeves then being under a charge of murder) The said Reeves said to him you are a Juryman and I have no statement to make until I go in the stand and more than that I have no business talking to you about my case. He the said Boyd answering Yes I am a Juryman and if you want to save your neck you had better make a statement to me. The said Reeves again stated he had no statement to make. He the said Boyd then replying you damned black son of a bitch I am just as certain to break your neck as I have this cane in my hand. Me and three others have got in for you.

What the conduct of said Boyd is Contempt of Court. It is therefore ordered that the said A. J. Boyd appear before this court forthwith to show cause why he should not be punished for contempt and that in case of his failure to appear forthwith he will be held in Contempt of Court and a warrant issued for his arrest.

Boyd was served with papers to appear before Judge Parker on September 28 at Cabin Creek, Johnson County, Arkansas, by Deputy U.S. Marshal J. H. Powers. There is no evidence in the file as to whether or not the juryman received jail time in this case.[5]

Bass Reeves made a motion for continuance on September 23, 1886:

The defendant says he is indicted in said court for the alleged crime of Murder and that he cannot safely proceed to trial without the testimony of James Young and John Brady. That he made application for said Young on the 22nd day of May 1886. And the said was allowed by the court, then he caused the issuance of subpoena for said Young pursuant to said application for some reason unknown to the defendant he is not present and he does not know whether he has been subpoenaed or not.

He can prove by said Young that he was present at the time of the alleged killing and that the same was an accident. That defendant was working at his gun and that looking at the deceased at the time of the firing of the fatal shot. Said Young resided at Fort Reno, I.T. and believing he is now there. By John Brady he can prove the same facts, substantially, that he can prove by the said Young, that said Brady was examined before the Commissioner in this case on the part of the prosecution. That said Brady is named on the indictment as a prosecuting witness and he had all the time relied upon the prosecution to have said Brady as a witness upon the final trial of this case. For that reason did not make official application for him. That subpoena was issued for said Brady at the instance of the prosecution as a witness herein which was surely served on the 26th of January 1886. But the said Brady, defendant is informed and believes is not present. And has not been during the present . . . but his exact whereabouts he does not know but is informed and believes he is now in the state of Arkansas in the region or direction of Hot Springs.

Defendant insists upon the presence of said Brady upon the trial of this case and states that he cannot safely prove to trial without him and the said Young. Who is . . . believed to be material witnesses for his defense herein. The defendant makes this motion also an application for said Brady as a witness for his defense and says he is poor and has not the monies to pay the fees of said witnesses . . .

That he believes the facts he expects to prove as aforesaid by said witnesses . . . That he has used all the diligence in his power to procure the attendance of his said witnesses but considered it unnecessary to apply for said Brady as he was marked upon the indictment as a prosecuting witness and summoned as such by the prosecution.

He believes by the next term of the court he can [illegible] the attendance of said witnesses if a continuance is granted him. That he does not make this application for delay but that Justice may be done here. That so far as knows there are no persons present by whom he can prove the same facts. Therefore the promises considered he prays . . .

[signed] Bass (his mark) Reeves[6]

On July 14, 1887, Reeves made an application for additional witnesses in his trial:

The defendant says he is indicted in said court for the crime of murder and that he cannot . . . proceed with trial without the testimony of the following witnesses in addition to those already asked for in his former application . . .

Lizzie Humphreys, Fred Swibke, who is now here in Fort Smith.

He can prove by said Swibke, that deceased was sick for several days prior to his being shot. [He] was suffering and complaining of bowel complications, that he continued to suffer and complain of this disease up to the time of the shooting.

He can prove by said Humphreys that deceased stay . . . at

Cherokee Town about one week and during this time he was sick with a bowel complications and said Humphreys waited on him during this time and that deceased left Cherokee Town suffering with this disease the same day of the shooting.

Said facts are true when . . . , that he has not the money and is unable to buy it for of said witnesses. Therefore he prays that . . . subpoenas at its expense of the United States.

> Bass Reeves
> Sworn and Subscribed before me this July 14, 1887
> Stephen Wheeler
> [signed] By E. Baglin, Clerk[7]

The murder trial for Bass Reeves eventually took place in October 1887, presided over by Judge Isaac C. Parker. The trial prosecutors were M. H. Sandels and Forester and the defense attorneys for Reeves were William H. H. Clayton, William M. Cravens, and Thomas Marcum. The defense attorneys were the best in Fort Smith.

The first witness for the government was Mary Grayson. She stated the last time she had seen Leach was at Cherokee Town in the Chickasaw Nation. Jim Grayson, her husband, a prisoner of Reeves, had taken sick and had sent for her. Mary went on to say there were four other prisoners beside her husband: Charley, Toby Hill, Big Wiley, and Lewis Tiger. She said there was a boy with Reeves named Johnny Brady. Mary described the shooting:

> Bass told him to drive the dog away and he said he was going to mush his dog.
>
> Q. Pet him.
>
> A. Yew Sir . . . Mr. Reeves told him to drive his dog away and he said he wouldn't do it an Reeves got up and when he started to get up Leach got about half way straight and the dog run off among the horses and then Bass shot Leach with his Winchester.
>
> Q. Just before that what was Reeves doing.
>
> A. He had been lying down on his coat and got up and took cartridges out of his coat pocket and shoved it into his gun and

worked the lever and loaded it . . . Him and Leach was face to face.

Q. What did Leach do when the shot was fired.

A. Nothing only fall.

Q. What did Reeves do.

A. Nothing only stood there . . .

Q. What became of Leach.

A. Brought him to uncle Nat. Cochran's the next day about 12 o'clock.

Q. How far was that.

A. Between 10 and 15 miles I guess.

Q. When he was carried to Nat. Cochran's what did you do.

A. I went over to my grandpa's about a mile. I staid all night that night and the next day I went to . . . home . . .

Q. Do you remember what he wanted him to drive the dog away for.

A. No sir.

Cross examination by Col. Cravens

Q. Your husband was under arrest and you went up to see him.

A. Yes sir.

Q. What time did you get to the camp that evening.

A. It was about 12 when I went to Cherokee town.

Q. Did you ride along with them that night you camped down where the shooting took place.

A. No sir, I was in the wagon. Jim Grayson and Bass was riding along together on horse back.

Q. Who did you ride with.

A. Me and my 2 little boys.

Q. You didn't ride in the marshal's wagon.

A. No sir . . . The other prisoners was in Bass' wagon.

Q. They were all prisoners.

A. Yes sir . . .

Q. Did he have any other prisoners at that time.

A. No sir, just Jim and these 4 Creeks.

Q. Did you try to talk Creek to them.

A. No sir.

Q. You didn't hear them talk English.

A. No sir.

Q. What time did you camp that evening.

A. About sun-down.

Q. How long after dark before the shooting took place.

A. I don't know, it was after dark though . . .

Q. How far was your wagon from Bass' camp.

A. As far as from here to the door.

Q. Did you sleep in your wagon.

A. Yes sir.

Q. Any one go after the doctor.

A. Bass got Jim to go after the doctor . . .

Q. Supper was over wasn't it when the difficulty took place.

A. Yes sir, it was after supper. These prisoners was all sitting up when the difficulty took place.

Q. You had laid down.

A. No sir, Reeves was lying down on his coat talking to Jim Grayson.

Q. They were just having a friendly talk were they.

A. Yes sir.

Q. Reeves appeared to be in a good humor.

A. Yes sir.

Q. You didn't hear him use an angry word did you.

A. No sir.

Q. When the gun fired how long had he been fixing the gun—he was squatting down by the fire loading it wasn't he.

A. No sir, he had laid it down. He was picking out the cartridges with his pocket knife.

Q. They were hung in the chamber and he was picking them out with his pocket knife.

A. Yes sir, looked like it to me.

Q. What were you doing.

A. I was sitting down.

Q. Where were your two children.

A. I had one in my lap and the other was standing up by me.

Q. Did you have much fire there.

A. Yes sir, they had a tolerable good fire.

Q. Leach—was he cook.

A. He cooked supper . . .

Q. Do you know Lizzie Humphreys.

A. Yes sir, she lived at Cherokee town.

Q. Do you know about Lizzie trying to get some medicine to cure his bowel complaint.

A. No sir, I wasn't at the camp at Cherokee town . . .

Q. You were surprised when you heard the gun fire.

A. Yes sir.

Q. You didn't expect to hear it.

A. No sir, not at all.

Q. Where was Leach from Bass when the gun fired.

A. he was (Shows diagram) right across the fire from Bass. He was shot right in there (Shows in the neck) . . .

Q. It didn't lodge in his neck did it.

A. I don't know.

Q. You don't think it lodged do you.

A. No sir, I didn't think it did. I never examined it at all. I never saw the wound until the next morning when he was lying down. Bass, when Leach was shot called for Jim and he sent Jim after a doctor.

Q. Didn't Bass say he was sorry he was shot.

A. I never heard him if he did. He never said anything to me after that.[8]

Next, Mary Grayson's husband was called to give testimony. James Grayson stated he had been brought into Fort Smith three or four times. The first time was for larceny and Deputy U.S. Marshal Bob Cochran had arrested him. Deputy U.S. Marshal Mershon had brought Grayson in for selling whiskey and for theft of a yearling. Judge Parker gave him ninety days in the jail for the whiskey charge. Bass Reeves had arrested Grayson on his last charge for assault and attempted murder. For this crime, Grayson received fifteen months in the Detroit House of Corrections. Grayson stated he was about forty years of age. James Grayson was questioned about the shooting of Leach:

Q. Do you know a man by the name of William Leach.

A. Yes sir.

Q. Where did you get acquainted with him—with Bass Reeves.

Q. What was his business with him.

A. He was cook.

Q. How long were you in camp while Leach was with him.

A. As near as I can recollect about two or three days after they arrested me, I took sick and he let me go to the house, I had 'amonia, and I wasn't with them until 7 or 8 days, and I got with them in March when they started down here.

Q. How long were you with them before Leach was left out of the party—How long were you in camp there with Leech.

A. We just camped one night after we left Cherokee Town after I had been left there sick.

Q. On this last night you were camped together there, I will ask you to state to the jury just what you all were doing, and Leach was doing, and what happened and all about it.

A. It was after we camped there and had done eat supper and was talking about a dog, and Leach was sitting down on a sack of corn on this side of the fire, and we was sitting on that side "pointing" and the fire was between us and this man, Reeves was talking to Leach, Reeves told he never traveled, and that he didn't know nothing, and Reeves said he was going to kill this dog, and Leach told him "He wouldn't" and he gets his Winchester, and this fellow shoved the dog off his lap, and he went to his coat and got cartridges and started to put them in his gun, this fellow then shot him. We was sitting right in front of the Tents (Shows where he was sitting) and the horses was back in that direction (shows). He had his gun cocked and his finger on the trigger and his hands just that way (shows presenting).

Q. Did he turn or move either way before he fired this shot at Leach.

A. Yes sir, he turned around to the left, around towards Leach. . . . It looked like the gun was right against him (Leach) as it burnt his face. He put his gun down and his nephew told him not to shoot anymore and he said, "I ain't going to shoot him" and then me and Bass took him, carried him and put him in the tent. He was struck right in there, the big part of the shoulder there (Shows right shoulder near the neck). It knocked a big hole where the ball came out in the soft part of the shoulder like.

Q. What was done for him that night.

A. He sent me after a doctor and I rode all night that night but found no doctor and came back next morning. The sun was up when I got back.

Q. What was done then.

A. We put him in my wagon and hauled him to Nat. Cochran's . . .

Q. How long had Reeves been talking to him about him not knowing anything etc.

A. A right smart while . . .

Q. During that time how did he and Leach get along together.

A. Well they couldn't agree very well. Leach couldn't cook to suit him. He would curse him every time he would go to cook or do anything.

Q. It was about the cooking.

A. Yes sir.[9]

During the trial Bass Reeves was questioned and gave direct testimony to what occurred on the evening that Leach was shot:

Before I would start anywhere when I was out on a trip, I would always examine my cartridges and gun and that night in examining my gun I found I had a .45 cartridge in the magazine and I couldn't throw it up in the barrel. I was down on my knee and had the Winchester laying up this way. (Shows by holding Winchester in position etc.) I reached my hand in my coat pocked and got my knife and put my hand back this way and either my knife or hand struck the trigger and the gun went off. (Shows by getting down to the jury and laying the gun across his left arm the muzzle pointing about 40 degrees). The gun went off then and the boy hallooed an said, "Lordy, you have hit Leach."

Q. Where was your gun lying when you picked it up.

A. In the scabbard. I had been working with gun some 3 or 4 minutes when it went off. I was trying to prie this .45 cartridge out with my knife. I had thrown out some cartridges.

Q. When you found you had shot him what did you do.

A. I throwed down the gun and told Jim Grayson to come and help pick him up and I took my handkerchief out and soused it in a bucket of water and put it on his neck.

Q. Did you intend to shoot him.

A. No sir.

Q. There was something said about a dog, what was it.

A. He was running around there and I said "You had better kill that dog, it is some little Indian dog and you had better kill it" and I never looked up. We hadn't had any words at all. He was all the help I had to work for me. Wilson was 30 miles behind. There was Johnnie and you couldn't trust him with 5 prisoners in that country, no how—you cant hardly trust yourself.

Q. Did it bleed much.

A. No sir.

Q. What Jim do.

A. He come right at once and we picked him up and I made a bed in the tent and him and me carried him in there.

Q. Did he complain much that night.

A. No sir. I then put Jim on my horse and told him to go after old man Nat. quick.[10]

Professor Nudie E. Williams of the University of Arkansas wrote the following analysis of the evidence that the jury had to consider:

> In its deliberations, the jury apparently considered several facts. There had not been any friction or argument between the deputy and the cook before the shooting incident. Most of the prosecutor's witnesses could not be considered impartial in their testimony against Reeves because he had arrested most of them at one time or another for criminal offenses. The deputy's reputation with a rifle was well known; if he had intended to kill Leach there is little doubt that he would have died instantly. Reeves made every effort to provide prompt medical attention for his wounded employee, especially under the circumstances. And finally, Reeves made no attempt to leave the country in the two years after the indictment and continued to perform assigned duties with his usual efficiency.[11]

On Sunday evening, October 15, 1887, at 7 p.m., Edward Hunt, the foreman of the jury impaneled by the Western District Court before Judge Isaac C. Parker, read the verdict to a crowded courtroom: "We the jury find the defendant not guilty as charged in the written indict-ment."[12]

The *Vinita Indian Chieftain* on October 20, 1887, reported:

> Fort Smith Court—Bass Reeves, the negro who has been on trial for murdering a prisoner, was acquitted a few days ago.

The *Fort Smith Weekly Elevator* on October 21 ran the following story:

United States Court Proceedings

> At the close of our last report ex-Deputy Marshal Bass Reeves was on trial for Murder. His case went to the jury Saturday, and they remained out until Sunday evening when they returned a verdict of not guilty.

According to the tax records for Crawford County, Arkansas, Bass Reeves sold his home in Van Buren in 1887. This was undoubtedly done to help pay the attorney fees he had accumulated. The Fort Smith Deed and Mortgage Records show that Bass Reeves bought a home on Lot 3, Block 2, Park Place Addition, in 1889. The city directory for Fort Smith gives this address as North Twelfth Street, Park Place, in 1890. The city directory for 1894–95 gives the address as 1313 North Twelfth Street. This home would have been at the time on the outskirts of Fort Smith. It was said that Reeves's murder trial depleted most of his savings and he never rebounded financially. The average annual salary for a deputy in the 1880s was five hundred dollars. The U.S. marshal got 25 percent of a deputy's take. Reeves during the 1880s averaged $3,000 to $4,000 a year. He was one of the top grossing deputy marshals of the Fort Smith court. Apparently, he lived with his wife and family at this address for a short period in the early 1890s. Later, as we follow Reeves's career, we find he worked out of the Paris, Texas, federal court in the mid-1890s and most conclusively did not reside in Fort Smith during those years, although his family stayed at this residence in Arkansas.[13]

The exact date is not known when Reeves was recommissioned a deputy U.S. marshal. There are a few cases on file in the Southwest Branch of the National Archives in Fort Worth, Texas, that indicate him working in 1888 for the Fort Smith federal court. In 1889 the Fort Smith court's jurisdictional land area was broken up. Muskogee was selected as the first court in Indian Territory. They only had jurisdiction over minor crimes; major crimes were referred to Fort Smith. Also in 1889, in Paris, Texas, the federal court for the Eastern District of Texas was given jurisdiction for the Chickasaw Nation and most of the Choctaw Nation in the Indian Territory. Earlier, in 1883, the federal court in Wichita, Kansas, had been given jurisdiction over the Cherokee Outlet and the Unassigned Lands, plus northwest Indian Territory. Then, in 1890, Guthrie, an Atchison, Topeka, and Santa Fe Railroad town, would become the federal court seat for the newly opened Oklahoma Territory, land that was earlier under the Wichita federal court supervision. Oklahoma Territory was located just west of the Indian Territory. There are stories that link Bass Reeves with the Paris, Texas, federal court in 1889. Noted deputies were given jurisdiction for more than one district on occasion, so it is likely this was the case with Reeves. Additionally, Reeves was a very familiar and seasoned veteran officer of the Chickasaw Nation, now under the Texas court's mandate.[14]

9.

Back on the Trail

One of the first well-organized bands of horse thieves to operate in Indian Territory was the Tom Story gang. Besides Tom Story, the gang had other talented men like "Peg Leg" Jim, Kinch West (who reportedly rode with William Quantrill), and "Long" Henry, who were all experts in the fine art of stealing and disposing of horses.

From 1884 until 1889 Tom and his gang were devoted exclusively to stealing horses in Indian Territory and selling them in Texas. They made their headquarters somewhere on the banks of the Red River in the Chickasaw Nation, and this strategic location allowed them to move in all directions to fully cover Indian Territory in their search for horses to steal.

Tom Story and his gang, however, were not above trying a new procedure. In 1889 they reversed their operation and stole a herd of horses and mules from George Delaney, who lived on the Texas side of the Red River. The gang stole his herd and drove them into Indian Territory in search of a market.

When he missed his herd, Delaney began to investigate on his own. Somehow he learned that Tom Story had stolen his horses and mules and that Story was expected to return to Texas in only a few days. Delaney immediately contacted the marshal's office at Paris, Texas, and a warrant was issued for the arrest of Tom Story on the suspicion of horse stealing.

Bass Reeves was then serving in Paris as a deputy U.S. marshal, and he was given the warrant.

Bass met Delaney and convinced him that if Tom Story was actually the man they wanted, and if he was returning to Texas, the best thing for them to do was wait for him along the way. Delaney agreed with this plan, and when Reeves decided that Story would cross the Red River at the Delaware Bend Crossing, Delaney agreed to go along as Bass's posse and wait for Story to return.

Reeves and Delaney made their camp close to the Delaware Bend Crossing on the Red River, deep in the brush that paralleled the trail across this ford. They fished and even hunted small game while they waited for Story. After about four days had elapsed, they learned from a man crossing the river who knew Story, that he could be expected late the next day.

As a result, Reeves was waiting for him in the brush on one side of the trail when Tom Story came riding across the ford, leading two of Delaney's finest mules, which he had failed to sell in the Chickasaw Nation.

When Story rode up, Reeves stepped out of the brush and challenged him. Story dropped the lead ropes of the mules in surprise. Bass told him he had a warrant for his arrest, and "right then and there, Tom Story committed suicide."

Tom attempted to draw his gun on Bass, thinking he had an even chance to beat him, as Bass still had his gun in its holster. But Story's gun hadn't even began to clear leather before Reeves had already drawn and fired his Colt pistol. Story was dead before he hit the ground.

Reeves and Delaney buried Tom Story there along the Red River. Delaney left for home taking his two mules along. Bass went back to Paris, Texas, and the Story gang quickly disintegrated, never to be heard of again.[1]

The famous American historian John Hope Franklin was born in Rentiesville, Oklahoma. Franklin's father, Buck Colbert Franklin, a Chickasaw Freedman, was born in 1879 in the Chickasaw Nation. In his autobiography, Buck Franklin told the following story of an incident that happened to his family when he was ten years old:

I recall a mild excitement at our home one evening in late September just as we children were returning from school. I saw many horses at the hitching post and our home surrounded by United States marshals from the federal court at Fort Smith, Arkansas. That was the only court at that time that served the vast Oklahoma and Indian Territories. If one wanted to file a complaint against an outlaw, he had to travel possibly two hundred miles, depending upon where he lived, to Fort Smith to do it. And because of the size of the area, no single warrant would be taken out; the clerk was ordered to hold the warrants until several had accumulated before taking them to the U.S. marshal's office to be served. The marshal would then send out as many as twelve of his deputies to try to run down, arrest or kill the men against whom the warrants had been issued.

A conservative estimate of 90 percent of the wanted men were murderers, cattle rustlers, and horse thieves (the latter two crimes ranking in penalty with that of murder, as did bank robbery and highway robbery). Some of them had prices on their heads, and the standard instruction was to bring them in "dead or alive." Such was the order against Cornelius Walker, for whom these deputy marshals were searching that evening at our home. Somebody had mistakenly informed the marshal that Walker was related to us and might be found at our house. John Swain, one of the deputies, had disputed this. He knew my dad too well, he said, to believe that he would shelter a criminal, even if he was a relative. But Jim Williams, who was in authority, overruled stopped them saying, "No harm will come from the search," and he opened the doors and told the officers to help themselves. Williams was the only one who accepted the invitation to search, remarking as he moved toward the door, "Cornelius and I will eat breakfast in hell in the morning."

At that very moment, Walker was at the home of dad's brother, Russell Franklin. Whoever had informed the officers had his facts wrong. Cornelius was a near relative of Aunt Reecie, Uncle Russell's wife. Swain and Bass Reeves, a Negro deputy, apologized to Dad for the embarrassment, but he told them to "forget it."

It was the custom of the marshal's office to send his men with a chuck wagon, a cook, and plenty of provisions, including plenty of blankets, sheets, and pillows. At daybreak, we learned that they had flushed out Cornelius Walker at my Uncle Russell's. Jim Williams, moving toward the door, called out to Cornelius to come out or he would break the door down. At the threshold he called out again, hesitated a brief moment, kicked the door ajar, and started in with drawn gun; but as he stepped across the threshold, the outlaw's carbine belched and the leaden bullet flew at the officer's head, blowing the top of it away and spattering the deputy's brain all over the floor. The women in the house were in a panic, and the outlaw quit the house, negotiating the distance between it and a tree, but Swain's revolver cut him down at the tree's roots. That was the last of Walker—and the last of Jim Williams, a brave but foolish man.[2]

The murder of Jim Williams took place on June 6, 1889, at Walker's house, which was located on Salt Creek, near Pauls Valley in the Chickasaw Nation. Jim Williams was the posseman for Deputy U.S. Marshals John Swain and Bill Carr. Cornelius Walker was a black man who was wanted for horse theft and selling whiskey in Indian Territory. During the gunfight in the Walker house, after Williams was shot, Swain shot Walker seven times. Swain evidently was using his Winchester rifle and not a pistol. Two men, Robert and Caesar Franklin, were arrested for being in complicity and resisting arrest.[3]

Buck Franklin said there were upwards of fifty African American deputy U.S. marshals in Indian Territory before Oklahoma statehood in 1907. The most prominent were Bass Reeves, Billy Colbert, Zeke Miller, Bob Fortune, and Neely Factor. Franklin went on to say he often saw deputy U.S. marshals, especially Bass Reeves, whose home was at Muskogee, and Bill Colbert, who lived at Atoka in the Choctaw Nation and knew his mother's people.[4]

On June 11, 1889, Bass Reeves asked for a warrant for a white man named Will Flannery for selling whiskey in the Choctaw Nation at Skullyville. Bass stated in the note that his witnesses were R. L. Martin, Walter Bolen, and H. M. Wallace. The writ for arrest was sent from the newly appointed U.S. marshal, Jacob Yoes, in Fort Smith. Yoes was a veteran of the Union Army during the Civil War, First Arkansas Cavalry, Company D. After the war, he was a Sheriff and an Arkansas legislator before becoming a U.S. marshal, officially in January 1890. The writ for arrest was signed by Deputy U.S. Marshal Wood Bailey. Bailey apparently was working with Reeves. Flannery was found guilty and given thirty-eight days in the federal jail and fined ten dollars.[5]

On August 19 and 21, 1889, Bass arrested two men for peddling whiskey in the Creek Nation fifteen miles west of Eufaula. The men's names were Peter Greenleaf and Sharper Hope, known as "Big Sharper." The men subpoenaed in the case were Jeff Brown, John Brassfield, and John Dedrick, all from the Eufaula area.

On October 4, before U.S. Commissioner Stephen Wheeler, Jeff Brown gave the following testimony:

> I reside near Eufaula, I.T. and know the defendant in this case. Along last spring I was staying at Brassfields, at Brassfields Ferry in the Choctaw Nation. Along about 3 o'clock one morning the defendant came there and staid until after breakfast in the morning. Sharper had two jugs of whiskey and Peter had a lot of bottles of whiskey in his saddle riders. I bought one pint of whiskey off Sharper and paid him 70 cents for it I believe. Brassfield and Johnny Dedrick also bought some of the whiskey.

> **Cross examination**

> Peter took one of the bottles of whiskey out of his saddle pockets and sold it to Dock Evans. It is about 95 miles from here to Brassfields ferry. Sharper was carrying the two jugs in a sack. I think they were gallon jugs. I saw Evans pay the money for the whiskey he got.

> L. A. Evans bought one quart of whiskey off Peter Greenleaf as stated above.

John Brassfield being duly sworn testifies

That the two men came to my house as stated with whiskey. I recognize the defendant Greenleaf as one of them. But I don't know whether the other one is or not. The Colored man that was there had long braided hair while this man has short hair.

The defendant Sharper Hope being duly sworn says

I know where Brassfield lives. I live about 20 miles from him. I did not go to Brassfields with Peter Greenleaf as has been stated by the witness Brown and Evans. It was my brother who was with him. My brother is a smaller man than I am, he wears his hair plaited. I never wore my hair that way since I was young. I have not worn it that way for 15 or 16 years."

Sharper Hope was discharged by the U.S. commissioner after he heard the testimony. Greenleaf was not discharged and was indicted by the testimony.[6]

Reeves sent a letter to Marshal Yoes from Wewoka, capital of the Seminole Nation, on September 28, 1889:

Dear Sir,

Please forward writs to Eufaula, P. O. Indian Territory

Name of Defendants	W.A. Gibson
Charge	Int. and Selling Whiskey November 1888 also August 1887
Witnesses are	Thomas West, Jackson Manual and Factor, Louisa Chupco.

By Thomas West we can prove that he bought one quart from Gibson, November 1888 and paid $2.50 for it. West was at time U.S. Indian Police.

By Jackson Manual we can prove he was present at the time West bought the quart of whiskey and saw him pay for it.

By Joe Factor we can prove that he bought 2 gallon of Whiskey off Gipson about Aug. 1889 and paid him $12.00 for the two gal.

By Louisa Chupco we can prove that Gipson live near here and that he does Introduce and Sell Whiskey and he is known as a whiskey peddler.

[signed] Bass Reeves
Deputy Marshal

Jackson Brown the Treasurer of the Seminole Nation informs us that Gipson is known to be a pardner) of Rober Crisop an old whiskey peddler who was killed by Sandy Walker and Bill Mc-Call Dptys of Marshal of Carrols in endeavoring to arrest them. The Collord people who were having a camp meeting at Bruner Town and Gipson was there and the boys had plenty whiskey. The Chief John Brown requested that we go there and he instructed his lighthorse to turn over all non citizens found selling or suspected of selling whiskey and from the information we had and his instruction we arrested Gipson and him now in custody and ask for a writ forth with.

[signed] Bass Reeves

By Dennis Bowlegs we can prove that he saw him with 2 gallon in September.

On October 9, 1889, W. A. Gibson plead guilty before the U.S. commissioner in Fort Smith.[7]

Bass Reeves was back in the Seminole Nation when he sent a warrant request to U.S. Marshal Yoes on December 26, 1889:

In the following case:	Ta Futsie (Seminole Indian)
Charge	Introducing Spts Liquors 2 gallons
	When Committed: 22nd Dec 1889
	Where Committed: Seminole Nation

Statement of Case.
He introduced 2 Galls whiskey. I caught him with same. I tasted it and it was whiskey, also Tee Jefferson tasted it and can testify to same.
What each Witness will State.
By Tee Jefferson—Will swear that this Indian had two Galls whiskey and tasted of it and will swear that it was whiskey.

Back on the Trail **155**

By Bass Reeves—I will swear to catching him with the whiskey and also tasted it and will swear it was whiskey.

Character of witnesses: Good

Please issue this writ and hold it until I come in. I will have the defendant with me.

[signed] Bass Reeves
Deputy Marshal[8]

A few days later Reeves sent a note to Marshal Yoes from the Creek Nation:

Eufaula I. T.
Dec. 30 1889

HON. JACOB YOES,
U.S. Marshal
Fort Smith, Ark.

Dear Sir.

Arrived here this 4 p.m. have 8 prisoners. Send mail to _____ P.O. where we will be By _____ next. After that we expect to be at Ft. Smith _____ by Jan 2nd 1890 Have got the three men who killed Deputy Marshal Lundy.

Respectfully
[signed] Bass Reaves

The above is a form letter that Marshal Yoes had developed for the deputies to use when corresponding from the field. The "three men" were Nocus Harjo, One Prince, and Bill Wolf, whom Bass arrested on December 27, 1889, in the Seminole Nation. They were wanted on a charge of murdering a white deputy U.S. marshal named Joe Lundy. Joseph P. Lundy was sworn in as a deputy U.S. marshal for the Western District of Arkansas on December 12, 1867. On June 10, 1889, Deputy Marshal Lundy was attempting to serve a warrant for horse theft on Harjo, an Indian. When Lundy located him near Econtuchka (now in extreme northwestern Seminole County) in the Seminole Nation, in the company of two other Indians, Harjo resisted arrest and shot Deputy Lundy to death. He had two accomplices with him at the time; they all escaped. They were on the "scout," a term used in Indian Territory for people on the run from the law, until later in the year when Bass Reeves arrested them. Bass served all the subpoenas for witnesses before the trial; the outcome of the trial is not evident in the case file.[9]

The year 1890 found Bass Reeves riding hard on the trail of wrongdoers in Indian Territory. This would be one of his most productive years in federal service since his murder trial in 1887. On March 6, 1890, the *Muskogee Phoenix* reported:

> Bass Reaves came in from the Seminole Nation with Robert Wolfe, "One" Jesse, "One" Walda, "One" Ulta, "One" Kinder, Tom Bruner, Joe Bruner and Thomas Payne, all charged with introducing and selling. Also Cyrus Williams charges with larceny.—Times.

On Reeves's next trip into the Seminole Nation he captured one of the most notorious Seminole Indian outlaws in the history of the Indian Territory. On April 29, 1890, the Little Rock *Arkansas Gazette* described the capture:

He's a Bad Indian: Capture of a Seminole Who Has "Seven Men" to His Credit

Fort Smith. April 28.—Deputy United States Marshal Bass Reeves brought in twelve prisoners from the "Indian" country today, among them To-sa-lo-nah, alias Greenleaf, a Seminole Indian who is wanted here on three separate charges of murder and who had been an outlaw for the past eighteen years, this being the first time he was ever arrested. About nine years ago he murdered a white man named Davis in the Chickasaw Nation, shooting him from the brush.

A few days later he murdered a man named Bateman in the same locality, shooting him down as he was plowing in a field. Bateman's body lay where it fell four days, and when the murderer fired the shot, the horse his victim was plowing with ran away, the plow struck a stump the point was broken off and is still sticking there. After this he murdered the mail rider near Old Fort Washita. He robbed all his victims. All of this time his business has been whiskey peddling, and every marshal that has ridden in the Seminole, Creek, and Chickasaw country has carried writs for him. Since killing the white men above mentioned he has killed four men of his own tribe, all of whom have assisted deputy marshals in hunting him. The last one he killed was Barna Maha. He first shot him down and then put twenty-four bullets in his body. For some time past it has been impossible for an officer to get any one to assist in hunting him as it was almost sure death to do so unless the hunt was successful. Reaves was in the neighborhood and learned that Greenleaf had just come into the country with a load of whiskey. He located him and at night got near enough and when he was selling his liquor to hear the Indians whooping and firing off their pistols. He waited until near daylight and then moved up close to the house. Just at daylight he and his posse charged up, jumped the fence, and before Greenleaf got fairly awake had him covered with their guns and he surrendered. After his capture people who had known him long doubted it and flocked to see it was really so, some riding as far as eighteen miles to convince themselves of his identity.

The *Fort Smith Weekly Elevator* reported on May 2, 1890:

Deputy Marshal Bass Reeves came in Sunday with Greenleaf, charged with murder; Cyrus Williams and Wm P. Bake, larceny; William Arnold, William Ripperton, Sam Mechum, "Watie" Mitchell, Shoartes, Tallahamasee, Noaka, O-con-a-harjo, Seba, all whiskey cases. Wm. Arnold gave bond. Greenleaf is a Seminole and his Indian name is To-sa-lo-nah. He has three counts of murder to answer in this court, and is alleged to have been an outlaw for eighteen years past, and yet this is the first time he has ever been captured.

Greenleaf was convicted in a jury trial in June on the charges of selling whiskey and sentenced to eighteen months in the Detroit House of Corrections. He was fined one hundred dollars. Apparently the federal court didn't have enough evidence to convict him of the seven murders he was accused of committing. There may have been a lack of evidence for the murder trials to go forward.[10]

On July 4, 1890, the *Fort Smith Weekly Elevator* reported on more criminals being brought into Fort Smith:

Jail Arrivals

Deputy Bass Reeves came in Friday with William Roberts, charged with murder; William Trammell, William Cully, Robert Albert, Thomas Jefferson, William Knight and Thomas Knight, all charged with introducing and selling liquor in the Indian country. Cully and Jefferson gave bond.

Peter Campbell and Hardy Colbert, introducing, etc. were brought in by Bynum Colbert . . .

Deputy Grant Johnson brought in Amos Hill, charged with introducing, etc.

The next outlaw Reeves dealt with was a notorious Seminole Freedman named John Cudgo. The name Cudgo is one of the few African names to survive in the United States. It is common among black Seminoles. John Cudgo would persist in committing crimes in the new state of Oklahoma. Bass arrested him on August 6, 1890. Reeves gave the following testimony before U.S. Commissioner James Brizzolara in regard to Cudgo resisting an arrest on horse theft charges:

I reside at Fort Smith, Arkansas and know the defendant in this cause. I had a commissioners writ for defendant for larceny being Deputy U.S. Marshal for the Western District of Arkansas. I went to defendants house in Seminole Nation to serve this writ on August 6, 1890. When he here the horses coming up he jumped up with his Winchester in his hands and he looked and seen there were three of us. I told the other boys to go around the house and I went on south side of house to right of front door near edge of porch. I jumped down off my horse and called him. I told him I had a writ for him. Defendant said he knew that but God damn me. I could not serve it. By this time he had sent his wife and children away from the house. Defendant said he knew I had the writs for him, that he never was going with me to Fort Smith. That this was his house that he built it, for me to get off his lawn. I told I had a writ for him and I was not going away without him. He told me to get away from there, that he would come to Fort Smith; that he was not going to go with any marshals, me nor any other God damn son of a bitch of a marshal, me especially. Then he said to sent the other parties away, that he was not afraid to talk to me. I told them to get back from the house and when I stepped around in front he had his Winchester up on his hands cocked and told me to go away, that he [be] allowed to die right there at home. I told him government law [did] not send me out to kill men but to arrest them. I seen that I could do nothing with him. I called defendant's wife first and asked her to go over and call Stephney to come over. Defendant told her not to go that if I wanted anybody to go to go myself. I told him I did not allow [myself] to leave until I got him. I then called Mr. Snell and sent him over after Stephney. Stephney came and told defendant that he was very foolish. To put down his gun and go with me. Defendant said by God he did not allow to go with me or other son of a bitch of a marshal. Stephney and I spoke to him for almost a quarter of an hour, he wanted Stephney to come in but he would not do it. Finally defendant told Stephney that he would not hurt him, to come into house and Stephney did so and defendant gave him his gun and came out and gave up. Defendant resisted and prevented us from arresting him for almost two hours. Defendant knew I was a Deputy Marshal. Defendant said he knew I had a writ for him. Defendant knew me; he has known me for almost eight or ten years. I was Deputy U.S. Marshal at the time. Mr. Easley was my posse. Mr. Snell was my guard. This occurred August 6, 1890.

Cross examination

There was no body at the house when we went there but defendant and his wife and children. His children are very small. Defendant jumped out with his gun from under the porch. I had my gun across my lap when he rode up. I had my gun too.

I had mine cocked. Defendant was in the house with door shut, about half too. Defendant said that he would go himself to Fort Smith when he got ready.

J. B. Snell duly sworn says

I reside in Crawford County, Arkansas. Know defendant on the morning of 6 of August, 1890. We went up to a house, just as we got within 50 or 60 yards of house; seen defendant come out from under the porch with a Winchester in his hands. We, Easley and I whipped around on the other side of the house. When we got around there he ran into the house, the woman and children ran out. Bass asked him his name. Defendant said John Cudgo. Then Bass told him to come out that he had a writ for him. Defendant said by God he would not come out. That, that was his house and his grounds that he had legally paid for it and ordered us to get off his premises. Bass told him to come out and act the man. That he wanted to talk to him. Defendant said that he would not come out that he would soon die there as at any other time. That if he would send the other men away he would to talk to him. That he was not afraid to talk to no one God damned man. Then Bass called me around and spoke to defendant telling him the best thing he could do was to come out and give up that gun. . . . Finally defendant said he would talk to old man Stephney and I went after him. When he came Stephney spoke to defendant for a considerable time outside then Stephney went into house and spoke to him in there for 15 or 20 minutes and finally Stephney came out with the gun and he gave gun to me. Defendant came out and surrendered to us.

Cross examination

Defendant said he would come to Fort Smith himself. Never heard defendant say anything about being chained until Stephney came. He whipped around house and defendant ran into house. I heard every word that passed between defendant and Bass.

James Easley duly sworn says:

I reside at Fort Smith, Arkansas. Know defendant on August 6, 1890. Bass Reeves, Mr. Snell and myself went to defendants house and defendant came out of door with a Winchester in his hands. Snell and I when Bass told us to go around house defendant jumped, went around house. [I] heard what passed between defendant and Bass Reeves. Bass Reeves said come out, I want to talk with you. Defendant said I am not coming no wheres. Reeves said why won't you come out and talk to me. Defendant said why you got a writ for me. Reeves said how do you know I have. Defendant said I know you have, why don't you come out like a man and say you have. Reeves said well John I have got a writ for you. Defendant said well you shall never serve it on me. Reeves said why. Defendant said because I will not go with you and be chained up and starved to death hauling me over the country. Reeves said, you had as well go with me as with anyone else. Defendant said well I ain't go with you . . . if you get any reliable man in this country I will go with him. Then Reeves said why won't you go with me. Defendant said I will no go with you or no other son of a bitch of a marshal. Then Reeves asked defendants wife to go after Stephney and defendant told her not to. Then Reeves sent Mr. Snell. Stephney came and would not go in house and staid outside for a few minutes. Then Stephney went into house and they spoke for some time and then Stephney came out with gun and defendant right behind him.

This testimony shows the negotiating tactics that Bass Reeves used when necessary. It sounds similar to the police negotiators of today who serve on the Hostage Rescue Units and Special Operations/Tactical Units of federal and urban police departments. The writ for resisting arrest was withdrawn on December 13 after two previous continuances on the hearings in October. The man identified in the above testimony as "Old man Stephney" was named Stepney Latta. In regards to the horse theft, Cudgo claimed he bought the horse from a Ben Jackson but still owed him five dollars after initially paying him ten dollars. There is no information on the outcome of the larceny charge in the case file.[11]

In 1907 John Cudjo and his brother, Ned, robbed a store and post office in Spaulding, Creek Nation. They killed a deputy U.S. Marshal named John Morrison who was also the town marshal of Sasakwa. John's brother was captured by a posse that included black Seminole Lighthorseman Dennis Cyrus, but he got away. In March 1913 John Cudgo killed another black man named Taylor in a knife fight. In November of that year, south of Wewoka, Oklahoma, a Seminole County deputy sheriff named John Dennis, in an attempt to arrest the felon, was shot and killed by John Cudjo when he exited his automobile at the home of the relative where Cudjo was staying. A running gunfight ensued with a mounted police posse, and Cudjo's horse was shot out from under him and he was wounded and captured near Holdenville, Oklahoma. Cudjo was transported to Wewoka to be put in the county jail prior to a hearing on the murder charges. A mob took Cudjo in custody once he arrived in Wewoka and lynched him from a telephone pole in front of the Seminole County Courthouse on the evening of November 4, 1913.[12]

The *Atoka Indian Citizen* on August 30, 1890, reported on Reeves's most recent trip into Indian Territory:

> Deputy Bass Reeves and Mr. Snell came in on the 14th with John Spott and one Legrist, Creek Indians charged with the murder of an old negro on Coal Creek, Creek Nation, about one year ago; John W. Baker and Little Moses, assault with intent to kill; Charles Woodard. John Cudgo, larceny; Robert Wolf, contempt; one Mart, John Wildhorse and Fihola, introducing, etc. The marshals were out 31 days. Little Moses, Woodard, one Mare and Fiohola gave bond.

On September 26, 1890, the *Fort Smith Weekly Elevator* reported:

Muskogee Items
Muskogee, I.T., Sept. 22—Deputy U.S. Marshal Bass Reeves arrested Jim Barnett here on Saturday, charged with larceny of horses. Barnett will be taken to Fort Smith for examination.

The most famous Indian outlaw in the history of the Indian Territory was a Cherokee named Ned Christie. Ned was born in the Rabbit Trap community of the Cherokee Nation on December 15, 1852. He was elected to the Cherokee National Council as a legislator in 1885 from the Going Snake District. Christie's father, Watt, had taught him to be a blacksmith and a gunsmith, which was his trade by profession. On May 4, 1887, Deputy U.S. Marshal Daniel Maples was shot by ambush and killed by whiskey peddlers in Tahlequah, the capital of the Cherokee Nation. Maples had been sent to Tahlequah from Fort Smith to curtail the liquor traffic in the town. Christie was accused of the murder.[13]

In 1918 a black man named Richard Humphrey would testify that he had witnessed the murder of Dan Maples. He told the *Daily Oklahoman* that the notorious Cherokee Bud Trainor was the killer, but Humphrey was too scared to come forward with the information at the time. Christie vowed not to be taken to Fort Smith for a crime he didn't commit and put up a five-and-a-half-year struggle against the U.S. marshal's deputies.[14]

Ned Christie had family and friends assist him against the numerous federal posses that were sent to capture him in the hills of the Cherokee Nation. Local people called the location Ned's Fort Mountain. Christie put up a valiant fight—many times he would nick and wound a lawman but never killed any of them outright. The noted Deputy U.S. Marshal Heck Thomas was one of the unsuccessful lawmen who attempted to capture Ned. In October 1890 the federal authorities in Washington DC granted a reward of one thousand dollars for the apprehension and capture of Ned Christie. Bass Reeves led an assault on Christie's fortified home after this reward was posted. Reeves may have been solicited for the job after his capture of the elusive and notorious Greenleaf. Of the many articles and books written on the hunt for Ned Christie, the assault by Reeves was never mentioned until my book *Black, Red and Deadly* was written in 1991.[15]

On November 27, 1890, the *Vinita Indian Chieftain* wrote the following story on Reeves's raid:

That Visit to Christy

The Muldrow Register has the following account of the raid recently made by the marshals upon the home of Ned Christie:
On Tuesday last U.S. Deputy Marshal Bass Reeves, of Fort

Smith, with his posse, made an attack on the home of Ned Christie in the Flint district, who is perhaps the most notorious outlaw and desperado in the Indian Territory, and the outlaw's stronghold was burned to the ground. Supposing that the owner had been killed or wounded and was consumed in the building, the news went out that he had met a violent death. But Christie has turned up alive, and may cause trouble yet; is said to be on the war path fiercer than ever and vows revenge on the marshal and his posse.

Ned Christie is perhaps the most desperate character in the territory and there is a large reward offered on his head. He has killed a number of men, among whom might be mentioned the Squirrel brothers, also considered "rough men." He is said to be a dead shot, has eluded the officers of the law for about four years and says he will not be taken alive.

It is thought by some today, including myself, that the framing of Ned Christie was a conspiracy. Christie was one of the most vocal critics against the railroads being given access to the Cherokee Nation. Plus, he was a member of the Keetoowah Society, the most conservative element of traditional Cherokees. Keetoowahs believe in the maintenance of traditional ways of the Cherokee people. They felt that giving the railroads access would just allow more white people to come in and usurp Cherokee land and rights. Ned Christy was eventually killed at his mountain fort on November 2, 1892. A sixteen-man posse under the leadership of Deputy U.S. Marshals Gideon S. "Cap" White and Paden Tolbert had been dispatched from Fort Smith and nearby communities. The posse had even secured an U.S. army cannon from Coffeyville, Kansas, to assist in the capture. This proved useless against Christie's double-tiered log fort. In the end, very little railroad construction took place in the Cherokee Nation.[16]

For a period after Reeves's raid, the newspapers carried stories that Ned had gotten revenge against the black deputy. The *Muskogee Phoenix* on January 29, 1891, wrote:

Fort Smith, Ark., January 26.—Word reached here to-night of the killing of Deputy United States Marshal Bass Reeves, near

Tahlequah, I.T., by Ned Christie, a well known outlaw. Reeves was a negro and well known in this city. Christie was being arrested for the murder of Ban Moffets some months ago.

Deputy Marshal Bass Reeves was killed Monday by Ned Christie near Tahlequah Christie is the outlaw wanted for the murder of Deputy Dan Maples several years ago. He is one of the toughest characters in the Territory. He has had two cabins burnt by Officers within a few months in a fruitless effort to capture him.

On the same day, the *Eufaula Indian Journal* wrote:

It is reported in the Republic from Tahlequah and in the Dallas News from Muskogee that Bass Reeves was killed Saturday near Tahlequah, while attempting to make an arrest. It is thought here that it is a mistake, as Bass was in Eufaula last week and with two wagons and supplies for several days and went west.

The *Van Buren Press* on January 31, 1891, wrote:

Bass Reeves Killed

Muskogee, Indian Territory, January 25.—Deputy Marshal Bass Reeves was killed yesterday by Ned Christie near Tahlequah. . . . Reeves is well known in Van Buren, having lived here for a long time. His death was not unexpected to those that knew him.

Later: The death of Reeves is doubted at the Marshal's office in Fort Smith.

The *Muskogee Phoenix* followed up with another story on February 5, 1891:

The report that Bass Reeves had been killed by Ned Christie in Flint District, Cherokee Nation last week, was without foundation. Reeves was 150 miles away from the reported place of killing at the time of the alleged killing.

On February 7, 1891, the *Van Buren Press* carried a retraction of their report on Reeves's death:

Last week the Press contained the announcement of the killing of Deputy Marshal Bass Reeves, and also the fact of its being doubted. It has been definitely ascertained that the statement was a hoax, and that Reeves was 150 miles from the Going Snake District, the home of Ned Christie, and from whose mountain fastness he never dares to venture.

The final article on the supposed death of Reeves appeared in the *Eufaula Indian Journal* on February 21, 1891:

Deputy Marshal Bass Reeves lacks lots of being dead as was reported recently from Muskogee to the Dallas News. He turned up Saturday from west with two wagons of prisoners going to Fort Smith. He had twelve prisoners in all; Eight for whiskey vending, three for larceny and one for murder. Two were U.S. citizens from Oklahoma, a white man and a negro; they had crossed the line and were selling fire water to Indians.

Earlier, on December 30, 1890, Bass Reeves had sworn out a warrant for the arrest of a black man named Bob Dosser. Dosser stole a horse valued at one hundred dollars from a white man named Sam Stratton in the Seminole Nation in June 1890. Judge Parker signed the writ for arrest. Dosser was brought into Fort Smith in February 1892 and given a $750 bond. In May he was released due to a lack of testimony from witnesses.[17]

Alice Spahn, Reeves's daughter, told Richard Fronterhouse that Bass Reeves subdued an outlaw named Bob Dozier, which possibly could have been spelled Dosser. Mrs. Spahn placed the conflict in the Cherokee Nation instead of the Seminole Nation where Dosser was arrested. She said Bass felt this police work was the high point of his career. Whether these two men were the same will be left to speculation and conjecture. Reeves will be cited later in this text for killing a horse thief in the Seminole Nation and no name is given for the outlaw. Carrie Cyrus-Pittman in the late 1930s told of an outlaw leader named Bob Dossay in the Seminole Nation who was killed by African Seminole Lighthorseman Caesar Payne. It is possible Payne was Reeves's posseman when he subdued Dozier. Reeves was the principal deputy out of the Fort Smith and Paris federal courts to work the Seminole Nation during the 1880s and early 1890s.[18]

Fronterhouse wrote:

Bob Dozier was another outlaw that deviled Bass for several years, even though they only actually met face to face one time.

Bob Dozier was a criminal strictly by choice. He had been a prosperous farmer for years, but the wild criminal life appealed to him so strongly that he made the cold, deliberate decision to give up his farm and a peaceful life and become an outlaw.

As a farmer, Dozier was very successful, and as an outlaw he was even more successful for several reasons. He was not a specialist who concentrated all his efforts in one particular phase of outlaw operations. He was smart and operated on the theory that diversification was more profitable and much safer. He stole cattle, robbed stores and banks, hijacked cattle buyers carrying large sums of money, held up stagecoaches, ambushed travelers as they crossed the Indian Territory, acted as a fence for stolen jewels, stuck up big money poker games when he could find them, delved into land swindling as well as other confidence man schemes, and was the ring leader of a stolen horse operation. Of course, during the rush of these activities, he killed several people, and it was rumored that he even resorted to torture in order to obtain the information his large scale operations required if they were to be successful.

In many respects, Bob's theories on criminal operations were remarkably astute. Because of his diversified activities, he never enraged any one particular group of people to the extent they banded together to support and aid the deputy marshals sent out to arrest him. Most people felt that as long as they were not personally involved, why should they be cooperative and furnish them information about the whereabouts of Bob Dozier. This attitude was widespread, and it may have been bolstered by the common knowledge that Bob always remembered a favor, but he never forgot a traitorous act.

With this disadvantage, the deputy marshals were completely hamstrung in their efforts to locate and arrest Dozier. He was able to avoid their every effort for years, until at last, Bass Reeves took the trail after him.

Bass knew a great deal about Bob Dozier. He knew what

Dozier looked like from the descriptions furnished by his victims, and he understood how Dozier operated to escape capture. With this knowledge, Bass theorized that a lone wolf pursuit, with perhaps a one man posse to help, would accomplish more than several deputies banded together because one or two men could move about and not arouse suspicions that might reach Dozier and scare him off.

For several months, Bass made no concrete progress in his attempts to arrest Dozier. He never made actual contact with Dozier even though he did come close enough to keep Dozier constantly on the run.

Dozier eventually learned who was after him. He sent word to Bass that if Bass didn't stop hounding him, he was as good as dead. Bass laughed and sent back the message that at least Dozier would have to quit running to kill him, and he was ready at any time to give Dozier his chance. However, nothing developed from this exchange, and Dozier kept on the move with Bass getting closer and closer.

Bass finally cut Dozier's trail in the upper Cherokee Nation. Bass was jubilant; this trail was fresh and hot, and he had another man along to help him.

Bass trailed Dozier deeper and deeper into the wilds of the Cherokee Hills, knowing he was only . . . an hour or two behind Dozier and the one other unknown rider with him. But late in the afternoon just before dark, a heavy, steady rain began to fall which began to blot out the tracks. To make matters worse, heavy lightning and thunder accompanied the rainstorm, which made the eerie Cherokee Hills seem even more foreboding.

After sunset and with all hope of tracking Dozier any further completely gone, Bass and his posse began to look for a dry place to camp for the night. They rode down into a wide heavily timbered ravine, using the lightning flashes to find their way down its treacherous slopes. The instant they reached the bottom of the ravine, the blast of a gunshot greeted them, and a slug whined past Bass' head.

Bass and his posse left their horses in a hurry for the cover of the trees, expecting more shots from the hidden ambushers. After a few minutes, Bass saw the dim shadow of a man slipping from tree to tree. He waited until the shadow was caught between two trees and fired two quick shots. The shadow dropped and fell. This eliminated one of the men but his two shots had given away his position to a second man who immediately opened fire. Bass jerked upright, took a reeling step away from the protective shield of the trees, and fell full length to the ground facing his attacker. He waited with his gun cocked and ready in his hand.

For several minutes the ravine was relatively quiet; only the rain and the crack of lightning could be heard. Bass lay waiting in the mud and rain, fully exposed. Finally, a man stepped from behind a tree laughing aloud, convinced that Bass was dead and his posse had run away. Bass smiled to himself as the lightning lit up the man's face. The long trail was over. He was facing Bob Dozier.

Bass waited until Dozier was only a few yards away before he raised up and ordered him to stop and drop his gun. Dozier stopped laughing, his eyes wide with surprise. He hesitated for a moment, then dropped into a crouch and attempted to shoot once again as Bass lay stretched out ready and waiting in the mud before him. Before he could level his gun, Bass shot first, hitting him in the neck and killing him instantly.

Thus the career of an outlaw that had laughed for years over the deputies' futile efforts to capture him was ended.[19]

1. Deputy U.S. Marshal Bass Reeves.
Courtesy Western History Collections,
University of Oklahoma Library.

Federal Official Family   Nov. 18, 1907.

(*Opposite top*) 2. The last official day of the "first federal family,"
including Bass Reeves (*far left*), U.S. Marshal Leo E. Bennett
(*rear center*), and Chief Deputy U.S. Marshal Bud Ledbetter
(*front, second from right*), at Muskogee, Oklahoma, on the first
day of Oklahoma statehood, November 16, 1907. Courtesy
Archives and Manuscripts Division, Oklahoma Historical
Society.

(*Opposite bottom*) 3. Muskogee, Oklahoma, municipal police
department, 1908. Bass Reeves (*front left*) was hired as a city
policeman in January 1908, at the age of sixty-nine. Paul Smith
(*front, second from right*) saved Bud Ledbetter's life in a shootout
in 1906. The building in the background is draped in bunting
in honor of slain Muskogee policeman L. F. Harvey. Courtesy
Daniel F. Littlefield Collection, North Little Rock, Arkansas.

(*Above*) 4. The U.S. Indian Police of the Union Agency,
Muskogee, Indian Territory, ca. 1890. Courtesy Archives and
Manuscripts Division, Oklahoma Historical Society.

(Opposite top) 5. Colt .45 pistol said to have belonged to Bass Reeves. The four-and-three-quarter-inch-barrel pistol, serial no. 233872, was shipped by Colt's Manufacturing Company on October 29, 1902, to Witte Hardware Company of St. Louis, Missouri. Leroy Champlain, a law enforcement officer in the Muskogee area, purchased the pistol from Reeves's daughter, Alice Spahn, in the 1960s. It is currently owned by Tom Odom of Huntsville, Alabama. Courtesy Tom Odom Collection.

(Opposite bottom) 6. Ned Christie, Cherokee outlaw, one of the most elusive fugitives in the history of Indian Territory. Bass Reeves made an unsuccessful attempt to capture Christie in November 1890; Reeves and his posse managed to burn down Christie's home, but the outlaw escaped. Courtesy Archives and Manuscripts Division, Oklahoma Historical Society.

(Above) 7. U.S. marshal's posse that killed Ned Christie. Deputy U.S. Marshal Paden Tolbert *(front center)* led the posse. Christie was killed in the Going Snake District of the Cherokee Nation on November 2, 1892. Courtesy Archives and Manuscripts Division, Oklahoma Historical Society.

(*Above*) 8. Deputy U.S. Marshal Bud Ledbetter on horseback in Vinita, Cherokee Nation. Ledbetter and Bass Reeves worked together for the federal courts of the Northern and Western districts in Indian Territory, headquartered at Muskogee, Creek Nation. Courtesy Archives and Manuscripts Division, Oklahoma Historical Society.

(*Opposite top*) 9. Lawmen in the Choctaw Nation, ca. 1900. *Left to right*: Amos Maytubby, Creek lighthorseman; Zeke Miller, Neely Factor, and Bob Fortune, all African American deputy U.S. marshals in Indian Territory. Factor said, "We were on our way to Deadman's Crossing when we had that picture made. Near Coal Creek we captured one murderer and two horse thieves . . . just a little later, another murderer, a white man who was later convicted and sent to the penitentiary" (*Black Dispatch*, March 25, 1937). Courtesy Western History Collections, University of Oklahoma Library.

(*Opposite bottom*) 10. Choctaw Lighthorse Police at Antlers, Indian Territory, 1893. Courtesy Western History Collections, University of Oklahoma Library.

11. Deputy U.S. Marshals John Swain (*left*) and Matt Cook at Purcell, Chickasaw Nation, 1892. Swain, who served with Bass Reeves in the Chickasaw Nation, was commissioned from 1882 until 1895, when he was killed, (not in the line of duty). Courtesy Archives and Manuscripts Division, Oklahoma Historical Society.

12. Choctaw Lighthorse Policemen, Indian Territory, ca. 1885. Courtesy Archives and Manuscripts Division, Oklahoma Historical Society.

13. Seminole Lighthorse Policemen,
Indian Territory, ca. 1885. The
policeman front right is possibly
Seminole Freedman Dennis Cyrus.
Courtesy Seminole Nation Museum,
Wewoka, Oklahoma.

14. The original federal jail at Muskogee, Indian Territory, 1895. Courtesy Archives and Manuscripts Division, Oklahoma Historical Society.

15. Federal courthouse at Muskogee, Indian Territory, 1899. Courtesy Archives and Manuscripts Division, Oklahoma Historical Society.

(*Above*) 16. Deputy U.S. Marshals A. J. Trail (*left*) and Paden
Tolbert in front of the new federal courthouse in Muskogee,
Indian Territory, ca. 1902. Trail and Tolbert worked with Bass
Reeves in the Northern District, Indian Territory. Courtesy
Archives and Manuscripts Division, Oklahoma Historical
Society.

(*Opposite top*) 17. Old U.S. courthouse and jail at Fort Smith,
Arkansas, ca. 1885. The jail was located in two large rooms
under the courtroom on the main floor. Outlaws called the jail
"hell on the border." Courtesy Fort Smith National Historic
Site, National Park Service.

(*Opposite bottom*) 18. George Winston, private bailiff of Judge
Isaac C. Parker, Fort Smith federal court. Courtesy Old Fort
Museum, Fort Smith, Arkansas.

Old U. S. Jail, Fort Smith, Ark.

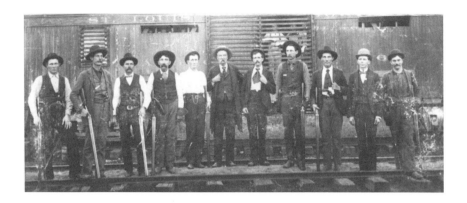

(*Opposite top*) 19. Indian Policeman Knox Tockawunna (Comanche) of the Anadarko Indian Agency with his wife, Esadooah. Courtesy McGalliard Collection, Ardmore Public Library, Ardmore, Oklahoma.

(*Opposite bottom*) 20. Anadarko Agency Indian Police, Anadarko, Oklahoma Territory, ca. 1890. Courtesy Fort Sill Museum, Lawton, Oklahoma.

(*Top*) 21. Federal lawmen of Indian Territory, in front of railroad cars loaded with prisoners. Courtesy Archives and Manuscripts Division, Oklahoma Historical Society.

(*Bottom*) 22. Prisoners waiting to be loaded onto prisoner train in Indian Territory. Courtesy Archives and Manuscripts Division, Oklahoma Historical Society.

23. Deputy U.S. Marshal Heck Thomas, a noted
officer of the Fort Smith court, who worked in
the Chickasaw Nation at the same time as Bass
Reeves. Courtesy Archives and Manuscripts
Division, Oklahoma Historical Society.

24. The Chickasaw Lighthorse Police guarding
a payment of one hundred thousand dollars
en route to the Indian Territory capitol of
Tishomingo. Courtesy Archives and Manuscripts
Division, Oklahoma Historical Society.

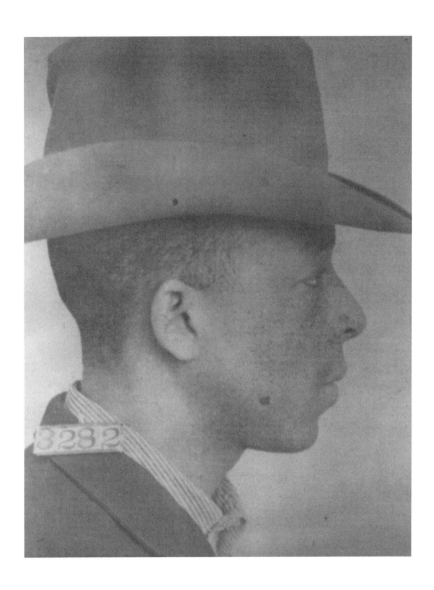

25. Ben Reeves at the time he was committed to Fort Leavenworth federal prison on February 13, 1903. Ben (or Bennie), Bass Reeves's son, was arrested by his father for the crime of murder. Courtesy National Archives and Record Administration, Kansas City, Missouri.

26. Portrait believed to be of Jennie Reeves,
Bass Reeves's first wife. Author's Collection.

27. African American family in a wagon at a Missouri, Kansas, and Texas Railroad siding in Muskogee, Indian Territory, ca. 1900. Courtesy Archives and Manuscripts Division, Oklahoma Historical Society.

28. The wagon yard at Muskogee, Indian Territory, ca. 1899. Courtesy Archives and Manuscripts Division, Oklahoma Historical Society.

(*Opposite top*) 29. Main Street of Fort Gibson, Indian Territory, ca. 1898. Courtesy Archives and Manuscripts Division, Oklahoma Historical Society.

(*Opposite bottom*) 30. The trading post at F. B. Severs Store in Okmulgee, Indian Territory, ca. 1885. Severs Store was the largest and most important store and trading post in the early days of Okmulgee, the capital of the Creek Nation. Courtesy Archives and Manuscripts Division, Oklahoma Historical Society.

(*Above*) 31. African American–owned business building in Muskogee, Indian Territory, ca. 1904. Courtesy Three Rivers Museum, Muskogee, Oklahoma.

DEPUTY U. S. MARSHAL'S OATH OF OFFICE.

NORTHERN *District of* Ind'n Territory.

I _Bass Reeves_____, do solemnly swear that I will
faithfully execute all lawful precepts directed to the Marshal of the NORTHERN
District of Ind'n Territory._____, under the authority of the United States,
and true returns make, and in all things well and truly, and without malice or
partiality, perform the duties of the office of Deputy United States Marshal of
the NORTHERN District of Ind'n Territory., during my continuance
in said office, and take only my lawful fees; and that I will support and defend
the Constitution of the United States against all enemies, foreign and domestic;
and I will bear true faith and allegiance to the same; that I take this obligation
freely, without any mental reservation or purpose of evasion; and that I will
well and faithfully discharge the duties of the office upon which I am about to
enter: SO HELP ME GOD.

his
Bass x Reeves
mark

Sworn to and subscribed before me, this ___1st___ day of
___April___ 189 8.

By H S Young

32. Deputy U.S. Marshal's oath of office taken by Bass Reeves on April 1, 1898. Courtesy National Archives and Records, Washington DC.

10.

The Winds of Change

On February 6, 1889, the U.S. Supreme Court for the first time heard appeals from the Fort Smith federal court. A month later, on March 1, Congress established a white man's court in the Indian Territory at Muskogee. This was a court of civil jurisdiction, upholding the civil laws of the state of Arkansas. The Muskogee federal court, we will remember, handled minor crimes. It had exclusive, original jurisdiction of all offenses against the laws of the United States not punishable by death or imprisonment at hard labor. Those crimes were referred to the Fort Smith federal court. Congress also gave to the Eastern Judicial District of Texas headquartered at Paris all of the Chickasaw Nation and a portion of the Choctaw Nation as far north as the Canadian River. The Paris federal court had jurisdiction over all federal law violations within their district.[1]

The U.S. Congress on May 2, 1890, approved an act that created the Territory of Oklahoma, comprising all area formerly known as the Indian Territory that was not actually occupied by the Five Civilized Tribes or the Indians of the Quapaw Agency in the extreme northeast corner, except the unoccupied part of the Cherokee Outlet and the Public Land Strip that was known as "No Man's Land." Guthrie became the territorial capitol of Oklahoma Territory. Later, on May 3, 1892, the Quapaw Agency was later put under the Third Federal District of Kansas, and on March 1, 1895, Congress divided the Indian Territory into three judicial districts, the Northern, Central, and "Southern.. The Northern District included the Quapaw Agency and the area of the Creek and Cherokee nations, with headquarters at Muskogee and court towns at Vinita, Miami, and Tahlequah; the Central District comprised the Choctaw Nation, with headquarters at South McAlester and courts at Atoka, Antlers, and Cameron; and the Southern District was made up of the Seminole and Chickasaw nations, with headquarters at Ardmore and court at Purcell, Pauls Valley, Ryan, and Chickasha. These courts were given exclusive, original jurisdiction of all offenses committed in the Indian Territory "except such cases as the federal courts at Paris, Texas, Fort Smith, Arkansas or Fort Scott, Kansas may have already proceeded against."[2]

With the opening of Oklahoma Territory in 1889, whites and blacks were allowed to settle on lands that were formerly for Native Americans. Oklahoma Territory legalized whiskey, while it remained illegal in Indian Territory. A number of whiskey towns sprung up in the new Oklahoma Territory. The most notorious of these saloon towns, Keokuk Falls, Violet Springs, and the Corner, were located in Pottawatomie County, which was located just west of the Seminole Nation. Pottawatomie County was opened for white settlement on September 22, 1891.[3]

Harve Lovelday, an early white homesteader of Pottawatomie County, made the following comments about the saloon towns:

> In old Oklahoma the West was West when the six-shooters worked out in the gambling halls and in the saloons of Asher, Avoca, Wanette, Earlsboro, Violet Springs, Corner, and Keokuk Falls about the time of 1889 and 1890. Earlsboro, Violet Springs, Corner, and Keokuk Falls were on the boundary line between the Pottawatomie country and the Seminole Nation while Asher, Avoca, and Wanette were along the boundary lines between the Pottawatomie country and the Chickasaw Nation . . .
>
> The Western people as man to man answered one another in Western style. The man who answered first was the man who was quick on the draw and on the trigger and all disputes were

settled just outside the saloons on the porches or they engaged in fistic fights . . .

These small Western towns were inhabited by Negroes, whites, Indians, half-bloods, gamblers, bootleggers, killers, and any kind of an outcast . . .

Bass Reeves, a coal-black Negro was a U.S. Marshal during on time and he was the most feared U.S. marshal that was ever heard of in that country. To any man or any criminal what was subject to arrest he did his full duty according to law. He brought men before the court to be tried fairly but many times he never brought in all the criminals but would kill some of them. He didn't want to spend so much time in chasing down the man who resisted arrest so would shoot him down in his tracks.[4]

Charles W. Mooney wrote that the ground in the saloon town of the Corner was covered with empty cartridge shells, and looked like gravel on a modern parking lot. He also stated that the modern term "bootleg-ging" came from the drovers, cowboys, and ranchers who would sneak a flat bottle of whiskey in each of their boots and smuggle it back into "dry" Indian Territory, where no legal liquor could be sold. Others were bold and tied their bottles and jugs on their saddle horns under cover of darkness, sometimes swimming the river when it was swollen. The term "Last Chance" was coined here at these saloons, as it was on the border that they had their last chance to get liquor before going into dry Indian Territory.[5]

Mooney wrote the following for the Shawnee, Oklahoma, newspaper:

Although Deputy U.S. Marshals were getting more numerous in the old Indian Territory and in the new Oklahoma Territory during the 1890's, an extreme variance with the custom, par-ticularly in the south, was a Negro Deputy U.S. Marshal. Bass Reeves was such a rarity.

The well known intrepid Marshal traveled extensively through what is now Pottawatomie county, and worked closely with the early day Sheriffs of the county before the turn of the century, as Sheriffs then could not pursue across the county lines, but Marshals could.

Reeves, although a quiet soft-spoken, . . . man, he had proved his mettle and prowess with his two big .45 caliber six-shooters, which materially enlarged his stature. He wore them butts forward for a cross handed draw. This gave him quicker access to the deadly weapons—a split second edge meant life or death. He used the pistols with deadly accuracy. A remarkable man, he was a credit not only to the Federal Court but to his race.

Reeves, was a master of disguise. Sometimes he dressed as a drover, cowboy, a gunslinger and outlaw, and he used aliases. Many times he had as many as 10 prisoners in an open wagon, handcuffed and chained together, en route to the federal jail at Pauls Valley, established in 1895. When not in disguise, he rode a big red stallion with a white blazed face. He was always neatly dressed, and was noted for his politeness and courteous manner. He carried a gourd dipper tied to his saddle bag which he used when he stopped at farmhouses for a drink of well water.

Perhaps the most famous and best remembered of all the disguises and accomplishments of the fearless early-day Marshal, was the time he dressed as an indigent tenant farmer. He drove through Keokuk Falls, then east of town in the Creek Nation. The cunning and sagacious officer had received a tip that some outlaws were holed-up in an abandoned log cabin about a mile east of Keokuk. Driving a yoke of flea-bitten, aged oxen hitched to a ramshackle wagon of outdated vintage and usage, he slowly lumbered along, approached the half hidden cabin in a cluster of trees. Driving close to the cabin, he deliberately got the wagon hung up on a large tree stump. When the unsuspecting outlaws came out to get him free, so he could be on his way and leave the quietude of their hide-out, old Bass calmly reached into his faded and patched overalls pockets, and came out with his two big .45 caliber six-shooters and got the drop on the careless outlaws. None challenged that authority.

He then disarmed all of them, gathered their weapons in the

wagon, and marched all six of them in front of his wagon on foot to the county jail at Tecumseh, a distance of over 30 miles. There, they were properly jailed by Sheriff Billy Trousdale, an later taken to the federal jail at Guthrie where they were convicted of robbery of the Wewoka Trading Post, then owned by Governor John F. Brown of the Seminole Nation . . .

May we ever remember the contribution to the heritage of this county by Bass Reeves, the formidable Negro Deputy U.S. Marshal.[6]

The Pauls Valley federal jail alluded to by Mooney was under the jurisdiction of the Paris, Texas, federal court in 1895. Current Oklahoma historian David A. Farris wrote the following concerning Reeves's work in Pottawatomie County prior to statehood:

Because Keokuk Falls attracted outlaws, it also attracted lawmen. Bass Reeves was one of the first black U.S. Deputy Marshals in Oklahoma Territory. In a land where racial inequality and the Ku Klux Klan thrived, Marshal Reeves wielded the same respect and authority as any of Judge Isaac Parker's lawmen. Reeves frequently rode through the Falls in pursuit of badmen.[7]

Although Reeves carried two Colt pistols, his main weapon was his Winchester rifle. The Winchester was the weapon of choice in the Indian Territory and on the western frontier; pistols were used as backup weapons or close-quarter defense options. Deputy U.S. marshals also used shotguns in their arsenal of weapons. Hollywood has placed too much emphasis on pistols in movie portrayals of the Old West. Later, when Reeves served the Muskogee federal court, he was known to carry three pistols, according to Richard Fronterhouse, who interviewed his daughter Alice Spahn: one on his hip, one in a shoulder holster, and one hidden away at the waist in the small of his back.

In 1887, the U.S. Congress set up the eventual disintegration of the Indian Territory when they passed the Dawes Severalty Act. The act allowed Indian lands to be cut up into 160-acre plots. The Native American families could claim at least one plot. The "surplus" lands would go to U.S. settlers. After the federal government opened the western part of the Indian Territory in 1889, they did the same with the 100,000-acre Cherokee Outlet in 1893, sometimes mistakenly called the Cherokee Strip. The Strip was actually in Kansas. Within days of the 1889 land rush, two new towns had sprung up on the Oklahoma prairie. In less than twenty-four hours, Guthrie boasted a population of fifteen thousand, while Oklahoma City claimed ten thousand. Among the new inhabitants of Oklahoma Territory with new homesteads was an estimated ten thousand African Americans who came primarily from southern states.[8]

One of the most important persons in the African American migration to the Oklahoma Territory was Edwin P. McCabe. McCabe served two terms in Kansas as the state auditor, making him the highest-elected African American official in the West. McCabe founded Langston City, a black town in Oklahoma Territory in 1889. Its post office was established in 1891. In 1890 McCabe urged the creation of African American towns throughout the Oklahoma and Indian territories. He hoped that the future state of Oklahoma would enter the union as a largely African American state and he would be elected governor. There would eventually be over thirty black towns and settlements in Oklahoma and Indian territories, more black towns than anywhere in the United States. About a dozen of these towns still exist. Boley in the Creek Nation was the largest and most prosperous. In 1905, Booker T. Washington, the leading black national politician said Boley was "the most enterprising, and in many ways the most interesting of the Negro towns in the United States." Because of McCabe's political ambitions, whites saw him as a serious foe to their settlement plans in the new territory. A newspaper from outside Oklahoma Territory stated in September 1891 that the closest McCabe came to being seriously injured was on one trip from Langston City to Guthrie through the Iowa Indian lands. He ran into three armed white men who ordered him to go back whence he came. He declined and they opened fire on him. One shot struck the pummel of his saddle, and being unharmed, he fled back to Langston, and then to Guthrie. In *African Americans in the West*, author Kennell A. Jackson states that at this explosive political time in Oklahoma Territory, Bass Reeves played an important role in keeping the peace. The deputy U.S. marshal patrolled the outskirts of Langston City. Reeves, according to the book, protected McCabe against death threats. I have not been able to corroborate this story with other sources, but it may be true. Langston City would later become the home of present-day Langston University, the only historical black college in Oklahoma, which my mother attended for one year. In 1897 McCabe became the deputy auditor of Oklahoma Territory, a post he held until 1907 when Oklahoma became a state. None of McCabe's plans were ever realized and he died in near poverty in Chicago in 1920.[9]

11.

Land of the Six-Shooter

Tulsa, Oklahoma, suffered the worst race riot in U.S. history in 1921. But violence was not new to Tulsa. Earlier, Reeves had made an impression on the frontier residents of this town, where many criminals sought refuge. J. M. Hall, the author of a 1927 book about the early days of Tulsa between 1882 and 1900, was the brother of H. C. Hall, the founder of Tulsa in the Creek Nation. H. C. Hall built the first store in Tulsa in 1882, and J. M. Hall was the first resident postmaster and had charge of the stores that supplied goods to the men building the Frisco Railroad from Vinita to Tulsa in 1882. Hall wrote the following concerning the U.S. marshal's force in the Indian Territory:

> Many United States marshals with their posses made regular sorties through the Indian country to serve warrants or quell disorders. Seeing them pass through the country one might easily have mistaken them for members of a cow ranch outfit. They had their wagons, tents and a cook. If they carried a warrant for a man in Tulsa they would make their camp at Bird creek or on the Verdigris. They would slip into town, get their man and take him to the camp. By the time they were ready to return to Fort Smith they might have had a dozen prisoners.
>
> The laws were violated often in the Territory with no reports made to Fort Smith. Sometimes months would elapse after a

crime and before the arrest of the suspect. In order to go to Fort Smith the early residents of Tulsa had to go to Monet, Mo., and change trains, or ride overland.

It was dangerous, too, for one private citizen to report another to the federal authorities. If the sentence gave promise of being anything heavier than a jail term retaliation was quite certain. The accused man would often kill the witness against him . . .

Many criminals from the States came into this country and lived under assumed names. That meant the marshals had to deal with the very worst type of men . . .

Bass Reeves, a negro deputy marshal, was one of the most noted officers of the early days. He was fearless. One night Bass went into the Hall store followed by a crowd of cowboys and others. The writer was talking to Reeves when a white man came in having the appearance of an outlaw. Reeves asked him to give up his guns. The man threw his hands on them and Reeves did the same thing with his. The white man didn't draw but he refused to surrender the weapons.

"You are a white man and I am a negro," Reeves said quietly. "White men do not like to give up to a negro. You give your guns to Mr. Hall and when you are ready to leave town he will give them back to you." The white man complied.[1]

This would be the last time Bass Reeves was mentioned in a book for nearly forty years. The next time would be in 1971 when William L. Katz published his book, *The Black West*, and Kaye M. Teall published *Black History in Oklahoma*, a resource book for the Oklahoma City Public Schools. Teall stated that Reeves was as good as any deputy U.S. marshal that worked the territories prior to statehood.

In January of 1891, Bass Reeves sent a note to U.S. Marshal Jacob Yoes at Fort Smith, asking for a writ to be sent to Okmulgee in the Creek Nation for John Jefferson, a citizen of the Seminole Nation, for introducing and selling whiskey. Reeves stated in the note that he had four witnesses and he had Jefferson as a prisoner. The Seminole Lighthorse police had turned Jefferson over to Reeves after making the initial arrest. In looking at Reeves's career it appears he had as good a working relationship with the Seminole Lighthorse police as with any Indian police in the territory.[2]

On March 5, 1891, the *Muskogee Phoenix* reported that Bass Reeves brought twelve prisoners into Fort Smith. One of the prisoners was a Creek Indian charged with murder named Hullabee Sam. This is probably the same Indian outlaw who Adam Grayson claims, as related in chapter 4, got away from Reeves because his horse was faster. Grayson told the story in 1938, giving the Indian's name as Hellubee Sammy. He stated this was the only person he knew who had evaded Reeves. It now appears that Grayson didn't have the full story.[3]

Later in the year, Reeves arrested a black woman named Evaline Hawkins for stealing a thirty-dollar watch from a white man who was a citizen of the United States. This incident took place at Wagoner, Creek Nation. The white man, John Hoalt, was drunk when he lost his watch, but he testified he was sure it had dropped out of his vest pocket while he was lying on the grass in town near the train station. The U.S. commissioner discharged Hawkins for the theft.[4]

Reeves arrested William Right for murder near Wellington in the Creek Nation on May 28, 1891. Right was accused of murdering his son, Joseph, with a club. In the testimony before the U.S. commissioner it was revealed that the son who was between twelve and fourteen years of age had been very ill for a long time. The crime may have been a mercy killing by the father. The criminal file on William Right had no information on whether a trial occurred or on the outcome of the hearing before the U.S. commissioner.[5]

Arrests made by Reeves in the territory continued to add intrigue and dynamics to his character in the local newspapers. The *Muskogee Phoenix* on May 28, 1891, reported:

> Sunday night about 12:30, officers Bass Reeves and Wiley Mc-Intosh arrest W. H. McDonald and one Cords, charged with killing John Irvin, the man found murdered in Blue creek, twelve miles west of Wagoner some two weeks ago. The officers had spotted the men for some time and arrested them at their house near Blue creek. The evidence against the two men is very

strong. They were known to have threatened the life of Irvin and cannot well account for themselves at the time the crime was committed. Our readers are familiar with the particulars of the finding of Irvin's body in the creek with a bullet hole in his head. The men were taken to Fort Smith and jailed.

Reeves would get an entirely different reception from the Fort Smith newspaper once he arrived with his prisoners. "McDonald" and "Cords" were really McDaniel and Card; they were white men whom Reeves arrested for killing John Irvin, a black man. It appears Reeves didn't have enough solid evidence to indict the two suspects. It also appears that in this case Reeves may have taken the law into his own hands. The *Fort Smith Weekly Elevator* was unrelenting in its attack on Reeves on June 26, 1891:

An Outrage: Two Innocent Men Arrested on a Trumped Up Murder Charge and Kept Chained for Nearly a Month

William H. McDaniel and Ben A. Card two hard working honest men, residing near Gibson station, were arrested on May 25 by Deputy Marshal Bass Reeves on a charge of murdering a colored man named John Irvin who it was well known, was drowned on the 25th of April and instead of bringing them in at once and allowing them to establish their innocence, he chained them and dragged them around over the Creek country . . . nearly a month, at the same time knowing, as he must have known, that there was no foundation for a case against them. McDaniel is a man apparently fifty years of age, and is recognized by his neighbors as a law abiding citizen, yet Reeves went to his house in the dead hour of night with three or four men, roused him from slumbers and when admitted went in and handcuffed him like a desperado in the presence of his frightened family and took him away. He and the negro Irvin who was drowned, were on the best of terms, and Irvin lost his life trying to swim a bayou McDaniel was the first man his wife sent for in her distress, and he kindly answered her summons. Her evidence alone would have cleared both these men.

This case was evidently trumped up on them by designing men for a purpose, and we understand that while Reeves was dragging them over the country, thieves invaded their premises, or at least those of McDaniel, and stole much of their stock. This report is likely true, as they live not far from Babe Mahardy, one of the most notorious harborers of horse thieves and cut throats in the Indian Territory.

On this same trip Reeves arrested a Negro girl about the same time he did McDaniel and Card, and carted her all over the country, yet when her case came up for examination there was nothing in it and she was discharged.

Now we protest against all such proceeding by deputy marshals, and we are satisfied Col. Yoes will not tolerate such capers on the part of his subordinates if the facts are brought properly before him.

The deputy arrested these men within four hours of Fort Smith, and should have brought them in at once instead of dragging them around over the territory chained up like wild animals, and we think such conduct on the part of officers ought to be severely punished.

In future we propose to make a kick every time we get on to such a case as the above, and in doing so we think our course will be endorsed by both Judge Parker and Col. Yoes as well as all other law abiding people.

I am sure Reeves was reprimanded by his superiors for arresting two propertied white men without sufficient evidence for an indictment. Given the time in American history that this incident occurred, it is almost beyond belief that an African American, even with a badge, would overstep his authority in such a manner with two white men. Black men were being lynched in surrounding states for much lesser actions. Reeves must have felt the two men bore some guilt in Irvin's death for him to take the action he took.

Later in the year Reeves was involved in a gunfight in the Creek Nation. He sent a letter to Marshal Yoes from Okmulgee on November 11, 1891:

Dear Sir

Arrived here . . . have six (6) prisoners. Send mail to Eufaula P.O. where we will be by Friday next. After that we expect to be at Fort Smith . . . by 16 or 17th. I had a writ for Ben Billy for whiskey and when I demanded him to surrender he and Tom Barnett fired on me and we had a fight in which I shot Ben Billy twice. When we got done off of our horses Tom Barnett fired and put ball in a tree just by Creekmore's head he fired two shots at Creekmore while Ben Billy was firing on me. . . . Tom Barnett fired 2 shots he threw his gun down and ran in the house Ben Billy fought until I shot him down. Please send a writ at once for Tom Barnett.

> [signed] Bass Reeves
> Deputy U.S. Marshal

Reeves also submitted a formal writ request where he stated that Tom Barnett fired twice at Milo Creekmore with a .38 Winchester. Both Ben Billy and Tom Barnett were resisting arrest when the shooting occurred. Evidently Ben Billy died because his name has a line drawn through it on the warrant request.

At the hearing for Barnett before U.S. Commissioner James Brizzolara in Fort Smith on November 19, Bass Reeves gave the following testimony:

I reside at Fort Smith, Arkansas and know the defendant in this cause. [I] am Deputy U.S. Marshal; myself, Milo Creekmore and Roland Nave went over to Sosa Barnett I had a writ for Ben Billy alias Ben Williams. We charged on the house and Ben Williams and defendant jumped out of house with Winchesters. I called at Ben Williams to halt and Ben Williams shot at me, then when Ben shot defendant jumped between the houses like; Milo Creekmore jumped down off his horse and jumped to a tree and defendant fired at him and put balls in tree Creekmore was standing behind. Defendant fired two shots, then defendant ran into house. Ben he just kept shooting until I shot him down. We captured them and took them to Okmulgee. Had no writ for defendant but caught him on a stolen horse. This was last Tuesday a week ago. Horse belongs to a white man name William McClure. I was Deputy U.S. Marshal; Milo Creekmore was also a Deputy; Roland Nave is and was my posse this was in Creek Nation. Ben Williams knew me very well. When I hailed him . . . I told him I had a writ for him and he answered with his Winchester. I am a Colored man; Creekmore is a white man and Nave is a Colored man.

Cross examination

This was about sun up. Ben fired twice and aimed to get around the corner of house when I shot him. Creekmore never fired a shot until he got off his horse. I had no writs for defendant and did not know him until then. I did not command defendant to halt. Ben's wife and two women and a small boy were at the house. Ben's wife was out in the yard when he shot. Defendant shot at Creekmore.

Milo Creekmore duly sworn says:

I reside at Van Buren Arkansas, am Deputy U.S. Marshal. When we charged house, I heard Bass call halt then someone shot and Bass shot. I got off my horse, in meantime Ben got to fence by gatepost and dropped right down on his knees and he would fire at Bass and then at me. I kept shooting at Ben Williams and walking to him and when I got up to a little tree there were two shots fired at me from corner of house and one of them hit the tree I was by. Ben he turned and went back running along fence, crossed over and when he did so Bass called to me to get on my horse and go around field to cut Ben off. I got on my horse and went about 100 yards saw Ben fall on the field. Then I got off my horse and went to Ben and then went with him to house and defendant was standing in yard. Bass asked him his name and he said it was Jim Willis. We arrested defendant and took them all to camp.

Cross examination

Could not see who fired at me. Never seen defendant with a Winchester. When I seen him he had no gun.

Roland Nave duly sworn says:

I reside at Muscogee, I know defendant, I was with Mr. Reeves and Creekmore when they made charge on Sosa Barnett's house. I was Bass Reeves posse. Reeves had a writ for Ben Williams. I seen defendant fire two shots at Milo Creekmore, he had a Winchester.

Tom Barnett did stand trial for assault with intent to kill in May 1892. The case file is not clear in regard to the outcome of the trial. This was another incident where outlaws made the mistake of trying to shoot it out with Reeves.[6]

Deputies Reeves and Creekmore arrested a white man named John Wamble for stealing ten head of sheep in December 1891 a few miles west of Muskogee in the Creek Nation. Reeves had written Marshal Yoes in August for a writ of arrest and received one for Wamble. In his note, Reeves stated that Wamble and his wife were U.S. citizens and had stolen the sheep from Sam Solomon near Muskogee. Solomon found his sheep later in the possession of R. L. Cramer who had purchased them from Wamble. In the testimony before U.S. Commissioner Stephen Wheeler on December 24, Simon Solomon said that while away from home freighting during the year of 1889, two of his sheep were taken by the Wambles and sold to a butcher in Muskogee. Solomon said he didn't speak to Mr. Wamble at that time concerning the two sheep. After he lost ten head of sheep, he said he did speak to Mrs. Wamble, who was his stepmother, and she told him they sold the sheep to pay a doctor bill of his father's. Evidently Solomon didn't agree with this method of payment and filed larceny charges. The U.S. commissioner discharged the case against Mr. Wamble.[7]

The *Fort Smith Weekly Elevator* on February 5, 1892, reported on the new jail arrivals:

The arrivals at the jail the past week have been sufficiently numerous to make things interesting . . .

Sandy Williams, larceny, Cherokee Nation, by Bynum Colbert . . . Ben Deer, introducing and selling, Creek Nation by Bass Reeves.

Bass Reeves received a letter from a resident of the Creek Nation asking for help in the theft of stolen cow in March:

Grane Creek I.T.
Mar 21, 1892

Mr. Bass Reeves
Sir Please get

A writ for one Frank Duken for Larceny, he killed and skin one of my cow with out my consent. Lee Arntrol, Boon Riley is the eye witnesses. Frank Duken he lives on Grane Creek on Willie Servier Place.
     Therefore I respectfully ask that you will make the arrest quick as you can.

Yours Truly
[signed] Geo. W. Hill

P.S. The value of the cow $300 Dollars. This was done on or about the 20th of February 1892.

Reeves swore out a warrant for the arrest of Frank Duken, a white man, on March 30 in Fort Smith for larceny of livestock. Reeves made the arrest, but upon the hearing before the U.S. commissioner, the defendant, whose real name was Frank Dugan, was released. In the criminal case file the witnesses' testimony is given but the testimony from Dugan is not found.

The *Fort Smith Weekly Elevator* on April 1, 1892, reported on the new jail arrivals in town:

Nessy Island, introducing and selling, was committed by Bynum Colbert, who arrested him in this city . . . Daniel Barnett, murder; James Barnett, Willie Lena, larceny; Ida Rice alias Rena Sunday, bigamy; Lillie Lena, Isaac Frazier, Perry Fixico, Hoti-bic-che, Henry Hope, Sanford Hightower, all whiskey cases were brought in from the Creek and Seminole Nations by Bass Reaves. Hightower gave bond.

On May 6, 1892, the newspaper listed Frank Dugan among the parties arrested and brought into Fort Smith by Reeves:

Aaron Jackson and Frank Dugan, larceny; One Johnson, Legist Thompson, Samanche John Chacahagee, David Koger and John Short, all whiskey cases, were brought in from the Creek and Seminole Nations by Bass Reaves. Koger and Legist Thompson gave bond and were discharged.

The *Fort Smith Weekly Elevator* listed Reeves's arrestees in the May 27 edition:

Jail Arrivals

Chas. Smith and William James, whiskey cases and Joe Fulsome, larceny, were brought in by Bass Reaves from the Creek Nation. Smith and James gave bond.

The same newspaper reported on new jail arrivals on June 24, 1892:

John Taylor was registered from Creek Nation by Grant Johnson, charged with introducing and selling. . . . Bass Reaves brought in Little John and Sam Davis from Creek Nation and Sam Haney, Walter Taylor, Robt. Bruner, Wallace and Willie Chism from Seminole Nation, charged with introducing and selling, and Chepaucaler alias Eugula for introducing and John Taylor for larceny.

Nancy E. Pruitt, an early settler, gave an opinion concerning black deputy U.S. marshals during the territorial era of Oklahoma in the Creek Nation:

Bass Reaves and Grant Johnson were colored officers. . . . They could talk Creek and the Creeks liked Negroes better than they did whites, (which) I suppose is the reason they had colored officers.[8]

A white woman named Mattie Bittle wrote Bass Reaves a letter in September 1892:

Sep the 24 1892
Mr. Bass Reeves sir

I though I would write a few lines to you. I never never can get to
see you. I want you to come soon as you can get here. my husband
on the first Sunday in August beat me all most to death. I was real
sick I wanted him to go for a doctor he said I need no doctor I was
able to work as he was I said I wished he had stade in the penitintry
he got a stick and beat me I don't think I can get over it they hindred
him as he would killed me he is in Redfork I gess

> Mrs. Matie Bittle
> My Witness is William
> Louis Arnold
> Lee Arnold Mollie Arnold
> Louis Arnold
> Mollie Arnold Was the one that hindred him from killing me
> [signed] Mrs Mattie Bittle

Bass Reeves was not able to investigate the case but his good friend
and colleague, Deputy U.S. Marshal Grant Johnson, did. On September
9, 1892, Johnson requested that a warrant for assault and battery with
intent to kill for George Bittle, a white man, be forwarded to the town
of Eufaula in the Creek Nation. In the request, Johnson stated that Mrs.
Bittle was in bed and was not expected to live. She was staying at William
Arnold's house and was badly hurt. Johnson's request for a warrant was
denied.

Deputy Johnson wrote a follow-up letter to Fort Smith:

> Eufaula I.T.
> 10/15/92
>
> Col Jacob Yoes
> U.S. Marshal
> Ft Smith Ark
>
> Dear Sir
>
> This woman died about the Seventh day after having been beaten
> by George Biddle and a short time previous to her death She stated

in the presents of several witnesses that she was satisfied that she could not live and that Geo Biddle was the sole cause of her death

Respt
[signed] Grant Johnson

This time Johnson was given a warrant for murder to arrest George Bittle. He made the arrest on October 26, 1892, at Red Fork in the Creek Nation. The outcome of this criminal case is not apparent in the archival file.[9]

Most whites that moved into the lands of the Five Civilized Tribes did so illegally; they were squatters. In the 1890 census there were 128,042 aliens living in the Indian Territory compared with 50,055 Indian citizens.[10]

Some whites rented land legally from Indians. As Daniel F. Littlefield Jr. explained,

> The invasion of Indian Territory by poor Americans were abetted by members of the Indian nations who realized that they could make good incomes from rents on improvements. At first, this process was controlled somewhat by a system of official permits that allowed noncitizens to live and work in an Indian nation. By the late 1880s and early 1890s, however, influential members of the Chickasaw, Choctaw, Cherokee, and Creek nations began to claim large tracts, which they broke up into small farms and rented to Americans, without any pretense of working the land themselves. In effect, they became landlords, who merely collected rents.[11]

On October 7, 1892, the *Fort Smith Weekly Elevator* reported on new federal jail arrivals:

Jail Arrivals

The register at the U.S. jail makes the following report this week: Jim Coody was registered from the Creek Nation by Grant Johnson. . . . Bass Reeves registered John Reynolds for introducing, Billy Tulsa for selling, and Barney McQueen for introducing and selling, all from the Seminole Nation. Walter Taylor, charged with larceny, was committed. Mitchell Bruner,

Caesar Add, Frank Jiles and Mack Jiles were registered by Bass Reeves for larceny. Jonas Goliah, for introducing and selling was registered from the Creek Nation by Bass Reeves.

Bass Reeves arrested a white man named Johnathon Steven Tilly on October 30, 1892, for assault with intent to kill and reckless firing of a gun and permanently crippling a man named Thomas J. Vanderlish. The arrest was made five miles east of Eufaula in the Creek Nation. At the time of the incident Tilly was going just by the name of Steve Tilly. Deputy U.S. Marshal Grant Johnson served all the subpoenas in the case. A jury trial in Fort Smith convicted Tilly on February 8, 1893. Judge Isaac C. Parker sentenced him to one year and six months of hard labor at the Detroit House of Corrections where he was admitted on April 7, 1893. Interestingly, in October of 1902, U.S. Marshal Leo Bennett of the Western District for the Indian Territory recommended and appointed Tilly to become the deputy U.S. marshal stationed at the town of Spokogee in the Creek Nation, a post Tilly held until statehood. As Tilly's granddaughter Willabelle Schultz wrote, "My mom always said she heard that Bass was so tough he could spit on a brick and 'bust it into!'"[12]

Later in the year, on December 6, 1892, Bass Reeves arrested an Indian named Robert Kelly for introducing and selling whiskey in the Creek Nation capital of Okmulgee. In a note to Marshal Yoes, Reeves stated that Kelly was selling the whiskey for two dollars a quart. Kelly was making quite a profit and doing a booming business until Reeves caught up with him.[13]

12.

Paris, Texas

On January 27, 1893, near Purcell in the Chickasaw Nation, Bass Reeves arrested a Creek Indian named Jim Bell for horse theft. Bell had been on the run since September 1890 for the larceny that he committed in the Creek Nation. Also in the fall of 1890, near Eufaula in the Creek Nation, Bell and Harry Sampson, also called Samsuagee, stole a horse from a white man named Newton Kelly. After stealing the horse, they shot and killed it for some unknown reason, most likely because they got scared and didn't want to be caught with the horse. Sampson was caught in October 1890, but Bell had been on the run until apprehended by Reeves.[1]

Reeves was back on the trail of outlaws when he took into custody two Creek Indians, Jimmy Rabbit and Willie Proctor, on April 18, 1893. They were arrested for introducing and selling whiskey. Reeves had sent a note earlier to Marshal Yoes stating that the two men were in the custody of the Creek Lighthorse police. Rabbit and Proctor were initially arrested by Creek Indian policemen Medicine Jack and Caesar, near Okmulgee. Both policemen served as witnesses during the trial.[2]

Historian Nudie Williams has stated that during the early 1890s, Bass Reeves's police work in the Indian Territory with fellow black Deputy U.S. Marshal Grant Johnson was legendary. It is regrettable that most of their exploits were not recorded or documented, and persons who could speak about them are deceased. They did arrest, in tandem, one white fugitive named Abner S. Brassfield in 1893. Brassfield would later serve as a policeman in the town of Eufaula before statehood. Brassfield killed a justice of the peace, William Ham, of Harrison, Arkansas, in October 1890. He was sentenced to twenty-one years in the Arkansas State Penitentiary. While his case was being appealed, however, he broke jail and escaped to the Indian Territory. Three years later, Reeves and Johnson along with a posseman named Andy Deering arrested Brassfield at a dance at Brooken, Creek Nation. Brassfield had family that lived in the Eufaula vicinity. Abner's brother Bill described what happened next:

> We hadn't been in this primitive setting but a few days when early one morning three men on horses rode up to the house. My brother, Abner, set on the middle horse, his hands handcuffed to the saddle horn, and his feet fastened by a chain that crossed under the horse's belly. On a horse on each side of him set a Negro United States Marshal, Grant Johnson and Bass Reeves. They would not let Abner dismount, just gave him time to say a few words. They had caught him at Brooken, which is twelve miles to the east of Eufaula; they were taking him to Little Rock. When Brother Abner broke jail at Harrison a $1500.00 reward had been placed on his head.
>
> We followed them into town and one in Eufaula, Johnson and Reeves turned my brother over to Andy Duren, as a guard while they went in search of breakfast. Duren was a deputy placed at Eufaula to keep watch over the inhabitants of its dozen or so residences, two stores, post office, and depot. It was in the front of the post office that Abner was permitted to dismount, his hands having been uncuffed and his feet unshackled. However, from my place on the sidewalk beside my father, I could catch glimpses of Abner through the crowd that milled about. Abner stood beside his horse, handcuffs dangling from one wrist, and the chain still attached to his ankle. Duren stood nearby.
>
> A few minutes later a well-known horse and rider appeared and the crowd parted to let them through. The horse was black, . . . went by the name of Niger. He had never been out run

in several years of competitive territorial horse races. His rider was his owner and my cousin, Abner Brassfield, and it was after Cousin Abner that my brother was named. Cousin Abner, then nearly sixty years of age, dismounted within a few feet of Brother Abner, but Niger walked up by Brother Abner's side. Into my mind leaped the thought that Brother Abner would try to make his get away on Niger. I later learned that almost everyone else thought the same thing but that's where we all were fooled, including Andy Duren.

Into Niger's saddlebag went Brother Abner's hand and when it came out it brought with it a .45 Colt, which we had aftertime named "Old Martha." Cousin Abner lived at Brooken and hearing of Brother Abner's arrest had hurried by our house after "Old Martha." This .45 Colt had been named "Old Martha" after Cousin Abner's wife who had given it to him.

The handcuffs still hanging from one wrist and the chain dragging, brother Abner backed away from the deputy sheriff. The crowd, by the way had suddenly diminished. Duren told brother Abner to stop. Where upon brother Abner retorted, "Go to h<2EM>l." The deputy jerked his gun and fired without taking careful aim. Duren's shot went wild and brother Abner's shot knocked the gun from Duren's hand severing the thumb from the hand. The deputy dived through the post office door. . . . Brother Abner took two parting shots at the door through which the deputy disappeared. His bullets embedded themselves in the woodwork of the door.

When Johnson and Reeves arrived on the scene a minute later, Father and Cousin Abner were placed under arrest and taken to Fort Smith; they were accused of plotting Brother Abner's escape. When the others of us reached home we found brother Abner seated on a chair on the porch with a Winchester between his knees. He had forced a neighbor to cut his chain and handcuffs off.

Dad and Cousin Abner made bond and came back home; made three or four trips to Fort Smith for trial but it was never held and the charges against them were finally dismissed.

Brother Abner stayed around for a few days and then went to Texas. Two years went by before we saw him again. At that time he returned and gave himself up to Grant Johnson. A detective in Texas had broken Abner's arm with a shot. Brother Abner served four years in the Arkansas prison at Little Rock and the Governor pardoned him.

For several years before statehood Brother Abner served on the law force at Eufaula.

Abner S. Brassfield's father's name was Sedrick Perry Brassfield and his cousin who assisted his escape was named Abner B. Brassfield. Deering stated in the hearing before the U.S. commissioner that the escape took place on July 21, 1893. At the hearing before the U.S. commissioner, Abner B. Brassfield was discharged. S. P. Brassfield went to trial over the escape and was found not guilty by a jury on February 6, 1894. This is the second documented case where a white man indicted for a serious crime was arrested by Reeves, served time, and later became a lawman.[3]

Police action by Reeves was reported in the *Muskogee Phoenix* on June 1, 1893:

Last week Robert Marshal, a colored Indian police, well known over the Indian Territory, was arrested by Bos Reeves and taken to Fort Smith on a requisition from Texas for one Robert Marshal Thompson charged with murder. Robert Marshal was not the man wanted and was released. Some years ago Robert Marshal was rather wild and wooly and several men it is said have died from getting troubled with him, but of late years he has been very orderly and law-abiding and an efficient officer.

On July 22, 1893, the *Van Buren Press Argus* reported:

Bob Reeves, colored, son of Bass Reeves, a brakeman on the Central Arkansas & Houston Railway, was killed at Varna, while coupling cars on Friday of last week. His remains were brought to his home in Van Buren and buried on Sunday afternoon. He leaves a wife and two children.

Robert Reeves was the oldest son of Bass Reeves. He had worked with his father as a guard during his teenage years, and his death no doubt was a blow to Bass Reeves and his family.

There are no case files in the National Archives on record that indicate Bass Reeves serving the Fort Smith court after 1893. That year, the number of Fort Smith court case files on record for Reeves is six. It is possible that Reeves's tenure with the Fort Smith court came to an end in 1893. This would correspond with the appointment of U.S. Marshal George Crump on May 29, 1893, to the Fort Smith federal court. Crump was the second former Confederate soldier and Democrat that Reeves would serve under. Crump and Reeves may not have gotten along very well. But Crump did hire other black deputy U.S. marshals for the Fort Smith Court, including Grant Johnson, Rufus Cannon, Bynum Colbert, Ike Rogers, and John Garrett. All the U.S. Marshals whom Reeves worked under at Fort Smith—Daniel Upham, Valentine Dell, Thomas Boles, and Jacob Yoes—were former Union soldiers and Republicans, except John Carroll and Crump.[4]

The record shows that Reeves did work for the U.S. Court for the Eastern District of Texas in the 1890s, which was located at Paris, Texas. The report of the attorney general for 1897 shows that Bass Reeves was stationed at Calvin in the Choctaw Nation under U.S. Marshal J. Shelby Williams for the Eastern District of Texas.[5] Calvin, located on the south bank of the Canadian River north of the Shawnee Hills, was close to the Seminole, Chickasaw, and Creek Nations, and Pottawatomie County, and it was on the Choctaw, Oklahoma and Gulf Railroad line.[6] What is not available is the exact date Reeves began his service with the Texas court. In 1916 a fire reportedly destroyed most of Paris, Texas, and most of the official documents were lost. Also, according to local historians, no federal records exist from this court pertaining to the Indian Territory.[7] But it is a great probability that Bass Reeves was transferred to the Paris court in 1893. Why Reeves left Fort Smith is not known. The reason for him leaving his family also is not known. His wife would succumb to illness a few years later in Fort Smith.

Another piece of evidence that Reeves left the Fort Smith area is that the Fort Smith Business Directory for the years 1894–95 lists Bass's son Newland as working for and living with Judge Isaac C. Parker. This also shows that the judge was a very close friend of the Reeves family.[8]

It was while serving the Texas court at Paris that Reeves patrolled the nefarious saloon towns of Pottawatomie County in Oklahoma Territory. Col. Charles W. Mooney, who grew up in the county and told several interesting stories about Bass Reeves's work there, claimed that in 1895 Bass worked out of the U.S. commissioners' court established at Pauls Valley, Chickasaw Nation. This court was under the jurisdiction of the federal court at Paris, Texas. In Mooney's book *Doctor Jesse*, which is about his father, Dr. Jesse Mooney, he stated:

> It was late in the summer when a messenger rode up for Dr. Jesse to go to the Corner Saloons on an emergency. The horse-back messenger told him, "Bass Reeves was shot in the leg and is calling for you." Dr. Jesse quickly saddled his horse and loaded his saddlebags of medicines and instruments, and started on the ten mile ride across the Canadian River into Oklahoma Territory. As he rode, his mind went back to when he first met Bass Reeves, the Negro Deputy U.S. Marshal. It had been about 8 years before at Belle Starr's house in "Younger's Bend" where the fearless Marshal rode up. Belle told the doctor that Bass Reeves was a good friend of hers and that she trusted him. Dr. Jesse recalled at the time, it was an unusual sort of friendship because Belle Starr was a spy during the Civil War for the Confederacy and reported to Dr. Jesse's father, she was dedicated to the South. For Belle to have anything to do with a Negro was unusual, let alone being a friend to a Deputy U.S. Marshal.
>
> When the doctor arrived at one of the three Corner Saloons, he found Bass Reeves half-standing and half-sitting on a barroom table. He had been shot in the left leg, above the knee. Still lying on the floor in a pool of blood was a young gunslinger with his drawn pistol still in his hand, dead.
>
> "What happened, Bass?" Dr. Jesse asked.
>
> "Just another young gunslinger who doubted my ability with these six-guns," the Negro Marshal said. "He was real fast, but like a lot of them, they couldn't shoot both fast and straight," Bass Reeves explained.
>
> The doctor soon extracted the offending bullet with his

tweezer-type probers, then properly medicated and bandaged the gunshot wound. Refusing the usual $3 fee, Dr. Jesse reminded the Marshal of their friendship for eight years and because both had been a friend of Belle Starr, there would be no charge for his service.

Bass Reeves was not only a fearless, aggressive, and most capable Deputy U.S. Marshal, he was somewhat of a rarity in the south; that of being a Negro Marshal. He was one of the first to fearlessly enter the nefarious Corner Saloons alone, where he had more than once been "called out" for a shoot-out by drunken gunslingers who doubted his skill and accuracy with his two six-shooters. He started holstering his pistols butts forward in 1885, the same year Belle Starr changed to this method. They both agreed this cross-body draw gave them quicker access to their deadly weapons, especially when riding horseback and a split second edge meant life or death.[9]

At the time of Reeves's death, territorial newspapers stated that he had never been shot during his long law enforcement career. The Corner saloons were located in a very remote area and Reeves may not have reported that he had been shot. One newspaper article, reproduced in chapter 18, said that Reeves had been shot in the line of duty, which corroborates Mooney's story

Mooney also wrote that Reeves and Belle Starr's son Eddie Reed had a working relationship. Eddie Reed was sentenced twice to prison by the Judge Isaac C. Parker and was pardoned both times after serving a short time in prison. The last time, his half-sister, Pearl Younger, had become a prostitute in Van Buren and Fort Smith to raise money to hire a lawyer to get him pardoned. Later, in 1893, Parker had Eddie Reed appointed a deputy U.S. marshal. The judge explained later that Eddie really never had a chance in life, so he gave him this trusted appointment. Judge Parker specifically requested Bass Reeves to break in Eddie Reed on his new position as a law enforcement officer. He knew Bass had been a personal friend of Belle Starr, and knew the capable Reeves would teach Reed the proper methods in performing his duties.

Reeves then took Eddie Reed "under his wing" and taught him the finer points of being a deputy marshal. For over three years Reeves considered Eddie to be his protégé. According to Mooney, Bass and Eddie investigated a murder together that happened about a half mile east of the saloon town of Keokuk Falls on May 15, 1895. The victim, Zachariah W. Thatch, was a well-respected man who had lived in Washington County, Arkansas, for several years. He had taken as a traveling partner a man named Casharego, alias Wilson.

Wilson, a man about twenty-six years old, was a known swindler, thief, and forger who had been out of the state prison in Tennessee less than a year before. He had been seen the evening before in the Red Dog Saloon in Keokuk Falls, where he had imbibed heavily before returning to his camp. Several persons later testified they saw Wilson and Thatch in camp together just before dark on that fateful night, and shortly after dark they heard two shots fired.

The next day the corpse was found floating face down in nearby Rock Creek just before its confluence with the North Canadian River. The body had lodged among some rocks and dead branches in the shallow creek. Two fingers on the right hand had been blown away, and the victim's head had been split open from a blow with an axe.

A few days later, according to Mooney, Bass Reeves and Reed arrested Wilson near the north bank of the North Canadian River on the Kickapoo reservation just north of the present town of McLoud, Oklahoma. The marshals were investigating the crime for the Fort Smith federal court.

Wilson at first claimed Thatch was his uncle, and said Thatch left the wagon and team with the camping supplies and equipment in his care and had gone farther west to hunt. When confronted with the corpse, Wilson identified the body, then confessed he was not the dead man's relative and that his real name was James C. Casharego of Conway, Arkansas; he denied he had murdered Thatch.

Reeves found a bloodstained axe in Wilson's wagon. Blood was still on Wilson's trousers, although his feeble alibi was that he had killed a rabbit and it had stained his trousers as he carried it back to his camp on the riverbank.

With more investigation, Reeves located the former campsite and thought it strange to find two campfires. He knew campers seldom build a second fire, especially not right against a tree. Wilson had burned a fire over the exact spot next to the tree where he murdered his victim and where his victim bled on the ground.

The extremely dry weather at the time of the fatal crime had caused the earth to crack open, and blood from the murdered man trickled deep into one of the fissures. Reeves and Reed dug down under the ashes and found the bloodstains. They collected several chunks of the bloodstained earth, which they carefully put in a saddlebag as evidence. Later, according to Mooney, Reeves testified at the trial in Judge Parker's court about the intensive investigation.

Wilson was sentenced to death and was the last man to be hanged on the famous gallows at Fort Smith. He was executed on July 30, 1896. Both Reeves and Reed witnessed the hanging.[10]

While researching the arrest of James Casharego, alias George Wilson, at the National Historic Site at Fort Smith, Arkansas, I found documents stating that Wilson was arrested by a Deputy U.S. Marshal Large, but no evidence on who might have assisted with the investigation and arrest. The file for the murder case contains no testimony of the witnesses at the trial. In a recent biography on Judge Isaac C. Parker, historian Michael J. Brodhead states that evidence in the James Casharego murder trial was found in the exact manner as discussed by Mooney, but Brodhead doesn't give the names of the deputies involved in the investigation.[11]

For many years in the twentieth century, a newspaperman named Alexander White Neville wrote a column for the *Paris (TX) News* entitled "Backward Glances." It talked about historical events that took place in the north Texas communities during the frontier days. In one columns, Neville talked about an incident that occurred in the 1890s that caused much racial violence. In Lamar County, Texas, near Paris, Jarrett Burns, a black man, got into a quarrel with his white neighbor named John Ashley. The feuding came to a head when Ashley shot and killed Burns. Additionally, Ashley's horses and mules began dying and eventually all his stock died. Next his house was burned. Ashley's friends believed Jarrett's relatives and black friends poisoned his stock and set fire to his home.

These incidents caused Ashley's friends to come to his assistance in retaliation. Not knowing if they were guilty of any crime, a mob hanged several black farmers on trees in the vicinity of Little Sandy Creek and Jefferson Road. Whites made threats that more African Americans would be hanged as soon as they were found.

The majority of blacks in the community left that area of Texas after Sheriff Gunn arrested about half a dozen and put them in jail, charged with being implicated in burning Ashley's home. Later, Sheriff Gunn heard that a mob intended to take the blacks from the jail and lynch them, a threat not to be taken lightly in Texas.

There were many federal prisoners in the jail at that time, besides the county prisoners. U.S. Marshal Dickerson summoned his deputies to Paris to protect the jail. It was reported that more than sixty deputy U.S. marshals were assembled for possible defensive action at the Lamar County jail. The residents of Paris, Texas, noted that one deputy stood out in the crowd of lawmen due to his size and color, Deputy U.S. Marshal Bass Reeves. The white mob never made an attempt on the jail, and cooler heads prevailed. It must have been a shock for some of the white Texas citizens to see this tall, stern-looking black deputy marshal from Indian country. Although he was assigned to the federal court at Paris, Reeves worked almost exclusively north of the Red River in Indian Territory.[12]

A white man, J. B. Sparks, who had been a pioneer in the territory, told a story concerning Reeves that occurred near Calvin:

> Bass Reeves was a Negro, but he was a U.S. marshal and made a brave officer. He was sent to get two outlaws near Atwood. He caught and arrested them and that night he went to Frank Casey's home and had them fix beds in the yard so he could sleep with both prisoners handcuffed to him.[13]

Without their father around, two of Bass's sons, Newland and Edgar, got in trouble with the law in Arkansas. On June 8, 1895, the *Van Buren Press* reported that according to the *Fort Smith Record*, Newland had received five years and Edgar one year in the Arkansas Penitentiary. The *Press* went on to say, "These are Bass Reeves' boys and have started early on a criminal life. They lived and were born in this city but for a long time have resided at Fort Smith."

Later in the year, on November 9, the *Van Buren Press* carried a story saying that the Arkansas governor had pardoned Ed Reeves, age sixteen, who was convicted of perjury in Sebastian County and sentenced to one year in the penitentiary, in order to enable him to testify against another party accused of the same offense, probably his brother Newland.[14]

In Fort Smith, Arkansas, the *Weekly Elevator* on March 27, 1896, carried a brief report: "Mrs. Bass Reeves, colored, died at her home in this city last Friday night. She was about 40 years old." However, the Fort Smith City Death Records reveal discrepancies with the newspaper report. Jennie Reeves was fifty-six years old at the time of her death. She probably looked much younger, hence the age given by the newspaper. Jennie had lived in Arkansas for about twenty-five years, which meant she moved into the state around 1870. She was born in Sherman, Texas. Her father's name is not listed, but her mother's name is given as Betty Haynes. Jennie died March 19, two days after the execution in Fort Smith of the notorious African Cherokee outlaw, Crawford Goldsby, also known as "Cherokee Bill," the most famous outlaw in the history of the Indian Territory. The cause of Jennie's death was peritonitis resulting from cancer. The duration of her illness was two years. The name of her doctor was J. G. Thomas. She was buried in the city cemetery now known as Oak Cemetery. It is apparent to me that Bass Reeves was not residing with his wife at the time of her death because a man named Green Saunders, Reeves's son-in-law (daughter Sallie's husband), paid for the burial, which was conducted by Birnie Funeral Home in Fort Smith.[15]

In June 1895 the Christian brothers, Bob and Bill, were being held in the Oklahoma County Jail in Oklahoma City for killing Pottawatomie County Deputy Sheriff Will Turner. On June 30, they made a successful jail break and in the process killed Oklahoma City Police Chief Milton Jones. The brothers, on the run from the law, put together a tough gang of desperados that included John Fessenden, John Reeves, Doc Williams, and a notorious black outlaw named Ben Brown. Lawmen hunted down and killed some of the gang members, but the Christian brothers remained on the run. About a year later, the federal court at Paris was still trying to locate them in the Indian Territory. On June 10, 1896, the newspaper in Ardmore, which was in the Chickasaw Nation, reported that a posse including Bass Reeves and black posseman Bill Colbert was involved in the federal hunt for the Christian brothers:

Close to Them: Deputy Marshals Chasing the
Christian Gang—An Ardmoreite in It

Paris, Tex., June 9.—Deputy Marshals Brockington, Chancellor, Gibbs, Reeves, Colbert and Lewis Williams, have returned from a trip into the Creek nation, where they went to try and capture the Christian gang. They trailed them to their rendezvous on the Deep Fork of the Canadian in the western part of the nation. As they approached the place which consisted of two cabins built of heavy logs with port holes, a negro named Will Stevenson came out and made fight. Brockington, Reeves and Williams had one cabin covered and Chancellor, Gibbs and Colbert the one Stevenson was in. When Stevenson attempted to shoot the officers fired, wounding him so that he only lived a short time. Dick Sanger, the negro in the other cabin, was with much difficulty induced to surrender. After capturing Sanger it was learned that the Creek authorities had offered a reward for him and Stevenson for robbing a man of $15,000 a few days before, and he was turned over to them. The Christian gang had been at the place only a short time before the arrival of the officers but had left. The cabins were in an unfrequented part of the country and were made for the purpose of defense. Had Stevenson not been killed at the beginning the officers would have had a hard fight.

Historians believe that the Christian brothers escaped to the New Mexico Territory where they formed a train-robbing gang called the High Fives.[16] But on June 18, 1896, the *Muskogee Phoenix* reported in the "Local Paragraphs" column that "Deputy Marshal Bass Reeves killed a horse thief whom he was trying to arrest in the Seminole country Thursday of last week." It is my assertion that Bass Reeves never went after the infamous outlaw Cherokee Bill and the Bill Cook gang during the mid-1890s because he was working for the federal court in Paris, Texas, at the time. Bill and the Cook gang fell under the jurisdiction of the Fort Smith court. Reeves's job as deputy U.S. marshal at the time was primarily patrolling the southern Creek Nation, and the Seminole and Chickasaw Nations. The Cook gang operated primarily in the northern Cherokee Nation and northern Creek Nation.

The Fort Smith federal court, under the leadership of Isaac C. Parker, was quickly coming to a close. New federal courts were installed in the Indian Territory at Ardmore for the Southern District, McAlester for the Central District, and Muskogee for the Northern District. These three courts would have full jurisdiction over federal crimes committed in the Indian Territory.

George S. Winston, Parker's black private bailiff, had served with the judge up until the appointment of Marshal George J. Crump by President Grover Cleveland to succeed Marshal Jacob Yoes. Parker was pressured to appoint a white Democrat, John Bloomburg, as bailiff to appease the new Democratic regime. Winston was a lifelong Republican, as were most African Americans during that era, because Republicans were in office when slavery was abolished. The Democratic Party had brokered the end of Reconstruction after the Civil War in the United States.

Winston was born a slave on February 5, 1846, near West Point, Georgia. After the Civil War, he joined the U.S. Army and mustered in at Jefferson Barracks near St. Louis, Missouri. He was sent to Fort Harker, where he was assigned to Company B, 38th Infantry Regiment. Later he was transferred to Company E, 24th Infantry, and was stationed at Fort Griffin and Fort Concho. Winston was given his discharge papers on May 15, 1870, and sought employment in Fort Smith, Arkansas. In the spring of 1872, Winston was appointed one of the six bailiffs to serve in the federal courtroom under Judge William Story. When Parker was appointed, he appointed Winston his private bailiff on the recommendation of all the court officers. Winston became a prominent member of the African American community in Fort Smith.[17]

The Democratic Party's takeover of all the federal political appointees in Fort Smith from the Republican Party occurred eight months before the end of Parker's reign as judge of the Fort Smith court. September 1, 1896, was the official end of Parker's court. Bass Reeves's long tenure with the court demonstrates that Parker and Reeves must have had a good working relationship. Parker had also presided over Reeves's murder trial. It is known that Parker, on occasion, could sway juries in his instructions and remarks. If Parker hadn't personally liked Reeves, he most likely wouldn't have come back to the district as a deputy U.S. marshal after the trial.[18]

In a documentary film on Isaac C. Parker's career, Bass Reeves's great-nephew, retired federal judge Paul L. Brady, described Reeves and Parker's relationship:

> They developed a very close working relationship. In spite of the widely diverse backgrounds, one a slave, one a former congressman, one educated, one who was not. Bass had no semblance of any formal education. They developed a very deep respect for each other. I think that perhaps this was based upon their overriding sense of duty and responsibility that they had learned earlier in their lives. Perhaps with some Christian backgrounds and some Christian teachings, because both were very versed in the scriptures from their early learning, he convinced Bass to join him in helping to establish the rule of law over the rule of men. And to bring law where there had never been any law before. He reminded Bass, that he would be in a position to serve as a deputy to show the lawful as well as the lawless that a black man was the equal of any other law enforcement officer on the frontier.[19]

Judge Isaac C. Parker said, "A coward can be honest, but a coward could never be a deputy." He died in Fort Smith on the morning of November 17, 1896, at the age of fifty-eight after an illness of several months.[20]

The Indian Territory was the most dangerous place in the "Wild West" during the late nineteenth century. From time to time the territorial newspapers would carry stories about crime and its impact on local citizens. The following editorial comes from the *Muskogee Phoenix* of September 10, 1896:

> Among the disagreeable facts about the Indian Territory that we can't conceal is the prevalence of crime. We try to draw the curtain over the horrible spectacle of the past year's aggregate

of crime but its no use. Cold facts stare us in the face and we are not doing our duty unless we give the facts publicly.

We have been looking over the files of the Phoenix for the past year and the grand aggregate of homicides is appalling in the extreme. No less than one hundred and ten killings, more or less willful and premeditated, were committed within the borders of this territory during the past twelve months. In the whole United States last year there were 6,200 homicides, about one for every 10,000 of our entire population. In the Indian Territory the rate was about one for every 3,000 inhabitants. This is startling but it is true. No state in the Union furnished half so many murders as the Indian Territory, population compared. People may doubt this but statistics prove it. A great many of these killings were justifiable and many never reached an investigation because they were between Indians and the United States courts had no jurisdiction. Many were never brought to light until all clues were obliterated by time and their explanation is still and will ever be a mystery.

It is not with a desire to arouse any sensational interest that we present these cold-blooded facts. One victim every third day in the year is the record, and it is a record that would better fit the dark ages than the nineteenth century. Such wholesale murder is a blot upon the record of any country and is a stigma upon civilization. We lay the cause of reckless state affairs at the feet of no race, but its existence is a flaming denunciation of the condition of affairs in our country. This wholesale taking of human life leaves its stamp upon the fair Indian Territory and is little wonder that we are stigmatized as a bloodthirsty and crime-producing community.

In Congress and throughout the states they harp upon the Indian Territory being the home of outlaws, the land of desperados, the hotbed of crime and murder. The Phoenix has denounced such accusations, has repudiated such statements and has maintained that the Indian country was no more the land of blood and crime than any other commonwealth. It is with a feeling of sorrow rather than of humiliation that we bow our head and acknowledge that the bloody record of the past twelve months belies our claims and refutes our boasts. In the face of the daily tragedies that are flashed before us, we must submit and cry out for deliverance. The very cause of humanity, the sanctity of home, the cardinal principal of self preservation, with one accord protest against a longer continuance of any system that makes possible such wholesale prevalence of the taking of human life. There is a limit to human endurance and the 70,000 law-abiding Indians and the 300,000 law-abiding whites will not continually submit to a state of affairs that subjects their property and their lives to more than the average risk attendant upon mankind in other civilized communities.

A year later Reeves was working in the Muskogee vicinity a few months before he was officially assigned to the federal court of that city under U.S. Marshal Leo Bennett. It appears that Reeves was reassigned from Paris, Texas, to the Northern District of Indian Territory during the last months of the administration of U.S. Marshal Samuel M. Rutherford, who was appointed U.S. marshal for the Northern District in March 1895.

On June 2, 1897, Bass Reeves arrested Louis Peters for unlawfully wearing a pistol as a weapon at Lee in the Creek Nation. Also at Lee, on June 3, Reeves arrested Samuel Manuel on a charge of obtaining property by false pretenses. Reeves arrested a William Wright at Muskogee on June 18 for stealing a cow. All three arrests were made on bench warrants signed by Marshal Rutherford. Manuel had obtained forty dollars by selling five steers that he didn't own to a Marion C. Lacey. In the *Muskogee Phoenix* of August 5, 1897, Bass Reeves was noted for bringing in fugitives from a black settlement called Sodom Town located near Wagoner north of Muskogee in the Creek Nation:

Commissioner Jackson's Court

David Ross and Hugh Perryman, two young negroes of Sodom Town, rode a horse each, the property of John McClellan, in town on last Saturday and proceeded to offer to trade them. T. B. Miller, a trader, recognized the horses and so notified them. He went to the court house to report the matter and the boys decamped on their own horses that were on the outskirts of town. Bass Reeves was soon in hot pursuit and caught them about eight miles west of town. The owner came and identified the horses, and now, in default of bail they lie in the bastile to wait the action of the grand jury next October in Vinita.[21]

An outside newspaper, the *Kansas City Star*, featured an extensive article on the Indian Territory in 1897. The writer described the Indian police he found on duty in and around Muskogee, including one black Indian policeman, who may not have been an Indian policeman at all, but deputy U.S. Marshal Bass Reeves:

> The Indian constabulary of the Creek and Cherokee nations are called "Light Horse police." In the Creek country many of them are citizen negroes, and they are a fine, dashing lot of men, fearless riders and if need be, savage fighters. One seen in Muscogee last week would have delighted the eye of Remington. He seemed to have dropped out of a Remington picture. He was coal black and sat on his white horse like a Prussian grenadier. He wore a reefer jacket buttoned to the chin; the large pearl buttons on it glinted in the sun. His head was covered by a wide brimmed black hat. His trim legs were encased in tight fighting breeches and riding boots, and his coat was bulged on the hips by the big cavalry revolvers strapped to his side. He was the type of officer who brings back his prisoner when he goes after him.[22]

The largest number of blacks assigned to the Creek Nation's Lighthorse police were located in the Muskogee District. The article could have been describing any one of them, but to me it sounds very much like Reeves, who was stationed at Muskogee at the time. The large black hat, the white horse, the two large pistols, and the erect sitting position on the horse sounds familiar. It wouldn't be the first time he was described as "coal black" by a white person. Reeves had probably achieved a good "suntan" from being constantly in the saddle.

The next move for Reeves was his last one in the Indian Territory. This would be the last federal court he would work for up to the time of statehood. Reeves never again worked the Choctaw, Chickasaw or

Seminole nations, where he had worked during the previous twenty years of his law enforcement career. The last ten years of his career took place primarily in the Creek and Cherokee nations. Much of this police work was in the city of Muskogee, the most important town in the Indian Territory. Judge Isaac C. Parker and the Fort Smith and Paris federal courts would now only be a memory.

Bass Reeves was deeply affected by the 1896 U.S. Supreme Court decision in *Plessy vs. Ferguson*. The case evolved from an incident that occurred in Louisiana in June 1892. A thirty-year-old shoemaker named Homer Plessy was jailed for sitting in the "white" car of the East Louisiana Railroad. It was said that Plessy was one-eighth black and seven-eighths white, but under Louisiana law he was considered an African American and therefore required to sit in the "colored" car. Plessy went to court in Louisiana and lost the case. He next appealed to the U.S. Supreme Court, which ruled that the precedent that separated facilities for blacks and whites were constitutional as long as the facilities were "equal." The decision by the Supreme Court was quickly extended to cover many areas of public life such as restaurants, theaters, restrooms, and public schools in the United States. Although this decision didn't immediately impact the Indian Territory, Bass Reeves felt he had been betrayed by the U.S. government. Reeves would now stand toward the rear at crowd gatherings and not be as vocal as he had been in the past.[23]

13.

Northern District, Indian Territory

By 1897 the Northern Federal District for the Indian Territory, with headquarters at Muskogee, now comprised the Cherokee, Creek, and Seminole Nations and the Quapaw Agency. Courts met in Muskogee in the Creek Nation, Vinita and Tahlequah in the Cherokee Nation, and Miami in the Quapaw country. Muskogee was a division headquarters for the Missouri, Kansas, and Texas (MK&T) Railroad, where thousands of cattle were shipped to markets. With the advantage of being able to fatten trail-weary herds of Texas cattle before shipment to slaughterhouses, Muskogee was definitely cowboy country. From the time when it was the end of the rail for "the Katy," as the MK&T was called back in the 1870s, Muskogee had been a rowdy and wild town. It remained a lively city up until statehood in 1907. Muskogee wasn't incorporated until 1898; before then, the town proper was policed by U.S. Indian Police who also had deputy U.S. marshal commissions. The business leaders appointed a city marshal from the Indian police. After 1898, Muskogee had a city police force, but once again, much of the police work fell to the deputy U.S. marshals of the Northern Federal District.

On September 21, 1897, President William McKinley appointed Dr. Leo E. Bennett as U.S. marshal for the Northern District of Indian Territory. Born in Kansas in November 1857, he was the son of Dr. James E. and Martha A. Bennett. The family moved to Fort Smith,

Arkansas, where Leo attended public school. Later he attended the prestigious Rugby Academy in Wilmington, Delaware, and the University of Michigan at Ann Arbor prior to attending medical school at the University of Tennessee. In 1883, after medical school, Bennett moved to Eufaula, Creek Nation, Indian Territory, to practice medicine. Besides his main occupation, Bennett started a newspaper in Eufaula, entitled the *Indian Journal*, in 1887. That same year, Bennett operated a store north of Muskogee on the MK&T Railroad. He made frequent trips to Washington DC and successfully obtained a post office at the small but growing railroad switchyard north of Gibson Station. This post office became known as the town of Wagoner. In 1888 Dr. Bennett sold his interest in the *Eufaula Indian Journal* and moved to Muskogee. He married a Creek Indian citizen named Lonie Stidham, the daughter of G. W. Stidham, and started a prosperous newspaper, the *Muskogee Phoenix*. On September 21, 1889, Bennett was appointed Indian agent for the Five Civilized Tribes, headquartered at Muskogee. Bennett was a Republican and became one of the founders of the party in Indian Territory. At the time of his appointment as U.S. marshal, Bennett increased the number of deputy U.S. marshals that served the Northern District to twenty-four. Some of the notable veteran deputies retained and placed by Bennett included J. F. "Bud" Ledbetter, Paden Tolbert, David Adams, Grant Johnson, and Bass Reeves. The presiding U.S. judge for the Northern District was John Robert Thomas.[1]

On September 30, 1897, two days after Bass Reeves arrested a murderer, a black man named George Cully, on the streets of Muskogee, the *Muskogee Phoenix* carried the following story:

Murdered and Robbed

Monday last Dick Carr, who had made a crop on the Scott Gentry farm at Choska, brought a load of cotton to town, sold it, got the money and started for home. He reached the Arkansas river after nightfall. The ferrymen, who were on the opposite side, heard the wagon and began pulling across. While crossing a gun-shot was heard. Having crossed, they waited for some time for the wagon to approach, and finally, at the suggestion of one that some accident had probably been met with, they searched for the wagon, which was found just at the bank of the river some distance from the water, as the river is very low. The team had gone but a few yards from the traveled roadway and stopped. Carr was found dead in his wagon with a bullet hole in the back part of his head, seemingly made with a small bored gun at very short range. Carr is supposed to have had $50 or $60 in money about him, but a few dollars in silver is all that was found on the body.

An alarm was sent out, a messenger sent immediately to Muskogee and search began for the murder.

Bud Kell left Muskogee for the scene of the crime with trained dogs and put them on the trail, but so much travel and the length of time which had elapsed rendered the work of the canines unsatisfactory.

Parties had seen a small negro, who gave his name as George Adams, but is known here as George Cully, following the road which Carr had taken, and is said to have inquired as to the passing of wagons ahead of him. He was riding and carried a small Winchester. Later in the evening he was seen passing back over the route he had traveled.

Search was made for this man and he was finally traced to this city where he was taken in charge and placed in jail. The actions of this man before the time of the killing and since lead many to think he is the murderer.[2]

Cully was the third person executed in Muskogee by the federal court. He is the only person that I can document that Reeves arrested and was later convicted in court and executed. The *Muskogee Phoenix* printed the following story a day before the execution:

Tomorrow George Cully, in jail for past two years will hang. Found guilty in October of 1897 before Judge Thomas; Cully is a negro about 5'8"150 lbs., charged and identified as the man who shot a merchant at Miami in attempt to rob store; just a little before he was arrested for the killing of Carr and has an unsavory reputation for several years. Cully lived with his aunt, Miss Peters west of town, came to town on September

27, 1897, and seen Dick Carr secure some money from Mr. Turner for load of cotton and when Carr left that night for his home at Choska he had followed him out of town and murdered Carr. He went back to his aunt's where he was captured a little later; man killed was white, 47 seven years old with a good reputation. Cully sentenced first time Christmas eve 1897 to hang February 25, 1898, his attorneys Twine and Lowery, gave him a lease on life but higher court confirmed; May 6, Judge Thomas sentenced Cully to hang July 21.[3]

Later that year, news of Judge Bennett's appointment as U.S. marshal reached the papers. The *Fort Gibson Post* ran the following story on October 21, 1897:

It's Marshal Bennett Now: He Assumed Charge of His Office Saturday Last

Muskogee, October 18—Saturday afternoon Hon. Leo E. Bennett was sworn in and assumed charge of the Northern District. The oath of office was administered by Judge Wm. M. Springer, after which the Judge congratulated the new marshal upon his preferment and promised his hearty co-operation in the performance of his duties. At the same time Judge Springer expressed his thanks to retiring Marshal Rutherford for the very able and efficient manner in which he had discharged his duties during his term of office.

On November 6, 1897, U.S. Marshal Leo E. Bennett sent his list of names he appointed as deputy U.S. marshals for the Northern District to the U.S. attorney general in Washington DC. There were forty names, an increase from the twenty-four he had earlier appointed. The deputy marshals were appointed by Bennett on October 10, 1897, and were given their respective duty locations in the district. David Adams and Orlando Dobson were stationed at Muskogee, Bud Ledbetter and Paden Tolbert at Vinita, Grant Johnson, the Creek Freedman, at Eufaula, and Bass Reeves at a town due west of Eufaula in the Creek Nation named Wetumka. This headquarters for Reeves gave him an opportunity to again team with Grant Johnson on various occasions.[4]

On October 22, 1897, Bass Reeves located and arrested a horse thief named Joe Justice and brought him into the court of U.S. Commissioner W. C. Jackson. Justice had stolen a chestnut mare from Mack Adair who lived near Fort Gibson, Cherokee Nation. Bud Ledbetter had subpoenas in regard to this arrest for Robert McPherson, Willis McPherson, and William Ward, but couldn't deliver them due to high water. The case file doesn't include the final disposition of this case but does include three witnesses giving testimony before the U.S. commissioner that Justice stole the horse.[5]

A farmer, Sam Austin, was arrested by Bass Reeves on November 9, 1897, and placed in the federal jail at Muskogee for selling mortgaged property. Austin sold one thousand pounds of cotton to E. M. Wright for $1.50 per hundred pounds. The cotton had a lien placed against it due to a mortgage agreement Austin had made with W. J. Parker and W. A. Lamon. A few months later, Lamon would have a run-in with Reeves.[6]

In January, Bass arrested a man named Frank Blackburn for horse theft. Reeves gave testimony before U.S. commissioner W. C. Jackson on January 25, 1898:

> I am a deputy U.S. marshal. On January 7th, 1898, I arrested defendants on the Verdigris. When I arrested him defendant Frank Blackburn wanted to go to a schoolhouse. I went with him and he talked to a boy. The boy was riding a bay horse that I afterwards captured at Annie Islands. Frank at first denied having a bay horse he afterwards admitted to having him and took me to Annie Islands where I found the horse concealed in a smoke house. He told me that he took up the horse on Thursday night. Said at first it was his mothers horse and afterwards said he took him up as a stray.
>
> [signed] Bass Reeves

Annie Island testified:

I know defendants Will Blackburn and Frank Blackburn. Sometime in January 1898 this month, Frank Blackburn came to my house riding a bay horse. He staid a few minutes and went away. On Friday he sent the horse back there by my little boy. I put the horse in a little house. The next day Deputy Bass Reeves came and got the horse. Defendant Frank Blackburn was with him at the time.

[signed] Annie Island

A man named Mose Andy testified next, and given his testimony he must have been acting as posseman for Reeves:

I know defendants. On January, Friday 7th, 1898, Bass Reeves arrested defendants Will Blackburn and Frank Blackburn for horse stealing. We received information that one of the stolen horses was at Annie Islands and we went over and found the bay horse. We brought the horse to Muscogee. Aaron Berryhill came in on Monday 10th, 1898, and found the horse to be his. He identified the horse as his and he was turned over to him.

He was farmer by Mose Jamison the man he got the horse from. Defendant claimed the horse a stray when he was arrested.

[signed] Ale Andy

Mose Andy signed his name Ale, but on the marshal's return it was given as Mose. The next and last person to testify was Aaron Berryhill:

I know defendants Will and Frank Blackburn. On or about January 6th, 1898, about four days before Deputy Bass Reeves arrested defendants. I lost one bay horse running on the range branded—C—I got my horse a few days after he was stolen from Deputy Bass Reeves here in Muscogee. The horse was worth about $30.00 The horse was taken without my knowledge or consent. I saw the horse on Wednesday morning before he was taken and Wednesday before I got him back on Monday.

[signed] Aaron Berryhill

All the people except Andy signed their testimony with an "x," including Reeves. The defendant pled not guilty. The outcome of the case is not apparent in the file.[7]

Bass Reeves arrested James McKellop for assault with intent to kill on February 15, 1898. The assault with a deadly weapon, a pistol, occurred on September 8, 1897, near Wagoner. McKellop was placed in the federal jail at Muskogee. D. L. Maxwell gave the following testimony before the grand jury hearing this case:

I live on Col. Robisons farm. I know the Phillips. I was at home on the 8th of last Sept. I live within a half a mile of them. On the morning of this day I was down towards their place, within a quarter of them when I heard the shooting. It was about eight o'clock, I had been in the field at work. The first of the shooting was rapid, four of five shots came in rapid succession, there was a pause, and then two more shots. All these shots came from the direction of and was close to Phillips house. I started towards the shooting to stop it because I thought some reckless fellow was doing it and endangering my hands who were at work.

When I heard the woman scream, I called the cotton hands cause I knew that something was wrong around there. When I got to the house the defendant was gone. I found Mr. and Mrs. Phillips injured. Phillips shot in each leg, and the woman had a shot in the ankle. The gun of Mr. Phillips was in the house, I don't recollect whether it was above the door or on the bed. We were very much excited; I think it was a cap and ball muzzle loader, I as I remember it, I examined it and it was empty. As soon as we arrived Phillips spoke up and said Jim McKellop had been there and shot them. We made arrangements to get a Doctor and I went to Muskogee and swore out a warrant against defendant. I noted fresh horse tracks in the yard. I saw the bullet mark on the door sill, it was fresh. The shots were loud and quick like a pistol shot and they all sounded as if they came from the same gun.[8]

With a larger number of whites moving into the Indian Territory, white attitudes and morals of the era became more prevalent and were accompanied by racial violence. Bass Reeves was called in on more than a few of these criminal cases. One of the most shocking occurred in the spring of 1898. It was detailed in the *Muskogee Phoenix* on Thursday, March 24, 1898:

A Mob's Horrible Work: A Saturday Night Tragedy Wherein Three Lives Were Lost—Bungling and Brutal Work of Assassins

A few miles north of Muskogee, between the Arkansas and Verdigris rivers, is a strip of country that has been the scene of many a dark deed and brutal murder in years that are past. It has at different times within recent years been the rendezvous of desperate and daring outlaws and criminals, and has always been regarded as a tough section. But in the annals of all the crimes of this section that which stained the record of Saturday night was perhaps the most uncalled for and brutal.

Ed Chalmers, a state-raised negro, was living in a little hut not far from Wybark with a white woman by the name of Mary Headley. They were said to be married and certainly claimed to their neighbors that they were man and wife. So far as is known they were both harmless and peaceable residents and were industrious farmers. The fact that a white woman and a negro man were married living as man and wife grated on the nerves of some of the residents of this section. This was but natural. The manner in which these neighbors took to show their dissatisfaction over this disgusting alliance was, however, most unnatural and uncalled for. A few of the near residents, all supposed to be white persons, assembled Saturday night and during the rain and storm proceeded to the humble home of these two poor ignorant sinners and transgressors of the law, and literally murdered them in cold blood. The details of the tragedy that took place at the lonely cabin in the woods on this dark night are not as yet fully known. The results of the raid were clear and distinct, however. Jim Mathews, one of the parties composing the mob, was found dead next morning by the M.K.&T. railway track, a mile from the scene of the killing. Whether killed by accident, by one of his own party or by the negro man in defending his life is not known. The white woman was shot to death in her bed and her negro consort was shot to pieces though he lived until nine o'clock Sunday morning. Here was the fatal error in the work of the midnight assassins. The negro man, the only human being on earth who saw and knew of the frightful raid, was not killed. Before he died the following morning he made a dying statement in which he named several parties as the guilty ones.

Early Sunday morning a messenger came running into Muskogee and informed the officers that a man and woman had been killed across the river. Scarcely had this messenger departed when word came that another man had been found near the Katy track with a bullet hole through his body. Deputy Bass Reeves was at once dispatched to the scene of the triple tragedy—the man who was found at the track evidently shot at the house where the two other parties were killed—and instructed to find all the facts so far as possible. Strange rumors of the complicity of certain white citizens in the horrible affair soon grew into reasonable certainties, and the actions of these parties on this night, the finding of their dead companion and the dying statement of the dead Negro, all coupled together, formed a web around certain parties that justified their arrest. Bright and early Monday morning Marshal Bennett was on the ground and in conjunction with his deputies arrested Ed Burnes, section foreman at Wybark; his two assistants, R. T. Mills and Robert Blalock; C. W. Gaines, station agent at Gibson, and W. A. Lamon, a merchant at Gibson. All are white men and all have heretofore borne good reputations. Rumor has it that others are also suspicioned, but we refrain from publishing names as we desire to do no one an injustice.

These five men were taken to Wagoner Monday and arraigned before the grand jury. What the result of the grand jury investigation is we have not yet learned. Excitement at Wagoner and the settlements across the river was at its height all day Monday and Tuesday and is by no means abated yet. The parties who stand charged with the frightful killings have many friends who insist upon their innocence and many theories to advance for the occurrence of the terrible tragedies. One thing is certain: It will only be a short time until all the facts are known and the guilt be placed where it belongs. No such crime as that, with the many circumstantial clues, can ever be hidden, and a few days, at most, will place the whole affair at rights.

For the good name of the Indian Territory and the Northern District in particular, it is to be hoped that the guilty ones, whether they be the ones now charged or others, will be speedily punished. It matters not how grievous was the crime of the negro man and white woman, they certainly afforded no excuse for the wanton butchery of the mob and those who imagined they or society were aggrieved knew or should have known that there was a lawful way to reach those who violate the laws of the land. There is no excuse under heaven for midnight raid and murder and each and every participant is equally guilty for the lives of all three who perished most foully on this night and as a consequence of this mob assault.

This incident became known as the "Wybark Tragedy." It was the second act of white mob violence within several months in the Northern District. The first one occurred in January in the Seminole Nation where two young Indians were burned to death because they were mistakenly identified as murderers of a white woman and her baby. That incident became known as the "Seminole Burnings." The *Muskogee Evening Times* on March 22, 1898, stated that the grand jury had indicted three men in the Wybark case: William A. Lamon, merchant at Gibson Station, north of present-day Okay, Oklahoma; George Gaines, the depot agent at Gibson Station; and Layton Sharpe. Ed Burns, section foreman, and his two men, Blalock and Mills, were implicated but released.[9]

The *Muskogee Evening Times* reported on March 24, 1898:

Head Suspects Turned Loose

The Times learns today that all the hand-car men arrested on the charge of complicity in the Wybark tragedy were released from custody yesterday. They should not have been arrested in the first place, as the matter of their having been at Blackstone switch, three miles above Wybark on that night cuts no figure.

Railroaders are a class of people who seldom mix up in any mob other than railroad strikes or in some way concerned.

From all available evidence, no one went to prison for this incident, which is different from the outcome of the Seminole Burnings, where individuals were sent to prison. In 1996 an elderly African American named Lawrence "Sundown" Downs from Wagoner, Oklahoma, remembered his parents talking about the arrest of the prosperous William A. Lamon, known as "Cap" Lamon. He owned two cotton gins and bragged he wasn't ever going to be arrested by any lawman. Downs didn't know what crime Lamon was arrested for.

> I just heard my folks talking. He [Reeves] was a pretty tough fellow they say. Bass Reeves was an officer of some kind. He was just a guy who was not scared, he was not no scared fellow. Bass arrested old man Lamon at Gibson Station, Lamon had a gin down there. He was in the cotton field and old Bass eased up on him that day and told him to put them up right there in the cotton field.[10]

Operating in the northern portion of the federal district, Bass Reeves arrested William Thomas and John Hunter near Talala, Cherokee Nation, for stealing eleven head of cattle. He committed the prisoners to the Muskogee federal jail on April 3, 1898, at 8 p.m.. Six witnesses, who lived in Talala or Bartlesville, testified against Thomas and Hunter. After Hunter was found guilty, his family tried to establish an alibi, saying he was at home at the time of the theft, and asked for a new trial. Hunter was given a new trial and found guilty again by a jury on December 7, 1898.[11]

Jacob Davis stole a mare in October 1897 and was later arrested by federal lawmen. In April 1898 Bass Reeves and Grant Johnson delivered subpoenas in the Muskogee and Eufaula area for the court in this case. Davis was found guilty by a jury trial.[12]

Research shows that in May 1898, Bass Reeves was assigned to work in the city of Muskogee to help curb the vice in town. Muskogee gambling dens and houses of prostitution were getting out of hand. Reeves arrested Myrtle Kidd on May 18 for maintaining a house of prostitution and arrested Mandy Jackson three days later on the same charge.[13]

Reeves arrested a "Myrtle" for vagrancy on May 17, and George Ray, J. R. Green, John Mackey, John Brown, Henderson Brown, Joe Carson, "Tahlequah Kidd," Bob Wallace, Peter Brown, Jim Thomas, Mat Thomas, Newt Steel, "Big Red," Howell Cobb, "One Virgil," and Samson Jones for gaming between May 16 and 25. Gaming in the Indian Territory was considered as unlawfully betting money and chips, "being then and there valuable things, on a game at cards, to wit: bragg, bluff, poker, stud poker, seven-up, three-up, twenty-one, vingtun, thirteen cards, the odd trick, forty-five, whist, draw poker, euchre, hearts, casino, high-five, pitch and cinch; contrary to the form of the statue in such case made and provided, and against the peace and dignity of the United States of America."[14]

On June 3, 1898, a lady named Lucy Evans, a cook and chambermaid for a rooming house in Muskogee, was arrested by Reeves for theft. She was accused of stealing a diamond stud pin and pearl stud pin from O. R. Wilson, an occupant named of the Robinson Hotel. The crime occurred on May 26. A jury trial found her innocent on December 16, 1898.[15]

On August 20 Bass Reeves arrested Jake McDaniel for selling whiskey at Ridge, which was located seven miles west of Taft, in the Creek Nation. McDaniel had bought 1 ½ gallons of whiskey in Oklahoma Territory and brought it to the Indian Territory. He sold a half pint to Jack Hawkins at Ridge on February 26. The witnesses against McDaniel were Hawkins, John Wear, and Jake Simmons, the famous Creek Freedman rancher. McDaniel pled guilty before the U.S. commissioner.[16]

On June 30, 1898, a double tragedy struck in a Muskogee house of ill repute run by Myrtle Kidd. Abe Liggins beat to death a John Gunter with a bludgeon and his brother did likewise to J. A. Shanhaltzer. Reeves arrested and brought both parties into the Muskogee federal jail on August 1.[17]

Reeves arrested a storeowner named R. H. Scofield on September 26, 1898, for receiving stolen property in Muskogee. Charles Hicks, an arrested felon, before the U.S. commissioner in regard to Scofield's activities:

> I know the defendant R.H. Scofield. He runs a second-hand business in Muscogee.

I have been bound over and am now in jail on the Burglary and Larceny.

The stuff I stole from houses I sold to defendant. He knows it was stolen. Every time I went to his store with goods he would ask me if it was "wet goods" and if it was I would say so and it was not I would tell him it was not. By "wet goods" I mean stolen goods.

I sold him an over-coat which I stole from Myrtle Kidd. It was worth about seven or eight dollars. I traded coat to defendant for a pair of second-hand shoes. I told him the coat was stolen.

I sold him a pair of pants which came from Operator Perry's. They were worth about $1.50. He understood that they were stolen. "I sold him a clock that came from Wagoner, I.T. He understood it was stolen. It was worth $12.00.

I have sent several things there by other parties.

It was understood that he would handle anything I would take to him.

He furnished me two keys, to be used in getting into houses, and told us to put him in a supply of anything that was valuable. He said he would not "turn me up" but couldn't pay me much for the goods. He made us a key to get the goods with. He said the key he made would fit any common door.[18]

A complaint of grand larceny was sworn against a seventeen-year-old man named Mike Horerine in the Central District of Indian Territory. As a fugitive from justice, Horerine was picked up near Claremore and lodged in the federal jail at Muskogee. His mother lived five miles west of Sapulpa. On November 18, Bass Reeves transported Horerine to the Central District jail at South McAlester for incarceration prior to trial.[19]

On August 4, 1898, Isaac Jones killed a man named Johnson Tiger with a knife. The case file isn't clear whether Reeves made the arrest of Jones. There is no name in the case file for the deputy U.S. marshal who made the arrest. Most likely it was Bass. He did handle the seven subpoenas for the murder trial on December 6, 1898. Gibson Taylor gave the following testimony to the U.S. commissioner:

Isaac Jones, Johnson Tiger and myself left the Mekusukey dance ground sometime after twelve o'clock to go to Earlsboro; I think Isaac Jones suggested it, but both Isaac Jones and Johnson Tiger spoke to me; each of us rode a pony and went very slow; it must have been four o'clock when we reached Earlsboro; we woke a man up and got a pint of whiskey; Johnson Tiger paid for it and put it in his pocket; we all three drank it up as we started back to Mekusukey over the same road; I drank least of all; before we got to the place where the trouble occurred the sun was up, it was getting hot and the whiskey was all gone; when we crossed a branch on the road coming home Johnson Tiger started his horse and rode on ahead; me and Isaac Jones were riding behind him and then Isaac Jones took after Johnson Tiger almost as soon as he left; nothing was said that I know of at the time they started and there had been no trouble up to this time; I then rode on slowly behind them and over took them and they were on the prairie at the edge of the road; Johnson Tiger and Isaac Jones were talking to each other and I rode right on without stopping and passed them; Isaac asked Johnson Tiger as I passed if he was drunk; I kept right on and when I turned back again I found Johnson Tiger was wounded; after I passed them I went on to the creek which is near by and stopped there a while and then I turned and come back and as I come back I met Isaac Jones and he had a knife open and in his hand; it was all bloody; I stopped and I said to him 'Isaac you have done something you ought not to have done' and I then took hold of his hand and tried to get the knife from him; were both on horse back and he said to me are you going back to that fellow and then he jerked it away and he went up the road towards Mekusukey a little ways to a little branch and then turned off; I then went on to the place where I had left them talking in the road and there I found Johnson Tiger lying on the road and I got down and spoke to him and he asked me says how did it happen I got hurt and I told him Isaac stabbed him with a knife I then left him and went to Mekusukey for assistance.[20]

This crime evidently was caused by the consumption of too much whiskey. The parties appear to be Indians who left the Seminole Nation, crossed the border into Pottawatomie County of Oklahoma Territory, and bought whiskey at Earlsboro, where the sale of whiskey was legal. Two of the parties subpoenaed by Reeves included a deputy U.S. marshal named N. M. Douglas and his posseman William Gates, both of Shawnee, Oklahoma Territory.

Bass Reeves arrested Cub Hanks, a noncitizen of the Indian nations, who stole a purse, clothing, and money amounting to seventeen dollars from a female named Patrice McIntosh. Reeves recovered some of the stolen items and presented the evidence in court. This incident occurred on December 2, 1898.[21]

As evidenced, the crimes that Bass Reeves was now attending to in the late 1890s were somewhat different than those he dealt with in the courts of Paris and Fort Smith. Reeves would spend some time in the saddle during his last ten years as lawman, but more and more he used a one-horse carriage or walked a beat. Moving into the twentieth century, Reeves would eventually become more a town cop with rural responsibilities. The days of riding his magnificent horses over the great expanse of prairie for weeks and months at a time, looking for desperados, were long gone. One aspect that didn't change was his ability to catch criminals who broke the law.

14.

Muskogee Marshal

By the late 1890s the white population had grown to more than two hundred thousand, from a total of sixty thousand in the Indian Territory in 1875. On March 3, 1893, Congress passed legislation authorizing negotiations with the Indians to the enrollment and allotment of their lands. Henry L. Dawes from Massachusetts was the chairman of this initiative, which became known as the Dawes Commission. Indians and Freedmen were given land allotments after enrolling, usually 160 acres; some received more, some less. This was the beginning of the end of Indian Territory. After all the allotments were given, the Indian Territory would be opened for settlement by U.S. citizens. This would bring about the end of the sovereign nations of the Indian Territory, and hasten Oklahoma statehood. An earlier act of Congress, the Curtis Act of 1898, laid the foundation for individual land titles in Indian Territory, by allowing noncitizens to own the lots on which they lived or did business. This act had a major impact on Muskogee because it authorized the segregation of town sites and the sale of town lots to the persons occupying them, whether they were whites or Indians.[1]

Muskogee always had a large African American presence, the original members being freedmen of the Muscogee Creek Indian Nation. At the time of the arrival of the Missouri, Kansas, and Texas Railroad in 1872, blacks made up the majority population of the small hamlet. When Muskogee incorporated in November 1898, the voting population of the

KANSAS

1. Peoria
2. Quapaw
3. Ottawa
4. Shawnee
5. Modoc
6. Wyandotte
7. Seneca

N

0 _____ 50
miles

MISSOURI

1
2
3 4 5
6
7

ARKANSAS

Miami

IRON MOUNTAIN & SOUTHERN RR

Verdigris

Nowata

Vinita

Cherokee

Grand

Claremore

Tulsa

Sapulpa

Wagoner   Tahlequah

Arkansas

Coweta

Creek

Muskogee

Fort Gibson

Boley

Okmulgee

Deep Fork

Checotah

Weleetka

North

Canadian

Shawnee

Eufaula

Seminole

Wewoka

Wetumka

Canadian

Purcell

Corner

Washita

Calvin

CHOCTAW, OKLAHOMA, & GULF RR

COLORADO

Ada

Pauls Valley

Choctaw

Chickasaw

MISSOURI, KANSAS, & TEXAS RR

ST. LOUIS & SAN FRANCISCO RR

& SANTA FE RR

Boggy Depot

Tishomingo

Ardmore

Hugo

Durant

Red

Paris

TEXAS

MAP 2. Indian Territory, 1890, after separation of territory
into Oklahoma Territory and Indian Territory

town numbered 1,088 African Americans, 744 whites, and 406 Native Americans. Although blacks had a numerical advantage, white businessmen and Indians had the upper hand in political affairs. This can be attributed to the lack of educational opportunities for African Americans at that time. All the newly elected leading officials were primarily white men. Blacks did have political clout and used it until statehood in 1907. Generally they aligned themselves with the Republican Party. There was a split in the black population between the Indian Freedmen, who called themselves "Natives," and the "State Raised Negroes," as they called the newcomers. The Freedmen, though generally less school-educated, were excellent independent ranchers and farmers. The blacks from other states, however, tended to be better school-educated but more economically dependent. The two groups did not get along until well after statehood, when state Jim Crow laws impacted both groups severely. Most of the time during the territorial era, the Indian Freedmen held close ties to the full-blood politics of the Five Tribes. They were some of the most ardent vocalists and agitators against the Dawes Commission.[2]

The oldest Baptist church in town was known initially as the Muskogee Baptist Church, serving both the Indian and black population. Later, it became a predominantly African American congregation known as Fountain Baptist Church. This is the oldest Baptist church in the state of Oklahoma today. Indian Freedmen would celebrate Emancipation Day each year in Muskogee on August 4. The celebrations would take place on the north side of Muskogee. Grant Foreman, author of a history of Muskogee, wrote, "Day and night, from one end of the camp to the other, could be heard the voice of the lunch vendor, the squeak of fiddles, and twang of banjos and guitars, accompanied by the voices of prompters on dance platforms. These celebrations were not limited to one day, but sometimes ran for a week, or as long as the interest was sustained, and visitors continued to arrive."[3]

The 1900 census credited Muskogee with an approximate population of 4,300. By 1906 the population was estimated at over 15,000. The town was growing in leaps and bounds. There was never any forced segregated residential housing in Muskogee based on race or ethnicity prior to statehood. Blacks, whites, and Indians lived together harmoniously in Muskogee, although there were areas where you found a greater concentration of African Americans living, both in and outside town. Tulsa's black community made great strides in the following decade due to the discovery of oil, but during the first decade of the twentieth century, Muskogee had one of the most progressive African American business communities, not just in the Indian Territory, but anywhere in the United States. According to the Muskogee city directory, by 1906 blacks owned the following businesses in town:

Attorneys 11
Auctioneers. 1
Baggage Delivery 2
Barbers. 6
Billiard Halls 4
Blacksmith 5
Boots and Shoes 1
Cigars and Tobacco 1
Clothing (Elliott Brothers) . . 1
Dressmakers. 8
Drug Stores 1
Dry Goods 1
Dryers-Cleaning. 1
Feed and Grain 1
Grocery Stores 28
Hairdressers 3
Hotels. 2
Insurance Company 1
Jewelers 2
Livery Stable 1
Meat Markets. 5
Millinery 2
Merchant Tailors 3
Newspapers 3
Notions 1
Painters 2
Paper Hangers. 1
Physicians 10

There were also seven African American lodges and societies in town. White and Indian consumers were also catered to by the black business establishments. The black-owned Elliot Brothers Clothing Store was considered the best in town. Muskogee had two black business districts, one on Second Street and one on Fon du Lac Street. In later decades, three of the greatest jazz musicians in history would come out of this community, violinist Claude Williams, pianist Jay McShann, and saxophonist Don Byas. The principal law enforcement officer for the black community in Muskogee at the turn of the century was Bass Reeves, and would remain so until statehood.[4]

It appears that Bass Reeves arrested principally African and Native American felons during his years in Muskogee. Research shows he would still arrest whites if the occasion called for it. There were also some major racial conflicts taking place in various towns in both Oklahoma and Indian territories during this time. Reeves would be involved in a few of these incidents that took place in and near Muskogee.

Clarence L. Sherman, a white resident of the Indian Territory during this period, told the following story concerning Reeves:

> One time a Negro deputy by the name Bass Reeves had the choice of some routine work or capturing a black man who had killed a fellow for a bale of cotton. Reeves said, "Let Sherman and Adams go to Muskogee and serve the papers," he said he did not want to get mixed up with white folks. "I will go and get this man or bring his boots." When we returned he had his man in the wagon. "What happened," we asked. "Well, he got in a log cabin and started firing at me, so I had to kill him," said the colored officer.[5]

I. F. Williams, another white resident of the Muskogee vicinity during this time, said:

Bass Reeves was a bad Negro and wasn't afraid to come out after the bad ones. He didn't bother much about the white outlaws but worried after the Creek and Cherokee Negroes and Indians. The United States officers arrested them when they stole or did anything against the whites.

He would sometimes make the arrest alone and bring the prisoners to the wagon in which they would be chained. I saw him one time when he had three prisoners who brought him a reward of $1000.00

He tried to hire me to go and guard the wagon, but I wouldn't go with him because he was a Negro and I didn't think a white man should work under a Negro. It sounds like it would be soft job to guard some prisoners who were chained to a wagon, but it was really as dangerous to capture them. Sometimes the prisoners had been surprised and caught without a fight but a marshal never knew exactly what would happen when he started after some men. After he got them in the wagon, the guards had to be careful or two or three of the friends of the prisoners would come up and throw guns on the guards and release the prisoners.[6]

Reeves was busy capturing wrongdoers in the new year of 1899. On January 25 he arrested Lewis Flowers for assault with intent to kill. Flowers had used a Winchester rifle to shoot James Anderson on November 10, 1898, at Wellington, Creek Nation, after an argument the night before between the parties.[7]

The following month, on February 27, Reeves arrested Aleck Johnson for assault with intent to kill. Johnson had used a knife to stab Joe Rector during a dance at Falls Store, Creek Nation, on October 22, 1898. Rector described what happened at the dance:

On Oct. 22nd 1898 at Falls Store about 9 miles from Muscogee, I.T. I was at a dance, I was standing by the side of house inside when defendant came along and stood on my feet. I told him to keep off. He said take your damn feet up and put them either in your pocket or mouth. I went in the room when they were dancing and was looking at the dance, he came up behind me and said something I didn't understand, he then threw his hand . . . in front of me and stabbed me in the shoulder with a knife. We were both pushed out of doors when, he again ran up and stabbed me in the back. John Morrison then grabbed him, threw him down and took the knife away from him.

I did not hit him with a whip. My side was against the wall. I was laid up about 2 weeks.[8]

The *Muskogee Phoenix* on March 30, 1899, carried a couple of reports on Reeves's police work:

Aaron Grayson, who was charged with assault with intent to kill, while being pursued very closely by Deputy Bass Reeves, swam the Verdigris river in order to escape being arrested.

Mann Manuel arrested by Deputy Bass Reeves and committed to jail by commissioner Jackson last Saturday.

Back in Fort Smith, Arkansas, Bass's son Edgar was getting into further trouble with the law. On April 22, 1899, the *Van Buren Press* reported that Edgar, in a fit of jealous rage, had cut the throat of his girlfriend, Emma Littlejohn, and had then escaped. There is no information available whether Miss Littlejohn lived or died, or if Edgar was apprehended by the law.[9]

On May 17, 1899, Reeves arrested Charley Peyton for horse theft in the Cherokee Nation. Columbus M. Evatt testified in court:

I know defendant. On about May 4th 1899 near Braggs I.T. I received information that defendant had my brown three year old mare branded bar L on left shoulder. I looked for mare and man. I received information that he had gone toward Tahlequah. I followed him several days and finally located the mare at old man named Ham in the Cherokee [Nation] near the Arkansas line. The defendant came in afterwards. Ham said defendant bought the mare there. And defendant took [the horse] over in a large hollow and had her hid. He claimed to have swapped for the mare from Alonzo Rummells. Where we found defendant in possession of mare is about 60 miles from where she was taken. She is worth about $50. She was taken off the range.[10]

Reeves arrested Allen Haynes in Muskogee on May 31, 1899, for stealing a twenty-five-dollar bicycle. It is interesting to note that during this era in Muskogee, a bicycle was called a "wheel." Will Ritter testified in court:

> I was riding my wheel on May 30th. I saw a boy named Shepard riding a wheel, I told him it was Bert Estes wheel. He said I will take you to the fellow I got it from. He took me where defendant was as I said, "Is this the boy you got the wheel from." I told defendant that was Mr. Estes wheel. He said, "I won it shooting craps down to the R.R. track from some little colored fellow." I asked him if he would know him if he would see him he said he would not. I reported to Mr. Estes where his wheel was.[11]

Another arrest made by Reeves for horse theft occurred on September 8. Robert Worthman was arrested at Muskogee and lodged in the federal jail. L. W. Willits later testified in court concerning the theft:

> I don't know defendant. On July 1st 1899 in Tulsa, I had one bay mare stolen from where she was hitched. I then hunted for her. I found her on September 8, 1899 in Muskogee I.T. in possession of Thomas Owen. Owen said he got her from defendant. She is worth about $50.00 I don't know who took her. Owen turned the mare over to me.
>
> The mare was taken sometime in the night. Charles Willits rode the mare there. I was not in town and don't know . . . when she was taken.[12]

In February 1899 a big fire burned many buildings in the downtown section of Muskogee. During the fire, there were a few thefts of personal belongings from residences and buildings. In October Bass Reeves arrested one of the persons accused of being involved in these crimes. A businessman named William Owen testified:

> I know defendant when I see him. On February 23rd, 1899, morning of the big fire. I had stolen from my room over my Drug store in Muscogee I.T. one ladies hunting case gold watch with the name of Mary H. Severs engraved in the back of the

valise about $60.00. Also a mint gold watch chain and a night [illegible] and Masonic chain with William Owen, Muskogee Country No. 1. I received information that defendant had my watch. The chain and clock were worth about $75.00. I went and asked defendant if he had the watch. He said he had not had a ladies watch.

Sanford Jones testified:

I know defendant. On or about October 20th, 1899 I saw defendant with a ladies gold watch at Jim Richardson's. I saw defendant pull out the watch and Mrs. Richardson wanted to trade but he would not let her see it. [13]

On December 2, 1899, Reeves arrested a man named Dick Fatt for making false testimony to the Dawes Commission for land allotment in the Creek Indian Nation. In testimony on April 3, he lied about the property he was trying to acquire by saying he had lived on the property and made improvements on it. He later testified that he filed on the property by instructions from a man named Pigler. Pigler told him that once he lived on the land for two or three years he would give Fatt all the improvements made to the 180-acre parcel. The land actually belonged to a Mrs. L. A. Berry. The government then filed perjury charges against Fatt, and Reeves made the arrest. [14]

Bass Reeves had made the transition to Muskogee very smoothly. He would gain a new family and friends, and he would become an indispensable deputy for Marshal Leo Bennett.

15.

A New Century

The following short notice appeared in the *Muskogee Phoenix* on January 18, 1900:

> Bass Reeves, the well known colored deputy marshal at this place, was married last Sunday at Muskogee.

Bass married Winnie J. Sumner, a previously wedded Cherokee Freedwoman originally from Tahlequah in the Cherokee Nation. Winnie had been born to Caroline Foreman and Dred Foreman. At the time of Winnie's birth, her mother was a slave of William P. Ross of the famous Ross family of the Cherokee Nation. In the 1900 U.S. Census, taken in June, Bass and Winnie lived on Altemont Street in Muskogee with three of Bass's sons from his previous marriage: Benjamin, born in June 1880; Homer, born in July 1882; and Bass Jr., born in April 1887. Also living in the house was one of Winnie's children from her previous marriage, Estella Sumner, born in July 1887. In the census report Winnie's age is given as thirty-one and 1869 as her year of birth. But the following year, when she and three of her children from her former marriage were trying to get on the Cherokee Freedmen Rolls, she gave a different age, forty-three, before the Dawes Commission. This would mean she was born around 1858, also consistent with her being born into servitude. Winnie's first husband's name was Ben Sumner, and they lived for some time in Kansas, where she had moved after the Civil War.

Winnie's first application with the commission was turned down, but on April 22, 1904, she and her children, Bennie, Charlie, and Estella Sumner, were admitted to the Cherokee Freedmen Rolls by the acting commissioner of Indian Affairs.[1]

Reeves's new marriage evidently did not hamper his police work. Reeves arrested Richard Edwards on February 6 for burglary. Edwards had broken into a store owned by a Creek Nation citizen named John Drew and stole merchandise on the night of December 16, 1899, at a place known as Pecan Creek.[2]

In contrast to his arresting parties for stealing cattle or horses, Reeves arrested Lee Peters and John Johnson on May 8, 1900, for the theft of five hogs and one sow, valued at sixty dollars, belonging to J. O. Cravens. The rustling took place at Ridge, in the Creek Nation, seven miles west of Taft. A jury convicted Lee Peters of receiving stolen property, and he was sentenced to one year and one day, to be served at the penitentiary at Fort Leavenworth, Kansas.[3]

Later in the month, on the 29th, Reeves arrested Sandy Gray and David Marcey, citizens of the Creek Nation, for committing an assault with intent to kill. Phillip Johnson had reported to individuals that Gray and Marcey had stolen their horse. Gray and Marcey caught up with Johnson near Okmulgee on the night of April 12. Gray shot Johnson three times with a .44 Winchester rifle. Johnson was hit in the arm each time he was shot. At the U.S. commissioners' hearing, Marcey was discharged and Gray was held on a five-hundred-dollar bond for a court date in Muskogee.[4]

Nero Harrison, alias Nero Nevins, of Checotah was arrested by Reeves on November 27, 1900, for adultery. Harrison convinced a young woman, Hattie Haverson, who lived near Ridge, that he was a single man and needed a wife. He talked her into leaving her mother's house with him under the pretext of getting married. After having relations with the man, Haverson found out that Harrison was married. This occurred in June 1900.[5]

On December 1, 1900, Reeves arrested a woman named Belle Williams on an arson charge. She was accused of burning down a house located near Ridge, Creek Nation, that was worth three hundred dollars.[6]

The arrest record of the U.S. docket of Muskogee for U.S. Marshal Leo Bennett during 1899 shows Bass Reeves making the following partial list of arrests in 1900:

Joe Arnold, age 22, Negro, Larceny, arrested June 5, 1900, received 364 days in the Fort Smith Jail.

Louis Banks, age 38, white, Assault to Rape, arrested October 24, 1899, received 21 years in the penitentiary in Columbus, Ohio. Began sentence on June 7, 1900.

Richard Bennett, Negro, age 24, Larceny, arrested November 10, 1899, received 2 years and 6 months at Fort Smith. Began sentence on February 25, 1900.

William Blake, Negro, age 28, Introducing and Selling, arrested January 5, 1900, sentenced to 90 days.

John Buckner, Negro, age 24, Larceny, arrested February 2, 1900, discharged.

Charity Barnes, Negro, age 21, Robbery, arrested April 16, 1900. Released on bond.

E. E. Buchanan, white, age 36, Larceny, arrested, July 27, 1900.

David Bennett, Indian, age 26, Aggravated Assault, arrested October 26, 1900. Discharged November 8, 1900.

Cy Brown, Negro, age 21, Aggravated Assault, arrested December 23, 1900. Received 30 days and a $5.00 fine.

Mark Chisolm, Indian, age 30, Larceny, arrested March 3, 1900. Received 2 years in the penitentiary in Columbus, Ohio. Began sentence on July 31, 1900.

Jim Coy, white, age 28, Larceny, arrested March 3, 1900. Released on bond.

Will Clussoe, Indian, age 17, Larceny, arrested April 2, 1900. Received 364 days at Fort Smith.

One Charley, Indian, age 31, Larceny, arrested July 16, 1900.

Abram Davis, Negro, age 40, False Pretense, arrested November 15, 1900.

Red Davis, Negro, age 27, Larceny, arrested June 27, 1900.

Ed Eryland, white, age 30, Assault to Kill, arrested February 2, 1900. Released on bond.

This gives the reader an idea of the crime, age, and race of the parties Bass Reeves was capturing at the turn of the century in the Indian Territory. While the majority of arrests were of African Americans and Indians, Reeves was still arresting some whites. This aspect of criminal justice is unique in American history; very few, if any, African American policemen outside the Indian Territory were empowered to arrest white citizens anywhere in the United States at the dawn of the twentieth century.[7]

The *Muskogee Evening Times* printed the following article on September 25, 1901:

Three Landed by Deputy Reeves

Sometime ago Orlando Dobson a deputy marshal and Bill Vann, his posseman, raised, it is charged, all sorts of disturbance over at Okmulgee. Dobson skipped out, likewise Vann was in the van in leaving for a hiding place. The marshal's office got news of Vann and that he was scouting over about Ft. Gibson. Deputy Bass Reeves was sent out for him and he "cotched" him. Reeves also caught two colored fellows John Wolf and J. C. McElway. The latter is a powerful negro and has two charges of whiskey, one charge of carrying concealed weapons, and one of wife beating, against him. All of them were taken to jail this morning where they will await trial.

Orlando Dobson had been one of the busiest deputy U.S. marshals associated with the federal court at Muskogee during the 1890s. Dobson and Vann were charged with disturbing the peace of the family of Mrs. J. L. Neal and for assault with the intent to kill a white man named Ed Fatima. All the parties lived at Okmulgee. This was another case of lawmen abusing their power in the territory.[8]

Reeves youngest son, Bass Reeves Jr., died of pneumonia in Muskogee on October 19, 1901. He was buried in the Muskogee city cemetery now known as Green Hill Cemetery. Bass Junior was fourteen years of age when he passed. After the funeral, Reeves continued his duties as town deputy.[9]

Reeves arrested Edward Walker for the crime of bigamy on October 23, 1901. He had married a woman in Van Buren, Arkansas, left the state, and set up another home in Muskogee with a lady without getting a divorce from his wife. It is interesting to note that this crime fell under the jurisdiction of the federal court.[10]

An article about the case appeared in the *Muskogee Phoenix* on October 31, 1901:

Had Too Many Wives

Deputy Bass Reeves came in Sunday with Ed Walker. Walker is a colored gentleman who sometimes preaches, or as he puts it, he is an exhauster of the scriptures. His time and mind is not wholly given to the sacred book and its teachings, however, for occasionally he finds time to make love to the fair sex of his own color with satisfactory results to himself. In one particular, Walker is a Mormon, at least he believes in that doctrine to the extent that a man is entitled to as many wives as he can get, and for having more than one darling to love, obey and worship him, he was lodged in the U.S. jail to await the action of the court.

Another article appeared in the same newspaper on the same day concerning Reeves making a sex-crime arrest:

Monday, Bass Reeves arrested John Hill, colored, who is charged with incest, his own daughter being the victim. Hill is also charged with assault, and has an unsavory reputation wherever he is known.[11]

The *Muskogee Phoenix* ran two articles on November 7, 1901, concerning Reeves's police work:

William Bussie, charged with assault to kill, was brought in Thursday by Bass Reeves and lodged in jail.

Yesterday Deputy Bass Reeves brought in the following colored gentlemen; Gabriel Jamason, Isaac Ponds, James Jimison, Early Griffin, Samuel Tucker, Grant Colbert, Calvin Jamison, and Washington Barnett; caught on the banks of the Arkansas River shooting craps. Commissioner Sanson fined Barnett and Ponds fifteen dollars each and the others ten dollars each.[12]

A week later the same newspaper ran the following two articles in which Reeves is mentioned:

Bass Reeves, Saturday brought in one Charley Wright with being perniciously active in trying to destroy his neighbors' hogs by dogging and otherwise mutilating them.

Serious Charge

Wm. Perryman, near Choska, Sunday appealed to the marshal to help him secure his grand-daughter, Lizzie White, aged 14, who had run away with one Tom Risby. Marshal Bennett sent Deputy Bass Reeves out to arrest the parties and he brought in the girl, who returned with her grandfather. Risby was not captured. It is likely he will be charged with abduction, as the girl strenuously denies any ground for more serious charge.[13]

Another article concerning Bass Reeves appeared in the same *Muskogee Phoenix* edition. It highlighted his law enforcement career in the territory and provided some unique historical data:

Life Full of Excitement: Deputy Bass Reeves Has Arrested More Than Three Thousand Men, Killed 12 of Them

Bass Reeves, a negro deputy marshal, working for the Muskogee court, claims that he has been a deputy for twenty-seven years; that during that time he has arrested more than three thousand men and women. He has, according to his statement, during that time killed twelve men. Two of them were brothers and belonged to the Bruner family of negroes, who roamed over the northwestern part of the Indian Territory for many years.

Reeves says that he was well acquainted with all the members of that family; fifteen in number, and that eleven of them died with their boots on. He also says that a Seminole Indian is the hardest man to arrest of any class of people he ever met; that he is always ready and if given a ghost of a chance he will shoot you and run.

When the civil war broke out Reeves was a slave and be-longed to Colonel George Reeves of Grayson county, Tex. Col-onel Reeves joined the Eleventh Texas Cavalry and fought with the South during the war. Bass was with his master during that time. He was in the battles of Chickamauga and Missionary Ridge. Later he was in the battle of Pea Ridge, Ark. And saw General McCullock when he fell.[14]

I mentioned earlier in the book why I felt Reeves reported the story about being a body servant during the Civil War. This would be one way for Reeves to make former Confederates and their sympathizers who worked around him more comfortable.

By the beginning of the twentieth century, Reeves had become a celebrity in the Indian Territory. But there would be no ego for him. He just wanted to be the best lawman he could be.

16.

Devotion to Duty

B ass Reeves was reappointed deputy U.S. marshal for the Northern District of Indian Territory, effective January 10, 1902. An
appointment form sent by U.S. Marshal Leo E. Bennett to the
U.S. attorney general in Washington DC on March 17, 1902, showed
Reeves and John L. Brown as the two most senior men in the district,
with twenty years service or more. Also appointed were Grant Johnson
of Eufaula with fourteen years of service; Dave Adams of Muskogee with
twelve years; Paden Tolbert of Vinita with twelve years; G. S. White, also
of Vinita, with ten years, and A. J. Trail of Claremore with four years of
service. Reeves and David Adams, a white man, were the two deputies
stationed at Muskogee. They would work together on numerous criminal cases in and around Muskogee. Many times, Adams would serve as
Reeves's posse. Bud Ledbetter, another white deputy whom Bass worked
with in Muskogee was not appointed at this time because he was the city
marshal in Vinita.[1]

According to historian Glenn Shirley, Muskogee was distinguished in
the Indian Territory:

> The city was permanent headquarters of the Dawes Commis-
> sion and its several hundred employees; the United States clerk's
> office was a busy place with a large staff; the recording officers
> of the territory, the main office of the Five Tribes added many

more employees to the government payroll; more government-franked mail left the post office than from any other in the United States except Washington; and Gen. Pleasant Porter had his executive offices and home there. The streets and hotels were jammed daily with Indians, lawyers, real estate speculators, adventurers, confidence men and grafters. Despite the efforts of local police, hop-ale and "uno" (you know) joints still supplied the thirsty. These shortcomings aside, Muskogee was, indeed, the most important commercial, financial, and industrial center in the Territory.[2]

As mentioned earlier, the Northern District, over which Reeves had jurisdiction, covered the Cherokee, Creek, and Seminole Nations. The May 31, 1902, *Cherokee Advocate* of Tahlequah reported on racial problems in the Cherokee Nation:

Twenty-Four Men Arrested

Muskogee, May 20.—Deputy United States Marshals Adams and Reeves came in Braggs to day with twenty-four prisoners who are charged with taking part in the race war.

The deputies made the arrest without resistance. All prisoners were bound over and will be tried in the United States court tomorrow.—Ardmore Appeal.

During this period in the Indian and Oklahoma territories there were some serious racial problems. In August 1901, because of some problems with newly arrived blacks, a white citizens' committee in Sapulpa, Creek Nation, had decided that all African Americans not of Creek Indian blood would have to leave town. In April 1902 the whites of Lawton in Oklahoma Territory threatened to drive the black people out of town, which led to fighting in the street between black and white citizens. The Oklahoma National Guard was put on standby for possible action. In April 1903 Deputy Adams took a posse to Braggs again due to rioting by blacks and whites. He arrested seventeen white and black men after one man had been wounded. At Wybark, ten miles north of Muskogee in the Creek Nation, a newspaper reported in 1904, "a white man was not allowed to stop after sunset and the negroes had everything their own way."[3]

The incident that resonates most with many who follow the life and career of Deputy U.S. Marshal Bass Reeves is the time he had to arrest his own son for murder. This tragic event took place in 1902. Richard Fronterhouse interviewed Alice Spahn, the youngest daughter and last living child of Bass Reeves, in December 1959. From this interview, Fronterhouse wrote:

> Bass and his deep-seated belief in the law are legendary. Nothing could deter him when he was forced to make a decision where the law was concerned. As proof of this, consider the time he arrested his own son for murder. (Author's [Fronterhouse's] Note. Since many innocent persons who are living today would be affected if the full story were told, no family names or dates are given in the following accounts, and only those facts essential to an understanding of what actually happened are given. The name "Bill" has been assumed by the author.)
>
> One of Bass' five sons, Bill, had married a beautiful Negro girl and was a native of the Indian Territory. They settled in Muskogee, Indian Territory and were happy at first, but Bill's work kept him away from home so much that this happiness was relatively short-lived. Bill's wife was a beautiful girl, and with Bill being gone so much, loneliness and the need for attention were probably the factors which caused the trouble to start.
>
> Bill realized that something was wrong with his marriage for his wife was drifting further and further away from him. He began to work harder than ever before in the hope that providing his wife with all the luxuries he could muster would win her back. This was a laudable course of action, but it only compounded the problem, for by working harder he was away from home even more. The situation progressed steadily from a small problem until it reached the point where Bill felt he had to try something else. He returned home unexpectedly one day to talk things over with his wife. He walked in and caught his wife with another man.
>
> Bill was hurt and mad, but he didn't do anything. He and his wife were reconciled with Bill completely forgiving her because

he honestly felt that he was directly responsible for the whole problem by being away from home so much. He found a new job that would enable him to remain at home. Bill's home life improved after this incident, and his wife seemed better satisfied and happier.

Bill and his father were very close; they had no secrets between them. One day, over a congenial glass of Forty-Rod, Bill told Bass about the trouble he and his wife had had and asked him how he would have acted in his place. Bass' answer was short and to the point. He is quoted as saying: "I'd have shot hell out of the man and whipped the living God out of her." This bit of advice must have made a lasting impression on Bill.

Shortly after telling his father about his previous troubles, Bill came home from work and found his wife again with another man. In the battle that followed, the man Bill had caught in his place escaped, bloody and beaten, but otherwise unharmed. However, in a hysterical rage, he killed his wife. Realizing what he had done, he ran away into the wilds of the Indian Territory.

Naturally, since a crime had been committed, a warrant was issued for the arrest of Bill with the charge of murder. However, since the warrant called for the arrest of Bass Reeves' son, the court and Chief Marshal Bennett in Muskogee were at a loss over what to do. Marshal Bennett wanted to send a deputy after Bill, but he also wanted to bring him in alive if he could. In addition to this, everyone concerned hated to go after the son of a man as respected and well-liked as Bass Reeves, particularly when the circumstances leading to the crime were considered. For two days the warrant lay on Marshal Bennett's desk with all of the deputies fearing that they would be chosen to serve it. Bass himself eventually solved the problem.

Bass was visibly shaken by what had happened. Perhaps he was remembering the advice he had given Bill and felt partly responsible. Whatever he thought, Bass went to Marshal Bennett and demanded the warrant. He told the marshal that it was his son who was wanted, and that it was his responsibility to bring him in. Marshal Bennett reluctantly gave Bass the warrant, and he left town on another manhunt.

Almost two weeks passed before he returned with Bill. He turned him over to the marshal, and Bill was bound over for trial.

During the trial, the damning fact that Bill had bolted and ran condemned him. He was convicted, sentenced to prison, and was quickly transferred to the Federal Prison at Leavenworth, Kansas. Bill stood up under the ordeal of his trial quite well; he didn't plead or whine in an attempt to influence the court towards leniency. He admitted killing his wife and then running away, never clearly elaborating on the reasons why he did it. Bass stood by him every moment, right up to the time that Bill boarded the train for Leavenworth.

When Bill reached Leavenworth, he was resigned to serving his full sentence. He became a model prisoner, establishing a perfect record unmarred by any prison demerits. This became an extremely important point in the chain of events that followed.

Many important, influential people in Muskogee, eventually learning of what actually led to the murder, felt that Bill had not been treated fairly. A citizen's petition was drafted and circulated expressing the opinions of this group, and it was presented to the proper authorities in an attempt to obtain Bill's pardon. This petition, coupled with the model prison record, resulted in a full pardon and Bill's subsequent release from prison. Bill returned to Muskogee to live, and became one of the city's most popular barbers.

Perhaps the one thought that best expresses the sentiments of the early citizens of Muskogee can be summed up by the expression so many people used when asked to sign the petition for Bill's release. They generally answered, "Sure, I'll be happy to sign it. He's got the blood."[4]

Bass Reeves's great-nephew Paul L. Brady described Reeves as

a tall, muscular man sitting astride his big sorrel. Bass rode slowly down the main street of Muskogee in Indian territory. He was delivering two prisoners to the first federal jail to be erected in that territory, and they would later be removed to Fort Smith for trial. Bass had nearly been killed when three men he had warrants for ambushed him deep in Creek Indian territory, where Bass' pursuit had taken him. He killed one in the ambush and got the other two to surrender. After delivering his prisoners to chief marshal Leo Bennett, Bass was looking forward to a well-deserved rest.

Bennett had another warrant that had to be served, though. He didn't want to assign another deputy to the case, but Bennett was disturbed to have to tell Bass that Bass' own son was charged with the murder of his wife and was a fugitive somewhere in Indian territory. Bass was visibly shaken with Bennett's news. Pacing the floor, he reflected how clearly the law had seemed defined for him, how concerned he had always been with enforcing it. And now it clashed markedly with his love for his own son. But, as the Muskogee Daily Phoenix reported, "with a devotion to duty equal to that of the old Roman Brutus, whose greatest claim to fame was that the love of his son could not sway him from justice, he said 'Give me the writ.'" Bass told Bennett it was his son who was wanted and it was his responsibility to bring him in. Two weeks later Bass returned with his prisoner, who was immediately bound over for trial.[5]

The *Muskogee Daily Phoenix* on June 8, 1902, carried the following story (We now know that Bass's son's name was Benjamin and not Bill. Benjamin was referred to as "Bennie" by family and friends):

Murdered His Wife: Ben Reeves Shoots Down the Woman in Cold Blood

Consumed with jealousy, crazed beyond endurance because the wife he married had told him she did not love him, a monomaniac who lived in the lights and shadows of his imaginary wrongs, angered until his blood became a furnace heated with all the fires of unrequited love. Ben Reeves yesterday at 11 o'clock in the morning sent a bullet from a .45 Colts' revolver crushing through the brain of the wife he had sworn to cherish and protect.

Like the jealous Moor he caught at "trifles light as air," and it needed not the finding of a handkerchief, nor the devilish, fiendish tempting of an Iago to tell this black man that his wife [was] untrue because he had set out to believe it, and the powers of the world were too feeble to convince him otherwise.

Reeves is well known to the people of Muskogee. He is a son of Bass Reeves, the colored deputy marshal, and has for the most part, been a quiet, orderly negro, working as a porter in different places.

He met his wife at her friend's house. They were standing together and he, it is said, was whispering terms of endearment into her not unwilling ears. She had previously dressed to come to the city from the house of Emma Solomon, upon the hill where negroes most reside. Dressed thus Reeves saw her. Their talk was calm and no premonition came to the woman that her life would be taken. She arose to leave the house. Reeves looked at her one moment. In that time visions of the dark but comely bride came before him. He saw her standing there, the one woman in all the world whom he loved; he thought of the happiness that had been snatched from him for some inexplicable reason, and at that moment he drew forth the deadly revolver and fired, the first ball striking his wife fairly in the face and going through her brain, the second a flesh wound. She died instantly. He then turned the gun on himself, but the ball only grazed his forehead.

He started to town and met his father, to whom he gave up. He was taken to the federal jail where he will remain until the September grand jury passes on his case.

The dead woman will be buried today. She had many friends who speak highly of her, and who assert that, she was not to blame. It is known that Reeves was insanely jealously and several families, where the woman boarded, have been disturbed at Reeves visitations at all hours of the night.

No other cause is assigned for the killing. The murderer refuses to talk, but in the absence on any statement the people believe that jealousy was the sole and only cause.

The newspaper story differs somewhat from the two preceding family stories of the incident. The exact sequence of events is probably somewhere in between all three reports. The newspaper story doesn't allude to a boyfriend (of Bennie's wife) being beaten up by Bennie at all. Telephones did exist at this time, so the marshal's office could have been alerted to the incident by this new means of communication, which also may have been the way Bass found out from U.S. Marshal Bennett. A fourth version is featured in a PBS television documentary that was produced in Oklahoma City in 1973. Rev. Charles Davis, an elderly Creek Freedman from Muskogee, was interviewed:

Bass Reeves came from Arkansas as one of those United States marshals. Bass was a kind, sympathetic man. But he was a brave man, and then mentally and physically strong. He could whip most any two men with his fist. He was a man that when he went after a group, now brother, he would bring you in, that's all. But he was a very kind and sympathetic. He never bulged in and caused trouble . . .

His son grew up here. He married one of the native women here and some how or another they got in trouble and he killed her, he murdered her. Leo Bennett was the head marshal here and he was arming his men. He got word that the boy had determined not to be arrested alive. Threatened them not to come to his house because he wasn't going to be arrested. Bass got a hold of it. Bass went to the office, Leo Bennett's office, and asked them not to go up there. "Some of you will be killed. Let me have the warrant and I'll go up there. It's a bench warrant and I'll do just what the warrant says, I'm going to bring him in dead or alive." Well the people who knew that, the colored people, they tell me a number of them followed him to the house where this young man was. Begging him and insisting on that he not do it, for fear he might get killed. But he went on, Bass did. Got to the house and yelled to this boy, his name was Bennie. "Now Bennie," he said, "You are no more my son, you committed a crime. And I have a warrant in my pocket for you, a bench warrant, either to bring you in dead or alive. And I'm going to take you in today, one way or the other. You can come out with your hands up or else your whole body will be down." Bennie came out, the people standing around hollered to him. Said, "Don't raise your hands because he will kill you sure. Bass will certainly get you." And he meant to do it. He arrested Bennie and took him in.[6]

Bennie was convicted and found guilty by a jury on January 22, 1903, in Muskogee. The presiding judge was C. W. Raymond. Bennie was sentenced to the U.S. prison at Fort Leavenworth, Kansas, for his natural life on January 24. He was received at Fort Leavenworth on February 13, 1903, where he stated he was born in Texas and his father was the only parent living. On the 1900 census for Muskogee, Ben's place of birth is listed as Arkansas. He also listed his father as being born in Texas, but the 1870 and 1880 census both listed Arkansas as Bass's birthplace. Bennie's vital statistics and age were given as twenty-one, five feet and eleven and two-fourths inches tall, weighed one hundred and seventy pounds, black hair and slate blue eyes, his color was listed as light mulatto. In the Trusty Prisoner's Agreement, Bennie listed his occupation as barber. He gave the following description of the crime that caused him to be incarcerated:

> On the morning of June 7th, 1902, at 11 a.m. I called upon my wife at her cousins house in Muskogee asked her if it was true she was having or did have improper relations with John Wadly, she answered me that she thought more of his little finger than she did of my whole body. By constant worry over her actions and breaking up of my home, and receiving such an answer I lost all control and shot her.

With whom do you correspond?

Bass Reeves, Father and Alice Spain [Spahn], Sister and Ernest Hubbard at Muscogee. Willie Turner at Vinita Okla.

Where and by whom were you arrested?

Muskogee by Bass Reeves my father who was Deputy Marshal . . .

Bennie stated he had two brothers living, Edward Reeves and Newton Reeves, and sisters Alice Spahn in Muskogee, Sallie Sanders in Fort Smith, and Georgia Johnson in Los Angeles, California. On September 22, 1911, Bennie sent his sister Sallie Sanders and her husband of Fort Smith a blank deed in the hopes of securing funds to aid in his efforts to obtain a pardon or commutation of sentence. When the deed was executed, he asked for it to be forwarded to A. C. Spahn at 816 Emporia Street in Muskogee. This was done through the chief clerk at Leavenworth prison. Bennie received a commutation of sentence from the Department of Justice, Washington DC on November 13, 1914. He served a total of eleven years and ten months at the U.S. prison at Leavenworth, Kansas. After his release, he returned to Muskogee. An elder of Muskogee, Pliny Twine, informed me that Bennie worked in a restaurant after his release from prison. Mr. Twine didn't ever remember Bennie having a family.[7]

The U.S. Congress on May 27, 1902, divided the Northern District of Indian Territory into two, creating a Western District. The Northern District would now comprise the Cherokee and Quapaw Agency, with headquarters at Vinita. The other court towns were Miami, Sallisaw, Pryor Creek, Claremore, Nowata, and Bartlesville. William H. Darrough, a former member of the Rough Riders of the Spanish-American War, was named U.S. Marshal, with Judge Joseph A. Gill presiding. The new Western District comprised the Creek and Seminole nations, with headquarters at Muskogee. The other court towns were Wagoner, Okmulgee, Sapulpa, Tulsa, Wewoka, and Eufaula. Leo Bennett was appointed U.S. marshal for the Western District, with Judge Charles R. Raymond presiding.[8]

The *Muskogee Phoenix* on July 3, 1902, ran a story on the officers of the new Western District. Bass Reeves, along with Grant Johnson and David Adams, were reappointed for the new Western District. Veteran officers Reeves and Johnson were the only African American deputies assigned to the new district.

On November 3, 1902, Reeves arrested John Anderson and Rosa Norman for adultery. Sam Norman gave testimony before the U.S. commissioner:

> I know Rosa Norman and Anderson. Rosa Norman is my wife. Rosa Hennix was her maiden name. I was married to her about six years ago. (Certified copy of marriage license and certificate introduced). We have never legally separated. John Anderson carried my wife away two years ago. They have been living together ever since in Creek Nation, Indian Territory.

Harry Ford testified:

> I am a farmer and a preacher. John Anderson and Rosa Norman lived on my place in same house. No one else in that house. House had one room. They lived there nearly a year. I saw them in bed together under cover, one morning about sunrise, in November, 1901. That was in Creek Nation, Indian Territory. I told them that I would not allow that sort of thing and gave them notice to leave.

Jourdan Hunter testified:

> I know Anderson and Rose Norman. I saw them in house together in one room. I saw them in bed together. They were covered up. It was early daylight. They lived in one room together for eight months. Anderson later moved over to Muskogee. I am certain the two defendants were in bed together.[9]

Later in the year, on November 11, Bass Reeves arrested Jamison Brown on a charge of grand larceny for stealing a horse on August 4, 1902, at Pecan Creek in the Creek Nation. Brown stole a horse, saddle, bridle, and blanket, which were valued at $117, from J. E. Crane. Before U.S. Commissioner Harlow A. Leckley, Crane gave the following testimony:

> My post office is Hitchita, I.T. my age is 32 years. My name is J. E. Crane. I was at a picnic about six miles west of Muskogee on August 4, 1902. Alfred Rector, Joseph Rector, Neely Manuel rode to the picnic place on Pecan Creek, about sunset. We rode horses. My horse was a bay mare. We tied are horses to two

trees, two horses to each tree. One of the boys said to Jamison Brown as we rode up, "You ain't gone yet?" Jamison Brown said, "No, I ain't gone yet. I ain't going quietly." I was right there on my horse when that was said. After hitching, we went off to get something to eat. We came back in about an hour to go away and my horse was gone, and the bridle, saddle and blanket were gone too. They were all worth about $100.00. I got on Joseph Rector's horse and Alfred Rector and Neely Manuel went with me to search for the horse. I inquired of the freighters along the road and learned that a man had passed them riding fast. We went on to the other side of Lee to another picnic ground and there I found my mare tied to a tree. The blanket was gone. Blood had run from the mare's shoulders to the hocks, and she was covered with sweat, and winded. Jamison Brown's coat was tied to the front of the saddle and Jamison Brown was on the dancing floor. I got my horse and we went back to Alfred Rector's house and stayed all night and until my horse could be ridden again.

Cross-examination by Mr. Wolfenberger

It was night when we went along the road looking for the horse, but near light, I think.

Brown never told me he had got the horse through mistake.

Re-direct by Commissioner

When we rode up to the picnic grounds at Pecan Creek, Jamison Brown passed right close to us and saw me on my horse. The blanket under my saddle was blue with a spotted colored border.

The above incident most likely took place on the Creek Freedman Emancipation Day celebration, which was always held on August 4. A jury trial found Brown guilty on January 3, 1903. He was sentenced to the U.S. prison at Fort Leavenworth, Kansas, for five years. The prison sentence would start from November 11, 1902. Brown was committed to Fort Leavenworth on February 13, 1903.[10]

On November 12, 1902, Reeves arrested George Bean, Will Bean, and William Penser for assault with intent to kill. The *Muskogee Phoenix* of November 20 carried a story about the assault in the city:

Negro Carving Affray: May Result in the Death of Joe Caesar, Colored

Joe Caesar, colored, was assaulted last night at 9:30 at a house on South Third street opposite the Ray marble shop, by George Bean, also colored, and it may be that Caesar will live, but it is quite doubtful. Bean cut Caesar a slash across the abdomen which reached the intestine and also cut some vicious slashes in his neck and shoulders, and Drs. Sims and Davis, colored, were engaged two hours in stitching up Caesar's anatomy.

It is alleged that Caesar had threatened to kill Bean and a man of the name Penser. They sought Officer McStravick and told him that Caesar had threatened them. McStravick was looking for Caesar when the scrap occurred.

Henry Bean, brother of George Bean, and Penser went to the house on Third street, Henry Bean claims they went to preserve the peace, and could not get to George before he assaulted Caesar. George Bean after he did the cutting went to U.S. Deputy Marshal Bass Reeves and gave himself up. Reeves afterwards arrested Henry Bean, Penser and the Bean brothers' sister, who was mixed up in the affair.[11]

The *Muskogee Phoenix* on November 27 reported that Joe Caesar had died. George Bean and Will Penser were charged with murder. Will Penser and Will Bean were charged also with complicity in the case. Caesar had made a deathbed statement concerning the attack on his life. In the case file the testimony appeared to give evidence that the Bean boys felt Caesar was responsible for the break up of their sister's marriage. Caesar then started seeing their sister and the Bean's developed an intense dislike for him.[12]

Also in the newspaper on November 27 was an article on new appointments with the U.S. Indian Police at Muskogee, which had jurisdiction over crimes committed among citizens of the Five Tribes:

The Indian Police

The Indian police force under command of Hon. J. Blair Shoenfelt, Indian Agent for the five civilized tribes, is the most
unique military organization in the United States. With jurisdiction over the Choctaw, Chickasaw, Creek, Seminole and
Cherokee nations, this organization exercises the authority of
police, U.S. marshals and U.S. troops. They are paid and uni-
formed by the U.S. government and perform a work not dele-
gated to any other branch of the service. The personnel of the
force is as follows:

> Creek Nation: Capt. John C. West, Muskogee; Private
> Wm. M. Sunday, Tulsa; I. K. Boone, Eufaula; Lewis Hari-
> aye, Weleetka; Samuel Haynes, Okmulgee; Thos. Williams,
> Frank West, Muskogee; Pleasant Berryhill, Beggs; Theo.
> E. Stidham, Muskogee.

> Cherokee Nation: Arthur J. Chamberlain, Vinita; John L.
> Brown, Webbers Falls; Samuel Edwards, Monata.

> Chickasaw Nation: Private Jas. E. McCauley, Ardmore;
> Samuel Victor, Dittle; Thos. W. Short, Kemp; Wm. D.
> McCarty, Sulphur.

> Choctaw Nation: Lieutenant, Alfred McCay, McAlester;
> Jas. Ward, Coalgate; Private, C. W. Plummer, Lehigh; Pe-
> ter Maytubby, Jr., Caddo; John Simpson, Carbon; B. J.
> Spring, Kinta; E.S. Bowman, Oak Lodge.

> Seminole Nation: Private Wm. H. Culley, Sasakwa.

The racial difficulties in the Indian Territory caused noted problems for the black deputy U.S. marshals after the turn of the century.
Zeke Miller, a black deputy who worked out of the Central District at
McAlester, Choctaw Nation, had almost started a race war in the mining
town of Bache in 1901. A white man named Dave Tatum was missing and
was last seen in the barbershop of Charley Williams, a black man. It was
assumed by some that Williams had murdered Tatum. Miller began a
search of all the black homes in Bache, and when that didn't turn up any
evidence, he ordered a search of all the white homes in Bache. Both the

black and white citizens were agitated over Miller's tactics, besides creating a lot of racial friction. A white deputy, Crocket Lee, was dispatched from McAlester to help quell the uproar. Miller was told to immediately stop the house searches. They found out later that Tatum had skipped town because he was under a criminal indictment and out on bond. Jack Walters, a black deputy U.S. marshal working out of the Southern District at Ardmore, Chickasaw Nation, had been hired to keep an eye on the black community on Wild Horse Creek. In 1901 Walters arrested a white man named Bob McGee for shooting another white man named Shelton. Walters made the arrest because he was the only lawman in the vicinity. Walters carried McGee to Ardmore by train. When he arrived at the Pauls Valley train station with his prisoner, a bystander resented the idea of a black man being in charge of a white man and used abusive language toward Walters. The black deputy made the bystander subside by threatening to shoot him with his Winchester rifle if he didn't keep quiet and leave him alone. A warrant was sworn out for Walters's arrest for disturbing the peace. The Pauls Valley authorities fined Walters ten dollars and court costs. Walters appealed to the U.S. district court in Ardmore. The white citizens wanted Walters to be dismissed but U.S. Marshal Hammer resisted their wishes and retained Walters. A few years later, in 1905, in the Central District, Robert Fortune, a black deputy who had earlier worked out of the Fort Smith court under Judge Parker, had been accused of trying to encourage black families to integrate a new school in Wilburton in the Choctaw Nation. The white citizens of Wilburton wanted the U.S. marshal to dismiss Fortune from the force. The U.S. marshal decided that Fortune wasn't guilty of the charges implied, but he ordered a white deputy to be placed in Wilburton to handle all the warrants for the white population. This incident marks the first time I am aware of that a black deputy U.S. marshal was told not to handle warrants for whites in the Indian Territory.[13]

17.

The Invincible Marshal

The Muskogee city directory for 1903 has Bass Reeves and his wife living at 325 West Court Street in Muskogee. This would confirm earlier information I received from Pliny Twine that Reeves lived at Fourth and Court. This location is right in the downtown area of Muskogee, which is today directly south of Arrowhead Mall Shopping Center. Reeves's neighbor across the street, at 320 West Court Street, was white Deputy U.S. Marshal David Adams and his wife, Henrietta

This area proved to be a prime spot for other town officials. At this time the Adamses' son, Harry, was living with his parents. He was a bailiff in the U.S. court in 1903. Adams and Reeves were the principal field deputies for the federal court at Muskogee in the ten years leading up to statehood. U.S. Marshal Leo E. Bennett lived not far from Reeves, at 115 South Fourth Street. The former U.S. marshal, S. M. Rutherford, lived at 121 South Third, and was a practicing attorney with Rutherford, Cravens, and English. Pleasant Porter, the principal chief of the Creek Nation, lived at 117 South Sixth Street. The U.S. Indian agent, J. B. Shoenfelt, lived at 129 South Fourth Street. W. H. Twine, the most important African American attorney in Muskogee, lived at 706 South Fifth Street. William Ragsdale, then a liveryman, and later to establish the most important African American funeral home business in Muskogee, lived at 511 West Fon du Lac. There were three African Americans in 1903 working as guards at the U.S. jail at Muskogee: J. B. Davis, E. L.

Robbins, and James Thomas. There was one white jail guard named G. S. White Jr., who most likely was the son of Deputy U.S. Marshal G. S. White who had worked the Fort Smith and Muskogee federal courts.[1]

Deputy U.S. Marshal David Adams started working in the federal court in Muskogee in 1889 under U.S. Marshal Tom B. Needles and later S. M. Rutherford. He worked a total of eighteen years, resigning on April 15, 1907, under U.S. Marshal Leo E. Bennett. Adams lived in Muskogee until the summer of 1922, when he died at home.[2]

Bass Reeves, the invincible marshal, continued to provide guardianship for the city of Muskogee. He arrested a white man, Sam Jackson, in Muskogee on March 7, 1903, for robbery. The victim, John Cloud, gave the following testimony before the U.S. commissioner in Muskogee on March 19:

> My post office is two miles north east of Ridge, Indian Territory; my age is 45 years. I have seen Sam Jackson, the defendant several times. On February 12, 1903 between 9 and 10 o'clock at night. I saw him on the railroad close to Okmulgee crossing. J. K. Ryders, Tom Box, and John Burgess were with me at that time. He came up behind us, another fellow was with him. The defendant jerked old man Ryders lose from me. Said they would take care of him. I had Ryders arm locked in mine. The other man (not here) helped jerk Ryders loose from me. Ryders said he would take care of himself. One of the men said we'll lock you up for being drunk. They claimed Ryder's was drunk. The defendant had a star on his coat. He drew a gun—a pistol. He told us that he would take me too. He made me walk around in front of him. He had his gun on me. I didn't see the other man with a gun. He had hold of Ryders. Both were trying to get their hands in Ryders pockets. One of them said if I put up $10.00, they would turn Ryders loose. I told them I didn't have the $10.00, but thought I could get it. I stepped back to Burgess. Then Sam Jackson, the defendant ran. Before I got back the other man ran too. The defendant held the pistol on

me. Burgess had walked away a little piece, Box was standing close.

Cross examination

The two fellers came up behind us. They claimed they arrested Ryders. They asked Ryders where he got his whiskey. Burgess had been waiting to go away on the train. I seen the defendant several times at the restaurant near the post office here in town. The night I spoke about he had a long black coat and white, kind of dude looking hat. Afterward about two weeks, I saw defendant on the street. I filed my complaint on March 7, 1903. I went to the officers at once. They said to pick him out and I looked for him the next day until nearly noon. I had him arrested on March 7, 1903 and taken before the Commissioners where I made complaint. The hat of defendant at time of arrest appeared whiter than the one now exhibited. The occurrence took place further than 200 feet from the station near the railroad. The other man was colored. By Commissioner—Defendant had a star on his coat plain to see. The occurrence took place right near the railroad, back of Pattersons and Spauldings.[3]

On May 21, 1903, at Braggs in the Cherokee Nation, Reeves arrested Chock and Joe Cordery for assault with intent to kill. Dr. D. T. Reece testified before the U.S. commissioner:

My post office is Braggs, I.T.; my age is 43 years. I am acquainted with the Cordery boys. I was called to Joe Cordery on May 21 to attend a wounded man. On the 22nd I was there also. At that time I heard a declaration made by George Brown the dying man. The substance of it was, "Joe Codery shot me. I had killed Mrs. Cordery's guinea. I went to pay her, she refused to take the pay. Told me to go settle with Joe. I went to Joe's house. Joe came to the door with his gun, told him to stop. . . . Joe then shot me and I shot at Joe then. And went in the house. The old man hit me on the head with a wedge. I took my gun and hit the old man." "Did you see Chock there?" "Yes he was out there but Chock did not do anything."

Wilson Cordery gave the following testimony:

My post office is Braggs, I.T. my age is 99 years. I am a Cherokee citizen. I am father to Joe Cordery and step father to Chock. I was present at Joe's house when George Brown was shot. George came to Joe's keeping behind trees with his gun presented. Joe went and got his gun. Joe yelled at George to hold up. Both fired about the same time. I think George fired first. George fired again. Joe could only fire twice. Joe went in house and shut the door. Brown came up and in. He was trying to shoot Joe on the bed, but his wife was pushing the gun away. I ran up and hit him on the head with a wedge. He then hit me with his gun and cut a gash on my head.

Chock was not there. He had not been there.[4]

The case file does not indicate to whether or not the defendants were convicted and sent to prison.

Bass arrested Willie Lowe for assault with intent to kill on May 27, 1903, and brought him before the U.S. commissioner. Lowe, along with Fred Taylor and Will Allen, shot at Stephen Franklin and cut him with a razor. Franklin gave the following statement on June 11, 1903, in Muskogee:

Ridge, I.T. is my post office; my age is 25 years. I acquainted with Willie Lowe—have known him since I can remember. I was present at a gathering at the Coal Creek Church house, a sort of supper in November, 1902, 13th or 14th. I was driving some cattle from Muskogee and saw that I could not get them home before night. I turned the cattle into a pasture and went to the church. I left my weapon at my brothers on my way to the church. After staying there awhile. The people asked to take away a loud boy who was drunk. I took him and started home. I got my revolver on the way. After we had gone some distance I met Fred Taylor, Willie Lowe and Mary Manuel. I said to them that as the ladies were going to the social we ought not be so loud. Fred Taylor said yes I think so and at that time reached his hand around me and took my gun, pointed it and his at my head and said he had been wanting to kill me for some time. I knocked the revolvers up with one hand and struck him with the other. I missed him but grabbed him again by the throat and knocked him down. As he fell he threw the revolvers to Willie Lowe. Willie Lowe struck me over the left shoulder with on of the revolvers. Noticed Willie Allen for the first time now. All them grappled with me and threw me down. Willie Lowe sat on me choking me saying [he] would kill me.

As I struck at Fred Taylor, I felt something give in my side. I had been cut about 2 inches deep with a razor.

Other people came and took them off of me. I was carried home.

Two shots were fired at me. One burned my right cheek, the other went through my hat knocking it off.[5]

There is no information in the case file as to the final deposition of the defendant in this case.

Reeves arrested a Paul Smith on June 24, 1903, for stealing a watch and chain worth sixty dollars from a man named Mike Ready on a MK&T Railroad excursion train from Kansas City, Missouri. The theft occurred, according to Ready, on the train between the towns of Wybark and Muskogee.[6]

On July 24, 1903, Bass Reeves arrested Will Sims for assaulting and robbing F. E. Bork at Oktaha on July 20.[7]

On September 15, 1903, Reeves arrested a white man Joe Napier, for raping a seventeen-year-old girl, who was either white or Indian, named Rebecca Davis. The girl lived with her stepmother in Muskogee, and Napier lived with the family. Rebecca told her black neighbors, R. C. and Alice Cotton, about the rape. She asked Alice for assistance, and Alice told her if she had been colored she would know what to tell her to do about the situation. Rebecca testified in court that Napier forcibly removed her from her home and carried her into the barn, about one hundred feet away, and raped her in a horse stall late at night. A doctor examined her and found she had been violated. The outcome of the case is not apparent in the criminal file.[8]

A tragic incident occurred in the Reeves family on December 28, 1903. Homer, the next youngest son after Bass Jr., died of fever in Muskogee. At the time of his death, Homer was twenty-one years of age. He was buried in Green Hill Cemetery. After statehood in 1907, African Americans were not interned in Green Hill Cemetery due to the discriminatory Jim Crow laws in the town of Muskogee.[9]

On January 1, 1904, U.S. Marshal Leo E. Bennett made J. F. "Bud" Ledbetter the chief deputy U.S. marshal for the Western District. Alice Spahn, Reeves's daughter, told Richard Fronterhouse that on one occasion Bud Ledbetter was sent from Muskogee to Checotah to quell an Indian stomp dance that had become a major disturbance due to whiskey consumption. She said that Ledbetter was unable to quell the mayhem and Bass was sent to Checotah on a special MK&T Railroad train. According to Mrs. Spahn, Reeves brought back twelve Indians, who were drunk and half dressed. Once they arrived in Muskogee, Reeves marched them through the streets to the U.S. jail.[10]

Mrs. Spahn also told Fronterhouse a story that involved the "letter trick" used by Bass Reeves. She said there were two men from Texas who were wanted for murder, one was a big man, one was a little man. Reeves had a warrant for their arrest.

The Texans met Reeves face to face on the road. Bass said, "Morning, gentlemen."

One of them replied, "I don't speak to black niggers." Then, "Ain't you Bass Reeves?"

Reeves answered, "No."

The Texans pulled their guns on Reeves and told him they would ride along until they met somebody who knew him. They rode quite a distance but didn't meet anybody. The Texans then told Reeves to get down off his horse because they were going to kill him, and asked if he had any last words he wanted to say.

Reeves told them he had a letter from his wife and asked if they would read it to him. Reeves got down off his horse and got the letter out of his saddlebags. The two Texans also dismounted. With a shaking hand, Reeves handed the letter to the big man. The Texan said, "What difference does it make?"

But when the big Texan took his eyes off Reeves and looked at the letter, which had been placed in the pommel of the saddle, Bass grabbed the big man's neck in a death grip with one hand and said, "Son of a bitch, now you're under arrest." With his other hand he took the gun away. The little Texan was so scared, he dropped his gun. Reeves secured both men and took them to Muskogee.[11]

Reeves arrested Jess Morgan on January 15, 1904, for assault with intent to kill. Morgan had attacked a Dennis Green on November 29, 1903, in Muskogee.[12]

Back in the saddle again on February 18, Reeves arrested Cornelius Nave at Fort Gibson, Cherokee Nation, for carrying a pistol unlawfully.[13]

On March 11, 1904, Reeves arrested a resident of the Creek Nation named Dick Lucky for selling cattle that he didn't own. On March 24 W. R. Whiteside gave the following testimony before U.S. commissioner Harlow A. Leekley:

> My post office is Muskogee, I.T.; my age is 50 years. I am loan inspector for the 1st National Bank, Muskogee. On June 26, 1902, I was in cattle business but working more or less for the bank. In February 1903 was the first time I knew about the Dick Lucky loan. A copy of the mortgage was given me and I was told to go out and get the stock or a settlement. I went out to Dick Lucky's. He was not at his place then. I saw Dick Lucky. I told him I had been told he had nothing. I think he told me he let Joe Primus have the money he borrowed. I asked him how many cattle he had. He said he might have two or three head around home. I asked him to show them to me. He did not show me any cattle. He said he had to go back to his wife. I made a search. I could not find any cattle described in the mortgage. I went to all the places Dick Lucky told me to. I was out to Dick's at two other times, but could never find Dick Lucky at home. . . . I can not swear from my own knowledge that Dick Lucky did not have the cattle described in the mortgage at time mortgage was given. I did not search the river bottoms. Dick did not tell me he had the cattle. My impression from his conversation was that he said he had only two or three cattle running around the place.

Nolan Williams also testified:

> My post office is Wagoner, I.T. my age is 43 years. I know Dick
> Lucky. Have known him about 12 years. I am in cattle business,
> have been in cattle business ever since I came here. I have had
> a pasture in Dick Lucky's neighborhood about a 5 years. I have
> had Dick's land leased about 3 years. Dick Lucky's place was in
> June 26, 1902 about 8 miles, S. E. of Catoosa. I had cattle in
> the pasture at that time. I knew all the cattle in the pasture. I
> did not see any of the cattle there described in the mortgage
> here presented. At that time (June 26, 1902) Dick Lucky had a
> cow branded J.P. That was all, except the calf of that cow. . . .
> I had 3500 head in the pasture. Winfield Scott had 3000 head
> in the pasture. . . . I never saw the cattle there, described in the
> mortgage.

Lucky had received $210 from the bank for the mortgage on the
cattle he didn't own. Lucky pled guilty on May 1, 1904, and was given
sixteen months' confinement at the U.S. penitentiary at Fort Leavenworth.[14]

On April 10, 1904, Thomas Matthews, who lived six miles northwest
of Muskogee, took his Winchester rifle and threatened to shoot A. L.
Gregory. This provocation by Matthews was for no reason at all; Gregory was on the road when he was approached and threatened. On April
12 Bass Reeves arrested Matthews. He was found guilty by a jury on
April 23 and fined fifteen dollars for his actions.[15]

On May 1 Reeves arrested a young man named Lonnie Smith in
Muskogee for assault to kill with a deadly weapon upon Henry Farris.
Farris gave the following testimony before U.S. Commissioner Leek-
ley:

> My post office is Muskogee, I.T.; my age is 27. I have seen
> Lonnie Smith. I last saw him April 30, 1904 in Muskogee. I
> was shot on April 30, 1904, twice—once in the mouth and once
> in the thigh. Five shots, I think, were fired. Lonnie Smith fired
> the shots. I had no arms of any kind. I was standing still when
> the first shot was fired. Then I ran away. Nothing was said at
> the time shots were fired.

Cross examination by W. H. Twine, Esq.

I had known Lonnie some time. I was not doing anything at time shots were fired. We had had a quarrel over a baseball suit some time before the shooting—downtown. He had struck me with a billiard cue and I had picked up a ball and hit him with it. I did not notice who was that at that time the trouble was going on. I made no threats. I have been arrested and convicted of burglary in Texas.

Cross examination by Commissioner

I saw Smith just before the shooting. I saw him coming out of the house. I saw a pistol in his hand. He ran around in front of me and began shooting.

James Henry, a witness, gave the following testimony:

My post office is Muskogee, I.T.; my age is 22 years. I know Henry Farris and Lonnie Smith. I was present on April 30, 1904, when Smith shot Farris. Just before the shooting we, Farris, I and a couple more boys, were going on home. We were near Ragsdale's stable. I saw a cab coming. The cab stopped at a house. We had got beyond the house. Lonnie Smith came running and began shooting at Henry Farris. There were over three shots fired. Henry Farris was shot in the mouth and in the leg. Farris was trying to keep another boy between him and Smith. Farris did not have any weapons. Smith ran away after he did the shooting. . . . It was about twenty minutes between the trouble at the billiard hall and the shooting at Elgin and 4th.

The outcome of the above case is not known; there is no information on the jury trial in the case file.[16]

On the same day Smith was arrested, Reeves arrested Abe Drew of Twine, Creek Nation, for murder. (Twine was later to be known as Taft, one of the thirty African American towns in the Indian and Oklahoma Territories.) Drew had used a pistol to shoot to death a man named George Colbert on May 1. In the application for allowance of witnesses at the expense of the U.S. Court for the Western District, Indian Territory, the following statement was given by Drew:

Comes now the defendant, Abe Drew, and shows that he is indicted for murder, in the above named Court, and that his cause is set for trial on the 25th day of January AD 1905 at Muskogee. . . . By Stephen Franklin and Fred Franklin he expects to prove that they were present when defendant shot the deceased and that the killing occurred at the house of Phoebe Glover and that defendant and the two Franklin boys were in Fred Franklin's buggy and had been to Tallahassee on business and on coming back Fred Franklin wanted to go by the house of Phoebe Glover to see Dinah Jemison and the defendant did not know that the deceased was there when they stopped. That when they stopped at said house Fred Franklin got out of the buggy and went into the house and just after Franklin went into the house the deceased came around the house and came in the door and then came back to the door and he then for the first time saw the defendant who was standing out in the yard and the deceased said God Damn look at Abe Drew and at the same time drew his pistol from his pocket and threw it on or towards the defendant and the defendant said to the deceased, George, don't you shoot me and at about the same time fired and the deceased fell backward with his pistol in his hand.

By the witnesses Wesley Warner, E. L. Drake and D. Criss, he expects prove that the deceased had threatened to kill the defendant at different times and told them to tell the defendant that he intended to kill him for him to get ready and that they communicated these threats to the defendant before the killing.

By Will McNeil and Frank Smith he expects to prove that they were present one day about a month before the killing when the deceased walked up to the defendant and knocked defendants hat off and pulled his pistol and threw it down on the defendant and Frank Smith ran in between the deceased and defendant and prevented the deceased from shooting defendant.

By Ella McIntosh and John Drew he expects to prove that the deceased was at their house about a week before the killing and the deceased came there and soon as he saw the defendant he drew his pistol and tried to shoot the defendant and they prevented him and ordered him to leave the place and the deceased said as he rod[e] off that's all right you sure saved him from getting killed meaning this defendant.

By Bass Reeves who is a deputy Marshal he expects to prove that he has known the defendant for a long time and that the defendant has assisted him as a posseman in arresting criminals for a long time and assisted witness in arresting the deceased and that he knows the defendant is a peaceable law abiding man and that the general reputation of the deceased was that of a desperate dangerous man.

That the defendant has no property except his homestead as a Creek citizen and is absolutely unable to pay for the attendance of said witnesses and he therefore prays that he be allowed said witnesses at the Governments expense.

Abe Drew

Drew surrendered to Reeves at Muskogee, who then put him in jail. Seeing how Drew worked with Reeves, they must have had a good relationship. The fate of Drew in his jury trial for the charge of murder is not available in the criminal case file.[17]

A humorous note appeared in the *Muskogee Phoenix* on May 6, 1904, concerning Reeves's police work:

Reeves Caught Him

For many days, Dr. Williams, Mr. Benedict and others in the same neighborhood have been missing their chickens, and finally the party taking them concluded to clean them out entirely, and had fairly started to do so. Instead of eating chicken however he will now order his meals from the bill of fare at the Lubbes hotel, where he was registered and given a room yesterday under the name of John Larrimore.

Mr. Lubbes was the well-known jailer in Muskogee.

The same newspaper a week later carried a story concerning Bass Reeves having to shoot a fleeing felon:

Shot in the Leg

Bob Johnson, colored, was lodged in jail yesterday by Deputy Bass Reeves, on a whiskey charge. Johnson has been on the scout since last August, and various attempts have been made to arrest him. He has been chased at shot at several times always getting away.

His arrest was effected at Wybark, and in order to stop him the officer was compelled to shoot him in the leg.[18]

The very next day, Reeves, along with a deputy U.S. marshal named Jones, arrested a John Wilkins near Coweta, Creek Nation, for the theft of horses and mules. Wilkins was locked up in the Muskogee federal jail.[19]

The *Muskogee Phoenix* on May 24, 1904, printed the following article:

Five Men Were Jailed by Deputy Bass Reeves in Twenty-Four Hours

Deputy Bass Reeves is determined to keep the number of inhabitants at the federal jail up to the standard. He made a trip to Falls City yesterday and on his return he was accompanied by Mose Raper, charged with introducing, [unknown] charged with introducing and selling, bond $2000; Will Clark, charged with selling liquor, bond $2000; Mansom Blue, charged with carrying a pistol and introducing and selling, bond for pistol $250 and whiskey $2,000.

Being unable to furnish bail, the entire outfit went to jail. The arrests were made on grand jury warrants.

D. S. Tyner, charged with threatening to commit an offense, was also taken in by Deputy Reeves and committed to jail.

On July 21, 1904, an African American newspaper, the *Muskogee Comet*, carried an item about a family visit Reeves received in the city:

Mrs. S. S. Sanders of Ft. Smith and Mrs. Paralee Steward of Van Buren are in the city visiting Deputy Marshall Bass Reaves. They are respectfully his daughter and mother.

The *Muskogee Democrat* on July 22, 1904, carried the following:

Numerous Arrests

Deputy Reeves made several arrests today, among them Will Cook, charged with petit larceny; Joe Drew, carrying a weapon; Will Reed, larceny; Pomper [Pompey] McIntosh, carrying a weapon and Grant Vaughn, disturbing religious worship.

Reeves's police activities were again highlighted in the *Muskogee Democrat* on July 27, 1904:

There Is Warfare in Little Africa: Colored Population Is Keeping the Courts Busy

Keep Bass Reeves Busy: Wife-Beaters, Introducers and Cain-Raisers Keep the Colored Deputy Going All Day Long

There is considerable warfare in Little Africa these days—not war carried there from any outside point, but the home grown article.

Jim Richardson, listed in the directory, a farmer, at 518 South Second street, but better known as the proprietor of a pawn shop, has been beating his wife Ophelia again. He beat her head and face and various parts of her body, administering a terrible punishment. He was arrested late last evening for that offense and was placed under $250 bond. He was arrested again on a charge of introducing and selling whiskey and was placed under a $2000 bond.

This morning he set out to beat his wife again, proposing to use a six-shooter for that purpose, she says. She came to the United States marshal's office, and asked to have him put under a heavy peace bond, so it is likely that he will be quelled pretty thoroughly some time soon.

Much sympathy is expressed for his wife who is said by those who know them to be an industrious and well-behaved woman, who has suffered a great deal at his hands.

Another bit of Afro-American discord, at 1114 South Second street, culminated in a shooting this morning. H. L. Brown a teamster, was shot in the leg by his wife Mamie Brown. She

The Invincible Marshal **267**

claims the shooting was accidental; that she had a pistol which he tried to take away from her and that in the struggle for possession of the weapon it was discharged by accident. He claims that the shooting was not accidental and swore out a warrant for her arrest. She was placed under bond in the sum of $1,000.

The same newspaper carried another piece concerning Reeves on July 29, 1904:

> Joe Cruns, charged with assault to kill, and Nero Nivens, charged with false pretense, were arrested yesterday by Deputy Bass Reeves.

Reeves arrested a white man named, J. A. Tatnull, on August 4, 1904, for burglary and larceny in Muskogee. From a store named Barbee and Company, Tatnull stole twenty pairs of shoes, twelve hats, and one pair of pants, a total of ninety-four dollars' worth of merchandise. On August 11 Bass Reeves testified before the U.S. commissioner:

> My post office is Muskogee, I.T.; my age is 66 years. . . . I am Deputy U.S. Marshal; I have seen the defendant. I arrested him at Johnson Green's shoe shop in Muskogee, day before yesterday. I found hats, shoes (a sack full) and other merchandise there in possession of defendant. I counted 12 pair of shoes and 11 hats, two pair of bootees and two pair of corduroy pants. 2 laundered shirts, a blue coat and vest, underwear, neckties; That's all. I brought items to Marshal's office. Small identified most of the goods as his. The defendant told me he met a colored fellow at stock yards who told him he had some things and that he had no place to store them. I understood the defendant to give that man's name as Carter. He said he was a black fellow.

Johnson Green testified:

> My post office is Muskogee, I.T.; my age is 38 years. . . . I have known defendant about four weeks. He has been living with me [during] that time. He rented a bed in my shoe shop about a month ago. He said he had roomed a few nights at Mrs. Jackson's. He said his home had been Houston, Texas. I left my shop

in his charge every evening. I went to shop last Sunday about
10 o'clock, but did not go into place he had rented. Monday
morning when I came down to work, he asked if it was not his
rent time. I said, "Yes." Well, he said he was fixed to pay me. He
said he had some shoes and that he had a buyer for the shoes.
Later he told me the buyer had refused to take the shoes. At
some time he hung a couple of pairs of shoes on the wall and
asked me to sell them for him. He let me have one pair for rent.
Then I went to dinner. When I came back, Bass Reeves came
in and made the arrest. I notified Bass about it, I got suspicious.
Bass came up and found the things under the bed, wrapped in
paper. There was a sack of shoes. I did not count the shoes.
Bass got the things and brought them to Marshal's office. I do
not know when the shoes were bought to my place.

J. A. Tatnull pled guilty to the crime of burglary and larceny in a
trial before Judge Charles W. Raymond on November 3, 1904. He was
sentenced to four years' confinement at the U.S. prison at Fort Leavenworth, Kansas.[20]

The *Muskogee Democrat* had a short item on Reeves's police work on
September 8, 1904:

Deputy Reeves made two arrests this morning. John Slaughter,
charged with larceny, and Ed. Jones charged with assault with
intent to rape.

On September 19, 1904, the *Muskogee Democrat* reported on the new,
modern federal jail in Muskogee:

Moved into the New Jail: Prisoners Transferred from Stockade to New United States Jail

In Column of Twos: Battalion of Bad Men Put on
Clean Clothes and March to New Quarters

This morning, without accident or incident, the prisoners in the
old prison pen under the hill were moved into the new United
States jail on Court street.

United States Marshal Bennett with typewritten list in hand
sat just inside the entrance of the old pen checking off names as

the prisoners were brought out in squads of 16 and marched up the hill in columns of twos, in charge of deputies and jail guards, to their new quarters. Before the transfer all the prisoners were required to take a bath and were given new clothes.

There were 173 prisoners transferred, six of whom are women. Ninety-three are negroes and the other 80 are Indians and whites. The offenses range from murder and rape down to disturbing the peace.

The estimate placed on the sacredness of human life in this vicinity is strikingly shown by the fact that 35, or more than one-fifth of the entire number, are charged with murder. Another striking fact is that nearly all of them wear broad-brimmed slouch hats, illustrating the close relation between slouch hats and criminal tendencies.

The excellent sanitary condition of the old stockade and care taken of the prisoners are shown by the fact that none of the prisoners are sick, all being able to march to the new quarters except one who was suffering from a gun-shot wound when put in and who has not yet recovered.

The old federal jail, the first in Indian Territory, had stood at Third and Denison streets and was surrounded by a twelve-foot wooden stockade.

On November 2, 1904, Bass Reeves purchased additional real estate in Muskogee for three hundred dollars. The address was 816 North Howard Street. Today the address is 509 and 509 ´ Howard Street. On March 14, 1905, Reeves sold this property to his wife for "Love and affection and ten dollars." The name on the deed was Jennie, but probably was meant to read Winnie. This would be the house where Reeves would die in 1910. It must have been a fairly large home, as the 1910 census recorded six people rooming there, besides Winnie and her daughter. I believe Reeves lived in his home on Fourth and Court streets in downtown Muskogee until the end of his police work. Undoubtedly, Reeves bought the large building on Howard so his wife could make some money with it as a rooming house.[21]

On November 18, 1904, Bass Reeves arrested a man named Scott

Gentry four miles north of Choska in Indian Territory, and brought him to the federal court in Muskogee. Gentry was the administrator for the estate of a deceased woman, Mary Owen. He was found in contempt of court for not filing a report of sale and annual report as ordered with federal court of the Western District of Indian Territory on November 14, 1904.[22]

Reeves arrested a medical doctor for selling illegal whiskey in the black town of Wybark on November 27, 1904. Dr. George W. Crockwell pled guilty and undoubtedly was fined for the indiscretion.[23]

On December 4 Bass Reeves arrested Henry Rosco in the Creek Nation for assault with a deadly weapon upon Roxie Rosco. Roxie may have been Henry's wife, but this information does not appear in the criminal case file. Henry was convicted and given ninety-five days in jail, to be served in the U.S. jail, Fort Smith, Arkansas, and was fined $14.40.[24]

A fourteen-year-old girl named Lillie McGriff was murdered in Boynton, Creek Nation, on November 12, 1904. Bass Reeves arrested Charley Wright and Morris Rentie on December 27, 1904, for the crime. Lillie's sister, Hattie, who was with her, testified before the U.S. commissioner:

> My Post office is Boynton, I.T.; my age is 16. I am Richard McGriff's daughter. Nov. 12, 1904 in the evening about dark my sister, Lillie and I went out to the [water] closet and just as we stepped outside the door of the closet, coming back to the house, someone fired a pistol at the corner of Kenefick Street. It was one man. When he fired I started to run to the house. Then we stepped back inside the closet; thinking the man would pass on by. When the man got even with the closet. He stopped and fired into the closet where we were. We both jumped out and ran toward the house. When I jumped out I looked and the man was going toward Rentie's. He was walking. The man I saw was a heavy set man. He had on a short, square-cut coat. I saw the man when he fired the second shot. I was looking through a crack in the side of the closet. My sister fell half way to the house. My sister did not speak after she was shot. The man was

about 12 feet from the closet when he fired the second shot. He presented the pistol or whatever he shot with right at the closet. . . . I could not recognize the face of the man who did the shooting.

Richard McGriff testified that Morris Rentie was wearing a short-cut coat that day his daughter was shot. Rentie testified that he weighed one hundred and forty-five pounds, therefore he was not heavyset as described by Hattie. Richard McGriff testified also that Rentie and Wright were walking in the direction of his house minutes before the shots were fired. The final disposition of the case is not found in the criminal file.[25]

18.

A Lawman to the End

As the final chapter closes in, Bass Reeves continues to refine his craftsmanship of a "lawman to the end."

On October 5, 1904, John Thomas was indicted on two counts: illegal cohabitation with Sarah Britt on October 1, 1904, and assault with intent to kill Pete Reynolds on October 4, 1904. Bass Reeves arrested Thomas on February 25, 1905.[1]

A shooting took place in the town of Porter in the Creek Nation on March 4, 1905. Alfred Barnett was indicted for trying to kill Edward King, shooting him several times with his pistol. Reeves arrested Barnett on March 8. King's wife, Josie, gave the following testimony before the U.S. commissioner:

> My post office is eight miles north of Wewoka, I.T. my age is 25. . . . I know Alfred Barnett. I, my husband, and Garnett were running a restaurant at Porter last winter. I was present at time my husband was shot February 22, 1905 at Porter. On Wednesday, February 22, 1905, my husband went into Barnett's shop-market and came back into restaurant where I was and he told me to go in and settle with Barnett. That Barnett had said he was "By God, going to have a settlement that morning." I went in and settled with him at his own figures. Just about that time my husband stepped up to the door. We started off to

restaurant. Barnett called my husband back and said "Your wife has been and settled with me and from now on Ganett's wife and your wife can attend to the account and you and Ganett can stay out of it." My husband replied, "That's all right," and started away from the door. Then Barnett kicked my husband, as he started away from the door. My husband had a hatchet in his hand at the time, but he did not attempt to hit Barnett with the hatchet. Barnett immediately went back into his butcher shop. My husband and I went on into our restaurant. My husband got his gun and I made him put the gun up. He started about his cooking. He was stooping down looking in the bottom part of the safe. I was standing in the middle door, with my face toward my husband. I looked around and Barnett had stepped into back door and up to me. He fired a shot as soon as he entered the door at my husband. He kept shooting. I tried to get out by him when he fired first shot. But I couldn't. Just before Barnett fired first shot, I could not see where my husband was, the house was full of smoke.

King was shot in the hip and the arm. Barnett was convicted by a jury trial on May 28, 1906, and was sentenced to eighteen months of hard labor at the U.S. penitentiary at Fort Leavenworth, Kansas.[2]

Reeves arrested Bessie Frazier, alias Thompson, and John Doe, alias Charlie Perryman and alias Charles Willard, on March 18, 1905, for forgery. B. F. Wood testified at the hearing:

My post office is Muskogee, I.T.; my age is 61 years. I have seen the paper shown me before, the first time on September 28, 1904. The defendant Bessie Frazier, signed by mark the name of Doretha A. Willard. Charlie Willard, defendant was with her at time she signed the deed. I looked over the abstract while he was there and showed Doretha Willard to be a young child and said he had known the woman for a long time and he knew her to be the proper party. He gave his name as Perryman. I am sure these are the same parties who were in my office in Muskogee when the deed was made.

Bass testified before the U.S. commissioner:

My post office is Muskogee, I.T.; my age is 66 years. I have seen the defendants before. I saw them yesterday. I took them back to jail. On the way to jail, I heard the woman ask Charlie Willard, "What in hell did you give me away for?" He said he could not say that he had not take her up to Wood's office, that he had taken her up there.

Bond was set at fifteen hundred dollars for each defendant and the trial date was set for April 18, 1905.[3]

The *Muskogee Democrat* on April 6, 1905, carried the following story:

Reeves Captures Negro at Fort Gibson and Spoils Much Booze

Walter McCarthen, a negro, was arrested at Fort Gibson last night by Deputy Bass Reeves, charged with selling whiskey. McCarthen was arrested in the first place by the Fort Gibson city marshal and had in his possession five pints of whiskey. The marshal telephoned to Muskogee and Bass went over and got him.

Although McCarthen had only five pints Bass says he had about half the people of Fort Gibson drunk. He worked for a lumberyard and kept the whiskey hid in the lumber.

Another article from the same newspaper discusses an arrest of robbers of the Missouri, Kansas, and Texas Railroad, or "the Katy" in Indian Territory, on April 25, 1905:

Reeves Makes Another Arrest of
Supposed Katy Freight Robbers

Seaborn Jones, a negro, was arrested today by Deputy Reeves, on the charge of being of the gang which has been robbing Katy box cars.

Mitchell and Young who were arrested at Young's house at Seventh and FonduLac, Sunday morning, confessed that Jones was implicated in the robbing of the box cars, and claim that he is the ring leader.

A lot more goods were discovered concealed in the house, which had been overlooked at the time of the first search. The goods include fine men's and women's shoes, sugar cured hams, shirts, etc.

On May 31 Reeves arrested Joe Tolbert for assault with intent to kill. Tolbert had shot Harry Jones by mistake in a rooming house in Muskogee on April 26, 1905. He was looking for a man named Waymon Reed. Jones was shot twice through his legs.[4]

Reeves made another trip to Fort Gibson, Cherokee Nation, on May 6 to arrest Louis "Monk" Williams for assault with intent to kill. On May 5 Williams had kicked the door in on a house that belonged to Lillie Hamilton. He fired twice with his pistol and she returned fire, but no one was injured. Fort Gibson policeman Martin V. Benge arrested Williams. Reeves traveled from Muskogee to pick up the prisoner and returned with him in custody to the federal jail.[5]

On July 20, 1905, the ubiquitous deputy Reeves made another arrest for assault with intent to kill. He put the handcuffs on James Mickens for trying to kill William Bean a half mile north of Wybark that same day. Bean testified before U.S. Commissioner Leekley in Muskogee:

> My post office is Wybark, I.T.; my age is 27 years. I am a farmer. On July 20, 1905, I was in [the] woods. Jam Mickens jumped on his mule and overtook me. I was going to my house. He told me to stop. I stopped when he told me the third time. Then he drew his Winchester on me and held it on me until he got right up to me. When he got within reach he struck me over the head with it. I had no weapons of any kind. He then told me to get on to the house. I went on to the house. Just as I got to the doorstep to step in, he made a shot at me. I got my gun and stepped back out and made a shot at him with a breech-loading shotgun. He shot more than once. I hit him when I shot at him. I am told. We had trouble the day before.

Cross examination by W. H. Twine

> I am from Alabama. Have been here I think since 1902. Have lived near Wybark and Falls City. On July 19, 1905 I had trouble with Makins, defendant.[6]

On August 12, 1905, Bass Reeves arrested Sandy Givens for assault with intent to kill. Givens had a heated dispute with his former girl-friend named Mettis Walker who was twenty years old. Ms. Walker lived in Clarksville, Creek Nation, a black town located eight miles east of Haskell. Before Givens shot at Walker while she sat on her porch, he told her, "If she wouldn't have him then couldn't any other damned son of a bitch have her."[7]

Reeves arrested Joe Grayson for attempted murder on September 5, 1905. Grayson had attacked George Frizzell with a club in the country five miles west of Haskell in the Creek Nation. Grayson pled guilty to the charge and on February 17, 1906, was sentenced to two and a half years of hard labor at the U.S. penitentiary at Fort Leavenworth, Kansas.[8]

An article appeared in the *Muskogee Democrat* on February 10, 1906, concerning Bass's good friend and colleague Grant Johnson:

Negro Deputy Marshal is Dumped by Bennett After 15 Years of Service

Eufaula, I.T., Feb. 9.—Grant Johnson, a deputy marshal, a negro, who has been on the United States marshal's force for fifteen years, has been dismissed from the service. Marshal Bennett refused to reappoint him this year because he thought he had become lax in his duties relative to the suppression of bootlegging. Johnson had made a remarkable record for bravery during his service for the government. He took pride in covering his district.

When Bud Ledbetter went to Eufaula and raided a number of drug stores and arrested owners for having whisky on hand, Johnson felt personally aggrieved. He wanted revenge and he got it. He decided to invade Ledbetter's own territory and discover something worth breaking up just as Ledbetter had done in his. So in the afternoon that the Eufaula raid was made, Johnson got on the train and came to Muskogee. That night he raided four gambling joints in Muskogee and single handed arrested twelve men and placed them in jail. The raids were made almost under Ledbetter's nose and the pique that Johnson felt was appeased.[9]

Johnson probably felt vindicated, but Bennett evidently didn't appreciate his chief deputy's actions. Johnson and Ledbetter had worked well together in earlier years. Some of Ledbetter's moves were done for political purposes. He had already held a couple of elected law enforcement positions and would be elected to more after statehood, including sheriff of Muskogee County. After statehood Johnson would serve on the Eufaula, Oklahoma, police department as the "Negro Policeman" for their African American community.

The Western District lost a black deputy in Johnson, but Bennett did appoint another African American as deputy marshal the same month in 1906. His name was James Garrett and he was stationed at Boynton in the Creek Nation. Garrett was evidently replacing an unidentified black deputy who was killed in Boynton in March 1905. The slain deputy had attempted to arrest a white man at a dance when he was shot by the offender.[10]

Another black peace officer had been killed in the Creek Nation in August 1905. The well-known black lawman, W. R. "Dick" Shaver, had held a deputy U.S. marshal commission under Judge Isaac C. Parker's court in Fort Smith in August 1890. In August 1905 Shaver had just been installed as the first town marshal of Boley, Creek Nation, the largest black town in the Indian Territory,. A week later, one of the deputies under Deputy U.S. Marshal D. M. Webb of Weleetka, asked for Shaver's assistance in hunting down a white outlaw named Andy Simmons. On the day that Shaver went out on the search with a deputy named Wood to the Simmons homestead, he was fired upon by Dick Simmons, Andy's brother. On August 18, 1905, the *Okemah Independent* reported:

> A spot three miles south of Boley, the colored village 14 miles northwest of here, was the scene of a double killing last Tuesday, in which Dick Shaver, colored marshal of Boley and Dick Simmons, a white man and outlaw for whom a $500 reward has been offered for sometime, both passed to their long home.
>
> On Monday word was passed out that Andy Simmons, an outlaw horse thief, for whom a reward of $800 has been offered for the past three years, had came in on the train. Deputy Wood, who works under Marshal Webb, of Weleetka, immediately

telephoned to Webb, who told him to get help and go out and get him, and if he couldn't get him to locate where he likely would be and to organize a posse and go after him.

Wood then got City Marshal Dick Shaver, of Boley and went out to the Simmons home but found none of them there. They rode over the country until dark and came back close to the Simmons place. Shaver remarked to Wood, "You ride on ahead. I want to see Johnson a minute. I know he will tell me if he has seen Andy." So Wood rode slowly for 100 yards, when the road turned taking him out of sight of Shaver. Shaver had called Johnson out into the road and Johnson had just come up to Shaver when Dick Simmons, dressed in black clothes, shirt and hat, raised up from behind the fence and spoke to Johnson, saying "Johnson, have you seen my horses," at the same time firing his Winchester at Shaver. The ball struck Shaver in the back on the lower left side, going clear through the body. Shaver tried to dismount falling from his horse. He raised himself on his right side and fired twice, almost simultaneously, the balls striking Simmons in the upper part of the right breast. The bullet holes were less than an inch apart. The third shot fired by Shaver struck Simmons in the palm of the left hand passing up through the wrist, coming out just above the wrist joint on the back.

Only one of the two shots fired by Simmons took effect. All three of the shots fired by Shaver were effective.

During the shooting they were about 20 yards apart. Simmons was dead when Wood and Johnson went to him and Shaver died in about thirty minutes. . . .

Shaver had been in this country for five years and was well liked by both blacks and whites and had the confidence of all. He had just last week been installed as the first city marshal of Boley. He leaves a wife and three children to mourn his loss as well as the whole community in which he lived. His funeral services were conducted at Boley, Tuesday evening under the auspices of the colored Odd Fellows. The funeral procession was nearly a mile long and was attended by something like five hundred negroes.

Near or on the same date as the *Okemah Independent* article appeared, the *Boley Progress* reported:

Mr. Shaver has lived in the Territory since boyhood and knew every nook and corner. Mr. Shaver leaves a wife and four small children to mourn his loss, besides four brothers, one of which happened to be in Boley from Eufaula, I.T. about the time of the tragedy.

This was a dangerous time to be a black lawman in the Indian Territory. But despite all the changes in Indian Territory and its new population growth, nothing deterred Bass Reeves from doing his job as efficiently as he could, as he had always done in earlier days.

Reeves identified a felon he hadn't seen in many years in Muskogee's federal jail. On February 24, 1906, the *Tahlequah Arrow* carried a story about the reunion:

Charged with Murder

Deputy United States Marshal John Cordell arrived in Muskogee Monday with two prisoners, Barney Fixico, and an Indian named "Wild Cat," who are charged with the murder of Billy Culley, a prominent Seminole, on February 3. Deputy Marshal Bass Reeves immediately identified "Wild Cat" as a prisoner who had escaped from him nearly twenty years ago while the two were on their way to Fort Smith. It was supposed that "Wild Cat" was long since dead.

On February 26, 1906, the *Muskogee Democrat* carried a riveting crime story:

Woman Murdered by Burly Negro

Jennie Cunningham, a white woman about twenty-seven years old, was murdered with a club and her little nine year old boy may die from a blow on the head with the same club. Last night in a small shack in Caesar Addition in the north part of the city. Jim Lewis, a Negro, is under arrest charged with the horrible crime.

It was a very brutal murder. The bloody club used to do the work is over three feet long and was formerly used as a stake for a wire fence. It has a knot about six inches from the end, which is bespattered with blood and covered with hair. The woman was found lying on the floor in a pool of blood with the back and left side of her head crushed in and the boy was in bed. Both had their clothes on.

The pictures on the wall and the bed clothes were spattered with blood indicating that the blows must have been delivered with considerable force. The little boy's hands were bloody and blistered as though he had put his hands up to ward off the cruel blows.

The murderer evidently did not meet with much resistance as the house did not present any scene of disorder, as though a scuffle had taken place. The woman fell where she was struck, as there was blood in that end of the house only. . . .

Jennie Cunningham was a woman about five feet tall with dark red hair, and was a friend of the woman known as "Sade" Williams, who is well known to the police and officials. She bore a soiled reputation and associated with negroes. She and "Sade" used to live together in the south part of town in a small house near Coody's creek.

Chief Carter was notified of the crime early this morning and made the investigation with Bass Reeves. He does not give any credence to the story of the Negro about another man coming to the house and driving him away, but believes that Lewis is the guilty man himself.

It is known that the negro under arrest has been familiar with the dead woman, and the child is a half breed. It is reported that they have been quarreling and that he threatened yesterday to "do her up." All the circumstances of the affair make the officials inclined to believe that they have the man. . . .

About 4 o'clock this morning Jim Lewis, the negro, about twenty-five years old, who has been employed at L. L. Ellis' store in the north part of the city, called at the home of Bass Reeves, deputy marshal, and told him a story of how some white man had called at the home of Jennie Cunningham while he was there and shot through the door, driving him away and shot the Cunningham woman. Bass was suspicious of Lewis and arrested him for the crime.

Lewis claims he went to the Cunningham home after his washing and that while he was there a white man came to the door and said he was an officer, and on being refused admittance shot through the door. He claims he became scared and ran out the back door and hid in the grass for some time and then went back to the house but didn't hear any noise and went home and went to bed where he staid until about 4 o'clock when he got up to notify the officers.

The little boy was taken care of by the woman "Sade," who procured medical attention for him, and made arrangements for the funeral of his mother.

At the home this morning a negro woman tried to talk to the boy but he could not speak, although he opened his eyes. His mouth seemed closed tight, but the woman opened it with a spoon and gave him some water, which he seemed to drink eagerly.

The dead woman has some relatives who will be notified if it is possible to learn where they are located. It is reported that an insurance policy was found among her effects. The body will be taken care of by the Home Undertaking company, a negro institution. The murdered woman had a sister and a son sixteen years of age living in Joplin, Mo. They will arrive in the city this evening and will make arrangements for the funeral.

The dead woman carried a policy in the Metropolitan Life Insurance company for $930.

Reeves could read people very well, and he most likely arrested the correct person is this instance.

A territorial newspaper, the *Ada Evening News*, carried an interesting story concerning Bass's son Ben on November 7, 1906:

Muskogee I.T., Nov. 6—To Indian Territory belongs the distinction and dishonor of having in the United States Penitentiary at Fort Leavenworth, Kansas, the model prisoner of the place, and the most untractable prisoner also. The former is Ben Reeves, a young Negro sent up for the murder of his wife, and the other prisoner is Lee Voss, also a Negro. The officers of the penitentiary state that there has never been a better behaved prisoner in that penitentiary than young Reeves. He is the son of Bas Reeves, a Negro deputy marshal at Muskogee, who has been in the government service twenty years. Young Reeves shot his wife and killed her in a fit of jealous anger. He was arrested and placed in jail by his own father. He got a life sentence. Lee Voss was sent up three years for robbery on a five year sentence. He will not work and sulks all the time.

From his early career in the 1870s, Bass Reeves was always dodging bullets, figuratively and literally. The *Muskogee Daily Phoenix* carried the following article about an attempt made on Reeves life on November 14, 1906:

An Attempted Assassination: Deputy Marshal Bass Reeves Shot At by Unknown Parties

An attempt was made to assassinate Deputy Marshal Bass Reeves near Wybark, Tuesday night while the marshal was scouring the country after criminals, for whom he had warrants. Reeves was driving under a railroad trestle a short distance from the town when he was fired on by an unknown foe. Reeves turned in the seat and fired several shots in the direction of the would be assassin. Reeves was not hit but the bullet splintered the wood in the trestle directly above his head. Reeves, who is a colored man, is one of the best known deputies in the western district and has been on Marshal Bennett's force for years. He is a valuable officer, especially in capturing negro criminals. He has been in a number of pitched battles, and today carries a bullet in one of his legs, received in one of his many fights with desperadoes.

Reeves's daughter Alice Spahn told of another assassination attempt near Wybark. When a man reported that some of his hogs had been stolen, Reeves went to the home of the man suspected of the theft. When he arrived in the morning the man was cleaning up, and Reeves noticed hog hair on the fireplace. Reeves had breakfast with the man and then informed him that he had a warrant for the pork theft. He then went on to tell him that if he gave evidence against the other parties involved he would help the man with the court case. The man confessed and showed Reeves where the hogs were killed and gave him the names of the other accomplices. While riding back to Muskogee around sundown with two of the men under arrest and handcuffed, a shot rang out. Reeves told the men in the buggy with him not to say a word, when another shot rang out; Bass fell back with his gun cocked. A shooter stepped out in the open and Reeves shot him in the stomach. The shooter and his confederate gave up on the spot and Reeves brought four men into Muskogee.[11]

On December 21, 1906, Reeves arrested a Johnson Vann, aliases John Vann and John Wolf, for impersonation. Vann had told land speculators that he was a Cherokee Freedman and wanted to sell his allotment property. The speculators paid Vann $250 and later learned he didn't own the land he had sold them.[12]

The year 1907 was the last year of the territorial period. On November 16 the new state of Oklahoma would rush in. Reeves was well known throughout the twin territories, and the largest newspaper write-up he would receive would come from the *Oklahoma City Weekly Times-Journal* in Oklahoma Territory on Friday, March 8, 1907. Portions of the *Weekly Times-Journal* article appeared earlier in the book. The following is the remaining text:

He Has Killed Fourteen Men: A Fearless
Negro Deputy of the Indian Territory

In Muskogee, I.T., lives Bass Reeves a negro. He has been a United States deputy marshal for thirty-two years and has killed fourteen men in that time.

"For thirty-one years, going on thirty-two, I have ridden as a deputy marshal, sir, and when Marse Bennett goes out of office I am going to farming for a living," is the simple way that Reeves tells the story of his life as an officer in a country at a time that every day's service was a hazardous one. Reeves has served under seven different United States marshals, democrats and republicans. With the expiration of the present federal regime upon the advent of statehood, he will, as he says, go to farming for a living, lying for the plow the six shooter, which in his hand has been a potent element in bringing two territories out of the reign of the outlaw, the horsethief and bootlegger, to a great common wealth.

Reeves is an Arkansas negro. He is six feet tall, 68 years old and looks to be 40. He was never known to show the slightest excitement under any circumstance. He does not know what fear is, and to him the one supreme document and law of the country is a "writ." Place a warrant for arrest in his hands and no circumstance can cause him to deviate. I saw him once arrest his own son charged with murder, take him to jail and place him behind the bars. It was for a most diabolical crime. The negro had brutally murdered his young wife. This was probably the most trying moment in the whole life of the old deputy. He walked into the office of Marshal Bennett and was told that there was a warrant for his son for murder, and asked if he did not want someone else to serve it. "Give me the writ," was all he said. . . .

During his lifetime Reeves had some mighty close calls. His belt was shot in two once, his hat brim shot away, a button on his coat was shot off, the bridle reins in his hand were shot in two. Yet he has never had the hood drawn in a fight, though fourteen men in all have had their lives snuffed out by his deadly gun and in not a single instance did he ever shoot at a man until the other fellow started the fight. . . .

Reeves has been tried for murder, but was never convicted, always proving that he was discharging his official duty. One time he was out with a posseman, so the story goes, when the latter became enraged and threw some hot grease on a favorite dog belonging to Reeves. Reeves whipped out his six-shooter and shot the negro posseman dead. He pitched forward into the camp fire, and the deputy was so enraged that he let the body lie in the fire until it was charred. Reeves denies part of this story, but he stood trial for murder on account of it and it cost him practically all he had ever made as a deputy marshal to keep out of jail for the offense.

The old deputy says the worst criminals and hardest to catch are Seminole Indians and [Seminole] negroes. They stick together better, fight quicker and fight to kill. A Seminole on the scout is always on horseback, never sleeps until after midnight and gets up with the sun; every minute he is not asleep he is on his horse. He does not get off to eat. He is given a piece of meat and bread, and sits in his saddle and eats it, watching all the time for and expected foe.

Even while he related his tale, Reeves commenced to shift uneasily and, when I asked him what was the matter, he said:

"There is a nigger across the street who ought to be arrested."

When I asked why, he said he could tell every time when a negro had been breaking the law just as soon as he saw him, and when I asked how he could tell, he said: "Every nigger who is guilty has a fear on him, and when he sees an officer he cannot hide it, but tries to get away as quickly as possible."[13]

Racial attitudes were quickly changing in the territories with Oklahoma statehood looming nearer. It is not known if Reeves actually used the word nigger or if the writer threw it in trying to color the dialogue. The same goes for the word "marse" instead of marshal; it is almost as if the interviewer is conveying that Reeves was calling Bennett "master." Considering his long service and remarkable dedication to duty, had Reeves been a white lawman it is quite possible he would have been as popular as any ever written about during the late nineteenth century, including Wyatt Earp, Wild Bill Hickock, Pat Garrett, or fictionalized characters such as Marshal Dillon of *Gunsmoke*.

The Seminoles that Reeves alludes to in his interview were the greatest foe the U.S. Army ever faced in the Indian wars. The African and Indian confederation of warriors in the southeast, known as Seminoles, killed more than a thousand U.S. soldiers in Florida. The U.S. Army would not lose as many soldiers in battle to any other Indian tribe in the nineteenth century. It stands to reason that Seminoles would make dangerous outlaws, just like many of them, such as African-Seminole Lighthorseman Dennis Cyrus, became outstanding lawmen in the Indian Territory. A contingent of the black Seminoles gave great service to the U.S. Army as scouts on the Texas frontier after the Civil War. They were known officially as the Negro Seminole Indian Scouts. Three of them won the Medal of Honor.

When I first started compiling information on Reeves I found a man who grew up in Muskogee named Rev. Haskell James Shoeboot. At the time I spoke to him in 1988, he told me he was ninety-eight years old. In my conversation with him, he was emphatic about telling me a story concerning Reeves he had witnessed with his own eyes. Reverend Shoeboot said that as a very young man, he would drive a horse-drawn hack for Chief Deputy U.S. Marshal Bud Ledbetter. Reverend Shoeboot related the following story concerning an incident that would have occurred late in Reeves's law enforcement career:

> Bud Ledbetter was in pursuit of a white outlaw who had committed a terrible crime near Gibson Station, Indian Territory, twelve miles north of Muskogee. Early in the day Ledbetter and his large posse were able to pin down the outlaw with gunfire. As the day progressed, Ledbetter and his posse did not make any gain in subduing the outlaw, and by early afternoon they had expended a large amount of ammunition. At this time, Ledbetter became very frustrated and requested the assistance of Bass Reeves. Reeves was sent for and arrived on the scene near sunset. The posse had stopped shooting at the outlaw as daylight was fading, so the desperado decided to make a run for it on foot. Posse members fired on the running target, but missed. Ledbetter hollered, "Get 'em Bass!" Bass replied, "I'll break his neck." At a distance of a quarter-mile, Reeves, with one shot from his Winchester rifle, broke the outlaw's neck.[14]

The most sensational gunfight in Muskogee happened just months before statehood. In 1905 an African American minister at Wagoner, named William Wright, organized a society of two hundred black members called the "Tenth Cavalry." Wright called himself "General Grant" in the circulars he distributed and claimed to be an agent of the president of the United States. President Theodore Roosevelt sent the Secret Service to investigate. Wright's Tenth Cavalry disbanded and Wright left town. Several years later Wright appeared at Muskogee with a new venture called the United Socialist Club. Each member wore a badge issued by a private detective company in Cincinnati, Ohio, and was promised 160 acres of land.

Wright also taught the scriptures, along with anarchy and his own version of voodoo. His followers were taught that they had the right to occupy any property they pleased without paying the owner anything. He also taught that the wearing of a conjure bag would render the wearer immune to death.

One of his followers was named Carrie Foreman. She took over a house that belonged to the realtors Rowsers and Young on Fond du Lac Street between Second and Third streets. Being unable to collect any rent from the woman, the owners sold the house to a Mr. Sitz. When Sitz went to collect his rent, he was referred to the woman's lodge. There he was informed that she was a member of the United Socialist Club and had the right to any property she chose and could keep it as long as she pleased. Sitz promptly went to the city marshal's office and swore out a warrant for Carrie Foreman.

Two city constables, John Colfield and Guy Fisher, were dispatched to serve the eviction warrant. When they arrived at the house and stated their purpose, the officers were seized by two male members of the United Socialist Club. Both were armed, one with a revolver and the other with a shotgun. A struggle ensued and Fisher escaped but was wounded in the shoulder. Colfield fell, shot through the chest, near the heart.[15]

On March 26, 1922, the *Muskogee Phoenix* gave the following description of the gunfight:

> About 2 o'clock in the afternoon of March 26, 1907, the quiet of the town was shattered when Charlie Kimsey, chief of police, dashed down the muddy, unpaved street in his buggy, drawn by a spirited sorrel horse, and drew up in front of the old federal courthouse at Second and Court Streets.
>
> There he repeated the report that had come to him that Po-

liceman John Colfield had been shot down by negroes barricaded in a big two-story building in the north end of town.

"Uncle Bud" (Ledbetter) was on the front steps. He grabbed two rifles and jumped into the buggy besides Kimsey. As they dashed away, a Phoenix reporter who was also at the courthouse, scrambled into the back of the buggy and clung to the seat for his life.

The other officers at the courthouse, among them Chief Deputy Marshal Ernest Hubbard and Deputy Marshal Paul C. Williams, were galvanized into action, and they arrived at the scene close behind Ledbetter and Kimsey.

As the chief of police drew up in his horse buggy in front of the building a rifle was fired and the zip of a bullet overhead caused "Uncle Bud" to leap out of the buggy, rifle in hand.

The shot was followed by another, and Chief Kimsey's horse was panic striken and it ran away. The reporter was thrown out of the back end of the buggy, but lost no time getting to cover. The horse dashed away with Kimsey, but as quickly as possible he regained control of the animal and hurried back.

Two negroes were standing on the front porch of the building as "Uncle Bud" jumped out of the buggy. He started toward them, and as he did so they opened fire on him, one with a rifle and the other with a revolver.

Almost as quickly "Uncle Bud" fired back, and one of the negroes flinched as the bullet struck him. "Uncle Bud" sought shelter behind a telephone pole and emptied his rifle at the two negroes, hitting them both several times but escaping unscathed himself.

Before he had fired his last shot from his rifle and thrown it down for his pistol, Paul Williams had reached his side and together they continued the fire. Other officers surrounded the house and opened fire.

When the first of the two negroes finally fell, the other stooped to take aim at Ledbetter, but was instantly shot through the head.

As "Uncle Bud" fired this shot, another Negro on the second

floor poked a rifle through the window and took deliberate aim on him. Paul Smith, a Negro policeman there with the other officers saw him and shot the Negro through the head, killing him instantly and saving "Uncle Bud's" life.

Another negro leaned far out of a window to take aim at an officer and "Uncle Bud" shot him through the stomach.

"Uncle Bud" was known to have killed at least two of the Negroes and Smith another. Later two others were found at some distance from the house, lying dead. They had been wounded and had dragged themselves away to die.

Two other negroes were wounded and four others were taken prisoner. Colfield and Guy Fisher, another officer, were shot, but both recovered. . . .

Following the fight, feelings were at a fever heat throughout the town, but at no time was a race war threatened because Negroes were as bitter in their condemnation of the socialist outlaws as were the white people.

Two thousand or more white people and negroes gathered together about the federal jail and for a time it was feared that together they might lynch the negroes who had been taken prisoner, but a heavy guard was maintained until the excitement died down.

Negroes who had been eyewitnesses to the fight made public statements commending the officers and declaring that nothing else could have been done under the circumstances.

Ed Jefferson, a prominent African American citizen, witnessed the initial shooting and called police. A short time later, he noticed several men had congregated at the house on Fourth Street, so he telephoned the U.S. marshal's office to inform them the city police would need reinforcements.

According to the *Phoenix* article, five members of the fanatical socialist group had been killed. Of the leaders, Tom Jackson had been shot through the neck and J. T. Terrill was shot in the groin. The latter escaped and was found the following morning in a shack in the Dean settlement, near an old brickyard in the south part of Muskogee. William

Wright, Milo Wilson, Richard Gootch, and Allen Andrews surrendered to the officers. Tom Jackson and James Brown were dragged out and taken to the hospital where Brown's arm was amputated. The house was spattered with gore where the wounded men had dragged themselves around. Frank Reed, another black city policeman, took the arrested men to jail and helped to handle the crowd gathered at the jail.[16]

In the articles I perused previously on this shootout in Muskogee, Bass Reeves's name was never mentioned. It wasn't until later, when I was conducting research for this book, that I found Reeves's name linked to this occurrence. The following appeared in the black newspaper, the *Muskogee Cimeter*, on March 29, 1907:

> The Democrat [newspaper] wants to know where the city police were when the deputy U.S. marshals engaged the desperate Negroes in battle. Reliable authority said they flew to the rescue in a closed carriage after the affray had ended. Twine says the Democrat knows that Paul Smith one of the black policemen was there on the ground close by Ledbetter and doing his duty like a brave man but the Democrat won't give him credit because he is black.
>
> The democrats know that they cannot win the battle with the Negroes' aid and they also know that their conduct toward the Negroes does not warrant them giving the Democrat their support. Hence the only hope for them is to buy, if they can sufficient votes to win.
>
> Let every true manly Negro stand up for the Republican party and persuade his brother to do likewise.
>
> Paul Smith has covered himself with glory and won the respect of the entire people by stand he took and by his obedience to duty. City officer stood by Ledbetter and put his life in the balance for his people, country, and his party.
>
> Desperate conflict between outlaws and officers; 3 Negroes dead and one white man seriously wounded, but no race riot.
>
> All this trouble (evening of 26th) about 4 o'clock on north 3rd Street, grows out of an anarchistic organization among some of our people, the foundation of which that nobody must work. An

old preacher is at the head of this society and his followers are densely ignorant. They believe in everything he tells them. This old voodoo assisted by others has worked up a crowd of fanatics that is dangerous to any community. No intelligent Negro can advise or counsel them. They are taught to believe that all property is held in common and that they can occupy any dwelling or business free of rent, than they must fight to death if they are disturbed by the real owners of the property. Situation might have been worse as there were a number of women and children in the house when the battle occurred. This same bunch had been digging all over the country wherever the spirits directed in search for buried treasure and have held meetings incessantly plotting against society. The industrious and sensible Negroes have neither time nor inclination to indulge in assisting these outlaws and it is a lie to call the affair a riot. It is just like the Democrat to send out such a lie as it did, probably for campaign purposes. Three colored men with the officers trying to preserve the peace. Paul Smith, Bass Reeves and R.C. Cotton. Said that Smith saved the life of one of the marshals. The battle was short but hot. The fanatics were desperate and showed the customary brute courage of all fanatics. All good people are with the law; while they deplore the incident, still all of us, black, white and red are proud of the fact that law and order reigns supreme in our city.

I also discovered that Reeves's daughter Alice Spahn talked about this particular incident in her interview with Richard Fronterhouse in 1959:

A secret order was not paying rent. The house was located on Fourth Street. The rent man was run off, this occurred on a Sunday afternoon. Ledbetter and two or three other police officers sent down to arrest them. The house windows were shot out by the police officers. Two men in crowd that had gathered on the scene were shot from an upstairs window. The crowd that had gathered ran in all directions. The police held the outlaws at bay in the house. Bass was sent for, his house was on the corner of Fourth and Court. Bass goes down to see what is going on, great excitement created in the town by the shootout. Bass sees that the disadvantage is on the street for the police. The crowd gathered is told to keep quiet by Bass, he then ask what window most of the shooting is coming from in the house. A gunman appears in the window pointed out by the crowd. Bass took careful aim and shot the man in the window with his Winchester rifle and wounded him severely. Shortly the rest of the men in the building surrendered and seven men were taken to jail.

Of the many criminal arrest made by Reeves, William Henry Twine was the attorney on record for the defendants in Muskogee. Twine, a unique individual, was the leading black attorney in Muskogee and publisher of the *Muskogee Cimeter* newspaper. Coming from Texas in 1890, Twine established with E. I. Saddler and G. W. F. Sawner the first black law partnership in Oklahoma Territory. The newspaper was founded in 1899 and ran for about twenty-five years. As an attorney, Twine defended many of the African Americans who were arrested by the deputy U.S. marshals and city police for various crimes.

It is not known whether Reeves and Twine developed an adversarial relationship. Twine's son Pliny told me he had never heard them having one. From my research, it appears Reeves was not mentioned much at all in the *Cimeter*. I also never located Reeves's obituary notice in that particular newspaper. It could have been that Reeves was identified with the Indian Freedman community, even though he was not one, whereas Twine was a leader of the State Negroes in Muskogee. It appears that Twine did have a good relationship with some of the leaders of the Indian Freedman community. He was one of the strongest black community leaders in Muskogee for years after statehood. He owned a building at 211 South Second Street, called the Twine Building in Muskogee, which was the home of the newspaper. Three of Twine's sons later became lawyers. W. H. Twine was called the "Black Tiger" because he was so vocal in defending constitutional rights of African Americans, and after statehood he prevented several lynching of blacks in Muskogee by leading armed black men in a show of force. Twine had a town named after him in 1902; he was one of its founders. At the time of statehood, 225 blacks, 21 whites, and four Indians lived in Twine, located ten miles west of Muskogee. In 1908 the town changed its name to Taft, in honor of the secretary of war and future U.S. president. W. H. Twine was born at Red House, Kentucky, on December 10, 1864, and died in Muskogee on October 12, 1933. He is buried in the Booker T. Washington Cemetery.[17]

On April 8, 1907, Reeves arrested a murderer named J. L. Ashford, who had killed a man named Drayton L. Chaney two days earlier in Muskogee. In this case Ashford and his cousin Chaney, who had a janitorial business together, had a fight over the money that was supposed to be shared. In the fight, Ashford shot and killed Chaney. Ashford was arrested by a city policeman named J. V. Peters and turned over to Reeves, who then escorted the young man to the federal jail.[18]

A few days later, on April 10, Bass Reeves arrested a young man named Mack Cobb for assault with intent to kill. On Christmas Day 1906, Cobb had viciously attacked Hector Grayson in Muskogee. The file doesn't indicate the final outcome of the court proceedings. In the early twentieth century, Mack Cobb would become a policeman patrolling the black community in Muskogee.[19]

Later in the year, on July 19, 1907, a newspaper article appeared in the *Muskogee Times-Democrat* providing evidence that Reeves was still as good a man hunter as in the days when he worked for Judge Parker:

Negro Assailant Caught at Summit

Will Smith, the negro who struck Henry Sites in the head with a hoe yesterday in a cotton patch west of Muskogee, was caught late yesterday afternoon on the railroad track near Summit, by Deputy Bass Reeves.

Deputy Reeves and Officer Grant Huddleston chased the negro from the scene of his attack upon Sites to the negro's home, and thence through a large corn field, using the blood hounds to trail the criminal. At the edge of the corn field, however, one of the blood hounds was overcome by the intense heat, and as its mate showed signs of collapse. Officer Huddleston returned to the buggy and took his dogs to town.

Reeves, divining that Smith had probably gone down the

Katy track, took after him. The fugitive was overtaken a mile down the track and brought back to Muskogee late in the afternoon.

On August 24, 1907, the Arkansas *Van Buren Press* carried a most interesting story on their famous former resident:

Paid Church Debt Selling Booze

Muskogee, Indian Territory, Aug. 21—Rev. Wilson Hobson, a Negro Baptist preacher, was arrested here, charged with selling liquor. He was placed under a $500 bond. It is claimed by the members of Hobson's church that he sold liquor to the members in order to pay off a church debt. The members wanted the whiskey and were perfectly willing that their pastor should sell it to them as long as the money went to pay off the church debt. Hobson was arrested by Bass Reeves, a Negro Deputy Marshal who was baptized by Hobson 3 years ago.

Not only did Bass Reeves arrest one of his sons for murder, he arrested the minister who baptized him. It is evident that Reeves was quite determined to uphold the law no matter the relationship he had with the offender.

On November 16, 1907, Bass Reeves had his picture taken with what the newspapers of the time called the "first federal family" of the Western District. It was their last official act. The following day, many of the duties of the U.S. marshal service would be given to the municipalities and counties of the new state of Oklahoma. There was no longer a need for a large force of federal police, the men who had helped bring law and order to the territory. There would be no more African American deputy U.S. marshals until late in the twentieth century. After statehood in Oklahoma, black men could only become the "Negro Police," with orders to only arrest blacks, in towns where there was a large black population. Reeves was not out of work long. On January 10, 1908, the *Western Age*, the newspaper of the black town of Langston, Oklahoma Territory, which had been founded by E. P. McCabe, carried a story on Reeves:

Negro Deputy U.S. Marshal a Policeman

Muskogee, Okla., Jan. 2.—Former Deputy United States Marshal Bass Reeves a giant negro, who was in many battles with outlaws in the wild days of Indian Territory and during Judge Parker's reign at Fort Smith, is on the Muskogee police force. Reeves was twice tried for murder while he was an officer. He is now over 70 years old and walks with a cane. A bullet in his leg, received while in the government service, gives him considerable trouble. He is as quick of trigger, however, as in the days when gun men were in demand.

Reeves was given a beat in Muskogee patrolling the area from the site of the Orpheum Theater, later known as the Ritz Theater, north to Fourth Street between the courthouse to the MK&T Railroad tracks. Bass was proud of the record he established on this beat. It is reported that, for the two-year period that Reeves patrolled this area, there was not even a minor crime committed. I was told by Reverend Shoeboot, who was a young man in Muskogee after the turn of the century, that Bass at this time would walk the streets of Muskogee with a sidekick who would carry a satchel full of pistols. If someone called Reeves's name, he would always put his back up against the wall before he turned his head to see who was calling his name. That is what one would describe as being prudent and cautious.[20]

The *Muskogee Times-Democrat* on November 19, 1909, carried a story concerning Reeves's health:

Bass Reeves Is a Very Sick Man

Bass Reeves, a deputy United States Marshal in old Indian Territory for over thirty years, is very ill at his home in the Fourth ward and is not expected to live.

Reeves was a deputy under Leo Bennett in the last years of the federal regime in Oklahoma, and also served in the old days of Judge Parker at Fort Smith.

In the early days when the Indian country was over-ridden with outlaws Reeves was sent to go through the Indian country and gather up criminals which were tried at Fort Smith. These trips lasted sometimes for months and Reeves would herd into

Fort Smith often single handed, bands of men charged with crimes from bootlegging to murder. He was paid fees in those days which some times amounted to thousands of dollars for a single trip. For a time Reeves made a great deal of money and was said to be worth considerable. He then shot a man whom he was trying to arrest and was tried for murder. The fight for life in the courts was a bitter one, but finally Reeves was acquitted on the testimony of a young negro girl. He was freed, but not until most of his money was gone.

The veteran negro deputy never quailed in facing any man. Chief Ledbetter says of the old man that he is one of the bravest men this country has ever known.

He was honest, fearless, and a terror to the bootleggers. He was as polite as an old-time slave to the white people and most loyal to his superiors.

His son shot and killed his own wife and Reeves, enforcing the law arrested his own son. The young negro was sent to the penitentiary.

While the old man is slowly sinking, Bud Ledbetter, who for years was in the government service with Reeves, is caring for the old man the best he can and is a daily visitor at the Reeves home. Police Judge Walrond, who was United States district attorney while Reeves was an officer, also calls on the old negro.

"While Reeves could neither read nor write," said Judge Walrond today, "he had a faculty of telling what warrants to serve on any one and never made a mistake. Reeves carried a batch of warrants in his pocket and when his superior officers asked him to produce it the old man would run through them and never fail to pick out the one desired."

Since statehood Reeves was given a place on the police force, but became ill and unable to work. For the past year he has been growing weaker, and has but little time to spend in this world. He is nearly seventy years old.

The same newspaper printed the following story on January 13, 1910:

Bass Reeves Dead

Bass Reeves, colored, for 32 years a deputy United States marshal in Indian Territory who served under the famous Judge Parker at Fort Smith and later at Muskogee, a man credited with fourteen notches on his gun and a terror to outlaws and desperadoes in the old days, died at home at 816 North Howard street late yesterday afternoon at the age of 72. Death was caused by Bright's disease and complications.

A more insightful story appeared in the *Muskogee Phoenix* on January 13, 1910, shortly after Reeves's death:

Bass Reeves Dead: Unique Character

Man of the "Old Days" Gone: Deputy Marshal Thirty-Two Years

Bass Reeves is dead. He passed away yesterday afternoon about three o'clock and in a short time news of his death had reached the federal court house where the announcement was received in the various offices with comments of regret and where it was recalled to the officers and clerks many incidents in the early days of the United States court here in which the old negro deputy featured heroically.

Bass Reeves had completed thirty-two years service as deputy marshal when, with the coming of statehood at the age of sixty-nine he gave up his position. For about two years then he served on the Muskogee police force, which position he gave up about a year ago on account of sickness, from which he never fully recovered. Bright's disease and a complication of ailments together with old age, were the cause of death.

The deceased is survived by his wife and several children, only one of whom, a daughter, Mrs. Alice Spahn, lives in Muskogee. His mother, who is eighty-seven years old, lives at Van Buren, Arkansas, where a sister of his also is living.

The funeral will be held at noon Friday from the Reeves' home at 816 North Howard Street. Arrangements for the funeral had not been completed last evening.

Bass Reeves Career

In the history of the early days of Eastern Oklahoma the name of Bass Reeves has a place in the front rank among those who cleansed out the old Indian Territory of outlaws and desperadoes. No story of the conflict of government's officers with those outlaws which ended only a few years ago with the rapid filling up of the territory with people, can be complete without mention of the negro who died yesterday.

For thirty-two years, beginning way back in the seventies and ending in 1907, Bass Reeves was a deputy United States marshal. During that time he was sent to arrest some of the most desperate characters that ever infested Indian Territory and endangered life and peace in its borders. And he got his man as often as any of the deputies. At times he was unable to get them alive and so in the course of his long service he killed fourteen men. But Bass Reeves always said that he never shot a man when it was not necessary for him to do so in the discharge of his duty to save his own life. He was tried for murder on one occasion but was acquitted upon proving that he had killed the man in the discharge of his duty and was forced to do it.

Reeves was an Arkansan and in his early days was a slave. He entered the federal service as a deputy marshal long before a court was established in Indian Territory and served under the marshal at Fort Smith. Then when people started to come into Indian Territory and a marshal was appointed with headquarters in Muskogee, he was sent over here.

Reeves served under seven United States marshals and all of them were more than satisfied with his services. Everybody who came in contact with the negro deputy in an official capacity had a great deal of respect for him, and at the court house in Muskogee one can hear stories of his devotion to duty, his unflinching courage and his many thrilling experiences, and although he could not write or read he always took receipts and had his accounts in good shape.

Undoubtedly the act which best typifies the man and which

at least shows his devotion to duty, was the arrest of his son. A warrant for the arrest of the younger Reeves, who was charged with murder of his wife, had been issued. Marshal Bennett said that perhaps another deputy had better be sent to arrest him. The old negro was in the room at the time, and with a devotion of duty equaling that of the old Roman, Brutus, whose greatest claim on fame has been that the love for his son could not sway him from justice, he said, "Give me the writ," and went out and arrested his son, brought him into court and upon trial and conviction he was sentenced to imprisonment and is still serving his sentence.

Reeves had many narrow escapes. At different times his belt was shot in two, a button shot off his coat, his hat brim shot off and the bridle reins which he held in his hands cut by a bullet. However, in spite of all these narrow escapes and many conflicts in which he was engaged, Reeves was never wounded. And this not withstanding the fact that he said he never fired a shot until the desperado he was trying to arrest had started the shooting.

On January 15, 1910, after Bass Reeves was buried, the *Muskogee Phoenix* followed up with another story. Some of the racial attitudes of the time come across in the article, but the respect given to Reeves is quite clear. For an African American to receive this type of salutation by a white newspaper in 1910 America was quite unusual and unique. It confirms the fact that Reeves was someone special.

Bass Reeves

Bass Reeves, negro, was buried yesterday and the funeral was attended by a large number of white people—men who in the early days knew the deputy marshal and admired him as a faithful officer and respected him as an honest man.

Bass Reeves was an unique character. Absolutely fearless and knowing no master but duty, the placing of a writ in his hands for service meant that the letter of the law would be fulfilled though his life paid the penalty. In the carrying out of his orders during his thirty-two years as a deputy United States marshal in the old Indian Territory days, Bass Reeves faced death a hundred times, many desperate characters sought his life yet the old man even on the brink of the grave went along the pathway of duty with the simple faith that some men have who believe that they are in the care of special providence when they are doing right.

The arrest of his own son for wife-murder, for which crime the young man is now serving a life sentence, is best illustration of the old deputy's Spartan character. He performed that duty as he did all others entrusted to him—and he was invariably given the worst cases—with an eye single to doing his duty under the law.

Black-skinned, illiterate, offspring of slaves whose ancestors were savages, this simple old man's life stands white and pure alongside some our present-day officials in charge of affairs since the advent of statehood. To them duty, honor and respect for law are but by-words, and their only creed is "get what you can and stand in with the Boss."

Bass Reeves would not have served under such a regime. Black though he was he was too white for that. His simple, honest faith in the righteousness of the law would brook no disrespect for its mandates, and some of the little ones in charge now would not have dared suggest such a thing to this man who feared nothing but the possibility that he might do wrong.

Bass is dead. He was buried with high honors, and his name will be recorded in the archives of the court as a faithful servant of the law and a brave officer. And it was fitting that such recognition was bestowed upon this man. It is fitting that, black or white, our people have the manhood to recognize character and faithfulness to duty. And it is lamentable that we as white people must go to this poor, simple old negro to learn a lesson in courage, honesty and faithfulness to official duty.

The probate on Bass Reeves's estate was handled on July 13, 1913, by his son-in-law A. C. Spahn, who was made administrator of the estate. W. H. Twine served as the notary public for the proof of publication. The estate was said to not exceed the value of five hundred dollars.

There were two claims presented and allowed. A. C. Spahn asked for $15.60 for the cost of advertising the notice of petition in the *Muskogee Cimiter* for two consecutive weeks. W. M. Ragsdale's funeral home asked for $74.60 and was allowed $50.00 by Muskogee County Judge Thomas W. Leahy. A. C. Spahn listed the following parties as heirs on the petition:

Winnie Reeves	age 65 years, residence, East First St. Los Angeles, Cal.,	Wife
Sallie Sanders	age 48 years, residence, Ft. Smith, Ark.,	Daughter
Alice M. Spahn	age 33 years, residence, Muskogee, Okla.,	"
Bennie Reeves	age 31 years, residence, Leavenworth, Kans.,	Son
Ed Reeves	age 28 years, residence, Independence, Kans.,	"
Mary Reeves	age 24 years, residence, McAlester, Okla.,	Grand-daughter
Rother Reeves	age 21 years, residence, " "	, Grand-son.[21]

Bass Reeves's life story is a true American saga of an individual leaving a legacy of commitment and contribution. It is a real "Wild West" story that fiction writers could never have imagined. Although never attaining great wealth or becoming an influential politician, Reeves made a significant impact on the lives of pioneers and homesteaders. A policeman's job entails being a public servant and to serve and protect. Reeves went above and beyond the call of duty. There is no evidence that he deferred to anyone on the basis of status, wealth, ethnicity, or religion. His accomplishments are all the more meaningful when you consider the discrimination black people had to endure during the late nineteenth and early twentieth centuries.

As a peace officer, Bass Reeves committed his life to making the Indian Territory a safer place for pioneers and settlers to live and work. He became the most feared lawman in the Indian Territory without becoming abusive or overbearing. The example of Reeves's career is an impetus for police officers today, worldwide.

Reeves rose above his humble beginnings as a slave and persevered and excelled as a federal lawman even though he was illiterate. His legend is one of the greatest frontier biographies in the history of our country. It ranks right along those of Daniel Boone, Davy Crockett, Buffalo Bill Cody, Will Bill Hickock, Crazy Horse, and Geronimo.

Bass Reeves's law enforcement career was a testimonial to the American creed of "truth, honesty, and justice." In 1995, after reading about the exciting exploits of Bass Reeves, Oklahoma native Russ Marker wrote the following poem, which I think is a fitting epitaph to the story of Deputy U.S. Marshal Bass Reeves:

An American Hero

He was U.S. Deputy Marshal Reeves,
The sworn enemy of killers and thieves,
Who devoted his life to serving the law,
One of the best the Old West ever saw.

He faced mortal danger a thousand times
From the perpetrators of countless crimes,
But for thirty-two years on a raw frontier,
Bass Reeves never showed an ounce of fear.

Although a dead shot when using a gun,
A rifle or a pistol, either one,
He always tried to avoid gunplay,
Believing an arrest was a better way.

But some hard cases, who thought they were tough,
Or else just didn't have sense enough
To play it safe and protect their skins,
Wound up paying dearly for their sins.

They defied the marshal and were shot forthwith,
Or danced on the gallows at old Fort Smith;
Where their rotten souls were consigned to hell,
And civilization was served quite well.

Now I'm sure there are bleeding hearts who'll sob
At the way Bass Reeves went about his job,
But to my way of thinking those folks are dense,
I pay no attention to all their nonsense.

You must bear in mind, those perilous days
Demanded courageous and drastic ways.

To pave the way for churches and schools,
Sometimes good men had to break some rules.

A part of the reason we've come this far,
Is because of those gents who wore the star.
And we need to remember now and again,
There were African Americans among those men.

Yes, sir, Bass Reeves was as good as they came,
He proved himself a champ in a deadly game.
And when it was finally his time to go,
He died a genuine American hero.

Epilogue

After Bass Reeves, there were other legendary African American policemen in the United States during the twentieth century. Two policemen from the Midwest were especially noted for their law enforcement careers: Ira L. Cooper from St. Louis and Sylvester Washington from Chicago.

W. Martin Delaney wrote:

> Probably the most significant African American police officer of this generation was Ira L. Cooper of St. Louis. Appointed in 1906 as one of the department's "negro specials," Cooper was its first college graduate and its most famous detective and crime fighter. During his career he overcame the racial restrictions imposed upon him by the St. Louis department to solve several important crimes. In 1917, for example, he exposed a $35,000 bank embezzlement scheme concocted by a black porter. (White police detectives had failed to solve the year-old case because none of them believed that a black man had the intelligence to commit such a crime.) In 1930, Cooper solved the Jacob Hoffman kidnapping and broke up a ring that was operating in the city. He also had the toughness that characterized black officers of the "crime fighter" generation; in 1911 he single-handedly faced down a mob and prevented a lynching

by threatening to shoot anyone who approached him and his prisoner. Unlike many of his black contemporaries in other cities, Cooper was rewarded for his intelligence and ability. He became the department's first African American sergeant and lieutenant and commanded a squad of black detectives. His reputation as a crime fighter and detective earned him listings in Who's Who in Colored America. When Cooper died in 1939, he was eulogized as "St. Louis' greatest police officer," and one city official remarked that "but for his color he would have been made chief of the department."[1]

The second policeman, Sylvester Washington, known as "Two-Gun Pete," was a legend in his own time while working for the Chicago Police Department. My uncle Roland Traylor told me about an incident in a pool hall on the south side of Chicago. As a young man, Uncle Roland frequented the pool hall, and one night during the 1940s Officer Washington came in with a squad and told everyone to get up against the wall. Uncle Roland said the police officers were looking for some felons but everyone was scared out of their wits because of the reputation of Officer Washington.

Washington began his service with the Chicago Police Department in 1934 at the age of twenty-seven. He got his nickname because he carried two pearl-handled .357 revolvers while on duty. Washington arrested over twenty thousand criminals during his eighteen years as a policeman, and was officially credited with killing nine men in the line of duty. After his retirement in 1951, Washington told reporters, "By my own count, it was twelve."[2]

Featured in a January 1950 issue of *Ebony* magazine, the famed patrolman said:

> Maybe my career has been fabulous, but if it has, it's only because I found out that the only way to keep law and order and get respect from a hoodlum is (to) earn a reputation for yourself as tough or tougher than the roughest in the street. And to earn that reputation, you've got to meet a thug on his own term: shoot it out with him, if that's what he wants. . . .
>
> . . . I grew up in Chicago. I've been here since I was 14 years

old. And I don't have to read a newspaper story to know how a man feels when discrimination cheats him out of a decent job. I don't have to be told how bitter he feels when he can't find decent quarters for his family, or can't stretch the few dollars from his job to provide food enough for his family. I know all these things and I can understand what drives people to crime. But when a guy pokes a gun in your face and threatens your life, you don't think about them at all.

You can only think about your own safety and the safety of the community you swore to protect.

Like I said, my job is not to deal with the reasons for crime, but to apprehend criminals and bring them to justice.[3]

Washington stated he could put fourteen bull's-eyes into a target out of fifteen shots, and had a marksmanship record of 147 out of a possible 150 with his pistols. He got his nickname from a writer for the *Chicago Defender* newspaper named Dan Burley, who wrote a story on Officer Washington cleaning up Fifty-eighth Street in Chicago. He said, "When the name 'Pistol Pete' was mentioned along the 58th Street stroll, all the drunks and prostitutes shiver, shudder and break for cover." Burley went on to say that Washington was like Buffalo Bill and Wild Bill Hickock rolled into one. Washington was stuck with the nickname after the Burley article came out, although he didn't particularly like it. Washington died of a heart attack in 1972 in Chicago at the age of sixty-five. Sylvester "Two-Gun Pete" Washington is still a legend today in the streets of Chicago.[4]

Appendix

Tom Wing, a park ranger at the Fort Smith National Historic Site, National Park Service, sent me information from U.S. Marshal Thomas Boles's account book revealing the income Bass Reeves received during the early 1880s. We can compare his figures to that of J. H. Mershon, one of the few deputies who was making more money than Reeves at the time, and to that of Addison Beck, who was making an average salary. At this time, the deputies were being paid solely in the form of reimbursements for food, supplies, and mileage for travel. The only extra money they collected was a reward if they captured a notorious outlaw.

Bass Reeves

April–December 1882 .... $1,706.67
January–June 1883 .... 1,755.64
July–December 1883 .... 1,799.52
February–June 1884 .... 1,392.93
September 1884–December 1885 .... 2,750.47

J. H. Mershon

May–December 1882 .... $1,445.32
February–June 1883 .... 1,771.63
July–December 1883 .... 2,295.53
January–June 1884 .... 2,605.21
September 1884–December 1885 .... 3,494.00

In correspondence dated December 16, 2002, Superintendent Bill Black of the Fort Smith National Historic Site informed me that the U.S. Marshals Service relieved Mershon of duty in 1887 because of overstating his fees to be reimbursed.

Addison Beck

April–December 1882	$1,340.56
January–May 1883	967.22
June–October 1883	842.11

The following information on Deputy U.S. Marshal Bass Reeves is located in the Returns of Fees and Expenses of U.S. Marshals and Deputy Marshals, June 1896–June 1912, Record Group 60, Archives 2, National Archives and Records Administration in College Park, Maryland.

While serving for the Northern District of Indian Territory, a few deputies such as Paden Tolbert, Bud Trail, and Bud Ledbetter made more money than Reeves. But Reeves was still near the top in terms of deputies reimbursed for fees and expenses paid out of pocket. By the turn of the century deputies were paid an annual salary of nine hundred dollars. Reeves's receipts for reimbursements from September 1898 to June 1900, which would be monies added to his annual salary, were as follows:

1898

September	$90.42
10/1–11/15	82.02
11/16–12/31	85.02

1899

1/1–2/15	$64.67
2/16–3/31	55.88
June	160.83
	538.83

1899

September	$113.24
December	172.39

1900

March	$226.08

June 260.64
                                            772.35

1900
September $245.62
December 203.00

1901
March $197.20
June 188.17
                                            833.99

The following items pertaining to Deputy U.S. Marshal Bass Reeves were located in the correspondence from U.S. Marshal Leo E. Bennett to the U.S. attorney general, Department of Justice, Washington DC for the years 1906–7. Both were explanations in regard to fees paid to Reeves for his expenses:

Bass Reeves

#4—PP.12 and 13. The only practical and usually traveled route from Coweta to Wagoner at this time is by rail, via Muskogee. Deputy had to stop over in Muskogee, enroute to Wagoner, and while here, he was ordered by the Marshal to take defendant before Commissioner at Muskogee, thus saving time and expense of taking prisoner to Wagoner. Under the ruling of the department (Treasury Department), this is the way services of this kind should be rendered, otherwise the extra expense in going to Wagoner would have been disallowed.

The two departments at Washington seem to be at cross purposes in this class of cases.

Bass Reeves

#6—P.78. Deputy Adams who acted as posse did not serve any process on March 14. This trip was made at night of March 14, as shown by explanation, attached to account, and defendant arrested about 3 o'clock a.m. Had Deputy served process on 3/13 or 3/14, he would not being a salaried officer but working on fees, would be entitled to his per diem as a posse.

Notes

Introduction

1. To my knowledge, there is only one town in Oklahoma named after a deputy U.S. marshal who worked the Indian Territory. It is Paden, which is named for Paden Tolbert, a white man and contemporary of Bass Reeves.

1. The Lone Ranger and Other Stories

1. Author correspondence with David Craig, Tulsa ok, October 2001; Smith, *Daltons!: The Raid on Coffeyville, Kansas*, 63.

2. *U.S. vs. Bass Reeves*, 1884, Fort Smith–Western District Court of Arkansas, Federal Criminal Court Records (hereafter fs), jacket #160; Fran Striker and George Trendle, *The Lone Ranger* radio show, 1933, wxyz, Detroit mi.

3. Sandy Sturdivant, Tulsa ok, correspondence with author, February 1999.

4. Burton, *Black, Red, and Deadly*, 171–73.

5. Alice Hendrickson, interview by author, Muskogee ok, August 2001, and phone interview by author, Phoenix il, September 2001. Ms. Hendrickson's father worked for the Midland Valley Railroad. The Three Rivers Museum is in the former Muskogee Midland Valley Railroad station. The Parler Collection is in the Special Collections of the University of Arkansas Library, Fayetteville ar.

6. Hortense Love, phone interview by author, Chicago il, October 1988.

2. Arkansas Son

1. *Muskogee Phoenix*, January 13, 1910; 1870 U.S. Census, Crawford County ar, 1880 U.S. Census, Crawford County ar; 1900 U.S. Census, Muskogee, Creek Nation, Indian Territory; Death Certificate, Paralee (Harralee) Steward, no. 342, 1915, Crawford County Courthouse Records.

2. Death Certificate, Paralee (Harralee) Steward; Brady, *A Certain Blindness*,

14; Swinburn and West, *History in Headstones*; 1880 U.S. Census, Crawford County AR.

3. "Lawman Remembered," *Springdale (AR) Morning News*, February 9, 2001; Grayson County Frontier Village, "Biography of William Steele Reeves," 550.

4. Brady, *A Certain Blindness*, 3–4.

5. "Negro Deputy Marshal at Muskogee a Good One," *Chickasaw Enterprise*, November 28, 1901.

6. Burton, *Black, Red, and Deadly*, 168; Speer, *Encyclopedia of the New West*, 340; Fulmore, *History and Geography of Texas*, 188; Grayson County Frontier Village, *History of Grayson County, Texas*, 550; Hale, "Rehearsal for Civil War," 228.

7. *Chickasaw Enterprise*, November 28, 1901; Cottrell, *Civil War in the Indian Territory*, 39; Edwards, *The Prairie Was on Fire*, 9–14; Brady, *A Certain Blindness*, 12.

8. Alice Spahn, Bass Reeves's daughter, was interviewed several times by Richard Fronterhouse. Some information was included in his seminar paper "Bass Reeves: Forgotten Lawman," 1960; Burton, *Black, Buckskin, and Blue*, 112–13; Zellar, "Occupying the Middle Ground," 49.

3. Van Buren and Fort Smith

1. U.S. Census, 1870, Crawford County AR.

2. Brady, *A Certain Blindness*, 14.

3. 1880 Tax Records, Crawford County Courthouse Records; Hopkins and Gray-McGaugh, *History of Crawford County, Arkansas*, 147.

4. U.S. Census, 1880, Crawford County AR; Richard Fronterhouse, correspondence with Bass Reeves's daughter, Alice Spahn, December 1959, letter in author's collection; *Van Buren Press*, December 23, 1882; January 13, 1883.

5. Brodhead, *Isaac C. Parker*, 42; Burton, *Black, Red, and Deadly*, 4, 156.

6. John Ward, interview, Indian Pioneer Papers, OHS; Warren, *Obituaries, Death Notices, and News Items Extracted from the Van Buren Press 1875*, 53. Deaths of deputy U.S. marshals were researched by Juliet Galonska, formerly park historian of the Fort Smith National Historic Site and currently exhibit and media specialist at Cuyahoga Valley National Recreation Area in Ohio.

7. Deed Record Book 5, p. 7, and Book Q, p. 35, Crawford County Courthouse Records; Fort Smith City Directories, 1890, 1894, and 1895, Fort Smith Public Library. The residence at North 12th Street was later given the address of 1313 North 12th Street.

8. "He Has Killed Fourteen Men: A Fearless Negro Deputy Marshal of the Indian Territory," *Oklahoma City Weekly Times-Journal*, March 8, 1907.

9. Galonska, "New Look at the Work of Deputy Marshals."

10. Burton, *Black, Red, and Deadly*, 4–5.

11. U.S. Park Service, *It Took Brave Men*.

4. On the Trail

1. Gideon, *Indian Territory*, 115–16.

2. *U.S. vs. Austin Ward*, 1876, Jacket #194, FS.

3. *U.S. vs. William Ausley*, 1878, Jacket #5, FS.

4. Burton, *Black, Red, and Deadly*, 182–83; Warren, *Obituaries, Death Notices and News Items* 1879, 48.

5. *U.S. vs. Simon James*, 1880, Jacket #102, FS; Harmon, *Hell on the Border*, 714; "Marshal's Grave Gets Stone at Last," *Fort Smith Times Record*, n.d., from J. H. Mershon vertical file, Fort Smith National Historic Site; Bill Black, superintendent, Fort Smith National Historic Site, phone interview by author, December 16, 2002; Friends of the Library, *Goodspeed Histories of Sebastian County, Arkansas*, n.p.

6. *Fort Smith New Era*, June 1, 1881; *Fort Smith Elevator*, June 3, 1881.

7. *U.S. vs. Bill Wilson*, 1881, Jacket #203, FS.

8. *U.S. vs. William Watson*, 1881, Jacket #198, FS.

9. *U.S. vs. Randall Stick*, 1881, Jacket #181, FS.

10. Williams, "Black United States Deputy Marshals in Indian Territory," 52; Fronterhouse, "Bass Reeves: Forgotten Lawman."

11. *U.S. vs. James Jones*, 1882, Jacket #108, FS. Diron Ahlquist, Oklahoma City OK, unpublished research on James Jones, copy in author's possession; Fronterhouse, "Bass Reeves: Forgotten Lawman," 3–6.

12. Affidavit of John Mullens, February 11, 1882, Kiowa Indian Agency Police Letters and Documents, p. 347.

13. P. B. Hunt to Commissioner of Indian Affairs, March 2, 1882, 168–71, Kiowa Indian Agency Police Letters and Documents; *U.S. vs. James Jones*, 1882, Jacket #108, FS. Diron Ahlquist, unpublished research on James Jones.

14. Fronterhouse, "Bass Reeves: Forgotten Lawman," 3–6.

15. Interview with Richard Fronterhouse, Morris OK, July 1992.

16. *U.S. vs. Jim Grayson*, 1882, Jacket #72, FS.

17. *U.S. vs. Frank Wilburn*, 1882, Jacket #208, FS.

18. *U.S. vs. Banks Grayson and Boston Williams*, 1881, Jacket #72, FS.

19. *U.S. vs. Charleston Holmes*, 1882, Jacket #90, FS.

20. *U.S. vs. Bass Kemp*, 1882, Jacket #111, FS.

21. *U.S. vs. Charles McNally and W. H. Winn*, 1882, Jacket #125, FS.

22. *U.S. vs. William Horton*, 1882, Jacket #91, FS.

23. *U.S. vs. Greenleaf and Pana Maha*, 1881, Jacket #75, FS.

24. *Van Buren Press*, August 26, 1882.

25. *U.S. vs. Robert Gentry*, 1882, Jacket #76, FS; Burton, 17.

26. Lem F. Blevins, Interview, Indian Pioneer Papers, OHS.

27. *U.S. vs. Isaac Frazier*, 1883, Jacket #65.

28. Adam Grayson, interview, Indian Pioneer Papers, OHS.

5. "No Sunday West of St. Louis, No God West of Fort Smith"

1. Speer, *The Killing of Ned Christy*, 22; *U.S. vs. Sammy Low*, 1883, Jacket #120, FS.

2. *U.S. vs. Cutsee Homachte*, 1883, Jacket #91, FS.

3. *U.S. vs. Wilson Willow*, 1883, Jacket #208, FS.

4. *U.S. vs. Sparney Harjo*, 1883, Jacket #168, FS.

5. *U.S. vs. Bill Haines*, 1883, Jacket #83, FS.

6. *U.S. vs. George Scruggs*, Jacket #185, FS; *U.S. vs. John McAllister and James Wasson*, 1883, Jacket #124, FS.

7. *Fort Smith Weekly Elevator*, October 17, 1883; *Arkansas Gazette* (Little Rock), October 17, 1883; *Muskogee Indian Journal*, October 25, 1883; U.S. Park Service, *It Took Brave Men*.

8. *U.S. vs. John Hobaugh, Mordecai Donagee, and Joseph McCaslin*, 1883, Jacket #91, FS.

9. *U.S. vs. Miles Jordan*, 1883, Jacket #109, FS.

10. *U.S. vs. Perfathohche*, 1883, Jacket #151, FS; Bureau of Indian Affairs Police Files, Muskogee OK.

11. *U.S. vs. Emarthla Chee*, 1883, Jacket #59, FS.

6. Gunman's Territory

1. *U.S. vs. One Jessie*, 1883, Jacket #104, FS; *U.S. vs. Mitchell Bruner (a.k.a. Michael Grayson)*, 1883, Jacket #7, FS.

2. *U.S. vs. Cotcher Fixico*, 1881, Jacket #68, FS.

3. Gideon, *Indian Territory*, 18.

4. *U.S. vs. Jim Grayson*, 1882, Jacket #72, 1882.

5. Owens, *Oklahoma Heroes*, 267.

6. "Little Stories of Men Whose Lives Overflow with Danger," *Daily Oklahoman*, January 8, 1911.

7. Fronterhouse, "Bass Reeves: Forgotten Lawman," 24–29; Morris, *Ghost Towns of Oklahoma*, 207. According to Shirk's *Oklahoma Place Names* (259), the town of Woodford, earlier known as Bywaters, was established by the Bywater

brothers in 1870. The name was changed to Woodford for the first postmaster, Woodford Smith, who established the post office on February 4, 1884.

8. Gideon, *Indian Territory*, 115–18.

9. *Oklahoma City Weekly Times-Journal*, March 8, 1907.

10. For gunfights by western lawmen, readers should refer to O'Neal, *Encyclopedia of Western Gunfighters*.

11. *U.S. vs. One Hanna*, 1884, Jacket #80, FS.

12. *U.S. vs. Arnie Stone*, 1884, Jacket #182, FS.

13. *Fort Smith Weekly Elevator*, September 12, 1884.

14. *U.S. vs. Chub Moore*, 1884, Jacket #207, FS. A good reference is Clark, *Lynchings in Oklahoma*.

15. *U.S. vs. John Bruner*, 1884, Jacket #7, FS.

16. *U.S. vs. John Bruner*.

17. *Oklahoma City Weekly Times-Journal*, March 8, 1907.

18. Nancy E. Pruitt, Interview, Indian Pioneer Papers, OHS; *Muskogee Phoenix*, November 14, 1901.

19. *U.S. vs. James Grier*, 1884, Jacket #77, FS.

7. Hell on the Border

1. *U.S. vs. Adam Field*, 1885, Jacket #63, FS.

2. Fronterhouse, "Bass Reeves: Forgotten Lawman," 41–43.

3. Harmon, *Hell on the Border*, 177, 256, 258; *U.S. vs. Luce Hammon, Hewahmucka, and One Wiley*, 1885, Jacket #80, FS.

4. *U.S. vs. One Weaver*, 1885, Jacket #199, FS.

5. *U.S. vs. Jonas Post and Jonas Stick*, 1885, Jacket #156, FS.

6. *U.S. vs. One Fegley, Charles Coley, and Ka Welles*, 1885, Jacket #63, FS.

7. *U.S. vs. George Perryhouse*, 1885, Jacket #153, FS.

8. *U.S. vs. One Hall*, 1885, Jacket #80, FS.

9. *U.S. vs. Debkerker Harper and One Henshaw*, 1885, Jacket #88, FS; Burton, *Black, Red, and Deadly*, 157.

10. *U.S. vs. Adeline Grayson*, 1885, Jacket #72, FS.

11. *U.S. vs. William A. Gibson*, 1885, Jacket #76, FS.

12. *U.S. vs. Thomas Post*, 1885, Jacket #156, FS.

13. Galonska, "Reforming 'Hell on the Border.'"

14. *U.S. vs. Fayette Barnett and Belle Starr*, 1885, Jacket #14, FS; Shirley, *Belle Starr and Her Times*, 188, 206.

15. Mooney, *Doctor in Belle Starr Country*, 190–91; Burton, *Black, Red, and Deadly*, 214.

16. *U.S. vs. Amos Gray*, 1885, Jacket #312, FS; *U.S. vs. William Anderson*, 1885, Jacket #6, FS. Crowder Nix's commission as a deputy U.S. marshal for the Fort Smith court in 1890 is on file in the Southwest Branch of the National Archives at Fort Worth TX.

17. Martin, "Marshals for Federal Court," 14.

18. *U.S. vs. Luce Hammon*, 1885, Jacket #80, FS.

19. *U.S. vs. Tobe Hill*, 1885, Jacket #88, FS.

8. Trial of the Century

1. *Van Buren Press*, January 23, 1886.

2. *U.S. vs. Bass Reeves*, 1884, Jacket #160, FS; Tammy Stamps-Heise, "Exploits Legendary: Former Slave Served as U.S. Deputy Marshal," *Springdale* AR *Morning News*, March 3, 2002. National Park ranger Tom Wing was interviewed for the article.

3. *U.S. vs. Bass Reeves*, 1884, Jacket #160, FS.

4. *U.S. vs. Bass Reeves*.

5. *U.S. vs. A. J. Boyd*, 1886, Jacket #12, FS.

6. *U.S. vs. Bass Reeves*.

7. *U.S. vs. Bass Reeves*.

8. *U.S. vs. Bass Reeves*.

9. *U.S. vs. Bass Reeves*.

10. *U.S. vs. Bass Reeves*.

11. Williams, "United States vs. Bass Reeves," 164–65.

12. Williams, "United States vs. Bass Reeves," 169; *U.S. vs. Bass Reeves*.

13. *Van Buren Press*, October 22, 1887.

14. Fort Smith Deed and Mortgage Records, 1887, 1889, Sebastian County Courthouse Records; Fort Smith City Directories, 1890, 1894, and 1895, Fort Smith Public Library; *Springdale Morning News*, March 3, 2002; Burton, *Black, Red, and Deadly*, 161.

9. Back on the Trail

1. Fronterhouse, "Bass Reeves: Forgotten Lawman," 35–37; Burton, "Black, Red, and Deadly," 198–99. A death notice for Kinch West was published in the *Muskogee Phoenix* on June 11, 1896. In this article West is associated with Quantrill's Raiders of Civil War infamy. West died at Catoosa, Indian Territory, from consumption (Herring, *Malice, Murder and Mayhem*, 1:33). In regard to the jurisdiction of Indian Territory in 1889, refer to Burton, *Indian Territory and the United States*, 152–53.

2. Franklin and Franklin, *Autobiography of Buck Colbert Franklin*, 26–27.

3. Owens, *Oklahoma Heroes*, 270.

4. Franklin, *Journey toward Hope*, 61–62.

5. *U.S. vs. Will Flannery*, 1889, Jacket 65, FS; Martin, "Marshals for Federal Court," 18.

6. *U.S. vs. Peter Greenleaf and Big Sharper*, 1889, Jacket #75, FS.

7. *U.S. vs. W. A. Gipson*, 1889, Jacket #76, FS.

8. *U.S. vs. Ta Futsie*, 1889, Jacket #219, FS.

9. *U.S. vs. Nocus Harjo, One Prince, and Billy Wolf*, 1889, Jacket #219, FS.

10. *Fort Smith Weekly Elevator*, June 6, 1890.

11. *U.S. vs. John Cudjo*, 1890, Jacket #216, FS.

12. Butler, "Night of Vengeance in Wewoka," 68.

13. Speer, *Killing of Ned Christy*, 23–39; Steele, *Last of the Cherokee Warriors*, 85.

14. Speer, *Killing of Ned Christy*, 37–38.

15. Speer, *Killing of Ned Christy*, 99.

16. Speer, *Killing of Ned Christy*, 114–22; Burton, *Black, Red, and Deadly*, 27.

17. *U.S. vs. Bob Dosser*, 1890, Jacket #243, FS.

18. Fronterhouse, "Bass Reeves: Forgotten Lawman," 48; Carrie Cyrus Pittman, interview, Indian Pioneer Papers, OHS.

19. Fronterhouse, "Bass Reeves: Forgotten Lawman," 31–34.

10. The Winds of Change

1. Shirley, *Law West of Fort Smith*, 192–93.

2. Shirley, *Law West of Fort Smith*, 194.

3. Gumprecht, "Saloon on Every Corner," 153.

4. Harve Lovelday, interview, Indian Pioneer Papers, OHS.

5. Mooney, *Localized History of Pottawatomie County*, 102–3.

6. Mooney, *Localized History of Pottawatomie County*, 296–97.

7. Farris, *Oklahoma Outlaw Tales*, 96.

8. Jackson, *African Americans in the U.S. West*, 81–82.

9. Jackson, *African Americans in the U.S. West*, 83, 85; Katz, *The Black West*, 248–49; Shirk, *Oklahoma Place Names*, 137; Dann, "From Sodom to the Promised Land," 374–75.

11. Land of the Six-Shooter

1. Hall, *The Beginning of Tulsa*, 39.

2. *U.S. vs. John Jefferson*, 1891, Jacket #377, FS.

3. *Muskogee Phoenix*, March 5, 1891.

4. *U.S. vs. William Right*, 1891, Jacket #266, FS.

5. *U.S. vs. Evaline Hawkins*, 1891, Jacket #217, FS.

6. *U.S. vs. Tom Barnett and Ben Billy*, 1891, Jacket #282, FS.

7. *U.S. vs. John Wamble*, 1891, Jacket #276, FS.

8. Nancy Pruitt, interview, Indian Pioneer Papers, OHS.

9. *U.S. vs. George Bittle*, 1892, Jacket #284, FS.

10. Calhoun and English, *Oklahoma Heritage*, 108.

11. Littlefield, *Seminole Burning*, 21.

12. *U.S. vs. Steve Tilly*, 1892, Jacket #272, FS; Diron Ahlquist, correspondence with author, July 2002. Ahlquist interviewed Tilly's granddaughter, Willabelle Schultz, on July 6, 2002.

13. *U.S. vs. Robert Kelly*, 1892, Jacket #517, FS.

12. Paris, Texas

1. *U.S. vs. James Bell and Harry Sampson*, 1890, Jacket #338, FS.

2. *U.S. vs. Jimmy Rabbitt and Willie Proctor*, 1893, Jacket #266, FS; *U.S. vs. A. B. Brassfield and S. P. Brassfield*, 1893, Jacket #266, FS.

3. William Roosevelt Brasfield, interview, Indian Pioneer Papers, OHS; Burton, *Black, Red, and Deadly*, 219–21.

4. Martin, "Marshals for the Federal Court," 12–19.

5. Littlefield and Underhill, "Negro Marshals in the Indian Territory," 82. In the article, footnote 26 refers to correspondence Underhill received from Vincent L. Wiese, General Services Administration, Fort Worth TX, which stated Bass Reeves had held a commission with the Eastern District of Texas at Paris.

6. Shirk, *Oklahoma Place Names*, 40. The town of Calvin was named for Calvin Perry, railroad official with the Choctaw, Oklahoma, and Gulf Railroad.

7. I learned in November 1987 from the staff of the library of Paris Junior College that a town fire in the late nineteenth century destroyed many municipal and federal documents.

8. Listing for Newland Reeves, Fort Smith Business Directory, 1894–95, Fort Smith Public Library.

9. Mooney, *Doctor Jesse*, 115–16; Burton, *Black, Red, and Deadly*, 196–97.

10. Mooney, "Bass Reeves, Black Deputy U.S. Marshal," 49.

11. Mooney, "Bass Reeves, Black Deputy U.S. Marshal," 50–51; James Casherago murder trial files, Fort Smith National Historic Site; Brodhead, *Isaac C. Parker*, 76–77.

12. Burton, *Black, Red, and Deadly*, 199–200. The original source of this information is believed to have come from "Backward Glances," *Paris (TX) News*, January 4, 1954. The column that I received from the junior college had no date.

The name John Ashley appeared in an index for "Backward Glances," a column written by A. W. Neville for the *Paris News*, http://gen.1starnet.com/back46–56.htm.

13. J. B. Sparks, interview, Indian Pioneer Papers, OHS.

14. Warren, *Obituaries, Death Notices and News Items*, June 8, 1895, 32, 57.

15. Birnie Funeral Home Records, book 2, p. 427, and Fort Smith City Death Records, book 2, p. 53, Fort Smith Public Library.

16. Owens, *Oklahoma Heroes*, 123; Shirley, *West of Hell's Fringe*, 283–301; *Daily Ardmoreite*, Ardmore OK, June 10, 1896.

17. Burton, *Black, Red, and Deadly*, 5–6.

18. Tuller, *Let No Man Escape*, 156.

19. *Isaac Parker: The Life and Times of a Hanging Judge*, documentary film.

20. *Isaac Parker*.

21. *U.S. vs. Louis Peters*, 1897, Docket #4224, Muskogee, Indian Territory, Federal Criminal Court (hereafter MUS); *U.S. vs. Samuel Manuel*, 1897, Docket #4233, MUS.

22. Quoted in "Report on the Five Civilized Tribes, 1897, by the *Kansas City Star*."

23. Judge Paul L. Brady, interview with author, April 1992.

13. Northern District, Indian Territory

1. Larson and Ritter, "Leo E. Bennett," 73–75; Shirley, *The Fourth Guardsman*, 58–59; Wadley, *Brief Indian History of Muskogee*.

2. Copy of Reeves's arrest record from the U.S. Docket of Muskogee, 1899, Richard Fronterhouse Papers. Reeves was documented as the arresting officer of George Cully, who was executed in Muskogee on September 21, 1899.

3. *Muskogee Phoenix*, July 20, 1899; *Fort Gibson Post* (Cherokee Nation), October 21, 1897.

4. Correspondence, Leo E. Bennett, U.S. Marshal, Northern District Indian Territory, Muskogee, to U.S. Attorney General, Washington DC, November 6, 1897, U.S. Marshals Vertical File, OHS.

5. *U.S. vs. Joe Justice*, 1897, Docket #4298, MUS.

6. *U.S. vs. Sam Austin*, 1897, Docket #4347, MUS.

7. *U.S. vs. Frank Blackburn*, 1898, Docket #4411, MUS. It is interesting to note that sometimes Muskogee was spelled with a "c" instead of "k" in the same document. The original spelling of Muskogee was with a "c." The Creek Nation in Oklahoma today spell it as Muscogee, which is also the name of the language

and the people. The name "Creek" for the Indian tribe came from the U.S. government.

8. *U.S. vs. James McKellop*, 1898, Docket #4417, MUS.

9. Liz McMahan, Wagoner OK, correspondence with author, December 1996. Littlefield's book *Seminole Burning* is also a good reference on the subject of racial violence in Indian Territory during 1898.

10. Lawrence Downs, phone interview by author, Phoenix IL, October 1996; Liz McMahan, correspondence with author, December 1996. McMahan, a newspaper reporter, conducted an interview with Lawrence "Sundown" Downs, who was a lifelong resident of Wagoner and at the time of the interview in his late eighties.

11. *U.S. vs. William Thomas and John Hunter*, 1898, Docket #4432, MUS.

12. *U.S. vs. Jacob Davis*, 1898, Docket #4291, MUS.

13. *U.S. vs. Myrtle Kidd* and *U.S. vs. Mandy Jackson*, 1898, Docket #4516, MUS.

14. *U.S. vs. "Myrtle"* (#4516); *U.S. vs. George Ray* (#4512); *U.S. vs. J. R. Green* (#4511); *U.S. vs. John Mackey, John Brown, and Henderson Brown* (#4509); *U.S. vs. Joe Carson* (#4505); *U.S. vs. "Tahlequah Kidd"* (#4498); *U.S. vs. Bob Wallace* (#4497); *U.S. vs. Peter Simon* (#4496); *U.S. vs. Jim Thomas and Thomas Mat* (#4495); *U.S. vs. Newt Steel and "Big Red"* (#4494); *U.S. vs. Hewett Cobb and "One Virgil"* (#4492); *U.S. vs. Samson Jones* (#4486). All cases 1898, docket number in parentheses, MUS.

15. *U.S. vs. Lucy Evans*, 1898, Docket #4729, MUS.

16. *U.S. vs. Jake McDaniel*, 1898, Docket #4608, MUS.

17. *U.S. vs. Abe Leggins*, 1898, Docket #4670; *U.S. vs. Felix Leggins*, 1898, Docket #4671, MUS.

18. *U.S. vs. R. H. Scofield*, 1898, Docket #4739, MUS.

19. *U.S. vs. Mike Horerine*, 1898, Docket #4679, MUS.

20. *U.S. vs. Isaac Jones*, 1898, Docket #4678, MUS.

21. *U.S. vs. Cub Hanks*, 1898, Docket #4717, MUS.

14. Muskogee Marshal

1. Wadley, *Brief Indian History of Muskogee*, 20; Foreman, *Muskogee*, 96.

2. Foreman, *Muskogee*, 98.

3. Foreman, *Muskogee*, 11, 126.

4. *Moore's Directory of the City of Muskogee, Indian Territory*, 1906, 360–72; Daniel F. Littlefield Jr., interview with author, March 2002. Dr. Littlefield is one of the preeminent scholars on the history of Indian Freedmen. A good resource

for Oklahoma's jazz music history is the Oklahoma Jazz Hall of Fame in Tulsa OK.

5. Merril A. Nelson, interview, Indian Pioneer Papers, OHS.

6. I. F. Williams, interview, Indian Pioneer Papers, OHS.

7. *U.S. vs. Lewis Flowers*, 1899, Docket #4750, MUS.

8. *U.S. vs. Aleck Johnson*, 1899, Docket #4755, MUS.

9. Warren, *Obituaries, Death Notices and News Items*, 1898–1902, 22.

10. *U.S. vs. Charley Peyton*, 1899, Docket #4839, MUS.

11. *U.S. vs. Allen Haynes*, 1899, Docket #4849, MUS.

12. *U.S. vs. Robert Worthman*, 1899, Docket #4920, MUS.

13. *U.S. vs. Henry Nelson*, 1899, Docket #4983, MUS.

14. *U.S. vs. Dick Fatt*, 1899, Docket #5009, MUS.

15. A New Century

1. U.S. Census, 1900, Muskogee, Indian Territory, 20; Applications of Winnie Reeves to the Commission of the Five Civilized Tribes, Muscogee, May 11, 1900, Fort Gibson, April 3 and 22, 1901, Fort Gibson, September 24, 1901, Muscogee, July 13, 1903, Department of the Interior, Washington DC, May 9, 1904, Cherokee Freedman Rolls.

2. *U.S. vs. Richard Edwards*, 1900, Docket #5043, MUS.

3. *U.S. vs. Lee Peters and John Johnson*, 1900, Docket #5112, MUS.

4. *U.S. vs. Sandy Gray and David Marcey*, 1900, Docket #5197, MUS.

5. *U.S. vs. Nero Harrison alias Nero Nevins*, 1900, Docket #5362, MUS.

6. *U.S. vs. Belle Williams*, 1901, Docket #5414, MUS.

7. Notes from U.S. Marshal Leo Bennett's docket book; Notes, Richard Fronterhouse Papers; Dulaney, *Black Police in America*, 15–18.

8. *U.S. vs. Orlando Dobson and Billy Vann*, 1901, Docket #5887–88, MUS; U.S. Marshal's Fee and Reimbursement Book, Muskogee, Indian Territory, Record Group 60, National Archives, College Park MD.

9. Green Hill Cemetery Records, Muskogee OK.

10. *U.S. vs. Edward Walker*, 1901, Docket #5907, MUS.

11. *Muskogee Phoenix*, October 31, 1901.

12. *Muskogee Phoenix*, November 7, 1901.

13. *Muskogee Phoenix*, November 14, 1901.

14. *Muskogee Phoenix*, November 14, 1901.

16. Devotion to Duty

1. Correspondence, U.S. Marshals Vertical File, OHS; Shirley, *Fourth Guardsman*, 95.

2. Shirley, *Fourth Guardsman*, 102.

3. Kaye M. Teall, *Black History in Oklahoma*, 202–3; Shirley, *Fourth Guardsman*, 104–6.

4. Fronterhouse, "Bass Reeves: Forgotten Lawman," 37–41.

5. Brady, *A Certain Blindness*, 2.

6. Rev. Charles Davis, interview in *Through the Looking Glass Darkly*, the first documentary on African Americans in Indian and Oklahoma Territories.

7. *U.S. vs. Ben Reeves*, Docket #6136, mus; Ben Reeves, prison file #3282, Trusty Prisoner's Agreement #3282, letter to Mrs. Sallie Sanders, Ben Reeves Prison File; Pliny Twine, interview by author, Muskogee ok, July 1995. Mr. Twine was the last living child of attorney and publisher William Henry Twine, who owned the *Cimiter* newspaper and was the leading black attorney in Muskogee prior to statehood. Mr. Twine told me that he remembered as a child seeing Bass Reeves passing his house in a one-horse hack to visit friends in his neighborhood.

8. Shirley, *Fourth Guardsman*, 95.

9. *U.S. vs. John Anderson and Rose Norman*, 1902, Docket #6317, mus.

10. *U.S. vs. Jamison Brown*, 1902, Docket #6237, mus.

11. *U.S. vs. George Bean, Will Bean, and William Penser*, 1902, Docket #6230, mus.

12. *Muskogee Phoenix*, November 27, 1902; *U.S. vs. George Bean, Will Bean, and William Penser*.

13. Burton, *Black, Red, and Deadly*, 240–41, 249–50; Robert Fortune information obtained from correspondence with the Wilburton Public Library, Wilburton ok, January 1989.

17. The Invincible Marshal

1. *Moore's Directory*, 1903.

2. Davis and Ritter, "U.S. Deputy Marshal David Adams."

3. *U.S. vs. Sam Jackson*, 1903, Docket #6533, mus.

4. *U.S. vs. Chock Cordery and Joe Cordery*, 1903, Docket #6651, mus.

5. *U.S. vs. Willie Lowe*, 1903, Docket #6644, mus.

6. *U.S. vs. Paul Smith*, 1903, Docket #6646, mus.

7. *U.S. vs. Will Sims*, 1903, Docket #6866, mus.

8. *U.S. vs. Joe Napier*, 1903, Docket #6965–6967, mus.

9. Green Hill Cemetery Records, Muskogee ok.

10. Shirley, *Fourth Guardsman*, 99; Alice Spahn interview, Fronterhouse Papers, September 1959.

11. Alice Spahn interview, Fronterhouse Papers, September 1959.

12. *U.S. vs. Jess Morgan*, 1904, Docket #7948, MUS.

13. *U.S. vs. Cornelius Nave*, 1904, Docket #6576, MUS.

14. *U.S. vs. Dick Lucky*, 1904, Docket #7627, MUS.

15. *U.S. vs. Thomas Matthews*, 1904, Docket #7678, MUS.

16. *U.S. vs. Lonnie Smith*, 1904, Docket #7509, MUS.

17. *U.S. vs. Abe Drew*, 1904, Docket #7590, MUS.

18. *Muskogee Phoenix*, May 12, 1904.

19. *Muskogee Phoenix*, May 13, 1904.

20. *U.S. vs. J. A. Tatnull*, 1904, Docket #7543, MUS.

21. Deeds and Records, Muskogee, Indian Territory, 1904 and 1905, Muskogee County Courthouse Records; U.S. Census, 1910, Muskogee, Indian Territory.

22. *U.S. vs. Scott Gentry*, 1904, Docket #7677, MUS.

23. *U.S. vs. George W. Crockwell*, 1904, Docket #7694–95, MUS.

24. *U.S. vs. Henry Rosco*, 1904, Docket #5079, MUS.

25. *U.S. vs. Morris Rentie*, 1904, Docket #7895, MUS.

18. A Lawman to the End

1. *U.S. vs. John Thomas*, 1905, Docket #7517–18, MUS.

2. *U.S. vs. Alfred Barnett*, 1905, Commissioners #3655, MUS.

3. *U.S. vs. Bessie Frazier and John Doe*, 1905, Docket #7874–75, MUS.

4. *U.S. vs. Joe Tolbert*, 1905, Commissioners #3717, MUS.

5. *U.S. vs. Louis Williams*, 1905, Commissioners #3735, MUS.

6. *U.S. vs. James Mickens*, 1905, Commissioners #3833, MUS.

7. *U.S. vs. Sandy Givens*, 1905, Commissioners #3880, MUS.

8. *U.S. vs. Joe Grayson*, 1905, Docket #8168, MUS.

9. Shirley, *Fourth Guardsman*, 127.

10. *Ada Evening News*, March 29, 1905.

11. Alice Spahn interview, Fronterhouse Papers.

12. *U.S. vs. Johnson Vann, alias John Vann, alias John Wolf*, 1906, Docket #9046, MUS.

13. This same article appeared two days later, on Sunday, March 10, 1907, in the *Washington Post*. Titled "Fearless Negro Deputy Marshal Has Killed Fourteen Desperadoes," it was the most national exposure Bass Reeves received from the media during his career.

14. Rev. Haskell J. Shoeboot, interview, Denver CO, August 1988.

15. Burton, *Black, Red, and Deadly*, 115–16.

16. Burton, *Black, Red, and Deadly*, 117–18.

17. Twine, *Family Histories*, 26–53.

18. *U.S. vs. J. L. Ashford*, 1907, Docket #9165.

19. *U.S. vs. Mack Cobb*, 1907, Docket #9166.

20. Fronterhouse, "Bass Reeves: Forgotten Lawman," 46–47; Rev. Haskell Shoeboot, phone interview by author, Phoenix IL, March 1988.

21. Muskogee County Probate Records, Bass Reeves, July 12, 1913, A. C. Spahn, Petitioner.

Epilogue

1. Dulaney, *Black Police in America* 105–6.

2. "Chicago's 'Two-Gun Pete' Dies of a Heart Attack," *Jet Magazine*, October 1971.

3. Sylvester "Two-Gun Pete" Washington, "Why I Killed Eleven Men," *Ebony*, January 1950, 51–57.

4. Washington, "Why I Killed Eleven Men," 51–57.

Bibliography

Brady, Paul L. *A Certain Blindness: A Black Family's Quest for the Promise of America*. Atlanta GA: ALP, 1990.

Brodhead, Michael J. *Isaac C. Parker: Federal Justice on the Frontier*. Norman: University of Oklahoma Press, 2003.

Bureau of Indian Affairs. Police Files. Indian Police Killed in the Line of Duty. BIA Office, Muskogee OK.

Burton, Art T. *Black, Buckskin, and Blue: African American Scouts and Soldiers on the Western Frontier*. Austin TX: Eakin, 1999.

———. *Black, Red, and Deadly: Black and Indian Gunfighters of the Indian Territory, 1870–1907*. Austin TX: Eakin, 1991.

Burton, Jeffrey. *Indian Territory and the United States, 1866–1907: Courts, Government, and the Movement for Oklahoma Statehood*. Norman: University of Oklahoma Press, 1995.

Butler, Ken. "A Night of Vengeance in Wewoka." *Oklahoma State Trooper Magazine* (Winter 2002): 65–69.

Calhoun, Sharon Cooper, and Billie Joan English. *Oklahoma Heritage*. Maysville OK: Holt, Calhoun, and Clark, 1984.

Cherokee Freedman Rolls. Application Files. Oklahoma Historical Society, Oklahoma City.

Clark, Charles N. *Lynchings in Oklahoma: A Story of Vigilantism, 1830–1930*. Norman OK: Self-published on CD-ROM, 2000.

Cottrell, Steve. *Civil War in the Indian Territory*. Gretna LA: Pelican, 1995.

Crawford County Courthouse Records, Van Buren AR. Death certificates; deed record books; tax records.

Dann, Martin. "From Sodom to the Promised Land: E. P. McCabe and the

Movement for Oklahoma Colonization." *Kansas Historical Quarterly* (Autumn 1974): 370–78.

Davis, Chick, and Al Ritter. "U.S. Deputy Marshal David Adams, Indian Territory Lawman." *Oklahoma State Trooper Magazine* (Summer 1997): 31–35.

Dulaney, W. Marvin. *Black Police in America*. Bloomington: Indiana University Press, 1996.

Edwards, Whit. *The Prairie Was on Fire: Eyewitness Accounts of the Civil War in the Indian Territory*. Oklahoma City: Oklahoma Historical Society, 2001.

Farris, David A. *Oklahoma Outlaw Tales*. Edmond OK: Little Bruce, 1999.

Federal Criminal Court Records, Fort Smith–Western District Court of Arkansas (FS), and Muskogee, Indian Territory (MUS). Record Group 21, Preliminary Inventory, Records of United States District Courts, Arkansas. National Archives–Southwest Region, Fort Worth TX.

Foreman, Grant. *Muskogee: The Biography of an Oklahoma Town*. Norman: University of Oklahoma Press, 1943.

Fort Smith National Historic Site, Fort Smith AR. Historical Files.

Fort Smith Public Library, Fort Smith AR. Birnie Funeral Home records; city death records; city directories; business directory; genealogy room.

Franklin, Jimmie Lewis. *Journey toward Hope: A History of Blacks in Oklahoma*. Norman: University of Oklahoma Press, 1982.

Franklin, John Hope, and John Whittington Franklin, ed. *My Life and an Era: The Autobiography of Buck Colbert Franklin*. Baton Rouge: Louisiana State University Press, 1997.

Friends of the Fort Smith Public Library. *Goodspeed Histories of Sebastian County, Arkansas*. Originally published in 1889; reprint: Columbia TN: Woodward and Stinson, 1977.

Fronterhouse, Richard. "Bass Reeves: The Forgotten Lawman." Unpublished seminar paper, 1960. Historic Oklahoma Collection, Division of Manuscripts, Western History Collections, University of Oklahoma Libraries, Box 69.

———. Research Papers. In author's collection.

Fulmore, Z. T. *The History and Geography of Texas as Told in County Names*. Austin TX: S. R. Fulmore, n.d.

Galonska, Juliet. "A New Look at the Work of the Deputy Marshals." Fort Smith National Historic Site, Fort Smith AR. http://www.nps.gov/fosm/history/court/newlook.htm.

———. "Reforming 'Hell on the Border.'" Fort Smith National Historic Site, Fort Smith AR. http://www.nps.gov/fosm/history/court/reformhob.htm.

Gideon, D. C. *Indian Territory: Descriptive, Biographical, and Genealogical; Including the Landed Estates, Country Seats . . . with a General History of the Territory.* New York: Lewis, 1901.

Grayson County Frontier Village. "Biography of William Steele Reeves." In *The History of Grayson County, Texas*, 550. Sherman TX: Grayson County Frontier Village and Hunter Co., 1979.

Green Hill Cemetery Records, Muskogee OK.

Gumprecht, Blake. "A Saloon on Every Corner: Whiskey Towns of Oklahoma Territory, 1889–1907." *Chronicles of Oklahoma* 74, no. 2 (Summer 1996): 146–73.

Hale, Douglas. "Rehearsal for Civil War: The Texas Cavalry in the Indian Territory, 1861." *Chronicles of Oklahoma* 68, no. 3 (Fall 1990): 228.

Hall, J. M. *The Beginning of Tulsa.* Tulsa OK: Scott-Rice, 1933.

Harmon, S. W. *Hell on the Border: He Hanged Eighty-Eight Men.* Fort Smith AR: Phoenix, 1899; reprint, Lincoln: University of Nebraska Press, 1992.

Herring, Edward, comp. and ed. *Malice, Murder and Mayhem in the Oklahoma and Indian Territories: Abstracts from Oklahoma Newspapers*, vol. 1: *The Muskogee Phoenix, January 30, 1896, thru December 31, 1897.* Mount Hope AL: self-published, 1999.

Hopkins, Eula, and Wanda Newberry Gray-McGaugh. *History of Crawford County, Arkansas, with Biographical Appendix.* Van Buren AR: Historical Preservation Association of Crawford County, 2001.

Indian Pioneer Papers, Oklahoma State History Museum, Oklahoma Historical Society (OHS), Oklahoma City. The Indian Pioneer Papers are a collection of oral interviews from the Federal Writers Project, which was funded through the WPA from 1937 to 1939. Early settlers were interviewed about conditions and life in pre-statehood Oklahoma, during the territorial era. Elderly African Americans were also interviewed about their status as former slaves. Interviews of the following persons are cited: Lem F. Blevins, William Roosevelt Brasfield, Adam Grayson, Harve Loveldary, Merril A. Nelson, Carrie Cyrus Pittman, Nancy Pruitt, J. B. Sparks, John Ward, I. F. Williams.

Isaac Parker: The Life and Times of a Hanging Judge. Documentary film produced by Michael Wilkerson. Tulsa OK: Barrister Productions, LC.

Jackson, Kennell A. *African Americans in the U.S. West.* Globe Mosaic of American History. Paramus NJ: Globe Fearon, 1994.

Katz, William Loren. *The Black West.* Doubleday, 1971; reprint New York: Touchstone, 1996.

Kiowa Indian Agency Police Letters and Documents, March 18, 1872–December 31, 1886, Microfilm #KA44, National Archives, Fort Worth TX.

Larson, E. Dixon, and Al Ritter. "Leo E. Bennett: Indian Territory Pioneer and Lawman." *Oklahoma State Trooper Magazine* (Spring 1995): 73–79.

Littlefield, Daniel F. Jr. *Seminole Burning: A Story of Racial Vengeance*. Jackson: University of Mississippi Press, 1996.

Littlefield, Daniel F. Jr., and Lonnie Underhill. "Negro Marshals of the Indian Territory." *Journal of Negro History* 56, no. 2 (April 1971): 77–87.

Martin, Amelia. "Marshals for Federal Court with Jurisdiction over the Fort Smith Area." *The Journal*, Fort Smith Historical Society, April 1979.

Mooney, Charles W. "Bass Reeves, Black Deputy U.S. Marshal." *Real West* (July 1976).

———. *Doctor in Belle Starr Country*. Oklahoma City: Century, 1975.

———. *Doctor Jesse*. Oklahoma City: Pro-Graphics, 1978.

———. *Localized History of Pottawatomie County, Oklahoma, to 1907*. Midwest City OK: Thunderbird, 1971.

Moore's Directory of the City of Muskogee, Indian Territory. For the year 1903 and 1906. Muskogee: Model, 1903, 1906.

Morris, John W. *Ghost Towns of Oklahoma*. Norman: University of Oklahoma Press, 1978.

Muskogee County Courthouse Records, Muskogee OK. Deeds and Records.

O'Neal, Bill. *Encyclopedia of Western Gunfighters*. Norman: University of Oklahoma Press, 1979.

Owens, Ron. *Oklahoma Heroes: A Tribute to Fallen Law Enforcement Officers*. Paducah KY: Turner, 2000.

Reeves, Ben. Prison File. U.S. Penitentiary, Fort Leavenworth KS.

"Report on the Five Civilized Tribes, 1897, by the *Kansas City Star*," reprinted in *Chronicles of Oklahoma* 48, no. 4 (Winter 1970): 416.

Sebastian County Courthouse Records, Fort Smith AR. Fort Smith deed and mortgage records.

Shirk, George H. *Oklahoma Place Names*. Norman: University of Oklahoma Press, 1965.

Shirley, Glenn. *Belle Starr and Her Times: The Literature, the Facts and the Legend*. Norman: University of Oklahoma Press, 1982.

———. *The Fourth Guardsman: James Franklin "Bud" Ledbetter, 1852–1937*. Austin TX: Eakin, 1997.

———. *Law West of Fort Smith: A History of Frontier Justice in the Indian Territory, 1834–1896*. Lincoln: University of Nebraska Press, 1957.

———. *West of Hell's Fringe: Crime, Criminals, and the Federal Peace Officer in Oklahoma Territory, 1889–1907*. Norman: University of Oklahoma Press, 1978.

Smith, Robert B. *Daltons!: The Raid on Coffeyville, Kansas*. Norman: University of Oklahoma Press, 1996.

Speer, Bonnie Stahlman. *The Killing of Ned Christy, Cherokee Outlaw*. Norman OK: Reliance, 1990.

Speer, William S., comp. and ed. *The Encyclopedia of the New West*. Marshall TX: U.S. Biographical, 1881.

Steele, Phillip. *Last of the Cherokee Warriors*. Gretna LA: Pelican, 1987.

Swinburn, Susan Stevenson, and Doris Stevenson West. *History in Headstones: A Complete Listing of All Marked Graves in Known Cemeteries of Crawford County, Arkansas*. Van Buren AR: Argus, 1970.

Teall, Kaye M., ed. *Black History in Oklahoma: A Resource Book*. Oklahoma City: Oklahoma City Public Schools, 1971.

Through the Looking Glass Darkly. PBS documentary film produced by Bob Dotson, directed by Mike Simmons. WKY Television Station, Oklahoma City, July 1973.

Tuller, Robert H. *Let No Man Escape: A Judicial Biography of "Hanging Judge" Isaac C. Parker*. Norman: University of Oklahoma Press, 2001.

Twine, Linda, comp. *The Family Histories of the Kentucky Twines, The Oklahoma Twines, and the Goggins*. Privately printed, n.d.

U.S. Census Bureau Records. National Archives, Washington DC. Mountain Township AR. Crawford County AR. Muskogee, Creek Nation, Indian Territory. (Van Buren [AR] Public Library and Muskogee [OK] Public Library.)

U.S. Marshals Vertical File. Archives and Manuscript Division, Oklahoma Historical Society Library, Oklahoma City.

U.S. Park Service. Fort Smith National Historic Site. *It Took Brave Men: Deputy U.S. Marshals of Fort Smith*. Documentary film. U.S. Park Service, 2000.

Wadley, Marie. *A Brief Indian History of Muskogee: The Indian Capital of the World*. Muskogee OK: Self-published, n.d.

Warren, Fran Alberson, comp. *Obituaries, Death Notices, and News Items Extracted from the Van Buren Press* (Chester AR: F. A. Warren, 2001).

Wilburton Public Library, Wilburton OK. Local history files. Deputy U.S. Marshal Robert Fortune file.

Williams, Nudie E. "A History of the American Southwest: Black United States Deputy Marshals in the Indian Territory, 1870–1907." Master's thesis, Oklahoma State University, 1976.

———. "United States vs. Bass Reeves: Black Lawman on Trial." *Chronicles of Oklahoma* 68 (Summer 1990): 154–67.

Zellar, Gary. "Occupying the Middle Ground: African Creeks in the First Indian Home Guard, 1862–1865." *Chronicles of Oklahoma* 76, no. 1 (Spring 1998): 48.

Index

court system in, 26–27, 30, 122, 125–26, 147–48, 171–72, 179, 203. *See also* Arkansas

Fort Smith National Historic Site, xviii, 2, 309–10

Fort Smith New Era, 87

Fort Smith Record, 200

Fort Smith Weekly Elevator, 61, 87–88, 92–93, 106–7, 111–12, 124–25, 147, 158–59, 163–64, 181, 185–87, 189, 201

Fortune, Robert, xi, 4, 152, *170-9*, 254

Franklin, Buck Colbert, 150–52

Franklin, John Hope, 150

Franklin, Russell, 151–52

freedmen: Civil War service of, 24; enrollment and land allotment of, 224; as policemen, 72; racial politics and, xi, 224–28. *See also* Indian Freedmen

Freeman, Morgan, 2

Fronterhouse, Richard, xix, 15, 47, 167–70, 175, 242–44, 260, 292

Galonska, Juliet, 27, 314n6

gambling, 219–20

Garrett, James, 278

Garrett, John, 4, 8

Garrett, Pat, 286

Geronimo, 10

Gibbs (U.S. marshal), 202

Gideon, D. C., 32, 79, 86

Gill, Joseph A., 249

Goble, Danney, 3

Goff, Allen, 81

Goldsby, Crawford "Cherokee Bill," 4, 10, 201–2

Gossett, Louis, 2

Grant, William, 61

Grey, W. J., 78

Guthrie ok, 8, 81, 148, 171, 175–76

Hadden, D. A., 81

Hall, H. C., 178

Hall, J. M., 178–79

Hammer (U.S. marshal), 254

Hariaye, Lewis, 253

Harmon, S. W., 8

Harrison, E. B., 122

Hawkins, Evaline, 180, 182

Haynes, Samuel, 253

"Hell on the Border," 119–20, *170-17*

Hell on the Border (Harmon), 8, 58, 110–11

Hendrickson, Alice, 17–18

Hickock, William "Wild Bill," 2, 23, 286

Holdenville ok, 163

horses: Bass Reeves and, 13, 37, 46–47, 52–53; matched races of, 44–46, 52–53; theft of, 57, 62–71, 78–79, 106–7, 159–63, 191, 213–14; Tom Story gang and, 149–50

Houston, Sam, 10

Howe, Arena, 35

Hubbard, Ernest, 248, 289–90

Huddleston, Grant, 294

Hughes, Tyner, 122

Hunt, Edward, 143

Hunt, Philemon B., 41–44

Hunter, William, 41

Indian Chieftain, 89

Indian Freedmen: defined, 4, 7, 118; legal jurisdiction over, 33; racial politics and, 226; racism and, xiii; statehood and racial separation of, xiv. *See also* African Americans; freedmen

Indian Journal, 210

Indian Police, *170-4*, *170-19*, *170-20*; as deputy U.S. marshals, 209; Five Civilized Tribes and, 252–53; in Indian Territory, 194; law enforcement by, 154; legal jurisdiction of, 51, 77; suspected crimes of, 37–44. *See also* Lighthorse police

Indian Police officers: Berryhill, Pleasant, 253; Boone, I. K., 253; Bowman, E. S., 253; Brown, John L., 240, 253; Chamberlain, Arthur J., 253; Culley, William H., 253; Edwards, Samuel, 253; Hariaye, Lewis, 253; Haynes, Samuel, 253; Maytubby, Peter, Jr., 253;

Parler, Mary Celestia, 17–18
Pauls Valley OK, 172, 174–75, 254
Payne, Caesar, 167
"Peg Leg" Jim, 149
Peoria Indian Nation, territory of, 12–13
Perryman, J. M. (Muskogee chief), 77–78
Pettit, Charles, 4, 7
Pickett, Bill, 10
Pierce, Frank, 91–93, 105–7, 112
Pierce, Jacob R., 39–42
Plessy vs. Ferguson, 208
Plummer, C. W., 253
politics. *See* Democratic Party; racial politics; Republican Party
Pompey, David, 113, 131–33, 135–36
Ponca Indian Nation, territory of, 12–13
Porter, Pleasant, 241, 255
Porter OK, 273
Pottawatomie County saloon towns, 172–73
Pottawatomie Indian Nation, territory of, 12–13, 28
Powers, J. H., 137
Prassel, Frank Richard, 5
prostitution, 197, 219–20, 281
Pruitt, Nancy, 104, 187
Pryor Creek OK, 249
Purcell OK, 172

quadroon, 124
Quantrill, William, 149
Quapaw Agency: federal court system in, 209; Oklahoma Territory and, 171–72; territory of, 12–13; U.S. court system in, 249

race riots, 178, 241, 253–54
racial politics: Democratic Party and, 291; in Muskogee OK, 224–28; Oklahoma and, xi, 203–4; "Tenth Cavalry" society and, 287–88; United Socialist Club and, 288–93
racial separation: law enforcement and, 31, 89, 117, 179, 236, 253–54; Oklahoma statehood and, xiv–xv, 278, 295; *Plessy vs. Ferguson* and, 208

racism: Bass Reeves and, xii–xv, 130, 133–37, 286; interracial marriage and, 215–18; Ku Klux Klan and, 175; law enforcement and, 87–89; lynching and, 94, 199–200; territorial politics and, 176–77, 203–4. *See also* discrimination; segregation
Ragsdale, William M., 255, 302
Ravage, John W., 13
Raymond, Charles W., 248, 249, 269
Reconstruction, 5–6, 203
Red Rock OK, 13
Reed, Eddie, 197–99
Reeves, Alice (daughter). *See* Spahn, Alice
Reeves, Bass, *170-1, 170-3, 170-32*; and son's arrest for murder, 242–49; assassination attempts on, 125, 283–84; baptism of, 295; as the "Black Marshal," 11; as blacksmith, 20; children of, xv, 25–26, 76, 194–95, 200–201, 230, 233, 236–37, 249, 260, 302; and commissioning as deputy marshal, 27–31, 122, 147, 240; criminal accusations against, 63, 71, 106–7, 112, 127–28; death of, 165–67, 296–98; illiteracy of, 4, 10, 109–10, 260–61, 297; income of as deputy marshal, 29, 147, 309–11; as "Invincible Marshal," 18, 256; as the "Lone Ranger," 11–14; marriage of, 25, 233; newspaper accounts of, 181–82, 284–86; as peace officer, 4–5, 89, 110, 299–301; physical description of, 32, 37, 46–47, 207; as policeman, xiv, 8, 207–8, 219–23, 228–32, 234–36, 296–97; as posseman, 32–41; as preacher, 53; reputation of, 16–17, 122, 173–74, 196–97, 302–4; shooting of cook by, 81–82, 103, 127–33, 137–39; as slave, xii–xv, 4, 19–24, 239; and trial for murder, 139–47, 204; use of disguises by, 11, 46–47, 54–55, 174
Reeves, Bass, Jr. (son), 236–37
Reeves, Benjamin (son), *170-25*, 242–49, 281–82, 302
Reeves, Edgar (son), 200–201, 230

Reeves, Edward (son), 249, 302

Reeves, George R. (slave master), 21–23, 239

Reeves, Georgia (daughter), 249

Reeves, Homer (son), 260

Reeves, Ira, 9

Reeves, Jane (sister). *See* Brady, Jane (Reeves)

Reeves, Jennie (Jane) (wife), 25, 33, *170–26*, 195, 201

Reeves, Mary (grandchild), 302

Reeves, Newland (son), 195, 200–201

Reeves, Newton (son), 249

Reeves, Paralee (mother). *See* Stewart, Paralee (Reeves)

Reeves, Robert (son), 114, 194–95

Reeves, Rother (grandchild), 302

Reeves, Sallie (daughter). *See* Sanders, Sallie S. (Reeves)

Reeves, William Steele (slave master), 20, 22

Reeves, Winnie J. Sumner (wife), 233–34, 270, 298, 302

Republican Party, 203, 226, 291

Robbins, E. L., 255–56

Robinson, Ed, 5

Roebuck, Dick, 4

Rogers, Ike, 4–5

Rogers, Will, 5, 10, 15

Roosevelt, Theodore, 288

Rosa, Joseph G., 2

Ross, William P., 233

Ruth, Jim, 4

Rutherford, Samuel M., 206, 212, 255–56

Ryan OK, 172

Sac and Fox Indian Nation, territory of, 12–13

Sacred Heart Mission, 28, 72

Saddler, E. I., 293

Sallisaw OK, 249

saloon towns, 172–73

Sandels, M. H., 139

Sanders, Sallie S. (Reeves), 201, 249, 266, 302

Sapulpa OK, 249

Sasakwa OK, 28, 72, 163

Saunders, Green, 201

Sawner, G. W. F., 293

Scales, Clint, 4

Schultz, Willabelle, 190

Searle, J. W., 122

Second Kansas Cavalry, 34

segregation, 226–28. *See also* discrimination; integration of schools; racial politics; racial separation; racism

"Seminole Burnings," 218–19

Seminole Indian Nation: federal court system in, 172, 209, 249; Five Civilized Tribes and, 4; and Indian Police, 253; law enforcement and, 71–72, 75, 122, 286–87; and Lighthorse police, *170–13*, 179–80, 287; racial violence and, 218–19; Reeves as fugitive slave with, 23–24; territory of, 12–13, 28

Seneca Indian Nation, territory of, 12–13

Shaver, W. R. "Dick," 4, 278–79

Shawnee Indian Nation, territory of, 12–13

Shirley, Glenn, 240

Shoeboot, Haskell James, 287, 296

Shoenfelt, J. Blair, 253, 255

Short, Thomas W., 253

Simpson, John, 253

Sixkiller, Sam, 7, 51, 122

slavery: American Indians and, 4; Reconstruction politics and, 203; Reeves's origins in, xii–xv, 4, 19–24, 239

Smith, Andrew, 122

Smith, Chris, 85–86

Smith, "Negro," 28

Smith, Paul, *170–3*, 290–92

Smith, Woodford, 316ch6n7

Snell, J. B., 160–62

South Carolina, 20

sovereignty, tribal nation, xiii

Spahn, A. C., 249, 301–2

Spahn, Alice M., 23, 167, 175, 242, 248–49, 260, 283, 292, 298, 302

Spokogee OK, 190

U.S. Congress. *See* U.S. government

U.S. deputy marshals: Adams, David, 210, 212, 240–41, 249, 255–56; Andrews, Elias, 122; Ayers, Jacob T., 34–43, 62; Bailey, Wood, 153; Beck, Addison, 34, 61–62, 78, 309–10; Brockington, 202; Brown, John L., 240; Bruner, Heck, 7; Caldwell, J. M., 34; Carr, Bill, 152; Chancellor, 202; Cochran, Bob, 143; Cook, Matt, *170-11*; Cox, Wiley, 62; Creekmore, Milo, 183–85; Dobson, Orlando, 212, 236; Douglas, N. M., 223; Fair, S. J. B., 128; Farr, John, 122; Gibbs, 202; Goff, Allen, 81; Grant, William, 61; Grey, W. J., 78; Hadden, D. A., 81; Hubbard, Ernest, 289–90; Hughes, Tyner, 122; Jacobsen, A., 81; Jones, James, 44; Jones, John P., 81; Jones, W. F., 122; Kell, Bud T., 106, 122, 211; Lacy, Thomas E., 34; Ledbetter, J. F. "Bud," *170-2, 170-8*, 210, 212–13, 240, 260, 277–78, 287, 310; Lee, Crocket, 254; Lundy, Joseph P., 156; Madsen, Christie, 81; Maledon, George, 34; Maples, Daniel, 164; McCall, Bill, 155; McIntosh, Wiley, 180; Mershon, James H., xii, 7, 33–34, 87–90, 122, 133, 143, 309–10; Morrison, John, 163; Pierce, Frank, 91–93, 105–7, 112; Powers, J. H., 137; Reed, Eddie, 197–99; Searle, J. W., 122; Smith, Andrew, 122; Swain, John, 151–52, *170-11*; Thomas, Heck, 37, 81, 103, 164, *170-23*; Tilly, Johnathon Steven, 190; Tolbert, Paden, 7, 165, *170-7, 170-16*, 210, 212, 240, 310, 313n1; Topping, Robert J., 33; Trail, A. J. "Bud," 7, *170-16*, 240, 310; Walker, Sandy, 155; Webb, D. M., 278; White, Gideon S. "Cap," 7, 165, 240; Williams, John, 62, 106, 122, 134–36; Williams, Lewis, 202; Williams, Paul C., 289–90; Williams, Zack, 48; Wingo, Sam, 122. *See also* U.S. marshals

U.S. deputy marshals (black): Cannon, Rufus, 4; Cleaver, Barney, 4; Colbert, Bill, 152, 202; Colbert, Bynum, 4, 62, 186; Cyrus, Dennis, 4; Escoe, Wiley, 5; Factor, Neely, 4, 152, *170-9*; Fortune, Robert, 4, 152, *170-9*, 254; Garrett, James, 4; Garrett, John, 4, 8; Jefferson, Edward, 5; Johnson, Grant, xi, 4–5, 159, 187–95, 210, 212, 219, 240, 249, 277–78; Love, Robert, 4–5; McNac, Wallace, 4; Miller, Zeke, 4, 152, *170-9*, 253–54; Nix, Crowder, xi, 4, 115, 123–24; Pettit, Charles, 4, 7; Robinson, Ed, 5; Roebuck, Dick, 4; Rogers, Ike, 4–5; Ruth, Jim, 4; Scales, Clint, 4; Shaver, W. R. "Dick," 4, 278–79; Smith, "Negro," 28; Thompson, Lee, 4; Walters, Jack, 4, 254

U.S. deputy marshals (Indian): Ellis, Jackson, 7; LeFlore, Charlie, 7; Sixkiller, Sam, 7, 51, 122

U.S. government: and Federal Bureau of Investigation (FBI), 8; federal court system of, 26–27, 122, 125–26, 147–48, 171–72; Indian Territory court system and, xiii–xiv, 28–31, 203–4, 209, 249

U.S. marshals: Bennett, Leo E., *170-2*, 190, 206, 209–10, 212, 232, 235, 240, 243–45, 249, 255–56, 260, 269, 277–78, 311; Boles, Thomas, 47–48, 56–58, 71–72, 76–78, 90, 106–7, 112–18, 123–24, 195, 309; Carroll, John, 124–25, 130, 195; Crump, George J., 195, 203; Darough, William H., 249; Dell, Valentine, 34, 195; Dickerson, 200; Hammer, 254; Ledbetter, J. F. "Bud," 289–90, 297; Needles, Tom B., 256; Rutherford, Samuel M., 206, 212, 255–56; Upham, Daniel P., 27, 195; Yoes, Jacob, 153, 156, 179, 182–83, 195, 203. *See also* U.S. Deputy Marshals

U.S. Marshals Service, *170-7, 170-21, 170-22, 170-32*; income and expenses of, 309–11; at Fort Smith AR, 26–27; horses in, 46–47; Indian Police and the, 209; in Indian Territory, 6–7, 27–31, 152; possemen of, 4–5, 11, 29, 32–33; racial tension and, 253–54; Reeves's career in, 296–301; Reeves's possemen in, 83–86, 103, 105–7, 113, 214, 265; Reeves's retirement from, 19, 207–8; reputation of, 7–8, 178–79; statehood and, 295; in Van Buren AR, 25–26; weapons used by, 175. *See* specific marshals

U.S. Supreme Court, 171, 208

Van Buren AR, 19–20, 25–26
Van Buren (AR*) Press*, 50, 200–201, 230, 295; proceedings of Reeves's trial reported in, 27, 133; Reeves's death as reported in, 166–67; shooting of Leach reported in, 128–29
Van Buren Press Argus, 194
Victor, Samuel, 253
Vinita OK, 172, 178, 209, 212, 240, 249
Vinita Indian Chieftain, 147, 164
Violet Springs OK, 172

Wagoner OK, 219, 249
Walker, Dale, 3
Walker, Daniel, 5
Walker, Sandy, 155
Walters, Jack, 4, 254
Ward, James, 253
Ward, Susan, 124
War of 1812, 20
Washington, Basse, 19
Washington, Billy, 82
Washington, Booker T., 176
Washington, Sylvester "Two-Gun Pete," 306–7
weapons, Reeves's legend with, 15–16, *170-5*, 175. *See also* marksmanship
Webb, D. M., 278
Webb, Jim, 82–89
West, Frank, 253
West, John C., 253
West, Kinch, 149
Western Age, 295

The Western Peace Officer: A Legacy of Law and Order (Prassel), 5
Wetumka OK, 212
Wewoka OK, 163, 175, 249
Whaley, George, 116
Wheeler, Stephen, 43, 71, 122–23, 153, 185
whiskey. *See* alcohol
whiskey towns, 172–73
White, Gideon S. "Cap," 7, 165, 240
White, Gideon S., Jr., 256
Who's Who in Colored America, 306
Wichita Indian Nation, territory of, 12–13, 37–44
Wichita KS, 148
Wilburton OK, 254
Wild Horse Creek OK, 254
The Wild West: Lawmen, Outlaws, Ghost Towns, and More (O'Neal, Crutchfield, Walker), 3
Williams, Claude, 228
Williams, Jim, 151–52
Williams, John, 62, 106, 122, 134–36
Williams, Nudie E., xii, xviii, 143, 191
Williams, Paul C., 289–90
Williams, Thomas, 253
Williams, Zack, 48
Wilson, Floyd, 83–85
Wing, Tom, 130, 309
Wingo, Sam, 122
Winston, George S., *170-18*, 203
women: African American, 180, 182, 250; assaults against, 49–51, 91–92, 243; bigamy and divorce of, 237; as crime victims, 62–71, 234, 280–82; domestic abuse of, 187–89, 236, 267–68; interracial marriage and, 215–18; as outlaws, 120–22; as prisoners, 35, 117–19, 270; prostitution by, 197, 219–20, 281; Reeves and, 129; sexual violence against, 259
Woodford OK, 85, 316ch6n7
Wright, William "General Grant," 287–88

Wyandotte Indian Nation, territory of, 12–13

"Wybark Tragedy," 215–19

yellow journalism, xiii

Yoes, Jacob, 153, 156, 179, 182–83, 195, 203

Young, James, 131–33, 137–38

Young, Lee, 6

Young, Otis, 7

Young, William, 22

Younger, Pearl, 197

Zeke and Ned (McMurtry and Ossana), 2